A History of the Town of Fair Haven, Vermont

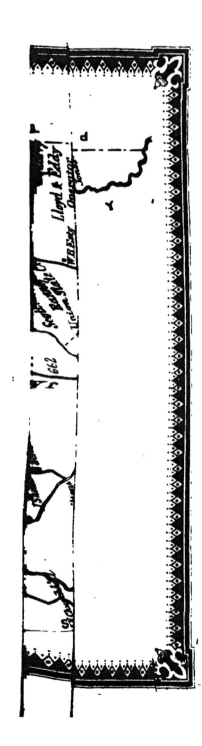

A HISTORY

OF THE

TOWN OF FAIR HAVEN,

VERMONT.

IN THREE PARTS.

BY ANDREW N. ADAMS.

FAIR HAVEN:

LEONARD & PHELPS, PRINTERS.

1870.

JAN 18 1898
(556)

PREFACE.

Aware that local history, on account of its special and matter of fact character, is of interest and importance only within a limited circle, and to those who are personally concerned, I do not anticipate that this history of my native town will be fully and generally read, or that it will answer the expectations of all into whose hands it may fall. It is not, probably, free from mistakes, and might be improved in plan and style; but it has been my aim to be impartial, to treat all persons and facts involved fairly, and as fully as possible. I have aimed rather to make the book a reliable compendium of facts for future reference and use than a smooth and entertaining story. I have not sought to give the name and family of all the present inhabitants, nor of such as have come into town within the last twenty-five years. The names of some have been unavoidably left out, or crowded out, who might with propriety have been mentioned as belonging to the earlier period which the book is intended to cover. I trust, however, that no essential or serious omissions will be found to exist; and believing that, in future years, when we who now live, have passed away, our children, and theirs, will find the book, with whatever defects it may have, both interesting and useful, and of more worth than it now is, or can be, to us, I commit it to its fate, bespeaking for it the fair regard and charitable criticism of my fellow-townsmen.

iv PREFACE.

I desire to express my thanks to several friends, especially to our venerable fellow citizen, Benjamin Franklin Gilbert, and to Mrs. Mary W. Palmer, daughter of Dr. James Witherell, of Detroit, Mich., for special assistance in my work. Much credit is due the publishers, Messrs. D. Leonard and E. H. Phelps, for the correct and elegant style in which their taste and oversight have caused the work to appear.

I may also express my obligation to the generous patrons abroad, who have waited so long and patiently, through delay and disappointment, for the completion of the book ; and in conclusion I may add, that it is due to the citizens themselves, and the vote taken by them at their annual meeting in March, 1869, that the book is now published.

A. N. ADAMS.

Fair Haven, Dec., 1870.

CONTENTS.

PART I.

CHAPTER I.

Preceding the Settlement..PAGE 9

CHAPTER II.

From the Settlement to the Organization of the Town in August, 1783.. 14

CHAPTER III.

From the Organization of the Civil Government to the Division of the Town in 1793... 54

CHAPTER IV.

From the taking of the first Census, in 1791, to the departure of Col. Lyon, at the close of the century................................ 92

PART II.

Lyon's First Store... 126
Lyon's Tavern House.. 128
Stephen Rogers' Tannery.. 131
Lyon's Dwelling House.. 135
Hennessy's Store... 137
The Old Dennis Tavern.. 139
The Iron Works... 141
The Paper Mill... 145
The Grist Mill... 149
Saw Mills.. 151
The Norton Place... 156
The Colton Place... 160
Beriah Rogers' Tannery... 163

vi   CONTENTS.

The Scythe Factory.. 165
The Cloth Dressing Works... 168
The Herring Place....................... 170
Seth Person's Store... 172
Elisha Parkill's Store.. 174
Richard Sutliff's Place.. 177
Joseph Brown's Cabinet Shop....................................... 178
The Old Hat Shop 180
Distilleries 181
Paupers and a Town Poor House..................................... 185
The Pound 188
The Park 190
Village Organization.. 195
The Town Hall 196
Burial Grounds.. 200
Mrs. Dyer's Legacy... 203
The Slate Business... 207
The Marble Business... 219
The First National Bank... 221
Literary and Library Societies 224
The Odd Fellows 226
The Masons.. 227
The Good Templars... 230
The Washingtonian Temperance Society.............................. 231
Fair Haven Young Men's Christian Association....................... 232
The Cambrian Cornet Band.. 233
Printing and Publishing.. 234
Military Affairs... 237
School Affairs.. 245
Ecclesiastical Affairs.. 257
Letter of Rev. Dr. Beaman... 273

PART III.

Biographical and Family Notices...................................... 281

APPENDIX,... 511

ERRATUM.—On page 268, eighteenth line from the top, read " Arminians"
instead of " Armenians."

PART I.

The Settlement and Growth of the Town prior to the Year 1800.

PART I.

CHAPTER I.

PRECEDING THE SETTLEMENT.

This town, comprising originally within its limits, what is now West Haven and Fair Haven, was in the time of the Revolutionary War a wild, unsettled tract of country lying along Poultney river and East Bay on the east side of Lake Champlain, which, in connection with Benson on the north, had been cut off and left south of Orwell and between the towns of Hubbardton, Castleton and Poultney on the east, and the Lake on the west, when those towns were incorporated by the government of New Hampshire in 1761.

A part of the territory was covered by Col. Philip Skeene's second grant, and was all included in the New York county of Charlotte, of which Skeenesborough was the county seat.

The inhabitants of the towns under the New Hampshire Grants, having organized a state government for themselves in March, 1778, under the name of Vermont, divided their new state into two counties, Cumberland on the east side of the mountains, and Bennington on the west side.

Vermont claiming westward to the Lake, the territory of Fair Haven—from what cause called by this

10 HISTORY OF FAIR HAVEN, VERMONT.

name we are unable to say—was thus brought within the bounds of Bennington county.

On the 27th of October, 1779, in the second year of the state, the General Assembly of Vermont, while convened at Manchester, granted petitions for acts of incorporation for the two towns of Fair Haven and Benson.

In the charter of the town, which was not made out and signed by the Governor until April 26, 1782, Fair Haven is bounded and described: "Beginning at a stake on the east side of Lake Champlain, 45 rods north of a certain cold spring on the east shore of said Lake, about 200 rods above a certain place known by the name of 'the Narrows'; from thence east 10° south 8 miles and 26 rods to a stake and stones in the west line of Castleton; thence south 10° west in the line of said Castleton and of Poultney, 8 miles and 238 rods, to a beech tree in the west line of Poultney, where the line crosses Poultney river; thence down said river at low water mark on the north-east side to East Bay; thence down on the northerly side of said Bay to Lake Champlain; thence down said Lake to the first mentioned bounds."

The grant was made in consideration of the sum of "Six thousand nine hundred and thirty pounds continental currency," to Capt. Ebenezer Allen, of Tinmouth, Col. Isaac Clark, of Castleton, and seventy-four others, of whom were Gov. Thos. Chittenden and his wife Elizabeth Chittenden, Ira Allen, Stephen R. Bradley, Doct. Jacob Ruback, and other prominent public men of that day. *See Appendix I.*

HISTORY OF FAIR HAVEN, VERMONT. 11

Among the original grantees, or proprietors, are the names of Col. Matthew Lyon, Oliver Cleveland, Philip Priest, Israel Trowbridge, Derrick Carner, and Eleazer Dudley, who were settlers in the town. By the conditions of the charter each proprietor was required "to plant and cultivate ten acres of land and build a house at least eighteen feet square on the floor, or have one family settled on each respective right within the term of five years next after the circumstances of the present war between Great Britain and America will admit of a settlement with safety." All pine timber suitable for masts and spars of a navy were reserved for the use and benefit of the freemen of the state. There were also reserved and appropriated to public uses one share for a seminary or college; one for the first settled minister in the town, to be disposed of for that purpose as the inhabitants shall direct; one for the benefit and support of the ministry; one for the County Grammar Schools, and one for the support of schools in the town.

The first deed or sale of land in the town was made at Manchester, on the same day with the grant, by Zadoc Everest, then of Manchester, to Elisha Hamilton, of Tinmouth, both of whom were among the grantees or proprietors.

Of the state of the country previous to this time it is difficult to speak with much historical certainty, on account of the absence of direct records. It is the mythical period in our history, in which imaginative and credulous minds can affirm what they like as truth and we have no data to correct them.

12 HISTORY OF FAIR HAVEN, VERMONT.

But while it is likely there were often related marvelous stories of danger and prowess in the cabin of the squatter or the camp of the hunter, by the bold and hardy adventurers who traversed the dense forests of these rough hills and valleys in pursuit of game, it will be our aim to write only what is known, or may justly be inferred to be matter of historical truth.

It is implied in the language of the Charter and the disturbed condition of the country generally, that during the Revolutionary War the territory of this town was not occupied or improved to any considerable extent. Along the shore of the lake and the borders of the bay and rivers, there were a few settlements commenced, as will be seen by subsequent records, but mainly the town was a wilderness, inhabited by wild beasts and traversed by hunters' trails. We hear of bears and wolves in the town after it began to be settled, and it is probable that the deer had, within our ancient borders, many a favorite haunt and runway.

The country of Western Vermont is supposed to have belonged to a tribe of ancient Iriquois Indians. but of their presence in the forests of this town we have no tradition.

Maj. Ebenezer Allen, of Tinmouth, and Capt. Isaac Clark, of Castleton, appear to have had "a hunting camp" on one of the large ledges in West Haven and not far from Benson line, with paths leading to and from the same in various directions, before the town was chartered, and probably before the state government was organized. The proprietors met at this camp, August 21st, 1780, to commence the survey of

HISTORY OF FAIR HAVEN, VERMONT. 13

their several proprietary pitches.

There are traces still existing confirmatory of early indirect records, that a body of Hessian soldiers came up the East Bay during the war, and, abandoning their boats at the foot of "Carver's Falls," cut a road thence through the woods on the New York side, to Poultney river at a point a little below its junction with the Castleton river, at the south end of the old Merritt farm, where they threw over a bridge long afterward known and called the "Hessian bridge," over which they crossed the river and cleared a road eastward toward Castleton and Hubbardton by way of the large hill south of Hiram Hamilton's, which, on account of their hollowing out a stump on the top of the hill, was called "Hessian Bowl Hill." By this "Hessian road," where it came away from the river, the surveys and deeds of Mr. Merritt's farm were afterwards bounded.

Another detachment of Burgoyne's army passed through this town after the battle of Hubbardton, in July, 1777, and it is thought, made a road south of the river, passing near Otis Eddy's, and along the north side of the cedar swamp below J. W. Estey's house, and thence crossing the Poultney river to the south and west, either creating or following what was long subsequently known as "Skeene's road." On a rude map of this region, printed in London, in January, 1779, by order of Governor Wm. Tryon, of New York, there are two roads branching out of one, about on the east line of this town, and diverging south-westward across the territory of Gen. Skeene.

CHAPTER II.

FROM THE SETTLEMENT TO THE ORGANIZATION OF THE TOWN IN AUGUST, 1788.

At what precise date the first residents, or those who were considered as squatters, came into the district which was incorporated into the town of Fair Haven by the General Assembly of the state in October, 1779, we have not now the means of determining; but we know from existing records that at or about the time the charter was obtained—which was done chiefly through the efforts of Maj. Ebenezer Allen and Gen. Isaac Clark, who had traversed the territory in their hunting excursions—there were a few persons resident in the town, and actual settlers began to come in and take up the land under the proprietor's titles.

Oliver Cleveland, an active pioneer in the settlement and organization of the town, was one of those who had made improvements in the towns before the act of incorporation, and appears to be the only one of the original settlers who is represented in the charter. He had come from Killingworth, Conn., and sat down with other members of his father's family, on what is now the New York, or Hampton side of

HISTORY OF FAIR HAVEN, VERMONT. 15

the river, then called "Greenfield," but which it was at that time expected would be in Vermont, the State line or boundary between the two States not being as yet settled and defined.

While residing there, near the river, the road then running close by the river bank, instead of over the flat as now, he had commenced clearing and improving the land which, about this time, became his home-farm in Fair Haven—the same that is now owned in part by Ebenezer Gould, of Hampton, and in part by Chauncey Wood. It extended from Poultney river to Poultney west line, and is said, in a survey made in 1794, to contain 205 acres, laid, all but 64 acres of it, on his own proprietary right.

At his death, which occurred in September, 1803, the farm became divided among his three sons, Josiah, Albert, and James. James' part, consisting of about 80 acres on the west side, was sold by him in Nov., 1807, to Pliny Adams, of Hampton, and passed from Mr. Adams' heirs to Sam'l Wood, Sen. Albert conveyed his 60 acres on the north and east to Oliver Cleveland, of Fort Ann, Nov. 13th, 1813, but probably continued to occupy it until it was sold to Charles Wood, of Hampton, in Sept., 1817. From Mr. Wood it passed through the hands of Mark H. Kidder and Daniel Smith to Sam'l Wood, Sen., in March, 1826.

Josiah had 60 acres on the south and lived on the same until near the spring of 1818, when he removed to Hampton and sold his farm to Charles Wood, and the same is now occupied by Chauncey Wood.

Mr. Cleveland was a rough, illiterate man, unable

16   HISTORY OF FAIR HAVEN, VERMONT.

even to write his own name, yet he was a man of great natural force and ability, and was trusted with the execution of much important business, being elected one of the Selectmen of the town from March, 1784, nearly every year till his death. He left a large family, whose names will be found in another part of this book.

The lands lying in the town to the south of Mr. Cleveland, between the river and Poultney line, had also been improved as early as this year, 1779, by Joseph Squier, Lemuel Hyde and William Meacham, persons who were resident on the Hampton or Greenfield side, but do not seem to have become citizens of the town.

At a meeting of the proprietors held at Castleton, October 4th, 1780, it was voted that John Meacham, Joseph Ballard, William Meacham, Lemuel Hyde and Joseph Squier might have the privilege of "covering their possessions with second division pitches, to be laid out in the form of the first when there is undivided land enough to lay them in such form;" and it appears from records in the archives of the State that these individuals, together with some fifty or more who had settled along the river and in what is now Hampton, considered themselves as within the bounds of the State, and had as early as the year 1779, and probably in the last part of the year, after Fair Haven was incorporated, and while the Legislature was still in session at Manchester, petitioned the authorities of Vermont for incorporation of the territory on which they resided as a town under the name of "Greenfield"—a name quite as significant as Hampton—but the boundary of the State being in controversy, the authorities did not grant it, and the petition was renewed in June, 1781, the petitioners expressing a strong desire to be under the government of Vermont, and evidently supposing the boundary, which was then established, to be to the westward of them. The catalogue of signers to this petition includes the names of several individuals who were then resident, or who afterwards became resident in Fair Haven; such as John Meacham, Joseph Ballard, Abel Parker, Solomon Cleveland, Abraham Sharp, Oliver Cleveland, Derrick Carner, Isaac Race, Benjamin Parmenter and Stephen Holt. *See Appendix II.*

From the State archives we also learn that in June, 1781, the settlers on the south side of East Bay and north of the old town of Skeenesborough, many of whom were from New Hampshire and the East, desired to be under the authority of Vermont, and supposed they were so, being on the east side of the Lake, and they accordingly petitioned our General Assembly, then met at Bennington, for an act of incorporation as a town by the name of "New Cheshire." Among these petitioners were Lemuel Bartholomew, Peter Christie, Robert Adams, and others whose names may be found in Appendix III.

John Meacham and Joseph Ballard, mentioned above, and by the proprietors at their meeting in October, 1780, as having possessions in town, were actual residents along the river to the north of Mr. Cleveland. Whether Mr. Ballard came before or after Mr. Meach-

18   HISTORY OF FAIR HAVEN, VERMONT.

am we are not able to determine, nor whence he come, but he must have been here, or on the Greenfield side of the river, as early at least as 1779, and it is probable that he came from Massachusetts or southern Vermont.

Mr. Meacham, with his wife and three children, came from Williamstown, Mass., either in the fall of 1779 or the spring of 1780, and built him a log house on the west side of the road, a little south from where Myron D. Barnes resides. His fourth child, Esther Meacham, born April 23d, 1780, it is claimed was the first child born in the town.

The land on which Mr. Meacham settled is now occupied by Mr. Barnes and Mr. Kidder. The north part, where Mr. Kidder resides, consisting then of 100 acres in a square form and extending on to the hill eastward, was covered in August, 1781, by two fourth division pitches of 50 acres each, which Mr. Meacham purchased of Col. Clark in June of that year. The south part, extending to and along the river, consisted of 50 acres laid out in October, 1784, 30 acres of it on the third division of the right of John How, or House, which Mr. Meacham had bought of James Smith, of Poultney, and the other 20 acres on the fourth division of Elijah Galusha's right, bought by Mr. Meacham of Col. Matthew Lyon. The east half of the 100 acres, it being the fourth division of Thomas Ashley's right, was sold by Mr. Meacham to Richard Beddow, December 18th, 1787.

On the 14th of April, 1790, Mr. Meacham sold 33 acres of the south part to Silas Safford, Esq., having previously sold 4 acres on the river bank to Isaac Par-

HISTORY OF FAIR HAVEN, VERMONT. 19

ker, of Watertown, Conn., and a few acres to Col. Lyon and Col. David Erwin. He sold the remaining 50 acres of the north part—the fourth division of the right of Ralph Watson—"excepting the house standing on the same," January 3d, 1794, to Col. David Erwin, bounding it as follows: Beginning at an elm tree in the southeast corner of the fourth division lot of Isaac Clark, thence running north 22 rods, thence east 60 rods to Richard Beddow's land, thence south on Beddow's west line 136 rods, thence west to the highway, and then north to the place of beginning.

Mr. Meacham appears to have been an acquaintance and friend of Col. Lyon in Massachusetts, and he is said to have worked with Richard Beddow at nailmaking in a shop which stood on the side hill east of Mr. Kidder's barns. He was a poor man and had a large family, which necessitated assistance from the town and the apprenticeship of his eldest son, John, afterwards a merchant in the town, and later an influential citizen of Castleton, by the authorities of the town, during his minority. Mr. Meacham was one of the members of the first board of selectmen chosen at the organization of the town in August, 1783, and was one of a committee chosen by the citizens in September, 1784, to draw up a remonstrance against the doings of a county convention. He removed from Fair Haven to Galway, N. Y., in 1794, and thence to Benson in 1800, where he carried on a brick yard, and was so injured by the caving in of earth which he was engaged in excavating that he survived but one week, and died in 1808 or 1809, aged 58 years.

20 HISTORY OF FAIR HAVEN, VERMONT.

Mr. Ballard's place of settlement laid next west of Mr. Meacham's, and consisted of 177 acres, besides some 60 acres bought by him at auction on the fourth division of Stephen Fay's right, and lying further to the west. The first 100 acres were laid out to him in August, 1781, on two fourth division rights purchased of Col. Clark in June, as follows: 45 acres in a square on Col. Clark's own right, the southeast corner being a noted elm tree in Meacham's west line; and 55 acres in a 45 rod wide strip, running west 219 rods to the river. The 77 acres were laid out in July, 1784, on the south of the above, 50 acres of it on the fourth division of Nathaniel Smith's right, bought on tax sale, and 27 acres on Elijah Galusha's right, purchased of John Meacham. In February, 1785, Mr. Ballard deeded the west part of his farm to his son, John Morrow Ballard, and the east part to his son-in-law, Stephen Holt, the division line running north 45° east from three elms standing together on the bank of the river, to the north line of the 55 acre lot. He re-deeded a portion of the Clark lot to Mr. Holt in November, 1792, and gave 45 acres, lying south toward the river, to his daughter, Drusilla Holt, with whom he appears to have lived, and perhaps died, about 1795.

The "Clark lot" was sold to Col. Erwin in June, 1794, he having bought Meacham's farm of John Meacham in January previous. Mr. Holt continued to reside on the south part until May, 1801, when it was sold to Henry Ainsworth, and passed through the hands of Danforth Ainsworth and Enos Wells to Barnabas Ellis,

HISTORY OF FAIR HAVEN, VERMONT. **21**

in November, 1813. It is now owned by Mr. Ellis' son, Zenas C. Ellis.

John Morrow Ballard sold his part to his brother-in-law, Solomon Wilder, of Whitehall, in March, 1795, and soon thereafter removed to Whitehall himself. The place is that where Charles W. Gardner now resides. John Morrow Ballard is said to have been a Methodist minister, and to have been partly of Indian blood; and beyond this we learn little or nothing of him. Jeremiah Ballard, a noted Methodist clergyman, of southern Vermont and Massachusetts, may have been a brother. He was in the town in December, 1795, when he quit-claimed to Mr. Wilder an interest in land which had been owned by Joseph Ballard. Samuel Cleveland, of Hydeville, a son of Solomon Cleveland, an intimate friend of Col. Matthew Lyon, and formerly resident in the town, relates that in his boyhood, while his father owned the mills, between 1796 and '98, he well remembers going to Mr. Holt's and hearing Lorenzo Dow preach there, Mr. Holt being known as a devoted Methodist. He also states that in that day the inhabitants were obliged to harbor or house their sheep at night to protect them from wolves, and in one instance Col. Erwin found a wolf in the pen with his sheep. The wolf had got in during the night and was unable to make his escape.

Besides these settlements, which appear to have been the earliest in the south part of the town, there were others lower down on Poultney river, which may have been of older date; as at the point where

22   HISTORY OF FAIR HAVEN, VERMONT.

the "Hessian road" came over the river, now on the Stannard farm, where a man by the name of Jonathan Lynde had improved a place. ·

The improvement may have been one cause that the Hessians crossed there, or Lynde may have sat down at that point because they *had* bridged the river and opened a road there. It is probable that he was one of a company of Dutch people who came into the neighborhood during the Revolutionary War, from the vicinity of Bennington, or country east of Albany.

The proprietors, at their first meeting, in June, 1780, called this place of Lynde's " an old possession on Poultney river," and voted to give him the privi- lege of holding it, "if laid out before the next meet- ing of the proprietors." The next meeting occurred in August, and as there appears no record of any sur- vey or deed to him, he must either have relinquished his claim altogether or sold it to John Smith, of Poultney, or to Michael Merritt—Mr. Merritt taking possession and surveying the same, this same month, on the first division of Mr. Smith's right.

A little above this improvement of Lynde's, Abra- ham Sharp, a Dutch settler on the New York side, then, at that point, called "New Haven," who came with his brother-in-law, James Vandozer, or Vando- zen, if not also others of his countrymen, from near Bennington, was given the privilege by the proprie- tors, in October, 1780, of "covering with some pro- prietor's right all his possession extending from the upper part of the lower falls on Poultney river to the

HISTORY OF FAIR HAVEN, VERMONT. 23

junction of said river with Castleton river, excepting Elisha Hamilton's lot, which shall not be covered by any other person to take away his labor." ҁ

Elisha Hamilton's lot, which was surveyed to him in August, 1780, on the first division of his own right as "lot No. 5," and laid where Hamilton Wescott now resides, being 100 rods north and south by 160 east and west, and reaching southward over the river and nearly to the river westward,—would thus appear to have been one of the earliest improvements in town; but whether improved by himself—he being said to be a resident of Tinmouth in 1779—or by some person of whom he purchased, we have no means of knowing.

The second division of Zadock Everest's right was laid out in July, 1781, next north of "lot No. 5," and was made to run west to the river; but it appears that Mr. Sharp had a claim by possession to all the lands lying along the river west of "lot No. 5," and to the west parts of both the Hamilton and Everest divisions, as also to the land which laid between the two rivers as they formerly run, the junction at that time being further down, below the present bridge, and the Poultney river sweeping westward around land owned by Mr. Sharp in Vermont, which is now, in consequence of a change made in the river about 1830, considered to be in the State of New York.

Mr. Sharp appears to have covered his claims in August, 1783, with surveys on the fourth divisions of the original rights of Jesse Sawyer and George Foot, the Foot division being deeded to him for the consid-

C

HISTORY OF FAIR HAVEN, VERMONT.

eration of £17 by Beriah Mitchell, April 5th, 1784, and both divisions being quit-claimed to him by Gen. Clark in December of 1783, as follows: "For and in consideration of the natural good disposition I feel toward Abraham Sharp, of Charlotte county and State of New York, and in order to quiet the old possession in Fair Haven, which the proprietors have granted a privilege to cover their respective possessions with any part of any proprietor's right * *. I do * * grant and quit-claim unto the said Abraham Sharp * * 100 acres, being two fourth divisions belonging to the original rights of Jesse Sawyer and George Foot, which I bought at vendue, and hold by deed from the collector, not yet laid out."

On the 23d of April, 1784, Joel Hamilton, who had come into possession of a half interest in "lot No. 5," and the Everest division on the north, for the consideration of the sum of £20, deeds to Mr. Sharp 20 acres from the west end of lot No. 5, and 30 acres from the Everest lot.

This Abraham Sharp was a noted hunter, and was called by the early inhabitants, "Old Abe." He married Jemima Vandozer, and had a son Abraham, who was the father of Robert. "Old Abe" was drowned on one of his hunting excursions, in the river near Granville, previous to March, 1789. Charles Rice was the administrator of the estate, which being insolvent, was sold, with the exception of the widow's interest, October 27th, 1789, to Elisha Kilburn, Jr., of Castleton. He sold the part lying north of the highway, about 30 acres, to Doct. James Witherell, in April,

HISTORY OF FAIR HAVEN, VERMONT. 25

1791, and 30 acres south of the highway to Charles Rice, in November, 1792, who sold it to Doct. Witherell shortly after, who finally purchased the whole estate.

James Vandozer, the brother-in-law of Mr. Sharp, purchased of Heman Barlow, of Greenfield, N. Y., in September, 1782, the first division of Joseph Haven's original right, "No. 45," laid out to Mr. Barlow, in September, 1780, south of the road and next east of "lot No. 5," being 100 rods east and west by 160 north and south, and this lot must have been improved, and may have been settled by Mr. Vandozer and his family at as early a period as the lands west of it. Tradition reports that it was occupied by Vandozer and his son-in-law, Simeon McWithey, called by the old people "McQuivey," who lived in a log house standing on the south side of the road, just west of Mr. O. P. Ranney's barns, in 1788.

Mr. Vandozer and his wife were old people and died at their place at an early day. He willed the west half of his farm to his grandson, Isaac McWithey, who sold a strip of about 12 acres off from the west side, to Isaac Cutler, Esq., in November, 1789, and the remainder to Russell Smith in August, 1795; Mr. Smith building a house on the same, which is now standing, east from John P. Sheldon's.

The other, or east part of the farm, was inherited by Simeon. and Sarah McWithey, who remained on the place, buying of Col. M. Lyon, in September, 1799, a building lot of 20 rods wide by 12 deep, on the north side of the road, on which they erected a dwelling

26   HISTORY OF FAIR HAVEN, VERMONT.

house. They sold the whole place to Lewis Stone, in January, 1812. From Mr. Stone it passed to Hezekiah and Harvey Howard, in November, 1818, and is now owned by Mr. O. P. Ranney.

Maj. Ebenezer Allen was allowed by the proprietors the privilege of covering with some proprietary right the possession in the north part of West Haven, which he had purchased of Joseph Hyde; and Benoni Hurlburt was granted a like privilege of laying out on some proprietor's right "a piece of land which he has had in possession a number of years, containing about 15 acres, provided he does not encroach upon any lands already laid out for public or private use." This lot of Benoni Hurlburt's laid on the bank of East Bay, south of Hiram K. Hunt's, and was sold by him in July, 1784, to Luman Stone, of Litchfield, Conn. Benoni Hurlburt's name appears on a petition in the Secretary of State's office, together with those of Joseph Carver, Joseph Haskins, Jona. Hall and John Vandozer, dated at Fair Haven, February 23d, 1782, in which the petitioners complain that they have been unjustly treated and deprived of their property and rights by those who obtained the charter of the town without informing them or giving them an opportunity to be represented in the same, though they were "persons who had for a long time before improved the land," having fled "from the southern parts of New England to Vermont to resume its liberties and promote its interests."

The committee to whom the petition was referred reported that on account of the adverse party not be-

HISTORY OF FAIR HAVEN, VERMONT. 27

ing cited to appear at the hearing, the petition be laid over till the next session, and that as the petitioners had made improvements and sowed and raised grain, an order be issued that they be not disturbed in their possessions in the meantime. But on the 26th of May following, Hurlburt, who had perhaps been bought over in the meantime, signs a remonstrance, dated at Cheshire, declaring that Carver is a transient person from Rhode Island, and had used his name on the petition without his knowledge or consent, and against his interests. *See Appendix IV.*

Who Joseph Carver was, or Jona. Hall or John Vandozer, further than what appears above, we are not informed, nor do we know where they located; but it is probable that they dwelt in the neighborhood of Hurlburt and not far from the falls on the Poultney river which are now known as Carvers Falls.

Joseph Haskins inhabited a spot just below the road south of where Otis Hamilton resides when the first surveys were made in 1780. There are several stories told concerning him. One is that "an old Indian" had made a pitch and built a log cabin on the place with a view to holding it, but Gen. Clark located the first division of his right over the same ground, surveyed and commenced building a saw-mill, on the north side of the Great Falls, now the "Dry Falls," when forsooth, the denizen of the log cabin, taking umbrage at such intrusion on his premises, and waxing fierce in his wrath, sought satisfaction for his revenge by digging away a neck of land above the falls so as to change the whole course and body of the

28 HISTORY OF FAIR HAVEN, VERMONT.

stream away from its ancient and natural bed over the falls, to the more western channel in which it now runs, thus destroying a valuable fall of water of some 150 feet.

It is related that "the old Indian" had a fight with a bear, whom he wounded, and came nigh getting beaten and devoured in the fray.

Another and independent tradition is that the man, Haskins, whoever he may have been, changed the course of the river; while several old people have incidentally remarked that Haskins was in part of Indian blood.

It has been claimed that the change in the course of the river was the work of freshets, washing away the loose, sandy soil of the plain.

It is no doubt true that the natural wear of the stream and the destructive effects of repeatedly recurring freshets in the drift alluvium of this old water-basin, had much to do with the change; but considering the early and decided character of the tradition, together with statements from some of the old people, that men were seen to come suspiciously away from the place of the change, leaving tools on the bank behind them, it would not be improbable that when the water had worn away the bank to a narrow isthmus, the spade of Joseph Haskins, or of some other man of the name—there being two others, Silas and Benoni Haskins, then in the country, either on the Vermont or New York side—had secretly helped or hastened the inevitable work already commenced by the stream itself.

HISTORY OF FAIR HAVEN, VERMONT. 29

Be this as it may, we have it as a historical fact that the stream was changed about the time of a freshet in the spring. of 1783, and that vast quantities of sand and earth were carried down into East Bay, thus filling up and impeding the navigation of the Bay, which, until then, had been accessible to vessels of 40 tons burden, and promised, had it continued of its original depth, to render the town along its banks a place of considerable commercial importance.

Harvey Howes states that when his father, John Howes, from Woodbury, Conn., first came into this country, sometime soon after the first surveys, probably in 1781 or '82, he came to Castleton, and thence followed down the "Hessian road" to East Bay, where the hulks of the Hessian's boats still laid, and the water in the Bay at that point was from 10 to 12 feet deep.

In fact, a town of considerable size was projected by the proprietors at a point just below the falls, as we shall see from the proprietors' records. The town plot, as drawn on paper and actually laid out at the head of the Bay, contained one acre to each proprietor's share, and is now in existence in the town clerk's office. Had the stream remained of its original capacity, the vast water power of Carvers Falls, nearly eighty feet in all, and the abundance of good timber which was then in the forests of the whole adjacent country, could scarcely have failed, with enterprise on the part of the owners, to render the Fair Haven of the early times a commercial mart of no mean importance to the whole western portion of

30 HISTORY OF FAIR HAVEN, VERMONT.

the State. The Bay, connecting as it did with Lake Champlain, would have afforded a cheap and easy channel through which vessels could have come in laden with ore and merchandise, and gone out freighted with cargoes of lumber, iron, nails, paper, lime, grain and produce, and finally, in our own day, with marble and slate.

As it was, it was made use of for many years, and as late as 1815, or later, by Asa Smith, Joseph Sheldon, Elizur and Chauncey Goodrich and others, as an outlet during the high water in the spring of the year for the rafts of timber and large product of the superior pine lumber which the region produced.

Of any further improvements or settlements in the town previous to its occupancy by the proprietors—other than those already spoken of—we find no trace or mention in the proprietors' records. It is not unlikely that there were others, especially in the West Haven part of the town on the shore of the lake; but the leading inhabitants, the principal settlers after Oliver Cleveland, John Meacham and Joseph Ballard, were those who came into the town after the act of incorporation, beginning about the year 1780.

Michael Merritt and Philip Priest deserve to be mentioned first in this connection, as they appear to have been here in August of this year, and may have come in the spring. They came from Killingworth, Conn., and settled in the west part of the present town, near the Poultney river. The land on which Mr. Merritt located has been already spoken of as that where Jona. Lynde had commenced improvements, border-

HISTORY OF FAIR HAVEN, VERMONT. 31

ing on the "Hessian road;" and we hear that Mr.
Merritt was able to furnish the early comers with corn
raised on his place before the other farms were ready
to grow it.

His farm was a first division lot of 105 acres on the
right of John Smith, lying on the intervale south of
Mr. Stannard's house, and where an old road went
through to the highway running past Hamilton Wescott's. In his deed to Mr. Merritt, John Smith says,
land "joining on the rode by the hussion bridge which
was formerly possessioned by Jonathan Lynds and
granted to him by the proprietors of fairhaven at their
meeting of the 16th July 1780." It was deeded by Mr.
Merritt to his son, Peter Merritt, in January, 1813, and
afterwards passed into the hands of Heman Stannard.

Mr. Merritt was on several important committees
for the proprietors; was chosen the first constable at
the organization of the town, filled the offices of town
clerk, treasurer and selectman, and served in other
public capacities. He had a family of eleven children,
all born in Killingworth, Conn., where he had married Lucy Chittenden. He died here August 18th,
1815, aged 77 years.

Mr. Priest was brother-in-law to Mr. Merritt, having
married his sister, Trubey Merritt, while in Connecticut. He located the first division lot No. 13, of his
own proprietary right—105 rods east and west by 160
rods north and south—in August, 1780, next east of
Mr. Merritt, and first built a log house on the ground
where Hiram Hamilton now lives. Here he kept tavern for a number of years. In June, 1788, he sold

D

32 HISTORY OF FAIR HAVEN, VERMONT.

Joel Hamilton 12 acres from the northeast corner of his home farm, and north of the highway, and a triangular strip of 3 acres south of the road. He must have removed about this time, or previously, to the residence occupied by him till the summer of 1800, on the knoll south of and opposite Mr. Stannard's house. He sold the balance of his farm to Mr. Hamilton, excepting about 25 acres sold to Charles Hawkins, partly in September, 1793, and partly in April, 1800, and went away to Chateaugay, N. Y., where he died, suddenly, about 1816.

Mr. Priest was an active man in the affairs of the town. He was employed by the proprietors, in August, 1780, to lay out a school lot, and charged them three shillings for one-half day in doing it. The first meeting for the organization of a town government was holden at his house, August, 28th, 1783, and he was made the first selectman. The town meeting of March, 1784, was also, like many of the meetings of the proprietors, held at his house; and we find his name as one of the selectmen as late as 1796.

Israel Trowbridge and Jeremiah Durand came into town from Derby, Conn., in the summer or fall of this year, 1780, both settling in the east part of the town, near the west line of Castleton, Mr. Trowbridge on the north, where the road enters the town from Hydeville, and Mr. Durand further south on the hill, near Alonson Allen's slate quarry.

Mr. Trowbridge was one of the proprietors named in the charter of the town, and located, in September, 1780, three divisions of his right—nearly 300 acres—

HISTORY OF FAIR HAVEN, VERMONT. 33

in one body along Castleton line and river, including all that is now D. P. Wescott's and Joshua Whitlock's, extending from Elijah Estey's farm eastward to the town line, and over land lying along the river, which, it is said, in one of the early surveys, a man by the name of Azariah Blancher, or Blanchard, "once pretended to own." He gave the second division lot, No. 34, lying south of the river, to his son, Levi, August 26th, 1786, who, upon the death of his father, sold it, in March, 1795, to Cornelius and David D. Board, of Castleton, from whom it passed, in November, 1805, to Hezekiah Whitlock, the father of Joshua Whitlock, who now occupies the place.

The remainder of the estate appears to have been divided by the Court of Probate among the heirs of Mr. Trowbridge, who, besides Levi, seem to have been Mary, the wife of Ralph Carver, of Castleton ; Elizabeth, the wife of Dr. Osee Dutton, of Derby, Conn.; Abigail, an unmarried daughter, who lived with Olney Hawkins; and Hannah, the wife of Olney Hawkins, who was a grand-daughter of Mr. Trowbridge.

Levi and Abigail sell the largest portion of the farm, in April, 1799, to Dr. Samuel Shaw, of Castleton, Levi retaining 52 acres on the east side adjoining the Castleton line, with the exception of one house, standing south of that in which he lived, he living not far from where Benjamin Hickock afterwards did, and the house on the south side of the road being the house which his father had occupied.

Levi sold the remaining 52 acres to Benj. Hickock, in October, 1804, and is said to have resided in the

34   HISTORY OF FAIR HAVEN, VERMONT.

Russell Smith house, on the west street, until his removal to the west.

Mr. Durand had married Sarah, a daughter of Mr. Trowbridge, while in Connecticut, and she had died there in 1777, leaving him an infant child, Hannah, who came with her aunt Abigail, called "Nabby," to Vermont, and became the wife of Olney Hawkins.

He located his land next south of Mr. Trowbridge's, in November, 1780, on the second division of Thomas Ashley's right, the lot being No. 68, and he getting a deed of the same from Col. Clark, in April, 1781. He sold a strip of 20 acres—32 rods east and west by 105 rods north and south—off from the west side of his lot to Wm. Buell, in 1791, and another strip of the same size to Charles Boyle, in 1793. He died in 1798; and the remaining 60 acres passed into the hands of Isaac Cutler, and from him, in 1807, to "Doct." Thomas Dibble. Dibble sold it to Elisha Parkill, in 1817; Parkill to Eli Barber, of Benson, in 1826, and Barber to Jonathan Capen, in 1833, who retained and occupied it until it was purchased by Alonson Allen, in 1851.

Curtis Kelsey, Sen., of Woodbury, Conn., came into this section of country in the summer of 1780, buying, in June of this year, of Josiah Grant, of Poultney, his proprietary right in Fair Haven, and locating the 100 acres of the first division, in July,—160 rods north and south by 105 rods east and west—where Elijah Estey now lives. The second division lot was laid in November, on the north and west of the first, and the third division in the following May, to the

HISTORY OF FAIR HAVEN, VERMONT. 35

north of the second, thus making nearly 300 acres. He removed his family from Woodbury to Wells in the spring of 1781, where they remained until the summer of 1782, when, having erected a cabin and covered it with bark, nigh where Mr. Estey's barn is, he moved into town with his family. He was chosen by the proprietors one of the overseers of the highway in November of this year.

Mr. Kelsey was one of the wealthiest persons in the town, only two standing higher in the Grand List of 1789 than he; namely, Matthew Lyon and Michael Merritt. In December, 1795, he deeded to his son, Lyman, about 83 acres from the west part of his farm —60 acres on the second division and 23 acres on the third division—it being the place owned not long ago by Stephen Fish, Esq. The other and principal portion of the farm he retained until 1821, when he sold it to his grandson, Harry Spalding, of Middletown, who was to give him, as a consideration, a support during the remainder of his natural life. The place was sold by Spalding to Mr. Estey, of Natick, Mass., in 1822, and has ever since remained in his hands.

In the year 1782 Silas Safford and his brother-in-law, Ager Hawley, came from Arlington and made the first settlement in the village.

Col. Matthew Lyon, who then resided in Arlington, had, in December, 1780, located the second division of Nathan Allen's right, and the first and second divisions of his own right—about 300 acres—on the land around the falls of Castleton river, the second division of Nathan Allen's right covering the ground where

36　HISTORY OF FAIR HAVEN, VERMONT.

the Common or Park now is, and extending eastward over the swamp to Mr. Kelsey's first division lot, No. 60, and his own rights coming over the river and falls from the south and west nearly to the south line of the Common. Subsequently, in January, 1781, he bought of John Hamilton, of Tinmouth, a second division of 105 acres lying next east of his own rights, which had been surveyed to John Smith, thus giving him possession of over 400 acres, all in one body. He must have visited the place at the time of the survey, 1780, and at other times following, prior to removing himself and family, which he did in the year 1783.

Preparing to make improvements on his land, and to build on the falls while yet resident in Arlington, he proposed to Mr. Safford to give him 80 acres of land as a premium to go to Fair Haven with his family and board the men whom he might employ in building his mills.

With Mr. Hawley, who was a mill-wright, he agreed to build a grist mill in co-partnership, Hawley to have one-third when the mill was completed. Safford and Hawley accordingly came to Fair Haven, camping on their arrival, the first night, in their covered emigrant wagon, near the river. Hawley built the first grist mill, either this season or the following spring, on the south side of the Lower Falls, a little below the present site of the old paper mill.

About the same time the bridge over the river and the saw mill on the north side were built.

In building the grist mill Mr. Hawley received bodily injuries from falling upon the frozen water

HISTORY OF FAIR HAVEN, VERMONT. 37

wheel while attempting to cut away the ice, which caused his death about eighteen months afterwards. He is said to have been buried in the old burying ground, northwest of James Campbell's. All the widow received for his interest in the property was the use of it two days in every seven, on which days her boy, Asa, then only 14 years old, acted as miller, and the inhabitants generally patronized him in preference to Col. Lyon's employee.

Widow Hawley married Derrick Carner, one of the proprietors of the township, whose name appears in the charter, and who is said by some to have been the first miller in town. He removed with his family to Hampton Corners, where he appears to have resided previously, in 1779 and '80, and thence he went to Underhill, Vt., where he and his wife died.

Mr. Safford built first a log house near the river, perhaps where Cyrus C. Whipple resides, or it may have been yet closer to the river bank. Here he had twenty-five men to board, and Mrs. Safford, who was a small woman, and mistaken for "a little girl" on one occasion, did the work of the house alone, the men assisting her by washing the potatoes at night and putting them on to boil in a cauldron kettle out of doors in the morning.

Mr. Safford did not reside long on this spot, but built a house 20 by 30 feet square on the place where Henry Green's house now stands. He was at this point in December, 1784, when the first highway was laid by the selectmen from Kelsey's north ledge to the river on Oliver Cleveland's farm, and is said

38 HISTORY OF FAIR HAVEN, VERMONT.

to have been here keeping a public house when Col. Lyon came, in 1783. He was here also in 1788, when the road was re-surveyed from the bridge northward.

At the time of the survey, in 1784, Col. Lyon's house is said to have stood near the north end of the bridge, the bridge being 23 rods south, 20° west of the northeast corner of Safford's house; and Ager Hawley lived 19 rods south by 5° west of the north end of the bridge.

These houses must have stood on Col. Lyon's land, and been owned by him, the contract upon which Mr. Safford came to town not having been written, and Col. Lyon deeding him no land according to the terms of the agreement.

In the spring of 1790 Mr. Safford bought the place where John Meacham lived—now Mr. Barnes'—and removed to that part of the town, opening there a public house, which he kept for a number of years. In the spring of 1814 he sold the place to James Y. Watson, of Salem, N. Y., and bought the farm lying next north of it of the estate of Eleazer Claghorn—the same place which Meacham had sold to Col. Erwin, and he to James Claghorn. Mr. Safford conveyed it, in December, 1825, to his son Alonzo, from whom it passed through the hands of Obadiah and J. W. Eddy, Abner and Rowley R. Mead, and Andrew J. Mead to Mr. Kidder, its present owner.

Mr. Safford died on this place. He was a justice of the peace from the commencement of the town for nearly forty years, acknowledging some of the earliest deeds on record, and filled other offices of trust

HISTORY OF FAIR HAVEN, VERMONT. 39

and honor in the gift of his townsmen. He had a large family, among whom Erwin was a prominent business man of the place for many years. The names of other members of the family will be given in a subsequent page.

Abel Hawley, father of Ager and of Mrs. Safford, was here with his children in 1784,.and died in town, October 16th, 1797, aged 77 years.

Among those who came into town in 1783, either before or after Col. Lyon, and settled in the central portion of the present town, were Joel Hamilton, from Brookfield, Mass.; Samuel Stannard, from Killingworth, Conn.; and Daniel Munger, with his son, Ashael, from Litchfield, Conn. Timothy Goodrich and Reuben Munger, Jun., may also have come about the same time.

Mr. Hamilton first settled on the west street, on the lot No. 5, of Elisha Hamilton's first division, of which mention has been made on a previous page. He was here in August, 1783, the place being called his "home-lot" at that time. In December, 1784, the river, it is said, ran between him and Sharp. He appears to have acquired the place through his uncle, Elisha, and his brother, Jesse, of Brookfield, Mass. In June, 1785, he deeds to Charles Rice his interest in the first division of Elisha Hamilton's .right, and the second division of Zadock Everest's right; and Rice deeds him in return the interest which he had in the first and third divisions of Everest's right, and the second, third and fourth divisions of Hamilton's right, besides the 50 acres which he, Joel, had deeded to Abraham

40   HISTORY OF FAIR HAVEN, VERMONT.

Sharp in April, 1784. After this he seems to have resided for a time on the side hill where John D. Wood now has an orchard, north of Harmon Sheldon's house, the hill taking his name, and being called to this day "Mt. Hamilton."

We hear that bears were accustomed to frequent the folds and pig-pens of this vicinity, and that Mrs. Hamilton was once accosted by a bear near her house on this place on Mt. Hamilton.

The house stood on land which had been surveyed to Charles Hawkins, in May, 1781, on the first division of the right of Benjamin Cutler; and Mr. Hamilton bought of Mr. Hawkins, in December, 1787, 20 acres from the southeast corner of this division, including the house he then lived in. He sold this 20 acres, together with 39 acres adjoining it on the east, from the second division right of Elisha Hamilton, to Dr. Simeon Smith, in April of the following year, 1788, and in June purchased of Philip Priest 15 acres, as has been stated in a former page, where Hiram Hamilton now resides, probably removing and taking up his residence on the same about this time. In the spring of 1790 he bought of Daniel Graham, of Suffield, Conn., one-half of the right of Jesse Belknap, the first division of which had been surveyed to Joseph Austin, in November, 1780, on the east of Mr. Priest's lot No. 13, and of the same form and dimensions. Buying of Mr. Priest, subsequently, the remaining portion of lot No. 13, Mr. Hamilton thus had over 200 acres in his home farm, on which he remained attending to various public and private duties, and keeping a mi-

HISTORY OF FAIR HAVEN, VERMONT. 41

nute diary of his farm work and other doings, until his death, on the 5th of June, 1826, when his nephew, Hiram, son of Rufus, became the owner of the property.

Mr. Hamilton was chosen constable of the town for eight years, from 1785 to 1792, and was deputy sheriff of the county for a number of years subsequently. A man of strong purposes and passions, he entered heartily into the Federalist side in politics, and was an open and determined political antagonist to Col. M. Lyon, with whom he seemed to be in almost interminable controversy during the last years of Lyon's residence in town.

Mr. Stannard resided for a short time toward the Lake in West Haven, but soon came and made his home on the spot where his son, Heman, so long resided after him. The place on which he settled was the first division lot, No. 66, of Asa Dudley's right, and was first surveyed in October, 1780, to Jeremiah Burton, but being purchased, in 1784, by 'Mr. Stannard and Timothy Goodrich in company, was re-surveyed to them in June, 1787, and by them divided, Mr. Goodrich settling on the east half, where Joseph Sheldon now owns and occupies, and Mr. Stannard on the west half.

Mr. Stannard bought the south half of Ebenezer Frisbie's first division lot, which lies just north of Mr. Sheldon's, of Dr. Simeon Smith, in February, 1797. He deeds to Heman, in March, 1815, his home place— 50 acres of Asa Dudley's right and 1 acre from Philip Priest's first division—and Heman leases it back during

42 HISTORY OF FAIR HAVEN, VERMONT..

his father's life. Mr. Stannard was an active and prominent man among the early settlers, and was frequently chosen on the board of selectmen. He died in April, 1815, in his 67th year.

Mr. Goodrich may not have come permanently into town, settling with his family, until the spring of 1784. He appears to have been a son of Waitstill Goodrich, of Woodbury, Conn., and to have had a brother Waitstill; the father giving to Timothy, in January, 1784, two-thirds, and to Waitstill one-third, of a half interest in Asa Dudley's right in Fair Haven. In March, 1801, Mr. Goodrich buys of Dr. Simeon Smith the 59 acres which Joel Hamilton had sold Smith, lying on Mt. Hamilton, and the north half of the Frisbie lot, now owned by John D. Wood. He sold this to his son, Chauncey, in August, 1818, Chauncey then living on it, and he being in Bethlehem, Conn., whither he is said to have gone and temporarily resided. The home farm where Joseph Sheldon now resides seems to have fallen to his son Elizur, upon the death of the father, in February, 1829.

The Mungers, Daniel and Ashael, settled on the intervale through which the road to the Sheldon saw-mill now runs, known universally in town as "the Munger road." Here, with them, also resided Joseph Snow, who had married Elizabeth, a daughter of Deacon Daniel Munger. Snow occupied a house which stood on the west side of the road, and Mr. Munger a house which was standing only a few years since, on the east side, where Harmon Sheldon now owns.

Daniel and Eunice, his wife, had received a deed

HISTORY OF FAIR HAVEN, VERMONT. 43.

from Judah Lewis, in June, 1783, while they were yet in Litchfield, of the right of Thomas Taylor, in the town, the first division lot of which, No. 15, had been surveyed to Joseph Taylor in November, 1780.

Daniel and his wife deed six acres of this division to Elizabeth Snow, and the other 94 acres to their son, Ashael, in December, 1793. Mr. Munger died here February 10th, 1805, in his 80th year, and Ashael occupied the farm with his family until the spring of 1817, when, having sold the place the previous October to Dr. Ebenezer Hurd, he removed to Michigan.

Elizabeth Snow had sold her 6 acres to Dr. Hurd in May, 1816, and the whole was deeded by Dr. Hurd to Dr. James Witherell, from whom it passed at length into the possession of Joseph Sheldon, Sen.

Daniel Munger was known as a deacon of the church, and is said to have superintended the building of the old meeting-house—now Daniel Orms' dwelling-house —about the year 1791, and to have found one of the first ministers who preached for the church, in the person of a Rev. Mr. Farley, a young man, who came hither from Poultney about 1803, and preached for a time, boarding with Maj. Tilly Gilbert, who then lived where the Vermont Hotel now stands. After Mr. Munger's death, his son, Ashael, became a deacon in the church.

Reuben Munger, Jr., was from Norfolk, in Litchfield county, Conn., having in October, 1782, bought the south half, or fifty acres of the first division lot of Ebenezer Frisbie, lying south of John D. Wood's place—now owned by Mr. Stannard—and removed on

44 HISTORY OF FAIR HAVEN, VERMONT.

to the same. He was on the place in the summer of 1785, when the road was surveyed north and west from the place called "the Narrows," to the eastward of his house. He seems to have removed to Middlebury prior to June, 1790, at which time he sold his place to Dr. Simeon Smith.

Lieut. Charles McArthur, of Nobletown, N. Y., bought of Col. M. Lyon, of Arlington, in July, 1783, 260 acres of land—the first, second and third divisions of Elijah Galusha's right—on the hill in the east and north parts of the town, ever since known and called from Mr. McArthur's national character and origin, Scotch Hill. This land had been surveyed to Mr. Galusha in April, 1781, and sold to Col. Lyon in November, 1782. It now constitutes the farms of Tilly Gilbert, Arnold Briggs and Joseph Sheldon, which extend from the hill down on to the intervale.

Mr. McArthur erected the first frame house of which we hear in the town—a low-studded, one story building—on the hill, over which the road then passed east of Tilly Gilbert's present residence, and there resided and died. The place was afterward occupied by his son-in-law, Elihu Wright, and is now owned by Mr. Briggs. His great arm-chair, which was one of the first brought into the town, is now in the hands of Mrs. Arnold Briggs, having been presented to her as a relic by Daniel McArthur, on his removal from town in 1835. It is of turned posts, straight backed, and in the style of the old-fashioned, splint bottomed ware.

Mr. McArthur's first wife, whom he must have

HISTORY OF FAIR HAVEN, VERMONT. 45

married in Arlington, was a daughter of Gov. Chittenden, and sister to Col. Lyon's second wife. He married Rebecca Stanton for his second wife, who survived him, and afterwards married Nathan Ranney.

He had a large family, among whom his lands were divided. He died October 8th, 1816, in his 74th year, and was buried in the village grave-yard. On his tomb stone is inscribed this epitaph: "An honest man is the noblest work of God."

Eli Everts, together with his brother Ambrose, must have been in the town, or vicinity, as early as the fall of 1783. In December, 1783, Ambrose is a witness with Beriah Mitchell to a deed from Isaac Clark to Abraham Sharp, and in April, 1784, both Ambrose and Eli witness to a deed from Joel Hamilton to Abraham Sharp.

They are said to have lived in a log house on the lower side of the road beyond Mr. Stannard's, at an early day, and as they resided on the place in December, 1784, when the road was surveyed from Eleazer Dudley's southward to Eli Everts', previously to their purchasing the land of Col. Isaac Clark, it is not improbable that they came first in 1783 into the house which had been built and occupied by Joseph Haskins, on Col. Clark's first division, lot No. 4. Haskins was on the place in the spring of 1783, when the great change in the course of the river bed occurred, and as there was trouble between him and Col. Clark, he may have decamped about this time, leaving Col. Clark to lease the place to Mr. Everts. The place was deeded to Mr. Everts, Nov. 20th, 1786, from a

46   HISTORY OF FAIR HAVEN, VERMONT.

tree "on the point of rocks on the north side of the river at the foot of the Great Falls, which the water has left dry," up the river to Michael Merritt's northwest corner, thence eastward to Mr. Stannard's land and around northward and westward, containing 100 acres on the first division of Samuel Herrick's right—No. 4—50 acres on the first division of Ira Allen's right and 14 acres on the third division of the same.

Mr. Everts must have built the old gambrel roofed house which formerly stood where Otis Hamilton's house is. In July, 1813, he sold 14 acres and 53 rods next west of Mr. Stannard's to Joel Hamilton. He sells above 11 acres to Lewis Stone, in February, 1809; and in April, 1816, he deeds the farm of 120 acres to his son, Milo. Milo sells it to Heman Stannard and Stephen Fish, in September, 1819. Mr. Fish bought out Stannard's interest in 1821, and carried on the place till 1827, himself living at the foot of the great hill, and having charge of the toll-gate on the turnpike, in West Haven. He then occupied it until May, 1835, when he sold it to its present occupant, Otis Hamilton.

Mr. Everts was called "Captain" by the people of his time. He was selectman of the town in 1793, and is spoken of as an old man in 1820. His wife's name was Jemima, and they had a daughter Millicent.

Millicent married a man by the name of Fuller, and was resident in Malone, N. Y., in June, 1826, when she appoints Linus Everts, of Cornwall, Vt., her attorney, and he sells about 21 acres adjoining the land of Jonathan Orms and Apollos Smith, to Stephen

HISTORY OF FAIR HAVEN, VERMONT. 47

Fish, in August, 1826. Milo was a student and teacher, and removed to Athens, Ohio, subsequent to his mother's death, about 1823, where he became Judge of Probate.

Richard Beddow, an Englishman, who had been a soldier in the army of Gen. Burgoyne, but deserted, or was taken prisoner and never returned, was early a settler near John Meacham,.on the hill east of Mr. Kidder's, in the south part of the town. He was a blacksmith and nailer, and worked at making nails with John Meacham, in a shop on his farm.

He married widow Rebecca Hosford and had a family of seven children. His sons removed to Warsaw, N. Y., whither he followed them subsequently to 1825, having in a fit of intoxication and violent temper, beaten his wife so badly as to cause her death. The farm passed through the sons' hands to Oliver Maranville.

Andrew Race is said to have lived in a small house near the school house in the south district; and his brother, Isaac Race, on the Hampton side of the river. Mrs. Sally Benjamin, a daughter of Isaac Race, who was afterward a resident of this town for many years, relates that when she was a child, she was playing beside the river bank and saw Col. Lyon's emigrant teams ford the river below Mr. Cleveland's on the arrival of the family in town.

We hear of a young physician of the name of Safford in the town as early as 1783, but he was no relation to Silas Safford, and appears not to have remained long in the town. Perhaps there were other residents

48   HISTORY OF FAIR HAVEN, VERMONT.

at the time Lyon commenced his works. We hear of several, among whom was Thomas Stonnage, a Dutchman, who cleared the land where Mr. Kittredge's house now stands. Benjamin Parmenter, or Parmetry, who married a daughter of Oliver Cleveland, and first built on the east side of the cedar swamp, afterward residing on land that Stonnage cleared, was also in the town at this early date.

In the north and west parts of the town—now West Haven—Beriah Mitchell, who had come from Woodbury, Conn., to Castleton, and thence to Fair Haven, in 1782, was settled on the farm now occupied by Mrs. Adelaide Hitchcock. He was constable in 1784, and one of the leading men of that day, but did not remain, returning to Connecticut in the year 1786.

The place on which he lived passed from him into the hands of his brother, Ichabod Mitchell, who came here in the year 1783, or thereabout, and kept a public house at the corner of the road.

James Ball and Perley Starr, who together bought the right of John Fassett, Jr., about where Rodney Fields now lives, had early commenced improvements on the same, but soon sold out and moved away. In the early part of 1783, sometime between January and April, Eleazer Dudley and Abijah Peet, both from Woodbury, Conn., came and located in the West Haven part of the town, Mr. Dudley on or near the "school lot," about where Nathaniel Fish resides, and Mr. Peet next north of Mr. Mitchell's, toward Benson. Thomas Dixon, written also Dickson and Dickinson,

HISTORY OF FAIR HAVEN, VERMONT. 49

in the records, came in from Castleton, locating next north of Mr. Peet's, on Benson line.

John Howe, Elijah Tryon, Elisha Frisbie, John and Henry Cramer, Timothy Lindsley, and others, came this year from Connecticut, and took up lands in West Haven. About the same time, also, or a little later in the year, came Heman Barlow, Cornelius Brownson, David Sanford, Samuel Lee, Amos and John McKinstry, and others, whose settlements belong to the history of West Haven.

DOINGS OF THE PROPRIETORS.

The first meeting of the proprietors to organize under the charter was warned by Ira Allen, Governor's Assistant, and was held at the house of Nehemiah Hoit, at Castleton Corners, June 14th, 1780. Col. Ebenezer Allen was chosen moderator, and Capt. Isaac Clark proprietors' clerk.

Capt. Clark, John Grant and Nathaniel Smith were appointed a committee " to survey and lay out a town plot on the most convenient place for trade and navigation, said plot to consist of one lot to each proprietor's right, containing not more than four acres, nor less than one." The committee were instructed "to lay out such roads as they should judge to be most convenient to the place of trade and navigation."

At this meeting it was voted to make a division of 100 acres of land, with 5 acres for highways, to each proprietor's right, and "that Maj. Ebenezer Allen and

50   HISTORY OF FAIR HAVEN, VERMONT.

Capt. Isaac Clark, as a compensation in part for their extraordinary trouble and expense in looking out the town and procuring a grant thereof, shall have the privilege of making the two first pitches in the first division, which pitches shall be called No. 1 and No. 2."

Lieut. Elisha Clark, Oliver Cleveland and Asa Dudley were chosen a committee to lay out the first division lots on the public rights. Capt. John Grant was chosen proprietor's treasurer.

It was voted that the 21st of August (1780) next, be the day to begin to survey the pitches. The next meeting was held by adjournment at the same place, August 16th. Of this meeting Capt. John Grant, of Poultney, was moderator, and Michael Merritt clerk.

It was voted to accept the plan and survey of the town plot reported by the committee, each lot containing one acre, together with one acre set apart for a public landing place for shipping.

Oct. 4th, 1780, the proprietors met again at Mr. Hoit's. Philip Priest, moderator. Voted to make a further division of 100 acres to each right to be called the "second division lots." Ensign Gershom Lake, Oliver Cleveland and Asa Dudley were appointed a committee to lay the public lots of this division.

At this meeting it was voted "that we will draw for the town plot lots in the same manner that we have drawn for the first and second-division pitches." Maj. Clark, Ensign Lake and Asa Dudley were "appointed and empowered to lay out a public highway from the west line of Castleton to the Great Falls, on lot No. 4, in the first division." Lot No. 4 was the lot laid

HISTORY OF FAIR HAVEN, VERMONT. 51

by Col. Clark, below where Otis Hamilton lives. It was directed that this main road from Castleton to the Great Falls should be six rods wide, and other roads which the committee might lay might be of any convenient width which they should think best.

December 14th, 1780. The proprietors met to draw for third division pitches of 63 acres each. Chose Michael Merritt, Philip Priest and Heman Barlow a committee to lay the public lots of this division. Chose Philip Priest collector, with power to enforce settlements.

June 7th, 1781. A proprietors' meeting was holden at the house of Maj. Isaac Clark, and voted to draw for a fourth division of their lands of 50 acres each. At a meeting, October 4th, Col. Isaac Clark and Jonathan Brace, Esq., were "appointed and empowered to act as agents for the proprietors of Fair Haven to vindicate the title of said township, as granted by charter of the General Assembly, in October, 1779."

April 8th, 1782. Isaac Clark charges the proprietors £3 and 6s. for two journeys to Bennington "to procure the charter and get it recorded," and £1 and 8s. for fees paid the Secretary for drawing and recording said charter. At an adjourned meeting, at Col. Clark's, Sept. 2nd, of this year, Eleazer Dudley was chosen on the committee to lay out public roads in lieu of Asa Dudley, and Philip Priest in lieu of Gershom Lake. Beriah Mitchell and Oliver Cleveland were constituted a committee to warn land owners when to work on the highways, and to keep the ac-

52   HISTORY OF FAIR HAVEN, VERMONT.

count of every man's work, and see that the roads were properly and well made.

The main highway from Castleton line to Mr. Dudley's camp, a point somewhere not far westward of the present division line between Fair Haven and West Haven, was surveyed, October 8th, of this year, 1782, *via* "muddy brook," Philip Priest's house, and the house of Joseph Haskins; Haskins' house being about 200 rods in a northwest direction nearly from Mr. Priest's then residence, and the road from Mr. Priest's house leading first south 38° west 12 rods, then turning westward and running from 27° to 38° north.

In November, 1782, Philip Priest and Curtis Kelsey were appointed overseers of highway work, and after several adjournments the last meeting of the proprietors in Castleton was held at Col. Clark's, the 8th of May, 1783; whence, after voting a tax of one penny per acre, 311 acres to each right, for highways and bridges, and appointing Heman Barlow, Thomas Dickson and Eleazer Dudley a committee to look after roads and open such new ones from the main road, already cleared, as best to accommodate the inhabitants, the meeting was adjourned to come together again November 3d, at the house of Philip Priest, in Fair Haven.

November 3d, 1783, the proprietors met at Mr. Priest's house, and after appointing a committee to settle with the Treasurer, adjourned to the first Monday of January, 1784, which meeting being convened, passed a vote limiting the special privileges previously granted to certain persons of covering their claims,

HISTORY OF FAIR HAVEN, VERMONT.

to the first day of February, and then adjourned to May 3d, when they met again, and having voted to raise a tax of one penny on the acre, dissolved the meeting.

CHAPTER III.

FROM THE ORGANIZATION OF THE CIVIL GOVERNMENT TO THE. DIVISION OF THE TOWN IN 1792.

1783. The important measure of organizing the civil government of the town was taken in a meeting of the settlers at the house of Mr. Priest, August 28th, 1783. Mr. Priest was chosen moderator, and Eleazer Dudley first town clerk. The first selectmen were Philip Priest, John Meacham and Heman Barlow. Michael Merritt was chosen first constable. No other officers were chosen until the following spring.

1784. The regular town meeting for the election of town officers was held at Mr. Priest's, March 22d, when Mr. Dudley was re-elected town clerk. Eleazer Dudley, Thomas Dickson and Oliver Cleveland were chosen selectmen; Daniel Munger, grand juryman; Philip Priest and Beriah Mitchell, listers; Beriah Mitchell, constable; Michael Merritt, treasurer; Ichabod Mitchell, John Meacham and Philip Priest, surveyors; Philip Priest, Michael Merritt and Eleazer Dudley, trustees, to take care of the school right, and the right for the support of the ministry. A vote was passed at this time to raise a tax of £6 and 10s. on the polls of the inhabitants, which was

HISTORY OF FAIR HAVEN, VERMONT. 55

rescinded at a subsequent meeting, held May 4th, and it was voted to raise the sum of £6 and 10s. "on the polls and ratable estate of the inhabitants."

Agreeably to a vote of the town the school lot was sold, in September, to Eleazer Dudley, for £75. At a meeting held September 22d, at Col. Lyon's house, the inhabitants voted, 1st, "That the county of Rutland extend seven townships north and south, and that Castleton be the county seat." 2d, "That they will remonstrate against the town of Rutland being a county town." 3d, They chose Col. M. Lyon, John Meacham and Heman Barlow a committee to draw a remonstrance against the doings of the county convention.

Several new roads or highways were surveyed in the town, in December of this year. Allusion has been made to that from Kelsey's ledge to Mr Cleveland's. The road previously running southward from a point 24 rods north of Silas Safford's house, i. e., from the village to Poultney river near Oliver Cleveland's, is called in the record of the survey, "a path." The new road now laid from this point was six rods wide, and farther to the west than the road now is, or near the cedar swamp. A road was laid this month from a point 12 or 14 rods east of Mr. Priest's barn northward and eastward to Mr. Munger's house.

On the 28th, Beriah Mitchell surveyed a six rod wide highway "beginning at a hemlock tree standing 22 rods northwardly of Col. Lyon's barn, thence running north 23° west 48 rods, thence north 30° west 40 rods, thence north 44° west 14 rods, thence north

G

56   HISTORY OF FAIR HAVEN, VERMONT.

56° west 26 rods, thence north 45° west 30 rods, thence north 52° west 22 rods, thence north 44° west 56 rods, to where it enters the old main road near ' Muddy Brook bridge,' so called." At the same time another road was laid from the middle of the large bridge between Abraham Sharp's and Joel Hamilton's, eastward, running north of east and then south, to where it intersected the old main road at a hemlock tree.

Moses Holmes appears to have come into town in the autumn of 1784, from Lenox, Mass., buying 30 acres of land of Joseph Ballard, adjoining Poultney river, and next north of John Meacham. This he sold to Matthew Lyon, November 29th, 1785, and bought another 30 acres, of William Meacham, at the extreme southern end of the town, November 30th. This land had been improved by Mr. Meacham, and was laid out on the third division of John House. It appears to have been owned afterwards by Samuel Beaman, of Hampton, as well as the Hyde lot, north of it, but we find no record of its transfer from Holmes. Holmes appears to have been in Hampton in April, 1788, but further than this we can get no trace of him. In April, 1790, Frederick Hill, surveyor, by direction of the selectmen of the town, laid out a highway, "Beginning on the middle of a bridge over Poultney river, near the southeast corner of said town, called Holmes' bridge." The road was laid eastward and northward to lands of Oliver Cleveland. There is slight reason to think Mr. Holmes may have been one of Col. Lyon's employees in the forge or mill.

HISTORY OF FAIR HAVEN, VERMONT. 57

David Punderson, who is alluded to in a vote of the town a little further on, in May, 1785, was chosen one of the listers at the annual March meeting of 1785, and must have been in the town as early as the year preceding, 1784. He resided on the upper side of the road, beyond Mr. Everts', but we learn nothing more concerning him.

1785. The annual town meeting for the year 1785 was held at Mr. Priest's, March 21st. Michael Merritt was chosen town clerk and treasurer. Philip Priest, Eleazer Dudley and Oliver Cleveland were chosen selectmen; Joel Hamilton, constable; and Silas Safford, David Punderson and Thomas Dickson, listers.

"Voted that Oliver Cleveland, Curtis Kelsey and Joel Hamilton be a committee to view the road from Mr. Priest's to Hubbardton river and Benson line, and make a report where it is best the road should go, by the first Tuesday of May, and that the above committee lay a burying place, by the road, south of Mud Brook."

This burial ground was located beside the old road, between the house now occupied by James Campbell and that in which John Allard resides. It was the first public burial place in the town, and had some thirty or forty graves made in it.

At an adjourned meeting, held May 3d, at Mr. Priest's, it was "voted that the road go from Philip Priest's barn to Samuel Stannard's, thence running in the old road through Eli Everts' field, to Mr. Punderson's," and "that two days labor be done on the roads

58 HISTORY OF FAIR HAVEN, VERMONT.

over what the law directs." The town was at this meeting first divided into three districts, whether school or highway districts is not stated, but we have reason to think this division pertained to the schools, if not also to the highways. The territory between Muddy Brook and Hubbardton river was to be the first district; that south of Muddy Brook the second; and that west of Hubbardton river the third.

A vote was passed that Elisha Frisbie should be deemed an inhabitant of the town; but another meeting, held in June, revoked the act by which Frisbie was given a habitation, and he was accordingly warned by the authorities to depart from the town in ten days. The circumstance illustrates a common practice of those days, that of ordering persons out of town to prevent their becoming a public charge.

We have on record the names of about fifty individuals who were warned away, many of them with their families, during the ten years which elapsed between 1803 and 1813. Some of these continued to reside here for years afterward, contriving a way to support themselves and their growing families, like so many of the other early inhabitants who were too poor to go away.

The main highway, laid by the proprietors, through the town, in October, 1782, we have seen, ran south from Mr. Priest's house 38° west 12 rods, then westward in a direction 27° to 38° north. The vote of the citizens at the meeting in May, of this year, was that the road go from Mr. Priest's barn to Samuel Stannard's. In June the selectmen caused a road to be surveyed "in

HISTORY OF FAIR HAVEN, VERMONT. 59

exchange of a highway leading from Philip Priest's barn to Samuel Stannard's house, it being part of a six rod highway, beginning at a hemlock tree standing in the east side of said highway, near said Priest's barn, in lot No. 13, division first; thence running south 30° west 20 rods to a maple tree, thence north 40° west 60 rods to a tree, thence west 30° north 24 rods to a tree at the south side of Mr. Stannard's house, and to the old road." There was also surveyed and laid out a highway "from Daniel Munger's to the country road," beginning in the north line of the highway between Reuben Munger's and Daniel Munger's, "near a place called the Narrows," thence running north and west "to the east side of the country road, in Capt. Brook's lot, about 100 rods north of the school house.

At a town meeting held September 5th, at the school house, agreeably to a warning for that purpose, it was voted that the selectmen see if a road can be obtained from Philip Priest's to Mr. Rice's, and that they "procure a deed of Mr. Priest to tolerate Michael Merritt to pass and repass through. his lands, where the road now runs, with some restrictions." In November, a road was laid from a hemlock tree marked "H," standing in the north side of the highway leading from Col. Lyon's to "Sharp's bridge," near the corner of Mr. Rice's field, to the south corner of Mr. Merritt's land, thence along his east line northward "to a tree in the west side of the highway which leads by Mr. Priest's to the Bay, about six rods west of Mr. Stannard's house."

The selectmen laid a road from a point in Castleton

60 HISTORY OF FAIR HAVEN, VERMONT.

west line south of "Screw Driver Pond," running southerly 32° west 420 rods "to Mr. McArthur's wheat field," and thence to the north side of the highway leading from Castleton to East Bay. This road is said to have run over the top of the hill, further east than the road now does.

Charles Rice, of whose land mention is made above, came hither from Brookfield, Mass., in the early part of this year. He had bought of Jesse Hamilton, of Brookfield, in February of the previous year, a half interest in the right of Elisha Hamilton, and in June, 1785, he buys of Joel Hamilton, of Fair Haven, "one-half in quantity and quality" of Elisha Hamilton's lot No. 5, and one-half of Zadock Everest's second division, both on the west street, toward "Sharp's bridge." Mr. Rice was first constable in town in 1793 and 1794. He removed from the west street to West Haven, and was keeping a public house nigh where Nathaniel Fish now resides, in the latter part of the year 1795, and also in the years 1798 and 1799. He was an eccentric man, and wrote on his sign :

> "Nothing on this side and nothing on t'other ;
> Nothing in the house, nor in the stable either."

His wife was Abigail Cutler, sister to Isaac Cutler, Esq. She died in West Haven, June 16th, 1820, in her 66th year. He removed to Canada before the war of 1812, and died there. They had two sons and one daughter.

Isaac Cutler, Esq., whose name we often meet in

HISTORY OF FAIR HAVEN, VERMONT. 61

the subsequent records of our early history, came hither also from Brookfield, in the spring of this year. He bought 75 acres of land of Mr. Rice on the 4th day of July, one-half from the east end of Zadock Everest's second division, on the north side of the road, and the other half from the east end of the Elisha Hamilton lot No. 5, on the south side of the road. Mr. Cutler built on this land the house afterward owned by Jacob Willard, and at a later period by Cyrus Graves, now the old house standing next east of Hamilton Wescott's farm house. It was opened and kept as a tavern by Mr. Cutler for some years, serving as a popular evening resort for the early settlers of the neighborhood. There was a nursery of apple trees. by the roadside a little east of the house, in 1797.

The place was sold by him—he having added to and sold from it—in September, 1798, to Philip Allen, of Salem, N. Y., and by Mr. Allen, in April, 1802, to Paul Scott, of Granville, N. Y. While owned by him it was occupied as late as 1816 by his father-in-law, Abel Parker. Mr. Scott sold 20 acres from the east side to Rev. Rufus Cushman, in April, 1808. He sold the rest of the place to Jacob and Azel Willard, in March, 1818. By them it was sold to Cyrus Graves, of Rupert, and passed into the hands of its present owner, Hamilton Wescott.

Stephen Rogers, a tanner and shoemaker by trade, who seems to have been a particular friend of Col. Lyon's, came from Branford, Conn., this year. He was followed soon after by his younger brothers, Ambrose, Beriah and Jared. Stephen started the first

62   HISTORY OF FAIR HAVEN, VERMONT.

tannery in town, under the patronage of Col. Lyon, under the hill on the west side of the Common. Hé also built the house where William Dolan resides, together with a shoe shop standing where Mrs. Ira Allen's house now is. In May, 1792, he bought of Col. Lyon 7 acres of land, extending from his house and shop back to the river, and including the tannery. He sold the place in March, 1801, to Calvin Munger, and went away to the West.

Col. Lyon, who, in 1805, was doing a large business in tanning, at Eddyville, Ky., sought and obtained him to go to Eddyville, whither his wife, whom he had left in Fair Haven, was assisted by the town to go to him, in August, 1811. She returned from western New York and died in Elizabethtown some years after.

Col. Lyon built the dam on his Upper Falls to bring water to his iron works, in July of this year, 1785, and in October (14th) he petitions the General Assembly of the State, which was then an independent sovereignty, to lay a duty of two pence per pound on nails, to enable him to build his works and supply the State. The place was called from this time, and for many years was known over the whole country about, by the name of "Lyon's works."

1786. Gamaliel Leonard came from Pittsfield, Mass., in 1785, to Greenfield, N. Y., stopping on Hampton Hills, and while resident there, in January, 1786, bought of Heman Barlow 120 acres on Poultney river, in Fair Haven. This land laid along the Falls north of the place where the old Skeene's road crossed.

HISTORY OF FAIR HAVEN, VERMONT. 63

It was surveyed as two 60 acre pitches, in April, 1781, on the third division of the rights of Joseph Haven and Stephen Rice, or Stephen Pearl (the survey bill says Rice, the deeds Pearl).

Moving into town in the spring of 1786, Mr. Leonard built him a house near the Falls, and commenced the erection of the second saw mill in town. The country east of Mr. Leonard was then an almost unbroken forest. A road was cut around the north side of the cedar swamp, and Oliver Cleveland drove a yoke of cattle on this road through the woods, which was the first team driven through to the saw mill. In 1788, Mr. Leonard, in company with Elias Stevens and Daniel Arnold, of Hampton, built a forge at the west end of the saw mill. Mr. Arnold sold his share of the forge to James Downey, Jr., in December, 1792, and Mr. Stevens sold his to Dr. Simeon Smith, in March, 1802.

Charles Hawkins, Sen., came into town from Smithfield, R. I., in the summer of 1786, buying, in August of this year, of James Hooker, of Poultney, one-half of Asa Joiner's right of land in the town, the first division of which was surveyed to him next south of the farms of Michael Merritt and Philip Priest, and just north of the entrance of Muddy Brook into Poultney river.

Here Mr. Hawkins built and settled, taking the freeman's oath in the town, in September, 1788, and removing and enlarging his house in 1792.

He had, several years previously, while resident in Smithfield, in January, 1781, purchased, in company

H

64   HISTORY OF FAIR HAVEN, VERMONT.

with his brother-in-law, James Bowen, of Smithfield, the original right of land in the town which belonged to Benjamin or Benoni Cutler, of Plainfield, N. H., and the first division of this right was surveyed to him in May, 1781; from which we infer that he had visited the town and located his land at this early date. He is said to have been a "gentleman" and a "blacksmith" in Rhode Island, and appears to have made a number of purchases and sales of lands in town. He adds to his home-farm by purchase of Philip Priest, in the spring of 1787, about 25 acres; and in the fall sells 20 acres to Joel Hamilton, in a triangular form, from the southeast corner of Benjamin Cutler's first division, including the house in which Hamilton then lived, said to have been in an orchard on the side of Mt. Hamilton.

In October, 1795, he sells to John Lamb and Lewis Bigelow the first and fourth divisions of John Paine's right, now constituting a part of J. W. Estey's farm. He had sold 26 acres on the north side to Isaac Cutler; and he afterwards sells 64 acres further eastward and laid on the first division of John Paine's right to Col. Matthew Lyon. In the spring of 1799 he quit-claims 52 1-2 acres from the middle of Benjamin Cutler's first division to James Bowen; Bowen having previously sold it to Jesse Olney, and Bowen quit-claims to him the remainder of the lot. In 1807 Mr. Hawkins deeds what is left on the west to his son, Charles.

Mr. Hawkins died here March 31st, 1810, in his 75th year, and his widow married Michael Merritt..

HISTORY OF FAIR HAVEN, VERMONT. 65

The home-farm was sold by his sons, Charles and Richard, to Dr. James Witherell, in October, 1813. Witherell sold it to Peter Merritt, in January, 1815. In September, 1821, Merritt sold it to Olney Hawkins, who occupied it till May, 1827, selling it in the previous June, 1826, to Heman Stannard.

David Erwin, afterwards known as "Colonel," and later as "General" Erwin, came hither from New Jersey, soon after the completion of Col. Lyon's iron works, and probably as early as the year 1786, he being in town and witnessing to the signing of a deed in March, 1787.

He is remembered by the older inhabitants as a man of marked ability, and the efficient superintendent, or foreman, of the slitting mill. The story is told that when he came to town, then a young man, he first engaged at very small wages as "blower and striker" in the shop where Col. Lyon's chief workman was manufacturing axes, pretending not to be skilled in any of the arts of Vulcan, and so was called "Lyon's fool." After a little while, when engaged in "striking" with his "boss," he put in the interrogatory, "Why not strike there?—and again, there?" The "boss" getting impatient of the fool's impudence, as he regarded it, swore out that he might make the axe himself, he appearing to know so much; when Erwin replied that he would do so if he would suffer him to try his hand. He accordingly took the fire and anvil, and in an unusually short space of time turned out his axe, which was declared to be a handsomer, better axe than any the shop had before produced. The "boss" threw

66 HISTORY OF FAIR HAVEN, VERMONT.

off his apron, put on his coat and cleared the shop, calling on Col. Lyon to settle up, averring that "the fool" had outwitted him and he would no longer work.

From this time "Captain Erwin," as he was first called, came to be Col. Lyon's foremost workman. He took the freeman's oath here in September, 1788. In May, 1789, he purchased of John Meacham three acres of land, on the bank of Poultney river, in the south part of the town. The next year he bought three acres more, and in January, 1794, he bought what land Mr. Meacham then owned, situated where Asahel H. Kidder now resides. He purchased 38 acres of Stephen Holt, adjoining his farm on the west, in the June following.

He sold the whole of this, with about 36 acres more laid to him on Elijah Galusha's right—about 110 acres —in November, 1798, to Henry Ainsworth, of Pomfret, Vt. In December, he bought of Ichabod and Aaron Brownell, of Colchester, Vt., the fourth division of James Brookin's right, lying south of Mr. Leonard's, on the bank of Poultney river. He also purchased about the same time the first and fourth divisions of John Paine's right, of John Lamb and James Sharp, and 20 acres of Joel Doud. He had laid out to himself on the right of Benjamin Richardson about 60 acres, in September, 1799, and bought of Col. Lyon 28 acres more. Together these lots constituted the farm which he sold, in September, 1800, to Josiah Norton, and on which J. Wellington Estey now resides.

Col. Erwin was ordered to meet with the regiment

HISTORY OF FAIR HAVEN, VERMONT. 67

under his command for parade, June 9th, 1796, his regiment being in the second division of the second brigade of State militia. He was called "General" Erwin, in 1799, and appears to have left the town about 1801 or 1802, and to have gone to northern New York. He leased the slitting mill, owned by Edward Douse, of Dedham, Mass., of Mr. Douse's attorney, John Brown, in December, 1800, until February, 1802. He was one, among others, licensed to sell liquors at the June training, of 1802. *See Appendix V.*

He is said to have had two sons, Walter and Moses, while in town, and afterwards to have been himself a member, or to have had a son who was a member of the N. Y. State Senate. Further than this we learn nothing of him.

Ethan Whipple, Esq., from North Providence, R. I., was one of the new comers of this year. He was a carpenter by trade, in Rhode Island, and had been a soldier in the war of the Revolution. Here he took up a large tract of land on the rights of John and Lemuel Paine, an interest in which he had purchased as early as 1781. He built the house where John Allard now resides, and sold the same to Adams Dutton, in 1831, and removed to the west street, buying the house and lot now occupied by Charles Clyne, of Joseph Adams, and residing there till his death. He was long a prominent and influential citizen of the town.

Ashbel Clark, who is said to have resided at Mr. Merritt's and Mr. Goodrich's, and afterwards to have

68 HISTORY OF FAIR HAVEN, VERMONT.

gone west, was here in November, 1786, and bought 50 acres of the first division of Ira Allen's right, of Col. Isaac Clark, located just above or eastward of Otis Hamilton's present residence. He took the freeman's oath in town in 1788, and sold his land, in December, to Dan Smith. He was assessed, in 1789, at £8.

Capt. Elijah Taylor come from Brookfield, Mass., this year. He was elected a juryman in March, 1787. He resided on the west street, having some claim on the farm of Charles Rice, a part of which he sold to John W. Throop, called "Troop," as late as June, 1795.

Capt. Taylor was never married. He was a great talker; had been in the battle of Bunker Hill; and used often to meet his neighbors and while away the long winter evenings in social chit-chat and story-telling over the merry cup at Squire Cutler's inn. He removed to Hydeville, then "Castleton Mills," where he died, about 1819.

The annual town meeting was held this year, March 13th, 1786, at Samuel Stannard's house. Michael Merritt was re-chosen town clerk and treasurer. Silas Safford, Thomas Dickson and Samuel Stannard were chosen selectmen.

At another meeting, held at Mr. Stannard's, September 5th, it was voted "not to divide the town into two societies," and to appropriate funds to build bridges in the west part of the town.

In December, at Mr. Stannard's, it was voted " that they will hire a minister," and Thomas Dickson was

HISTORY OF FAIR HAVEN, VERMONT. 69

made a committee "to treat with Benson committee how they shall proceed." A tax of two pence on the pound to be laid on the List of 1786 was voted, it is to be inferred, for the support of the ministry.

1787. Dr. Simeon Smith, of Sharon, Conn., came hither this year, and bought lands extensively in the West Haven part of the town. He built a saw mill on Hubbardton river, and commenced a forge on the Falls, afterwards owned by Gen. Jonathan Orms. He resided on the school lot, so-called, which he leased from Eleazer Dudley, in February, 1789. He there built the house which was afterwards occupied by Maj. Tilly Gilbert.

Dr. Smith was a leading and influential citizen of the town, and previous to the division in 1792, was chosen selectman in the years 1789, '90 and '91. He was chosen representative to the General Assembly, in 1789 and 1792, and again in 1797. He was the delegate of the town to the State Convention at Bennington, in January, 1791, which for Vermont, adopted and ratified the Constitution of the United States; and in 1789 was elected one of the Assistant Judges of the Rutland county court. In 1792 he was Probate Judge for the district of Fair Haven. He died February 27th, 1804, aged 70 years, bequeathing to the town of West Haven the sum of $1,000, then a relatively generous amount, to be kept at interest for the period of 60 years, after which time to be devoted to educational purposes as follows: "to have one good grammar school kept in West Haven, near the village where I now live, the overplus for

70   HISTORY OF FAIR HAVEN, VERMONT.

the benefit of other schools and the support of a gospel minister, well educated and regularly instructed in the ministry, and if any over, for the support of the poor and needy in the said town of West Haven, under the direction of the civil authority and the selectmen of said town."

Dr. Smith's second wife was Catharine Cutler, sister to Isaac Cutler, Esq. She survived him, inheriting by his will one-half of all his estate, which was estimated at $80,000, and afterward married Christopher Minot, Esq., of Boston.

Dr. Stephen Hall came from Connecticut, where he lost his left hand while cutting cornstalks for molasses, during the Revolutionary war. He bought a building lot of Capt. Elijah Taylor, in March, 1788, on the corner of the west street and the road leading to Mr. Hawkins'. He was also chosen one of the listers in town in the same month.

He is the first physician who is mentioned as owning land in the town. Selling his place, together with an acre purchased of Elisha Kilburn, to Dr. James Witherell, in October, 1791, he removed to New Lebanon, Columbia county, N. Y. He resided in Canaan, of the same county, in the spring of 1802.

Timothy Brainard, of East Hartford, Conn., in August, 1787, purchased of Asa Tyler, of Hampton, the farm lying next south of Oliver Cleveland's, between Poultney west line and Poultney river, and came and took up his residence on the same. He resided here until 1817, when, having sold the place

HISTORY OF FAIR HAVEN, VERMONT. 71

to his son, David Brainard, he removed to Elizabeth-town, N. Y.

At the March meeting of this year, held again at Mr. Stannard's, Silas Safford was chosen town clerk; Michael Merritt, Thomas Dickson and Eli Everts, selectmen; Mr. Merritt, treasurer; and it was voted that "the sign-post be erected on the hill by Col. Lyon's new barn," from which it is inferable that Col. Lyon had then recently built on the premises of the old tavern stand. The sign-post stood, a little over 30 years ago, near the southeast corner of the old shed which then and until as late as 1853 occupied the present site of Mr. Adams' brick store.

On the 18th of February, 1787, Michael Merritt, town clerk, by order of the citizens of the town, signs a petition to the General Assembly, to have the county seat of Rutland county at Castleton. This petition was joined in by Wells, Benson, Orwell, Poultney, Castleton and Hubbardton; but certain persons had intimated that Fair Haven and Benson ought not to be considered, whether because these two towns were later organized, or on some other ground, we are not told. The petition coming before the General Assembly, in March, Col. Lyon, who was a member from Fair Haven, moved that it be filed and postponed to the next session—votes, 25 yeas, 19 nays.

In May, 1787, it was ordered by the selectmen that the road coming across James Brookins' division from Muddy Brook [from] where it strikes the west line of Nathan Allen's division, and turns southwestward to the road leading from Lyon's mills to Mr. Merritt's

72   HISTORY OF FAIR HAVEN, VERMONT.

should "continue four rods west of said line, and the highway now traveled in lieu of this, is flung up."

1788.   Maj. Tilly Gilbert came to this town from Brookfield, Mass., in the spring of 1788, in company with Gideon Tafft, who had taken up land in the town, and resided here for a short time, but afterward settled in Whitehall. Maj. Gilbert was then quite a young man. He put up at first at the public house kept by Silas Safford, on the spot where Henry Green now lives, and was employed by Col. Lyon to teach a school, perhaps in the old school house on the Green.

He studied medicine with Dr. Hall, on the west street, and also taught school in Benson and Orwell. Removing to Benson about 1791–2, his connection with the history of our town does not really commence until his return, in about 1800, and will'require attention at a later period.

At the March meeting, held at Mr. Stannard's, March 13th, Dr. Simeon Smith was chosen moderator; Mr. Safford, town clerk; and five persons were chosen on the board of selectmen, of which. Col. Lyon was chairman. Dan Smith, of the West Haven part of the town, is named as one of the listers, together with Stephen Hall and Gamaliel Leonard. It was voted "that hogs be yoked with a yoke of four pieces below the neck, half the depth of the neck, and above the neck the depth of the neck, from the 10th of May to the 15th of October."

In April the road from the north end of the bridge near Col. Lyon's mills, was altered so as to run " north 20° east 22 1-2 rods to the northeast corner of the house

HISTORY OF FAIR HAVEN, VERMONT. 73

where Silas Safford now lives, thence north 7° west 28 1-2 rods, then west 10° north 36 rods, then north 10° east 36 rods, then west 10° north 50 rods, until it intersects the highway as it now runs that goes to Skeenesborough;" the first three sections to the southwest corner of the Common, where it turns north 10° east, to be six rods wide, the remainder only four rods wide.

The road which led northward to Mr. Priest's—perhaps across the ground which is now the Park—was at the same time declared exchanged "for the two rods addition now made to the road that runs westerly from Col. Lyon's towards Skeenesborough," and the road which "ran northerly from the said spot 28 1-2 rods from the house where Silas Safford, Esq., now lives"—[i. e., from Col. Lyon's toward Kelsey's]—was altered "so as to have the west line of the said highway begin at that place and continue north 10° east, until it intersects the west line of the said highway to the northward."

We are told that there was a frost on the 20th of June, òf this year, which was so severe as to destroy the wheat and other crops on which the settlers relied for subsistence, and in consequence many suffered of famine during the winter of 1788–9.

By a warning from Silas Safford, justice of the peace, a proprietor's meeting was held at Mr. Safford's house, August 26th, Col. Lyon being chosen moderator. After chosing Mr. Safford clerk the meeting was adjourned to the first Monday in October, but the

74   HISTORY OF FAIR HAVEN, VERMONT.

proceedings of the adjourned meeting are not to be found.

There was a citizens' meeting at Mr. Priest's house, September 2d, when it was voted " That the selectmen do repair the bridge which crosses the river between this town and Greenfield, and tax the town for the cost, if a tax is not granted by the General Assembly for that purpose." It was also voted to memorialize the General Assembly for "a tax of two pence on the acre for repairing bridges and highways in this town."

An alteration was made in the middle school district so that Daniel Munger should belong to the south district. Thomas Dickson was elected trustee for the north district; Michael Merritt for the middle, and Col. Lyon for the south. Thomas Dickson, Simeon Smith and Isaac Cutler were chosen a committee to hire a minister to preach at two different places, and it was voted that the minister preach one-half the time at Matthew Lyon's, and the other half at or near Eleazer Dudley's. The committee were empowered to lay a tax to pay the minister.

Jehiel Mitchell, who was a carpenter by trade, and came hither from Litchfield, Conn., was here in the summer of this year. He was a brother to Beriah and Ichabod Mitchell, of West Haven, and he built ",a red shop" on the south side of the road, opposite Dr. Hall's, on the west street.

Isaiah Inman came from Massachusetts with his family, in the fall of this year, stopping, at first, with his brother-in-law, Charles Hawkins, Sen. He located

HISTORY OF FAIR HAVEN, VERMONT. 75

east of Dr. Simeon Smith's, and the "country road," nigh the romantic and beautiful lake in the north part of the town, called from him, "Inman Pond." He did not reside long in the town, but removed to Hampton, N. Y., in 1792, and sold his place to Theophilus Woodward, of West Haven.

Thomas Dibble, called "Doctor Dibble," who came from Nobletown, N. Y., and here married a daughter of Oliver Cleveland, was in town about this time. He dwelt, previously to 1807, south of Wellington Estey's place, on the bank of Poultney river. In 1807 he purchased the farm which had been settled by Jeremiah Durand, and resided on the same until 1817.

1789. Dr. James Witherell, who had come to Hampton from Mansfield, Mass., the preceding year, stopping for a time with Samuel Beaman, came into town this season. He took the oath of allegiance here in September, 1790, and in April, 1791, he purchased about 30 acres of land of Elisha Kilburn, of Hampton. The land was situated on the border of the river, north of the highway, in the west part of the town. He purchased, in October following, the house in which he was then living, and the acre and a half of land at the corner of the road, of Dr. Stephen Hall, whose place as a physician he seems to have taken. He afterwards purchased of Charles Rice and others a large portion of what now constitutes Hamilton Wescott's farm. Dr. Witherell, known also as "Judge Witherell," was for over twenty years a public and influential citizen of the town, being several times a representative in the State Assembly, a Judge

76   HISTORY OF FAIR HAVEN, VERMONT.

in the county court, and likewise a Member of Congress while resident in Fair Haven.

He removed to Detroit, Mich., about 1810, where he held a responsible public office as one of the United States Judges of the Territory, and was long one of the chief men and officers of the State. His son, Judge Benjamin F. Witherell, who was long a resident of Detroit, has prepared a biographical sketch of his father, which will appear in this volume, together with resolutions passed by the bar and court at the death of Dr. Witherell.

Among the new comers of this year was Frederick Hill, who bought a house lot of Isaac Cutler, on the south side of the west street, and just east of Squire Cutler's, in November, probably about where John P. Sheldon now resides. Mr. Hill was town clerk in 1790 and '91, but soon sold back to Mr. Cutler and removed to Rutland.

The March meeting was held at Mr. Priest's, and Dr. Stephen Hall was chosen town clerk; Silas Safford, Isaac Cutler and Simeon Smith, selectmen. It was voted that the committee appointed last year to hire a minister and provide for the expense, continue to serve for the year ensuing.

At a meeting, September 1st, 1789, adjourned from the house of Mr. Priest to Samuel Stannard's, Simeon Smith being chosen moderator, and Fred. Hill clerk, *pro tem.*, it was voted that the first school district be divided into two, "beginning at a point on East Bay due west from a point where a certain brook running [runs] through a lot of land lying and adjoining

HISTORY OF FAIR HAVEN, VERMONT.   77

north upon the lot which Ensign Dan Smith lives on, thence running due east to the highway running southerly from a place called the Hamilton farm, thence due north to the north line of the town, and that the district south and east of the above line and within the line of the aforesaid first district, be known by the name of the fourth district."

Jabez Newland bought of Col. Lyon 100 acres of land, where the late Oliver Proctor so long resided, in this year. He sold 50 acres on the north side, in September, 1792, to Joshua Artherton, and the other 50 acres he sold to Beriah Rogers, in February, 1797.

In October of this year, Col. Lyon invokes the State by a petition to the General Assembly to sell him 100 acres of land granted to the Society for propagating the gospel in foreign parts, and also for £800 State scrip, to be paid back in two years. The petition was referred to the next General Assembly.

1790. The March meeting for 1790 was held for the first time "at the school house in the middle school district." At a meeting holden in September, Simeon Smith, Esq., Capt. Thomas Dickson and Ensign Isaac Cutler were chosen a committee to hire preaching, and were instructed to hire for the year ensuing "to the amount of £60, to be paid in grain, beef, pork or iron, and that the selectmen make a rate for that purpose, to be collected by the collector of town rates and paid to the said committee."

Beriah Rogers is said to have come into town this year, from Branford, Conn., and to have made his home for a number of years following with his brother,

78 HISTORY OF FAIR HAVEN, VERMONT.

Stephen, on the west side of the Common. In February, 1797, he bought of Jabez Newland 50 acres of land, on Scotch Hill. This he sold in March, 1799, to Ethiel Perkins. In August, 1797, he bought of Pliny Adams, of Hampton, N. Y., a house and 17 1-2 acres of land, where Zenas C. Ellis resides, making several additional purchases subsequently.

On this place he seems to have made his home until he removed to Hampton, about the spring of 1808. In 1802, he bought of Josiah Norton, Esq., the piece of ground on the west side of Eliel Gilbert's garden, where L. J. Stow and his mother now reside, and commenced a tannery. This he sold, after his removal to Hampton, in April, 1808, to John Quinton and Thomas Christie, of Whitehall, N. Y., for $500.

Mr. Rogers was a justice of the peace in the town for a number of years, and filled other positions of importance and influence while a resident here. He sold his home place, in January, 1809, to Lanson Watkins.

Charles Boyle and Olney Hawkins took the oath of allegiance at the freeman's meeting, in September of this year. Mr. Boyle, in company with Robert White, of Lansingburgh, N. Y., bought of Col. Lyon, in January, 1792, 2 acres of land on the east side of the old highway leading from Lyon's works to Castleton, including a small red store standing on the same.

He owned, also, the west part of the second division of Thomas Ashley, on which Mr. Durand resided. At his decease, in 1799, he owned the second division of Nathan Clark, bought of James Brookins, in Decem-

HISTORY OF FAIR HAVEN, VERMONT. 79

ber, 1792, and 85 acres of land, known as the "Handy lot," bought of Col. Lyon; in March, 1793; and William Lee, of Rutland, was appointed his administrator.

Olney Hawkins was a son of Charles Hawkins, Sen. He bought of Dr. Witherell, in January, 1797, an acre of land, on the west street, on the corner of the road leading to Charles Hawkins', together with the buildings thereon standing, "except a store built by Nathaniel Dickinson;" also a strip of about six acres, extending along the north side of the highway running to Sharp's bridge, and lying south of land sold by Dr. Witherell to Abijah Warren, excepting on this strip "a small barn built by John W. Throop."

He afterward, in July, 1802, purchased of Mr. Warren, 35 acres adjoining his land on the north. He carried on the blacksmith business on his place. In May, 1821, he sold his whole place to Cephas Carpenter, of Ira.

William Buell, a gold and silversmith, who came from Arlington, and occupied the place at the foot of the hill where Cyrus C. Whipple resides, and there repaired watches and sold silver ware, must have come into town this year. In April following, 1791, he bought a piece of land of Jeremiah Durand, and was assessed in the Grand List. He was chosen second constable in 1794; is said to have been an Englishman, and to have had a son William. He married, for his second wife, Polly Baldwin, of Rutland. Her first child was deaf and dumb. He died in town, and his widow went back to Rutland.

80 HISTORY OF FAIR HAVEN, VERMONT.

Nathaniel Dickinson, mentioned above as having built a store near Dr. Witherell's, on the west street, took the freeman's oath here in 1791. He came hither from Massachusetts. His wife was a sister to Maj. Tilly Gilbert. In June, 1795, he was keeping Col. Lyon's public house when Col. Lyon sold the same to David Mack. He kept the same house, or some other, for several years afterward, even as late as 1803.

Mr. Dickinson bought 65 acres of land of John Brown, on the west street, in October, 1797, which he sold to Dr. Witherell in March following. He owned one-half the grist mill. He was constable in 1802. He resided in West Haven in 1809, where he died in July, 1811—his wife having died in December before.

Abijah Warren, to whom allusion has been made above, was from Litchfield, Conn. He was a son-in-law of Dea. Daniel Munger, and was probably here as early as this year, and may have been here at an earlier period. He appears to have first bought a building lot on the road north of Dr. Witherell's toward Mr. Hawkins', in June, 1796,—adding to it, in April, 1797, 30 acres more, all of which he sold to Olney Hawkins, in July, 1802. He is said to have been a very sanctimonious man, and to have lived in the grist mill house after this time, where he had a large family.

John W. Throop, called "Troop" by his cotemporaries, who is mentioned as having built a barn near Dr. Witherell's, and elsewhere as having bought land on the west street, of Capt. Elijah Taylor, in June,.

HISTORY OF FAIR HAVEN, VERMONT. 81

1795, was from Pomfret, and is said to have kept a store on the west road. His wife's maiden name was Vail. Together with some of his wife's brothers, he removed to Kentucky, where, from the letters which Col. Lyon wrote to his friends, it appears he was a worthless drunkard. Elijah Galusha married one of his daughters.

Besides those already named as residents of the town at this time, there were Benjamin Stevens, who is assessed in the List of this year at £8, and who, in September, 1798, bought an acre of land of Col. Lyon, north of the village, toward Ethan Whipple's, which he sold, in February, 1801, to Joel Hamilton; Israel Markham, who owned a small blacksmith shop, standing just under the hill, near where Mrs. William Miller now resides; and probably others who were resident here for a longer or shorter period.

At a town meeting held at the school house near Mr. Stannard's, in July, 1791, Mr. Ethan Whipple, Col. Matthew Lyon and Maj. Lemuel Hyde were appointed as a committee "to give a deed of release to Simeon Smith, Esq., of the first division of the school right," provided he should give deeds of land "of equal value and which will rent as well." Frederick Hill, the town clerk, having removed to Rutland, a meeting was called, in December, which chose James Witherell town clerk, and voted "to dismiss the committee heretofore chosen to hire preaching."

1792. At the annual meeting, March 5th, 1792, Dr. James Witherell was chosen town clerk, but the records appear to have been kept by John Brown, a

82   HISTORY OF FAIR HAVEN, VERMONT.

young man of education, who came hither from North Providence, R. I., in the spring of 1792, and taught school in the town. Becoming a resident, he was chosen town clerk in 1793, and continued in the office until February, 1801; during which time the town records are made with great elegance and beauty of penman- ship. Mr. Brown was a brother-in-law of Ethan Whipple, Esq., having married his sister, Mary Whip- ple, in Rhode Island.

He bought of Col. Lyon, in May, 1793, 2 acres of land, on the old road just south of Mr. Whipple's, and built the house where Orrin Kelsey and family after- wards resided, now James Campbell's. Buying a farm of 65 acres of Charles Rice, near Dr. Witherell's, on the west street, in March, 1798, he removes there- on, and advertised his other place for sale in the "*Fair Haven Telegraph*," in December, 1795. In October, 1797, he sells the 65 acres on the west street to Na- thaniel Dickinson, and removes into the public house in the village, which he seems to have kept a number of years. In September, 1798, he sells his house and 3 acres, toward Mr. Whipple's, to Paul Guilford. He removed to St. Albans in March, 1801. He died March 16th, 1805, aged 39 years. His wife died April 11th, 1805, aged 39 years.

The warning for the March meeting called the peo- ple together to choose town officers, and "to see if they will agree to petition the Legislature of this State to divide this town into two, and to see if they can agree on a dividing line." James Witherell and

HISTORY OF FAIR HAVEN, VERMONT. 83

Lemuel Hyde were appointed agents to petition the Legislature for the division of the town.

At another meeting, held the 22d inst., and for the first time at the meeting house, Oliver Cleveland was chosen an additional selectman, and it was voted "to hold future town meetings here, and also the freeman's meeting, for the election of the next Member of Congress, and a Member of Convention.

James Witherell, Silas Safford and Philip Priest were chosen a committee to join a committee from West Haven, "to settle the public accounts which lie in common between the two towns."

On the question that the dividing line be at Mud Brook, the vote stood—yeas 9, nays 48; that it be at Hubbardton river, yeas 9, nays 48; that it run, as now, from Poultney river to a line on the hill parallel with the west line of the Brook's lot, and thence along the Great Ledge to Benson, yeas 48, nays 7. "But as there is a number of persons who dissent from the line which the majority think the most commodious, voted that Isaac Cutler, Silas Safford and Ethan Whipple be a committee to confer with the aforesaid dissentients, in choosing a disinterested committee to point out a dividing line, which line the inhabitants will petition the Legislature to establish." The meeting was then adjourned to March 27th.

At the adjourned meeting, Cornelius Brownson, Ethan Whipple and Lemuel Hyde were made a new committee to settle the town account with the treasurer, Mr. Merritt, and it was voted to call the west or north part of the town "*West Haven.*"

84   HISTORY OF FAIR HAVEN, VERMONT.

September 4th the citizens met again by adjournment, and voted "that they still continue determined to divide the town into two, and that the dividing line be established as it was previously voted. Col. Lyon, Samuel Stannard and Philip Priest were chosen a committee to meet a committee from West Haven to settle the claim of each town to lands granted by the Legislature for the ministry and for schools. This meeting was adjourned to January 4th, 1793.

In the meantime Messrs. Witherell and Hyde make their petition on behalf of the town on the 8th of October, the Legislature convening at Rutland. The petition recites that they desire division,

"1st, Because 'the public road goes more than 16 miles from the northwest to the southeast corner, at which extremes the town is inhabited.'

"2nd, Because it is 13 miles from the southwest corner to the east side of the town.

"3d, Because there is a "Great Ledge," which nearly divides the east from the west part.

"4th, The west part of the town having better land than the east part, yet a large share of it remaining in a state of uncultivation; and the east part having natural accommodations for water works, and great roads through it, makes it consider its future importance;—so that each part has its expenses while not considering the expenses of the other part, they cannot agree on a center as one town, yet when divided there is not the least difficulty, each being ready to agree on a center for itself.

"5th, The town being longer than a 6 mile square

HISTORY OF FAIR HAVEN, VERMONT. 85

town, the inhabitants have always expected to be divided, and although at times they might disagree about the place where to divide, yet each extreme has scarcely ever failed of wishing to get rid of the other, which has at times created difficulties which we do not wish to mention."

They then state the fact of an agreement at three several times on a line, and request to be divided, with the privileges of other towns, excepting that they should have but one representative to the two towns.

Against this petition the following persons protest or remonstrate that "they think the town so small that a division will be injurious, the Grand List being only £2283 and 10s., the number of freemen not exceeding one hundred, and the land on the west of the line of a vastly superior quality, therefore they pray that the town may not be divided:—but if it is to be, that the dividing line may extend so far westward as to take in one-half of the whole number of acres in the town, and so far as to Hubbardton river." The names are: Samuel Stannard, Alexander McCotter, John Howes, Isaac Turner, Abraham Utter, Jonathan Orms, John Warren, Amos Lay, Russel Smith, Ansel Merritt, Martin Merritt, James Merritt, Daniel Cushman, Philip Priest, Timothy Goodrich, Daniel Munger, Peter Cramer, Henry Cramer, Jr., Dan Smith, Joel Hamilton.

By an Act of the General Assembly, passed on the 18th, and signed on the 20th October, 1792, at Rutland, the west line of Fair Haven, as it now is, was established, and West Haven erected, with all

86   HISTORY OF FAIR HAVEN, VERMONT.

the privileges of a separate town, excepting that the two towns were to meet together and choose one representative.

The two towns accordingly had but one representative and held their freeman's meetings together until March 3d, 1823, when it was "Resolved, that the town of Fair Haven is by the Constitution and Laws of the State of Vermont, entitled to a representative in the General Assembly of the State, in its own right, distinct from any other town, and that the first constable be directed to notify the annual meeting in September next, for the choice of Governor, Lieut. Governor, councillors and representative to the General Assembly, to be holden at the centre school house, in said Fair Haven."

The General Assembly, also, at its session of this same year, decided that the clause of the act limiting the two towns to one representative was repugnant to the provisions of the Constitution of the State, and was therefore void. Since this time the two towns have each had their annual representative.

The populations of the two towns, respectively, as given in the census reports of the State, were, in 1791, about the time of the division: Fair Haven, 375; West Haven, 545. In 1800 Fair Haven is reported to have 411 inhabitants, and West Haven 430. From this time West Haven steadily increases to 774, in 1840; Fair Haven increasing to 714, in 1820, after which time it fell off to 633, in 1840.

Up to this year, in which the town was divided— the larger portion of the territory going to West

HISTORY OF FAIR HAVEN, VERMONT. 87

Haven—we have seen the town steadily filling up with population, and improving, until it stands, in relative importance, on account of its mills, its central location, and the enterprise, intelligence, and wealth of its inhabitants, on an equal footing with many other towns of greater extent and more inhabitants.

But before taking leave of our twin-sister on the west, with whom we struggled along through so many hardships and privations in our early days, and before seeking out the new scenes and acquaintances of the years to follow, it will be pleasant to look back upon the geography of both sections, topographically and geologically, in the light of present knowledge and observation, and see if there be not something in both reciprocally complementary of that in which either may be wanting.

TOPOGRAPHICALLY, we see the plain around the village then covered with heavy pines, cut away where the Park now is, and leaving the large stumps still thickly standing, to remove them at a later date, requiring many "bees," or public working parties, at which times many gallons of spirituous liquors, so commonly used at that day, were consumed. The heavy pines and hemlocks were standing over most of the plain, roads only here and there being cut through them. The chief settlement and point of trade seemed to be on the west street, around the corner where the road led northward to Mr. Hawkins' and Mr. Merritt's.

The general surface of the town is hilly, the hills rising in two instances only, to the dignity of moun-

K

88 HISTORY OF FAIR HAVEN, VERMONT.

tains: "Bald Mountain," covering the whole southern extremity of West Haven, along the east shore of the Lake, and "Mount Hamilton," the eminence just northward of Messrs. Wood's and Sheldon's, in Fair Haven, so named from Joel Hamilton, Esq., who resided in the old orchard on its southern slope at an early day.

The town to the northward of Mt. Hamilton, as far as Benson line, is taken up with the Great Ledge coming down on the west, covered with its ever green forests, and seeming to equal in distant beauty the forests of ancient Lebanon, as you look northward from the summit of Mt. Hamilton, while just below you, in front and at your feet, on the east side of the Great Ledge, and embosomed in the green hills on every side, lies the charming little lake in its secluded and native beauty, which has been known among us by no better name than its earliest accidental designation, "Inman Pond."

As viewed at the still dawn of a summer evening, there are few scenes which God has elsewhere made, surpassing in exquisite loveliness, the silent, quiet grandeur of this, our own home scenery. From Mr. Hamilton's eastward, Scotch Hill, fringed with its opening quarries of slate, and the wide, fertile intervale between, are seen below you, sweeping off to the southward, where the village greets your eye in the distance. Altogether, there is no spot for many miles around so well worth a visit as Mt. Hamilton.

A little to the west of Oliver Proctor's former residence is a range of hills, called, in olden times, "Porcupine Ledge." South and east of this, along the

HISTORY OF FAIR HAVEN, VERMONT. 89

east border of the town, and traversed by the road to West Castleton, is Scotch Hill, so named from the Scotch people who settled it.

"Glen Lake," formerly called "Screw Driver Pond," from a supposed formal resemblance to a screw-driver, and which has its outlet in Lake Bomoseen, in Castleton, furnishing at that point an abundant water fall and power for manufacturing purposes, lies partly in the northeast corner of the town.

To the west of Porcupine Ledge, and east of Mt. Hamilton, is the large marsh fed from Inman Pond, which has long been known as "Beaver Meadow." This meadow furnished, for many years, a supply of cranberries to the residents of the town and village, who were permitted, by the generosity of the proprietor, to go on an appointed day of each autumn and glean of the annual harvest, and this cranberry meadow was at the same time a mill-pond in the spring of the year, from which water was taken by Joseph Sheldon, Sen., to run his saw mills, at the outlet, where he carried on an extensive lumbering business for many years.

As seen from Scotch Hill, the saw mill, now owned by Daniel Orms, and ensconced among the trees at the head of the valley, through which the small but perpetual stream, called Mud Brook, flows to Poultney river, on the west, presents a beautiful and picturesque appearance.

The view of Fair Haven village, as seen from some points on Scotch Hill, overlooking at the same time Hampton hills and the mountains to the south and

90 HISTORY OF FAIR HAVEN, VERMONT.

west, is one on which the lover of the beautiful in landscape scenery will delight to gaze and linger. There is one other view, that from the road or hill north of Otis Hamilton's, looking westward on Bald Mountain, with Poultney river, Carvers Falls, and the powder mills in the deep gorge of the foreground, which for wildness and grandeur in a warm, hazy summer afternoon, is worthy the attention of the painter and artist. Just south of this point, and below Mr. Hamilton's house, are the Dry Falls, as they are called, and the old river bed on the flat, where not the river only, but ancient ocean currents once flowed.

The Castleton river receiving the waters of Lake Bomoseen just outside of the borders of the town, comes in on the east and winds circuitously into the Poultney river on the west side, furnishing several good manufacturing privileges· in the village. On Hubbardton river, also, flowing through West Haven, from the ponds in Benson, into East Bay, are several good mill powers. Following down the Poultney river, besides the Falls at the powder mills, where there are also a saw mill and grist mill, and was once a fulling mill and factory, below that point we find Carvers Falls, a deep, narrow opening in the limestone rocks, through which the combined waters of Castleton and Poultney rivers fall down at first about twenty feet, and then about sixty feet, perpendicularly, into East Bay. At this point there were, at one time, on the New York side, a saw mill, forge and store.

GEOLOGICALLY viewed, West Haven exceeds in spec-

HISTORY OF FAIR HAVEN, VERMONT. 91

ulative interest, but Fair Haven in economical value. At the bottom of the extreme southern promontory of the town, opposite the railroad depot and steamboat wharf, in Whitehall, is found the only specimen in the State, of the oldest, or bottom rocks of the globe, the primordial crust of the Azoic, or Laurentian formation. This fragment of igneous primordial gneiss extends only three or four miles along the Lake northward. Over, or on this, rests the first fossiliferous formation, the Lower Silurian, with which commences the existence of organic life on the globe. There are several varieties of the Potsdam Sandstone found on Bald Mountain, interesting specimens of which are to be seen in the State cabinet.

Overlying the sandstone is a large development of calciferous sand rock, composed of lime and sand, which extends far northward and across the Lake, and is found to contain fossils of the genus Maclurea. This formation "enters Vermont from Whitehall, south of the mouth of Codman's creek, in West Haven. In the northwest part of West Haven it unites with a spur that runs up to the very southern extremity of the town, upon the east shore of Lake Champlain."*

Next above this appears the Trenton Limestone. "A little more than a mile west of the West Haven post-office it appears as a light blue limestone, capping several small hills with a very small easterly dip. It extends west to Codman's creek. There is but little thickness to it, while the calciferous sand-rock beneath is enormously developed."*

*Geological Survey of State.

92   HISTORY OF FAIR HÁVEN, VERMONT.

Fossil corals are found in this limestone further north in Vermont. Utica Slates come in above the Trenton Limestone, and first appear about a mile west of the post-office; their inclination being greater than that of the underlying rocks. Then there* are the Hudson River limestones, alternating with clay slates or shales, throughout the central and eastern parts of West Haven. In the western part of Fair Haven is a large range of Talcose or Talcoid shist, running north and south; and east of this, extending into Castleton, is the extensive slate group, or Taconic range, called by the State geologists, from the town of Georgia, in the north part of the State, where all its characteristic fossils are found, "Georgia slates." These slates were quarried and worked in this town by Alonson Allen, as early as 1845, and might with great propriety have been denominated *Fair Haven Slates*.

CHAPTER IV.

FROM THE TAKING OF THE FIRST CENSUS, IN 1791, TO THE DEPARTURE OF COL. LYON, AT THE CLOSE OF THE CENTURY.

From the year 1791, the time of the taking of the first census, until the close of the century, when the number of inhabitants is reported as only 411, though the increase of population is small, as compared with the previously rapid growth of the town, there are several important facts and changes to be noted. In the first place, the number of inhabitants in 1791 was large, as compared with many other towns in the State, at that time; Burlington, for instance, though organized nearly as early, numbering only 332.

The area of the town is smaller than that of any other town in Rutland county, excepting Ira gore, and fully one-third part, especially the northern section, is unsuited to habitation; while the southern portion, bounded west on the Poultney river, is very narrow, being scarcely two miles in its widest extent, and at the same time much broken by rough ridges of slate on the east, and by the cedar swamp on the west.

94   HISTORY OF FAIR HAVEN, VERMONT.

Yet, as early as 1791, settlements were made, as we have seen, in about every accessible portion, and even in some places which have since been abandoned, as, for example, on the old "Skeene's road," running over the river south and west of J. Wellington Estey's, where Mr. Dibble early resided, afterward Mr. Bullard, and later Mr. Bristol. Then on the west street, beyond Hamilton Wescott's place, where the road went through to Mr. Stannard's, and there are now no dwellings or residents, there existed, at this period, a considerable settlement, or village. The Mungers and Mr. Snow were in the north, on the Munger road, where there have been no residents for many years. Mr. Beddow occupied on the hill east of Mr. Kidder's, and Mr. Ballard and Mr. Holt west of Mr. Kidder's, where there are now no habitations. At a later period, there were residences on the hill above Alonson Allen's slate quarry, and in the old orchard north of the Proctor farm, which are now entirely gone.

Where the village now is there could have been no settlement of much account, aside from Col. Lyon's iron works, grist mill and saw mill, at the beginning of this period—1791—Col. Lyon himself owning all the land. A road had been laid, as we have seen, in December, 1784, from the works northwest to Muddy Brook, on which Ethan Whipple located, in 1786; and a portion of this road across what is now the Park, was thrown up and declared exchanged for another, six rods in width, which was

HISTORY OF FAIR HAVEN, VERMONT. 95

laid, in April, 1788, across what is the south end of the Common.

Col. Lyon having built a new barn on the hill, prior to December, 1784, had probably soon after erected his house, on the corner of the road, and Stephen Rogers had built a house and shoe-shop, at the west end of the new highway, on the land of Col. Lyon, and perhaps had also commenced his tannery, under the hill, west of the house.

North of Mr. Rogers', on the east side of the street, and about opposite Ira C. Allen's present residence, there was a school house, as early as 1790. The old church, which stood on the public ground, north of the school house, and which was never encumbered with the luxurious innovation of brick and mortar— called "the Lord's barn," and "Lyon's den"—was in use in the spring of 1792, and must have been built as early as 1791.

Col. Lyon had also built the small red store, which he sold to Boyle & White, in January, 1792, on the spot where Thomas Hughes now lives. Besides this he must have built the paper mill not far from this time, and perhaps also the building east of Mr. Rogers', nearly opposite where Joseph Adams' marble residence now stands, which was used, soon after this time, as a store and printing office, and later as a dwelling house, and was taken down and removed by Maj. Tilly Gilbert, in 1810.

Further than this there does not seem to have been any improvements where the village now is. Mr. Safford, having bought a place of John Meacham, in

L

96 HISTORY OF FAIR HAVEN, VERMONT.

the south part of the town, in April, 1790, had removed thither from the village, and there opened a public house on the spot now owned by Mr. Barnes.

During the next few succeeding years, notwithstanding the small increase of population, many and great changes are made, and Fair Haven becomes what tradition has reported it, a place of business equal in importance to any north of Bennington.

In the village, Lyon first sells Robert White, of Lansingburgh, N. Y., and Charles Boyle, of Fair Haven, on the 23d of January, 1792, the little red store and two acres of land. He next sells, in May following, seven acres to Stephen Rogers, including the house and shop which Rogers had built.

In 1793, Lyon is said to have commenced the publication of a newspaper, called *The Farmer's Library*, in one part of the paper mill building, and to have continued it three or four years, notwithstanding the sparseness and poverty of·the settlers, and the very limited demand for such a publication. There were, at the time, but three other papers in the State, the *Gazette*, at Bennington; the *Herald*, at Rutland; and the *Journal*, at Windsor. The paper called the *Fair Haven Gazette*, during a part of its existençe, was printed by Col. Lyon's son, James Lyon, and Judah P. Spooner—James having learned the printing business at Philadelphia—and was issued by Lyon, no doubt as a political sheet, he being before the people of the district as a candidate for Congress, as " the representative of the commercial, agricultural and manufacturing interests, in preference to any of their law characters,"

HISTORY OF FAIR HAVEN, VERMONT. 97

from the admission of the State into the Union, in March, 1791, until his election on the fourth trial, in 1796.

This paper was probably succeeded by *The Farmer's Library, or Fair Haven Telegraph*—"a Republican paper, printed by J. P. Spooner and W. Hennessy, at Fair Haven, Vt.;" the first number of which was issued July 28, 1795, and copies of which are now in the writer's hands. This paper, published by Mr. Spooner, alone, after March, 1796, was a Republican paper, and supported Col. Lyon. It was continued as late as 1798, and was printed in the building which stood on the north side of the highway, nearly opposite Joseph Adams' dwelling house. Persons are living who remember this printing office. It was occupied as a dwelling house by Luther Bibbins, in 1805, and by Isaac Cutler and Harvey Church in 1810, and was shortly after taken down and removed by Maj. Tilly Gilbert.

The motto of Mr. Spooner's paper—"The freedom of the people cannot be supported without knowledge and industry"—shows the appreciation in which the people then held knowledge and industry in relation to a free government. The name of the paper was again changed, in November, 1797, to *The Farmer's Library, or Vermont and New York Intelligencer.* There are copies of both of these papers now extant. Besides this there was published by Mr. Spooner, in 1796, '97, and '98, *The Vermont Almanac and Register*, giving the dates of the grants, and the rateable property of each town in the State, also "an account

98 HISTORY OF FAIR HAVEN, VERMONT.

of the Masons, literary societies, attornies, ministers, and religious assemblies, the officers of the militia, the Members of the Legislature, the names of the Civil officers, and times of holding courts in Vermont." These almanacs and registers were advertised as for sale by the post-riders and at the office, for one shilling each.

There are several interesting advertisements and facts in the old papers printed in Fair Haven. In December, 1795, Mr. James Brown, "late post-rider from Fair Haven to Randolph," advertises that on account of ill health he is obliged to discontinue his business. At the same time, Jeremy Dwyer, the father of Mrs. Orren Kelsey, who had come hither by the personal solicitation of Col. Lyon, in 1793, and resided, in 1795, in the house above the grist mill, "proposes to ride from the printing office in Fair Haven, to carry the newspapers through Castleton, by the old fort, thence through Hubbardton, Sudbury, Whiting and Cornwall to Middlebury Falls; thence to return through the westerly part of Cornwall, Whiting, Sudbury, and the east part of Shoreham, Orwell, Benson and West Haven—every other week to reverse the route. Any person on his route wishing for papers from Bennington, Rutland, Albany or Lansingburgh, or the Rural Magazine, printed at Rutland, shall have them delivered on reasonable terms." Orren Kelsey advertises "to carry the newspapers from the printing office in Fair Haven through West Haven, Benson, Orwell, Shoreham, Bridport, Addison, Panton and Ferrisburgh."

HISTORY OF FAIR HAVEN, VERMONT. 99

In March, 1796, the *Telegraph* says: "The measles have been very rife in this and the neighboring towns for some time past, and we learn that five persons have died of that disorder in Middletown in the course of a few weeks." * * "The small pox is also prevalent in the neighboring towns. * * Travelers seem greatly alarmed to hear of people having it on the main road, particularly at a tavern a little to the southward of this town." Abner Fuller advertises that he "has lately set up the blacksmith business, a few rods north of the printing office, in Fair Haven."

Samuel Stannard, proprietors' clerk, publishes a notice of an adjourned meeting of the proprietors of Fair Haven and West Haven, to meet at the house of Charles Rice, innholder, in West Haven, on the 2d Monday of April.

Mr. Hennessy advertises in June, 1796, that he has taken the slitting mill; and William Buell that he "still carries on the gold and silversmith's business, repairing watches, etc.," and has on hand "several silver-mounted swords, which he will sell cheap."

In the January paper of 1798, James Lyon, postmaster, publishes a list of letters remaining in the post-office at Fair Haven, January 1st, among which are letters for persons in Poultney, Middletown, Granville, Pawlet, Sudbury and New Hartford, and one each for Nathaniel Dickinson and James Witherell, Esq., of Fair Haven. The paper states that an extensive band of thieves who had troubled the neighborhood, had been broken up and the culprits punished, one of them by whipping—the "whipping-post."

100 HISTORY OF FAIR HAVEN, VERMONT.

being an institution at that time, and for many years subsequently.

Nathan Durkee, a bachelor, whose name first appears in the Grand List of 1793, and who came here from Pomfret and died here at the public house, advertises in January, 1798, that he "has lately received, and is now selling, at his store in Fair Haven, at the corner, opposite Brown's tavern, a small assortment of English and India goods, for cash, country produce or ashes."

The following shows the political spirit of the Fair Haven newspaper: "Much has been said against the French Council of Ancients ordering a Quaker to be turned out of their House, for obstinately persisting in keeping on his hat, contrary to the rules of the House. The high-flying Federalists in this country reprobate their conduct and call it persecution, and yet would oblige citizen Lyon, one of the Members of the House of Representatives, to be dragged in procession before the President, although he has repeatedly declared that it was against his conscience and opinion to join in that ceremonial."

A March number of the paper contains an address of Col. Lyon to his constituents, and the following little bit of precious news for the gossip of the time: "Married, at Orwell, on the 4th inst., Mr. Thomas Little, of West Haven, aged 58 years, to the amiable Miss Elizabeth Craw, aged 17."

There were a number of other publications, and several books, some of which are still in existence, which were printed in the town during this period—among

HISTORY OF FAIR HAVEN, VERMONT. 101

these, "The Life of Franklin," a small volume, and a French story or novel, entitled "Alphonso and Dalinda."

We have seen "A Brief and Scriptural Defence of Believers' Baptism by Immersion, by Sylvanus Haynes, pastor of the Baptist church of Christ, in Middletown, Vt.," which was printed here by Mr. Spooner.

There is still preserved the first two numbers of a semi-monthly duodecimo magazine, *The Scourge of Aristocracy and Repository of Important Political Truths*," which was commenced here October 1st, 1798, when Col. Lyon was running for Congress, and the *Rutland Herald*,. under Dr. Samuel Williams, refused to publish communications in his favor. It was edited and published by James Lyon, but contained several articles from his father. The subscription price was three dollars and it was continued but one year. The second number contains Col. Lyon's celebrated letter to Gen. Stevens T. Mason, Senator from Virginia, written by him October 14th, 1798, while a prisoner in jail, at Vergennes; and, judging from the tone of the several articles, whether original or selected, which appear in the first two numbers, it·is evident that the name of "*Scourge*" was well chosen. It is enough to say here that intense and bitter opposition to the principles of the Federal party, the standing army, the stamp act, and the alien and sedition laws, is its prevailing burden and characteristic.

In January, 1794, Lyon sells to William Hennessy the two south fires in his forge, together with a hammer and anvil and coal house. Hennessy was a warm

102 HISTORY OF FAIR HAVEN, VERMONT.

political friend of Col. Lyon, and appears to have been in the town before this time, being assessed in the List of 1793 at £6. On the 25th of September, 1793, while under the influence of strong drink, and engaged in an angry political discussion, at Castleton, with his fellow-townsman, Joel Hamilton—Hamilton having about this time gone over to the Federal party—Hennessy assaulted Hamilton and put him out of doors, endangering his life, for which Hamilton claims damages of Hennessy, in the March term of the county court of the year 1794, to the amount of £150; Hennessy replying that 'Hamilton had first assailed him. The court awarded Hamilton £1 and 4s.

There appears to have been a standing irreconcilable political quarrel between Mr. Hamilton and the Republicans of that time, which led to much difficulty and trouble while Lyon remained in town, and, indeed, long afterward. Lyon called Hamilton to answer, in the November term of the county court, 1793, to the charge that he, "Lyon, the plaintiff, was chosen selectman at Fair Haven, in March, 1791, and sought to discharge his duties as a person of good repute and credit, free of deceit, fraud or falsity"—yet the defendant, "maliciously intending to hurt and injure his good name and reputation, and to cause him to be esteemed and reported as a person perjured and foresworn, and who had acted corruptly in his office," did on the 17th of June, 1793, at Rutland, in the *Farmer's Library*, Vol. 1, No. 12, "falsely and maliciously devise, speak, tell, print and publish divers false, scandalous and horrible lies of and concerning said plaintiff."

HISTORY OF FAIR HAVEN, VERMONT.   103

The substance of the falsehood was that Hamilton, who was constable at Fair Haven, and presided at the freemen's meeting, in September, 1791, "complained and charged Lyon with being very officious at that meeting in procuring votes for himself, for Member of Congress, even from New York; causing persons to be admitted to the freeman's oath who had not been in the State a week; that Lyon wrote a letter to the commanding officer of a military camp, in the State of New York, who had his men embodied on that day, soliciting him to dismiss his company, that they might come to Fair Haven and vote; that Lyon made use of threats, etc., to terrify him [Hamilton] to perjure himself by aiding him in his wicked designs"—making out false returns, etc.

Lyon charges that these accusations injured him in his reputation so that some of his neighbors refused to have any common acquaintance or discourse with him, and demands to recover of Hamilton the sum of £2,000 lawful money. The court awarded him 20s. damages and costs. As an offset to this Hamilton brings a suit of replevin against Lyon and Charles Rice, the constable, in the March term of court, 1795, for the recovery of his horse and mare, taken from him October 4th, 1793, and unlawfully detained, laying his damages at £100. The court awarded him 2s. damage, and cost of £6, 14s. and 6d.

It may not be out of place to state in this connection, as among the results of the violent political strife of this period, that not only these lawsuits, but others, of which we have no records, grew up from acts of

M

104   HISTORY OF FAIR HAVEN, VERMONT.

aggression committed against persons and property.

Mr. Hamilton's orchard was entered and his fruit trees maliciously girdled, from motives of political spite, about the year 1800. It was generally understood to have been done by a party of young men, or boys, chief among whom was a son of Charles McArthur, who fled to the south or west, while a number of others, who were supposed to have been implicated, were arrested, fined and imprisoned. These were Erastus Goodrich, Davis Olney and Joseph Davidson. Goodrich was an apprentice to Gen. Jonathan Orms, and Gen. Orms, while believing him innocent, hired money of Dr. Shaw, of Castleton, and paid the three fines, of $100 each, to get the young men out of prison. This affair was a memorable one among the people of that time.

While Lyon was exceedingly popular among his own party and personal friends, doing much to court their favor, and frequently throwing open his house for hospitable entertainment of his workmen and party friends, he was yet a rough, wilful man, and had many strong enemies. When, therefore, in the summer of 1798, he made himself liable to prosecution under the famous "sedition law" of that year, there were not a few ready and willing to see the law executed upon him. He was accordingly indicted for sedition on account of words he had written and published in the *Vermont Journal*, and being brought to trial before a court composed of Federal judges, in October of this year, he was convicted and sentenced to four months imprisonment and to pay a fine of $1,000 and

HISTORY OF FAIR HAVEN, VERMONT. **105**

costs. Being committed to jail, at Vergennes, during the winter, he was treated with much rigor, and his friends in Fair Haven were obliged to send him a stove to keep him warm.

About the time of Lyon's trial, at Rutland, a political opponent, John Cook, of Poultney, was appointed by the Legislature a justice of the peace, in opposition, it was said, to the almost unanimous voice of the town. Impelled by the excitement of the times, and instigated, also, it was said, by Mrs. Lyon, who furnished powder for the operation, a number of the young men of Fair Haven, who were friends of Lyon and enemies to Cook, undertook, in the night time, to undermine and blow up Cook's office, at Poultney, but he getting intelligence of the plot, was able to frustrate it. Some of the young men, however, who were engaged in the undertaking, among them Jeremy Dwyer, Jr., were obliged to flee the State for their liberty.

Lyon being re-elected to Congress while in prison, was enabled at the expiration of his term of confinement, on the morning of the 9th of February, 1799, to proclaim himself, immediately on his exit, on his way to Congress, and thus protect himself from re-arrest, which had been contemplated by his enemies. His journey to Philadelphia was a triumphal procession through the several towns of the State, he being transported in a carriage drawn by four horses, with the American flag flying at the head of the procession.

The relation of Col. Lyon's public and political life to the historical events and business of Fair Haven

106 HISTORY OF FAIR HAVEN, VERMONT.

will be further seen in the account of changes which occurred in a very few years.

Mr. Hennessy buying of Col. Lyon, in May, 1794, a piece of land 12 rods square, on the corner north of the tavern house, and 6 rods from it, with an east front on the four-rod highway which ran past the little red store of Boyle & White, toward Castleton—built ón the middle of the lot, nearly opposite Boyle & White's store, and facing the east, a large double house, or store. This formed the main building which, at a later day, was remodeled into a public house, or tavern, by Royal Dennis, with a piazza on the west side, and a wing running back eastward over the old road.

Mr. Hennessy seems to have been a man of much business and activity, but not very successful. Besides the forge fires, which he bought of Col. Lyon, at the beginning of the year, and the store which he had built, in July, 1795, he associates himself with Mr. Spooner, in the publication of the *Fair Haven Telegraph*. This he gives up the next spring, and leases Col. Lyon's slitting mill, selling his store, also, in July, 1796, to George Cadwell, Lyon's son-in-law, of Hampton, N. Y. With the store he sells only a strip 7 rods wide from the north part of the 12 rod square piece, leaving a piece 5 rods wide—now lying in front of Mr. Graves' store—which he sold to Elijah G. Galusha, and which was subsequently deeded to the town, by Alexander Dunehue.

Mr. Cadwell sold the store in August, 1797, together with the 7 rod wide strip of land, to Isaac Cutler and Stephen Rogers; and it may have been this store, or

HISTORY OF FAIR HAVEN, VERMONT. 107

the Boyle & White store, on the corner, opposite Brown's tavern, in which Nathan Durkee had his stock of merchandise, in January, 1798, Brown occupying the Lyon tavern house that winter. Messrs. Cutler & Rogers sold the store, in March, 1798, to John Taylor, of New York, by whom it was owned until 1804, and then sold to John Meacham.

Mr. Hennessy owned a half acre of land on the north side of the highway, above the iron works, for a short time in 1797. He had a barn, in April, 1798, about where Harris Whipple's house stands, and a nailer's shop, said to stand in the highway, about 4 rods north of the dwelling house of Dr. Clement Blakesley. He had taken the shop from Israel Markham, on attachment, and now both barn and shop were taken by Morgan & Boardman, of Troy. His forge fires were taken possession of by Abraham Leggett, of New York, in April, 1798, under an attachment.

In June, 1795, Col. Lyon, having previously built his dwelling house on the place where the Vermont Hotel now stands, and the same building which was appropriated by Mr. Fish, for an L, or wing—sells to David Mack, of Middlefield, Mass., his tavern house, on the corner, and ten acres of land, the house being at the time leased and occupied by Nathaniel Dickinson. It was sold by Mack, who never occupied it himself, to Dr. Simeon Smith, March 7th, 1798, by whom it was again sold to Isaac Cutler, in 1803.

In July, Col. Lyon sells to Asa Smith and Heman Huffman his grist mill and saw mill, and provides "that the saw mill shall never at any time draw the water

108
HISTORY OF FAIR HAVEN, VERMONT.

away from nor injure the paper mill standing, or that may stand, opposite to said mill. Nor shall the grist mill take the water from the paper mill to injure it in its motion any time from twelve o'clock at noon to twelve o'clock at night." There is to be allowed no waste of water by leaky gates and flumes on either side. The ground in front of the mills is to be reserved as common ground for a mill yard.

At the same time he conveys to Asa Smith one and a half acres of land, on the east side of the highway, opposite the saw mill, extending in area from the river to the road leading to the forge, excepting from this the house on the east road, formerly occupied by David Erwin, and lastly by Thomas Wood; and excepting on the north and south road the place at the foot of the hill, where William Buell then resided, now Mr. Whipple's. This was conveyed back to Lyon, by Simeon Smith, in August, 1796.

In August, 1796, having re-purchased of Huffman and of Simeon Smith the mills he had sold to Huffman and Asa Smith, Col. Lyon again sells one equal half of the two mills to Solomon Cleveland, of Hampton, N. Y., Cleveland moving into town and re-building the mills, with Jonathan Orms for his millwright. Cleveland, in April, 1798, sells his equal share to Pliny Adams, of Hampton.

Col. Lyon sells one-half the saw mill, after three years time, in August, 1799, to Eliel Gilbert, of Greenfield, Mass.—a brother of Maj. Tilly Gilbert—and with it one acre of land, on the west side of the highway, above the mills, including the house in which

HISTORY OF FAIR HAVEN, VERMONT. 109

Clement Blakesley then resided, the same which had been occupied by Jeremy Dwyer, a few years before, and by Silas Safford, Esq., at an earlier day.

Mr. Adams, about this time, sold his share of the grist mill and saw mill to Stephen Rogers. Rogers sells his half of the saw mill to Tilly Gilbert, in September; and Lyon closes off the remaining share of the grist mill to Nathaniel Dickinson. Thus, in September, 1799, the saw mill is owned by Eliel and Tilly Gilbert; the grist mill by Stephen Rogers and Nathaniel Dickinson.

In August, 1797, Lyon leases to Moses Scott, of Waterford, N. Y., and James Lyon, of Fair Haven, for the term of nine years, the saw mill "now building" on the Upper Falls, over the iron works, they to finish the mill and deliver it back in good order at the expiration of the team of the lease, with "one saw-gate with two good saws in, one with one good saw in, and one with a gang of good saws, and with every appurtenance and tool thereto belonging." He also sells them all the pine timber standing or lying on his land, on the southeasterly side of Castleton river, and north and east of the road leading from the new bridge, over his Upper Falls, toward Jeremiah Durand's, they to have nine years to cut the timber in, except that they are to cut from the western half during the first four years.

James Lyon mortgages his half to Stephen Holt, in January, 1798, Holt having become surety for him in the sums of $40 and $50 respectively, for which judgment had been obtained against said Lyon,

110   HISTORY OF FAIR HAVEN, VERMONT.

in favor of William Baxter. In April he again mortgages the saw mill to his partner, Moses Scott, to secure him on a note of $2,000, which said Scott had endorsed with him, in March.

James Lyon, besides acting as a printer of his father's paper, is said to have been, at one time, superintendent of the paper mill, and again to have tried his hand at selling his father's iron, a work in which he was mainly successful in getting rid of a good sleighload of the iron, together with a valuable span of horses, without bringing home with him any appreciable equivalent. He is said to have married a worthy and beautiful young lady in Waterford, N. Y., and to have resided at one time in the east part of the Boyle & White house, occupying the front for a printing office, and having with him as apprentices two young men, Jacob Hoffman and Edward Ritchie. It is said, also, that the house at the foot of the hill, where Cyrus C. Whipple resides, was used for a printing office. In which of these offices the *Scourge of Aristocracy* was published, it is impossible to tell.

James Lyon built the house which stood where John D. Goodwin now resides, east of the church, sometime previous to 1798, and was post-master here in January of that year. He commenced the publication of the *Scourge* in October, 1798, continuing it for one year. In November he acted as clerk, or agent, for his father in a lottery scheme, and had a book store in town, perhaps at the Boyle & White stand. His father had purchased, at Rutland, of John Wood, of Kingsbury, N. Y., formerly of Pittsford, Vt., the

HISTORY OF FAIR HAVEN, VERMONT. 111

grant, or charter for a lottery, paying $500 for the same. The scheme comprises one prize of $1,000, "to be paid in a house and farm of good land and conveniences, on the main road in Fair Haven; one of $1,500, to be paid in a farm in West Haven, containing 500 acres, about five miles from Whitehall, on East Bay; and fifty ten dollar and six dollar prizes, to to be paid one-half in cash and one-half in books, at cash prices, at the book store in Fair Haven," where the lottery is to be drawn, and where James Lyon is said to keep a complete assortment, and choice of books will be given. James Lyon countersigns the tickets as clerk.

From the lottery business Col. Lyon is said to have obtained means to pay his fine and costs, after his liberation from prison, and to have realized a surplus of $3,000. However this may be, it appears that at the expiration of his second term in Congress, in the year 1800, his business in Vermont, as well as his personal and political relations, were such that he did not deem it prudent to return hither to reside, but turning his feet westward, established himself near the Cumberland river, in Kentucky, at what is now Eddyville, Lyon county.

As he had done in Fair Haven, so here in his new home he engaged with his wonted energy in politics and business, taking out his family, transporting type and machinery on horseback, over the Alleghany mountains, with which to establish the first printing office in Kentucky, persuading others to immigrate to his new abode, and using every means to build up his

112   HISTORY OF FAIR HAVEN, VERMONT.

place. In 1802 he was elected to the Legislature of Kentucky, and in 1803 or 1804 to Congress, where he remained by re-election till 1810.

In writing from Washington, to Judge Witherell, in January, 1805, he makes urgent inquiry as to what had become of Stephen Rogers, and if he could not obtain him to come to Eddyville, both for Rogers' sake and his own, as he had one hundred hides of leather, taken off his own cattle the previous summer, and tanned by a negro man, whom he owned, but he would prefer Rogers' tanning and shoe-making, as Rogers formerly worked for him. He wants Rogers, he says, to rise again in life, and enclosed money to get him to the Monongahela river, in March. He shall not remain, he says, to the close of Congress, as he has more gun-boats to build, and shall have to erect a forge to make the iron for them in the summer. He wants a bloomer and refiner who will teach the negroes.

Gen. Whitehouse, he says, is doing well, and wants his wife, "Patty," to come to Eddyville, and he gives money and directions for her to remove.

He inquires about Ithamar Hosford, Mrs. Beddow's son, if he is worth encouraging to come to the West. He says James Lyon is engaged in ship-building, on his own account, and this business has made money circulate, and attracted many traders to the place. He wants more ship carpenters and joiners; inquires about his friend Cutler, if he has not got what is to be had of Dr. Smith's relics, with which he could come to Kentucky; says he would do anything in his power for him, and "could fix him in a store or tavern."

HISTORY OF FAIR HAVEN, VERMONT. 113

Alluding to his lottery business, he says he has sent money to Boston to buy up those tickets James sold there, and there are tickets yet at Baltimore—"has not had time to look over the last year's packet, and dreads to do it—wishes he could have a more pleasant account of the business," etc.

In another letter, written prior to this, he says it would not be convenient for him to come to Vermont this year, but "I wish you, seriously, to acquaint yourself with the situation of the lottery business; see how many tickets friend Cutler has taken up; how many there are in the hands of others, who claim payment or are uneasy. Hyde will make a noise for nothing. I want much to get this business settled in a way that cannot be said to be injurious to my reputation, and not being able, as I contemplated, to go and finish the drawing of the lottery, makes me reflect again whether it is not best to buy in the two dollar prizes, and the two and three dollar tickets that are out, for value received. Make no noise about this; consult friend Cutler about it, and write me what has become of my books at Rutland; he had charge of them." James Lyon, he says, is worth a good deal of money, by good luck and good management. He sends regards to all his friends; says he once wrote Dickinson to find mother McArthur something to drink, and wishes to have him paid if there is anything due.

In October, 1798, Col. Lyon, "for the consideration of the friendship he bore the town of Fair Haven," deeded to the town five pieces of land, "the first being an acre for a burying ground, to be laid out with-

114   HISTORY OF FAIR HAVEN, VERMONT.

in one year, in convenient form, by the selectmen, including the graves already made, on the spot southwesterly from the meeting house. The other four pieces are four six rod square pieces, on the four nearest corners of my land to the meeting house, and containing 96 rods, so as to make the Green 18 rods square, including the highway."

These four corners were formed by the crossing of the roads at right angles, and the 18 rod square constituting the public Common, covered the land on which the old meeting house—now Dan Orms' dwelling house—then stood, and included the ground now occupied by the school and town house, and that on which the Methodist church stands.

In August, 1799, Lyon sells to Eliel Gilbert, of Brookfield, Mass., "all that part of a lot of land which I now live on, the second division of Nathan Allen's right, which lies east of the highway to Castleton, except two acres sold to Robert White and Charles Boyle, and except such part of the acre I have sold to William Hennessy and Thomas Whitehouse as may be included in the said Nathan Allen lot."

He conveys also the land which is now the public Green, or Park, "30 rods east and west, and about 44 rods north and south, which lies between the road going to Castleton and the road going to West Haven, from my now dwelling house, and the road going from the meeting house to the Castleton road, excepting 144 rods in the southeast corner, sold to William Hennessy," and "excepting also six rods square, deeded to the town of Fair Haven, for a Green, near the

HISTORY OF FAIR HAVEN, VERMONT. **115**

meeting house"—and besides this, a piece on the plain, to the north of the ten acre lot, where John D. Goodwin resides, coming down from the north end of the Nathan Allen lot, on the west side of the highway running to Castleton, to within 54 1-2 rods of the highway leading east from the meeting house, and likewise a small piece under the hill, between the south line of the Nathan Allen lot and the road running east to the bridge above the iron works.

In September, 1799, Col. Lyon sells to Josiah Norton, of Castleton, his paper mill and 32 acres of land ,on the first and second divisions of his own right, running west on the south side of the river and coming eastward on the north side to the main road, at the southeast corner of land which he had sold to David Mack, thence south on the highway 1 1-2 rods to the house where Clement Blakesley then lived— now Henry Green's—thence west on Eliel Gilbert's north line, and south on Gilbert's west line to the river. At the same time he sells to Mr. Norton 10 acres, including the house which James Lyon had built, east of the church, "Beginning nine rods east 10° south, of the middle of the north end of the meeting house [which then stood a little forward of Dan Orms' now residence], thence east 10° south 24 rods, in the north line of the highway to the west line of the highway which runs toward Kelsey's, thence north 10° east 54 1-2 rods, thence west 10° north 30 rods, thence south 10° west 48 1-2 rods, thence east 10° south 6 rods, thence 6 rods to the first mentioned bounds."

116   HISTORY OF FAIR HAVEN, VERMONT.

This six rod square piece was one of the four corners Lyon had previously deeded to the town. In December, 1801, Mr. Norton, who had purchased the second and third divisions of James Brookins' right of Col. Lyon, in November, 1800—which covered two of the six rod square corners, and came over the old highway to his west line, north of the meeting house —then re-deeded, by quit-claim, to the town, the two squares on the west, with that which was the old six rod wide highway, lying back of the old meeting house, as follows: "Beginning in the centre of the north end of the meeting house, thence east 10° south 3 rods, thence north 10° east 6 rods, thence west 10° north 12 rods, thence south 10° west 18 rods, thence east 10° south 6 rods to the highway."

Col. Lyon, while at Philadelphia, in March, 1800, sold to Edward Douse, of Dedham, Mass., his slitting mill and iron works, and an extensive tract of land lying south and east of the river. In November he closed off to Mr. Norton what remained to him in the town, including the saw mill on the Upper Falls, at the expiration of Scott & Lyon's lease.

Mr. Norton takes up his residence, in 1800, in the house built by James Lyon, east of the church, where he succeeds Lyon as post-master, and also keeps a small stock of merchandise for sale. This same year he buys an extensive tract of land of Col. David Erwin—Col. Erwin's farm, on the plain, toward Mr. Leonard. He was chosen town clerk in 1801, re-elected in 1802 and '03, but he fell down and died suddenly, of apoplexy, or disease of the heart, in March 1803, when

HISTORY OF FAIR HAVEN, VERMONT. 117.

his property was divided among his heirs. He was a man much respected while resident in the town.

Tilly Gilbert, who had returned to the town in 1799, succeeded Esquire Norton as town clerk, in April, 1803. He first moved into and occupied the house of Boyle & White, opening a store of goods in the west end. Upon Col. Lyon's removal from town he took up his residence in the house vacated by Col. Lyon's family, on the spot where the Vermont Hotel now stands, the place being then owned by his brother, Eliel Gilbert. Maj. Gilbert succeeded Mr. Norton, also, in the post-office, which he kept in the old store for about a year, being followed by Andrew McFarland, who kept a store of merchandise in the same place in 1805, Maj. Gilbert about that time erecting a store for himself, under the hill, near the place where John G. Pitkin now resides.

Thus, within the village, around the mills, at the close of the century, the property which was all owned by Col. Lyon, in 1790–1, has all changed hands; the iron works are owned by Edward Douse, of Dedham, Mass., except the two south fires in the forge, which belong to William Lee, of Poultney; Josiah Norton owns the paper mill and lands south and west of it, the saw mill on the Upper Falls, and the house and land east of the church and west of the Castleton road; Tilly Gilbert owns the lower saw mill in company with his brother, Eliel, of Brookfield, Mass., who has a deed of all the land on the east side of the village, excepting Boyle & White's store and two acres; Stephen Rogers and Nathaniel Dickinson

118　HISTORY OF FAIR HAVEN, VERMONT.

own the grist mill, and Rogers has a place on the west side of the village; Dr. Smith, of West Haven, owns the tavern house and land, and John Taylor, of New York, the Hennessy store north of the tavern.

Outside of the village there were also some changes during this period. On the west street, Russel Smith, of West Haven, bought of Isaac McWithey, in August, 1795, a strip of land 44 rods along the south side of the highway, by 160 rods deep, adjoining Isaac Cutler's farm, on which he commenced to build a house for himself. In March, 1797, he bought another piece of Mr. Cutler, adjoining his own on the west, but dying soon afterward, his farm was sold, in 1804, by Michael· Merritt, guardian of his heirs—Olive, Sally and Lydia—to Salmon Norton, from whom it passed to James Witherell, and from him again to Tilly Gilbert, who sold it, in January, 1807, to Paul Guilford, Jr., of Conway, Mass.

In September, 1798, Philip Allen, of Salem, N. Y., a carpenter and joiner, who is said to have built a "portico" to the old meeting house, purchased Isaac Cutler's farm, and removed on to the same, occupying it until 1802, when he sold it to Paul Scott, of Granville, N. Y.

In March, 1795, Solomon Wilder, of Whitehall, N. Y., buys a farm of his brother-in-law, John M. Ballard, on Poultney river—where Charles W. Gardner now resides—and occupied the same until as late as 1811, when he deeded it to his son, Keyes Wilder.

Henry Ainsworth, of Pomfret, bought of Col. David Erwin, in September, 1798, a farm of 110 acres, where

HISTORY OF FAIR HAVEN, VERMONT. 121

Brownell, of Colchester, and John Lamb, of Fair Haven—the same he sold, in 1800, to Josiah Norton, Esq.

Jeremiah Durand had sold off portions of his farm to William Buell and Charles Boyle, and had died prior to 1799.

Israel Trowbridge had also died, and his son, Levi, had sold, in March, 1795, the second division of his father's original right—the farm on which Hezekiah Whitlock afterward settled—to Cornelius and David D. Board, of Castleton. In the spring of 1799, Levi and Abigail, his sister, had given Dr. Samuel Shaw, of Castleton, a deed of a large part of their home-farm —now D. P. Wescott's place—reserving only a small portion along Castleton town line. A man by the name of Content Allis occupied Shaw's portion, toward Kelsey's, about one year. Shaw sold the place in the summer of 1800, to Jacob Slyter, sometimes written "Slaughter," of Poultney.

On the west street, Frederick Hill, who had a place just east of Isaac Cutler's—perhaps where Rev. Rufus Cushman afterwards resided, now John P. Sheldon's —and was town clerk in 1791, removed, as we have seen, to Rutland, leaving the place to Mr. Cutler. Beyond Esquire Cutler's, besides Dr. Witherell, there were Charles Rice, Capt. Elijah Taylor, John W. Throop, Abijah Warren, Olney Hawkins, John Brown and Nathaniel Dickinson, all owners of real estate during this period. These seem to comprise the principal points and incidents of change during the period.

In the public transactions of the town there are several facts deserving of mention and record. At

122 HISTORY OF FAIR HAVEN, VERMONT.

the March meeting, 1793, Samuel Stannard was chosen trustee for the north school district, and Dr. James Witherell for the south district.

At a meeting in June a tax was voted of 2d. on the pound on the List of 1793, "to purchase town books, weights and measures." Oliver Cleveland, Curtis Kelsey, Philip Priest and Ethan Whipple were appointed as a committee "to view the river between Capt. Taylor's and Mr. Leonard's, and report to the meeting whether they think a bridge can be built that will stand in high water." The committee made report that they deemed it feasible to build a bridge over the river there.

It was voted "that the south part of this town be set off for a school district, from where an east and west line strikes the fork of the road that leads to Mr. John Meacham's."

At a meeting held in July, 1793, Col. Matthew Lyon was chosen delegate to a convention to be held at Windsor.

The March meeting, 1794, voted "that there be a new school district established, to be called the northeast district, and that the southwest corner of the lot of land laid out on Israel Smith's right be the southwest corner of said school district, and that a parallel line north 10° east, and another east 10° south, divide said district from the other district or districts."

It was then voted "that the northeast school district extend southward so far as to take in Abraham Sharp's house and improvements, and so far west as to include Asahel Munger's farm."

HISTORY OF FAIR HAVEN, VERMONT. 123

At a meeting in April, 1794, the selectmen were directed to repair the bridge over the river toward Elisha Kilburn's, in Hampton, and to apply two-thirds of the highway work of the year in that direction. They were authorized to let out the building of the bridge by the job, if they judged best.

In October, 1794, Curtis Kelsey, Sen., petitioned the Legislature, then in session at Rutland, "to establish a school district in Col. Lyon's vicinity, and relieve him, he being nearly the only farmer in the district, and having a large List; while Lyon's hands have no list, but many children, and Lyon, by his influence over the listers, has prevented any assessment of his forge, saw mill, grist and slitting mills. * * Neither," he says, "have the merchants been assessed who have stores of Lyon."

At the freemen's meeting, in September, 1794, the vote of the citizens stood—for Governor,

Thomas Chittenden,	74
Isaac Tichenor,	23

For Lieutenant Governor,

Jonathan Hunt,	69

For Treasurer,

Thomas Tolman,	49
Samuel Mattocks,	19

In December the vote for Representative to the Fourth Congress stood:

Col. Matthew Lyon,	60
Isaac Tichenor,	6

The meeting of September, 1794, was held at the school house, "a little north of Mr. Samuel Stannard's,"

124 HISTORY OF FAIR HAVEN, VERMONT.

and voted "to accept the proceedings of the committee for dividing the school lands," and that the committee "be and are hereby empowered to give quitclaim deeds in behalf of the town."

In October, 1797, at a meeting called at the meeting house, and adjourned to Nathaniel Dickinson's, a tax was voted of sixteen cents on the pound "to repair bridges and highways, payable in cash, wheat, rye, Indian corn, nails, bar iron or labor, at the current prices of said articles," Timothy Brainard, Samuel Stannard and Ethan Whipple being chosen a committee "to superintend the expenditure."

October 2d, 1799, Michael Merritt, Philip Priest, Charles McArthur, Isaac Cutler, John Brown, Nathaniel Dickinson, Jonathan Orms, Timothy Goodrich and Ethan Whipple petition the General Assembly of the State, convened at Windsor, as follows: "Being deeply impressed with the most lively sensibility of the inestimable advantages to be derived from social compacts, when formed in designs to cultivate useful knowledge,—pray that for the aforesaid honorable purpose your petitioners may be incorporated into a body politic, by the name of Fair Haven Library Society, with such powers, privileges and immunities as you in your wisdom shall deem adequate to such purpose." The charter of this society was granted October 23d, 1799. Whether any action was ever taken under this charter we are not informed.

PART II.

Miscellaneous Sketches.

MISCELLANEOUS SKETCHES.

LYON'S FIRST STORE.

This was a small, red building, which now constitutes the southwest part of Thomas Hughes' dwelling house and store. It was built as early as 1791. The first sale of land made by Lyon, within the limits of the village, was the sale of this store and two acres lying east of the old highway, which ran through the town in a north and south direction, close by the west end of Mr. Hughes' house. The sale was made in January, 1792, to Robert White, of Lansingburgh, N. Y., and Charles Boyle, of Fair Haven, the land being a portion of the second division of Nathan Allen's right, and bounded as follows: "Beginning at the point where the east side of the highway begins to take a course north 10° east, said point is about 7 1-2 rods nearly northeast from the northeast corner of the house built by Matthew Lyon; thence runs north 10° east 12 rods, thence east 10° south 26 2-3 rods, thence south 12 rods, and thence west to the bounds begun at." In this deed Col. Lyon reserves to himself the privilege of keeping public houses of entertainment on his own lands, not, how-

P

127　　HISTORY OF FAIR HAVEN, VERMONT.

ever, prohibiting them from selling spirituous liquors at retail, as was then customary in country stores.

Mr. Boyle died here about 1799, and William Lee, of Rutland, as his administrator, sold his half of the store and land to Cephas Smith, in 1801, and Mr. Smith sold it to Dr. James Witherell, in April, 1805.

Mr. White having also died, Salmon Norton, his administrator, deeds the south acre, or half, of the lot, on which the store stood, to Dr. Witherell, and Dr. Witherell, in May, 1805, quit-claims to Norton the north acre, or half of the lot. In July, 1806, Dr. Witherell sells the south lot to Joshua Quinton, of Whitehall, N. Y. It remained in the hands of Mr. Quinton and his son, Joshua, being variously occupied, through many years.

Tradition reports that James Lyon occupied the east part as a dwelling, and had his book store and post-office in the west part, as early as the year 1798. Maj. Tilly Gilbert kept a store and post-office in the building in 1803. Andrew McFarland occupied it for a store in 1805. It was afterwards occupied for a store by John Quinton and Thomas Christie, and as late as 1824 by Dr. Charles Backus, who resided in the east part of the building.

In May, 1847, it was deeded by Joshua Quinton, Jr., to Olive Kelsey. She resided on the place, leasing the small store which had been built by her brother, James N. Kelsey—now the back part of Mr. Bosworth's building—to Evan G. Evans and John W. Jones, of Middle Granville, N. Y., in March, 1855, for three years.

HISTORY OF FAIR HAVEN, VERMONT. **128**

She sold the whole place, in March, 1860, to Israel Davey. He sold the store and a lot 34 feet on the front, to Hezekiah Bosworth, of Hampton, N. Y., in July, and the house and lot to Thomas Hughes, its present owner, in August, 1860. Mr. Hughes has built the large two-story building now used as a store and jewelry shop, and has added various improvements to the dwelling house.

LYON'S TAVERN HOUSE.

This house, the second erected on the hill, was built by Col. Lyon, prior to 1787, and probably as late as 1785, on the south part of the division of Nathan Allen's right, a little above the north line of the first and second divisions of his own right, and on the corner of the roads. It was occupied by Col. Lyon himself at first, and probably kept by him as a public house for a number of years, till, having built a private residence on the opposite side of the street, where the Vermont Hotel stands, he removed into that, and rented the hotel to Nathaniel Dickinson, who was occupying it in June, 1795, at which time it was sold by Col. Lyon, together with 10 acres of land lying south and west-

129 HISTORY OF FAIR HAVEN, VERMONT.

ward of it, to David Mack, of Middlefield, Mass. Mr. Dickinson kept it as a public house as late as 1798, it being sold, in March of that year, by Col. Mack to Dr. Simeon Smith, of West Haven, and John Brown is said to have occupied it. Dickinson is said to have kept a tavern in March, 1798 and '99, and in 1801, '02 and '03. Brown is mentioned as keeping the house in April, 1800.

It was sold by Dr. Smith, in February, 1803, to Isaac Cutler, Esq. He owned it until September, 1809, when he sold it to Thomas Wilmot, of Poultney. Mr. Cutler does not appear to have kept it himself during the whole of the time he owned it. Royal Dennis, who came here in 1807, kept the house about two years. Mr. Cutler sold one acre off from this place—it being the same that is now occupied by Mrs. William Miller—to Joel Beaman, in November, 1808.

By Mr. Wilmot the house was essentially enlarged and improved, in 1811 or '12, the columns which are now standing being put up at that time, and a balcony floor put in above, and various artistic devices being lavished on the wood-work of the rooms. After Mr. Wilmot's decease, in January, 1813, the house was kept for a number of years, and as late as 1816 and '17, by John Beaman, who also took charge of the silversmith shop which stood west of Mr. Wilmot's house, and near Alonson Allen's present office. Beaman is said to have owned this shop in July, 1817.

Mr. Wilmot had sold to Elisha Parkill, in January, 1811, a lot where James Miller's house stands, for a site for a store, and another store-lot to Erwin Safford,

HISTORY OF FAIR HAVEN, VERMONT. 130

in April following, where Mr. Miller's shop now is.
Mrs. Wilmot sold to Mr. Safford, in January, 1820, a
lot for a grain store, just west of Joseph Adams' now
residence. In August, 1823, she sold to Joseph
Brown a half acre of land where Alonson Allen resides. She also sold to the town, in August, 1824, a
lot 40 feet square, for a pound, where Widow Ira
Allen's barn now is and back of it. She having purchased the old Lyon house, on the opposite side of the
street, leased her tavern house, in August, 1829, to
Moses Colton, for five years. On the same 11th day
of August, she purchased of John P. Colburn, attorney
for Samuel Dennis, of Boston, the old "Dennis tavern,"
then occupied by James Greenough, and agreed with
Mr. Colton that it should not be kept open for a public house.

At the expiration of Mr. Colton's lease, July 30th,
1834, Mrs. Wilmot again leased it for a term of five
years, to her son-in-law, Spencer Ward, but Mr. Ward
only remained two years, throwing up the lease in
July, 1836, and going away to Chautauqua county, N.
Y., Mrs. Wilmot taking the hotel herself, and employing John D. Stannard as her agent, to whom she afterward, February 9th, 1838, sold the place.

Mr. Stannard kept the house open to the public until
about 1850, when it was closed for a time, and afterward was opened and kept, in 1857, by Royal Bullock,
for one year. Mr. Stannard sold it, in May, 1853, to
Joseph Adams, its present owner. Mr. Adams removed
the old barns and shed in the following summer, and
re-fitted the house which was kept as a public house

131   HISTORY OF FAIR HAVEN, VERMONT.

for a number of seasons thereafter by his son-in-law, David B. Colton. The brick store was erected by Messrs. Adams & Allen, in the summer of 1854, on the spot which had been occupied by Lyon's barn and shed. Mr. Adams' new marble residence, and the dwellings of his son and son-in-law, and that also of Corril Reed, as well as the store which he owns and occupies, on the south of Mr. Adams', have all been built on the land of the Lyon tavern house, sold by Lyon to David Mack, and by Mr. Stannard to Mr. Adams.

STEPHEN ROGERS' TANNERY.

The second sale of land by Col. Lyon, within the limits of the present village, was made to Stephen Rogers, in May, 1792, and consisted of about seven acres of land on the bank of the river, on the west side of the Common. Mr. Rogers was a tanner and shoe-maker, who worked for Col. Lyon. He had built the northeast part of the house now occupied by William Dolan, which must have been the third house built on the hill. The northeast corner of his purchase was 51 feet north from the northeast corner of his dwelling house, and the southeast corner was on the line of the old pound then established and existing,

HISTORY OF FAIR HAVEN, VERMONT. **132**

and the land laid partly on Lyon's own first and second division right, and partly on the second and third divisions of the Brookin's right.

Lyon prohibits to Rogers in this sale the establishing of a tavern or house of entertainment, or store, or shop for the sale of merchandise or imported spirits on the premises for fifteen years, without his consent, if living, on penalty of reversion, meaning to retain such right on his own premises.

Rogers had established his tannery under the hill, west of his house, and built a small shop where Mrs. Allen's house now stands, and he there made the leather and boots and shoes worn by Lyon's men and the inhabitants. In October, 1799, he made an additional purchase of 2 3-4 acres to his place, with a front running north 10 rods from the point 50 feet north of his house.

He sold the whole to Calvin Munger, his brother-in-law, in March, 1801. Mr. Munger sold a strip of three rods in width from the north end, to Christopher Minot, of Boston, in October, 1805. Mr. Munger died in April, 1806, and the place was occupied by Rufus Guilford, who purchased the same in February, 1809, Mrs. Rebecca E. Munger and Tilly Gilbert giving the deed. In March, 1810, Mr. Guilford sold the place to Isaac Cutler, and it was said to consist of 12 acres. Mr. Cutler sells another strip of one rod in width to Mr. Minot, in November, 1811. In April, 1812, he sells to Harvey Church about one acre and 23 rods, including the dwelling house occupied by Church, the shop and the tan-yard. Mr. Church gives Samuel

133 HISTORY OF FAIR HAVEN, VERMONT.

Hemmenway, of Shoreham, a mortgage on his place, October 13th, 1812, for notes running to 1817.

Mr. Cutler had built for himself the house now occupied by Owen Owens—for a long time the parsonage of the Congregational society—where he continued to reside until his removal to West Haven, about 1827. He deeded his place of 10 acres to Col. Joseph Watson, a son-in-law of Dr. James Witherell, as early as June, 1818, reserving the right to occupy the same.

By him it was deeded to Nathan B. Haswell, of Burlington, in December, 1832. Haswell conveyed it to William C. Kittredge, in December, 1838, and Mr. Kittredge, in May, 1839, deeded to the Congregational society the house and garden lot, reserving in his own possession the land lying back of the hill, along the river, which he afterward sold, with his home-lot, to Ira C. Allen, in January, 1866. The house was occupied by Rev. Amos Drury during his pastorate in the town, from 1829 to 1837. It was sold by the Congregational society to Owen Owens in January, 1866.

Mr. Church carried on the tannery and shoe shop until August, 1827, when he failed in business, and deeded his place to Francis S. Hemmenway, of Shoreham, by whom, in November, 1830, it was conveyed to Isaac Patch and Theophilus T. Parmenter, of Brandon. Mr. Church had, in June, 1819, deeded a small piece near his tannery to Erwin Safford, with the privilege of water from his spring for Safford's distillery.

Messrs. Patch and Parmenter run the tannery and manufactured shoes in the shop for a few years, perhaps

HISTORY OF FAIR HAVEN, VERMONT. 134

as late as 1834, when they failed, and the place went back to Mr. Hemmenway, who is said to have been guardian of Calvin Munger's children, as well as brother to Mrs. Rebecca S. Munger. He sold the place again, in April, 1839—one acre and 23 rods, excepting the land and privilege sold by Mr. Church to Erwin Safford, in 1819—to Alonson Allen, and it was occupied from that time by his brother, Ira Allen. The old grain house was bought by Alonson Allen of William C. Kittredge, and removed to this lot in the spring of 1840, and transformed into a dwelling house.

Mr. Allen sold the house and north portion of the lot to Heman Foot, in March, 1842, the front being 58 feet in width, reserving the use of water from the well. Mr. Foot sold the same to Joseph Adams, April 20th, 1843. It was occupied and thoroughly reconstructed by Mr. Adams, in 1846. He sold it to William Dolan, April 30th, 1853.

Mr. Allen deeded the south portion of the place to his brother, in February, 1853.

135   HISTORY OF FAIR HAVEN, VERMONT.

LYON'S DWELLING HOUSE.

This house, which was built by Col. Lyon, where the Vermont Hotel stands—and now constitutes the back wing, or extension of the same—previous to 1795, was sold by him, in August, 1799, to Eliel Gilbert, of Greenfield, Mass., together with other lands, he describing the place as that whereon he then lived, and a part of the second division of Nathan Allen's right, extending on the south to the road leading to the iron works, and including a small piece from the first and second divisions of his own right, excepting the two half acres sold to Thomas Whitehouse and William Hennessy, situated above the road to the iron works.

Mr. Gilbert sold his lands to his brother, Tilly Gilbert, in November, 1802, including this house, which Tilly then occupied. Tilly Gilbert built for himself a dwelling house on the bluff where his son, Benjamin F., now resides, and in April, 1805, he sold the Lyon house and a lot consisting of about six acres to Dr. James Witherell. It was occupied for a time by Dr. Witherell, and was sold by him to his son-in-law, Dr. Ebenezer Hurd, in July, 1809.

In June, 1817, Dr. Hurd deeded, by way of mortgage, to Rollin C. Mallory, a strip of 10 rods wide, along the north side of the road leading to Davey's iron works, extending from land owned by Mr. Davey on the east to the turnpike on the west. This land

HISTORY OF FAIR HAVEN, VERMONT. 136

is now covered by the residences of Messrs. Ketchum, Williams, Lloyd and Pitkin.

After his removal to Detroit, in May, 1819, Dr. Hurd quit-claimed this strip of nearly two acres to Dr. Witherell, and Dr. Witherell quit-claimed it to Mr. Mallory. In May, 1820, Mr. Mallory sold it to Jacob Davey. It was made use of by Mr. Davey for many years. As late as 1830 he had a large cooper shop on the point of rocks near where John G. Pitkin lives.

Dr. Hurd re-deeded the main place to Dr. Witherell, in May, 1817, and by him it was sold to Lucy Wilmot, in April, 1826. Mrs. Wilmot conveyed it to Spencer and Ann Ward, in April, 1834. In June, 1837, Spencer Ward quit-claims his share to William W. Ward, of Silver Creek, N. Y., who deeds it back to him in March, 1839, and in August following Spencer and Anna convey it again to Mrs. Lucy Wilmot. December 14th, 1840, Mrs. Wilmot sold it to Seth J. Hitchcock, of West Haven, for·$900.

Mr. Hitchcock, in June, 1843, sold a lot 48 feet wide, where Richard E. Lloyd's house stands, to Azel Willard, Jun., for a site for a store. In May, 1843, Mr. Hitchcock sold the place to Adams Dutton, and bought Mr. Dutton's farm, north of the village. Mr. Dutton moved onto the place in the spring of 1844, and resided there till April, 1851, working a slate quarry at Cedar Point, and constructing machinery for the manufacture of slate pencils. He sold the place in April, 1851, to Israel Davey; and Mr. Davey, after selling off the building lots, now occupied, east of the hotel, sold the residue to Served Fish, April 1st, 1858. Mr.

137 HISTORY OF FAIR HAVEN, VERMONT.

Fish built thereon the present Vermont Hotel, a three story brick building, which has proved inadequate to accommodate the wants of the public for a hotel in the town.

Mr. Fish kept the house as a hotel until March, 1866, when he sold it to David Offensend, who kept it open about two years, and then leased it to David McBride. The house has been popular and liberally patronized while occupied by Mr. McBride. It was sold, in March, 1869, to Charles C. Knight, of Whitehall, N. Y., who came into occupation of the same April 6th, 1870.

HENNESSY'S STORE.

In May, 1794, Col. Lyon sells to William Hennessy, for £17 and 10s., a piece of land 12 rods square, lying six rods north of his dwelling house, and on the west side of the old four-rod-wide highway which led past his house toward Castleton. On this lot Mr. Hennessy built a large, square double house, nearly opposite the Boyle & White store, facing the east, and with a store in one side.

Mr. Hennessy, who had been an associate proprietor of the *Fair Haven Telegraph*, and had owned a part of Lyon's forge, sold out this store in July, 1796, to

HISTORY OF FAIR HAVEN, VERMONT. 138

George Cadwell, of Hampton, a son-in-law of Col.
Lyon. With it he sold only the north part, or a strip
seven rods wide, of the 12 rod square lot, which he
had bought of Col. Lyon, thus leaving a strip of five
rods by 12 rods on the south of it. This was sold to
Elijah G. Galusha, and afterward given to the town by
Alexander Dunehue, in 1814.

Mr. Cadwell sold his part and the store in August,
1797, to Isaac Cutler and Stephen Rogers. They sold
it, in the following spring, to John Taylor, of New
York. He retained it till May, 1804, when he sold
to Peter B. French, of Hampton, and Mr. French, in
December, sold to John Meacham, of Hampton. Mr.
Meacham had been a resident in Fair Haven, and afterward became a resident of Castleton, where he died.
He carried on business in this store less than a year,
the road meantime being changed, in August, 1805,
from the east to the west side of his building, thus leaving his lot but four rods east and west by seven rods
north and south, or with the old highway, which was
set over to him, eight rods east and west. Mr. Meacham sold this to Salmon Norton, in September, 1805.

Mr. Norton soon after purchased the north acre of
the Boyle & White lot, and connecting the two, sold
the whole to Alexander Dunehue, in April, 1807, and
with it another lot or addition, eastward, which he had
purchased of Tilly Gilbert, thus preparing the way for
what will be better remembered by many now living
as the OLD DENNIS TAVERN.

THE OLD DENNIS TAVERN.

Royal Dennis, who had been keeping the tavern house of Isaac Cutler for about two years, in May, 1809, bought of Alexander Dunahue about 1 1-2 acres, including the old Hennessy store, on the spot where Mr. Graves' block now stands. He built a wing or extension eastward over the old highway, constructed piazzas on the west side, and generally remodeled the building, making thereof a spacious and convenient hotel, which was kept by him for many years, and became generally known throughout the country. Mr. Dennis deeded it to his brother, Samuel Dennis, of Boston, in May, 1822, and removed to Hartford, N. Y., in 1823.

The house was kept by John Beaman for several years. He was the landlord in 1825, and prepared the celebration dinner on the 4th of July of that year. The house was kept by Joseph Brown in the year 1827. In 1828 and '29 it was occupied by James Greenough, and was sold to Mrs. Lucy Wilmot in August, 1829, who, on the same day, leased the Lyon tavern house to Moses Colton, contracting that no tavern should be kept at the Dennis stand. She sold the Dennis house to John J. Davey in February, 1838, prohibiting his opening it for a tavern for fifteen years. The building was completely remodeled by Mr. Davey, he putting in offices and basement rooms on the south side, and

HISTORY OF FAIR HAVEN, VERMONT. 140

a large store, entered by high stone steps, on the west side. The store was occupied by Alonson Allen, about 1840, and until it passed into Leonard Williams' hands, in January, 1845; Mr. Williams, at that time, purchasing it of the mortgagee, Jonathan Atherton, of Cavendish, Vt., to whom Mr. Davey had mortgaged it in February, 1838.

By Mr. Williams the building was again completely transformed, the old one being, in fact, displaced by another of a different but scarcely improved construction and appearance. Mr. Williams also removed the old stable of the Dennis tavern, which stood where Norman Peck now lives, and built the present dwelling house of Mr. Peck in its stead. He sold the two houses, store and two acres of land, to his brother, James Williams, of Hydeville, in June, 1848, and James Williams deeded to his son, James E. Williams, in March, 1851.

James E. Williams sold the store building, then occupied by Messrs. Adams & Allen, and three-fourths of his land to Ira Allen, May 10th, 1854, reserving to the north tenement the use of water from the well, and the right of way along the north side of the store building, and past the east end of the same. In order to secure this right, Simeon Allen purchased the north house and lot, April 1st, 1861, the lot being 48 feet and 10 inches in width, south from the southwest corner of Increase Jones' home-lot. On the 2d of April, Ira Allen sold to Matthias Ludlum the store and land adjoining, south of the center line of the passage or roadway between the two houses as they

141   HISTORY OF FAIR HAVEN, VERMONT.

then stood. On the 30th of April, 1862, Mr. Ludlum transferred the premises to his father-in-law, Augustus Graves, of Salisbury, and Mr. Graves immediately erected the building now standing on the corner, and occupied by his son, for a store, on the land of the old roadway at the east end of the store built by Mr. Williams, afterwards removing the same to the present corner, and placing the old part farther to the east and south, and at the same time extending the north wing of his dwelling house.

Simeon Allen sold the north house and lot to Norman Peck, of Hampton, in January, 1866, and Mr. Peck soon after erected on this lot the building now used as the printing office of the *Fair Haven Journal*.

THE IRON WORKS.

Col. Matthew Lyon built the dam on the Upper Falls, to bring water to his iron works, in July, 1785. He must have built the works during the season, bringing his machinery on wagons from Massachusetts. In October he petitioned the General Assembly of the State, which was then an independent sovereignty, to lay a duty of 2d. per pound on nails coming

HISTORY OF FAIR HAVEN, VERMONT. 142

into the State, to enable him to build his works and supply the State. The town was called "Lyon's Works," and known for some years after this time, in the whole country around, by this designation.

The iron business was carried on here by Col. Lyon under various superintendents—Gen. David Erwin being remembered as for a number of years the managing foreman, or boss—until Lyon's removal to Kentucky, in 1800. The business appears to have been partly the manufacture of axes, hoes, and various agricultural implements, but mainly the making of iron from the ore imported from abroad, into nail rods, the rods being manufactured into nails by hand. It was not until several years later that machinery was invented to cut the nails directly from the rolled plates.

Col. Lyon is reported to have kept a large number of men in employment about his works. In January, 1794, he sold to William Hennessy the two south fires in his forge, together with a hammer, anvil and coal house. Mr. Hennessy failed, and the forge fires were taken possession of by Abraham Leggett, of New York, in April, 1798, under an attachment. They came into the hands of William Lee, of Poultney, in August, 1799, and he sold them to Alexander Dunehue, of Castleton, in March, 1804. Dunehue sold them to Cornelius D. Board, of Castleton, in April. Board sold them to Salmon Norton, in April, 1805, and in April, 1808, Norton sold them to Jacob Davey.

Col. Lyon, having decided to leave Vermont, sold the works, while at Philadelphia, in March, 1800, to Edward Douse, of Dedham, Mass., selling with them

143 HISTORY OF FAIR HAVEN, VERMONT.

all the land lying south of the road running past the works and east of the turnpike, and the extensive tract afterward purchased by Jacob Davey, lying south and eastward from the river.

The slitting mill was leased by John Brown, attorney for Mr. Douse, on the 25th of December, 1800, to David Erwin, until the 15th of February, 1802, Erwin to pay for the use of the same in iron rods as fast as they were manufactured, but Erwin does not appear to have retained it; and Mr. Douse leased the works to Dan Smith, of West Haven, in July, 1801. Mr. Smith started the works and finally purchased them of Douse, in July, 1803. In October, 1807, Jacob Davey, who had come into town in the spring of 1804, and taken charge of the works for Mr. Smith, purchased them of Smith, with the six acres of land extending westward to the turnpike. He also leased for seven years the 300 acres east and south of the river, with the privilege of buying, and in June, 1812, purchased the same.

The works were burned down in November, 1815, and re-built by Mr. Davey. In May, 1829, Mr. Davey sold one-half interest in the works to Edmund Kingsland, Jonathan Capen and Jacob D. Kingsland, and they took charge of the business, making $500 each in the first six months and losing what they had made in the second six months. Mr. Capen and Jacob Kingsland sold to Edmund Kingsland in the spring of 1831. Mr. Capen hired the works one year, in 1832, and made $1,000 in running them. Mr. Kingsland

HISTORY OF FAIR HAVEN, VERMONT. 144

sold to Mr. Davey, and Mr. Davey offered them for sale for $3,000.

In 1838, Alonson Allen leased the works for five years; and ran them till they were burned down a second time, March 17th, 1843. Mr. Davey, with his customary energy, re-built them the same season, and leased them to his son-in-law, Artemas S. Cushman, and his son, Israel Davey, then of Castleton.

Mr. Davey died in October, 1843, and in November, 1845, the works were sold at auction to Artemas S. Cushman; Israel Davey, administrator, deeding to him, June 26th, 1846, and Mr. Cushman conveyed back to Israel Davey an undivided three-fifths interest in the same. Mr. Davey bought out Mr. Cushman, January 26th, 1853. In August, 1859, he deeded one-half interest to Benjamin S. Nichols, of Whitehall, N. Y. Mr. Nichols deeded back to Mr. Davey, in August, 1865, and Mr. Davey died in August, 1869, sole proprietor of the works, which have been kept in operation for the benefit of the estate by Rufus C. Colburn.

THE PAPER MILL.

The paper mill in Fair Haven was started by Col. Matthew Lyon, about 1790 or '91. His son, James, is reported to have had charge of it at one time, and they must have made the paper generally used, both for writing and printing purposes, in the town, and most of the country about. We have no information as to the men who were employed in the mill while it was owned by Col. Lyon, but we have specimens of the paper, both in blank books and printed sheets, which was manufactured during the period. Some of this is very coarse and muddy, and indicates the imperfection of the hand process, or art of manufacture then practiced.

The mill was sold by Col. Lyon, with 32 acres of land, to Josiah Norton, Esq., of Castleton, for $1,500, in September, 1799. The land ran wést on the south side of the river, and came east on the north side to the southeast corner of the land sold to David Mack; then south on the highway 1 1-2 rods, to the house where Clement Blakesley lived; thence west on Eliel Gilbert's north line, and south on Gilbert's west line to the river.

At Mr. Norton's decease, in the spring of 1803, the paper mill and land attached was set to his eldest son, Salmon Norton. By him the mill and a half acre of

HISTORY OF FAIR HAVEN, VERMONT. 146

land was sold to his brother-in-law, Alexander Dune-hue, of Castleton, July 30th, 1804, for $1,695. He sold the land west of the paper mill and that lying north of the river, where the marble mill now stands, to John Herring and Moses Colton, in November, 1809. The mill was rented by Dunehue, in 1805, to John Herring, Moses Colton and Joel Beaman; and they, after running one year, divided their stock of paper on hand, Herring and Colton taking their shares south, to Troy and New York, and Beaman selling his in Montreal.

The mill being burned in March, 1806, Mr. Dunehue sold the site to Herring, Colton & Beaman, for $800, and they re-built the mill. Herring and Colton bought out Beaman in April, 1811, paying him $1,300. Herring sells to Colton, March 25th, 1813, the paper mill and 25 acres of land. In October, Herring deeds to Alexander Dunehue the land north of the river, now occupied by the marble mill. Mr. Colton sold one-half the mill, in April, with one-half acre of land, and the Beriah Rogers tannery lot, on the north side, to George Warren, for $2,400—the amount he had paid Herring. The mill was thus in the hands of Messrs. Colton & Warren, from April, 1813. In January, 1819, they took David C. Sproat into partnership, and conducted business under the firm name of Colton, Warren & Sproat for several years, engaging also in distilling whiskey and selling merchandise.

Mr. Colton deeded to the company, in January, 1825, 12 1-2 acres of land south of the road leading to Mr. Leonard's, which he had purchased of John Quin-

147 HISTORY OF FAIR HAVEN, VERMONT.

ton and Thomas Christie; and in December, 1826, he quit-claimed to Messrs. Warren and Sproat this same 12 1-2 acres, the paper mill, with land running west along the river 26 rods, and the store, distillery and grain-house, which Colton, Warren & Sproat bought of Colton & Crane, in February, 1823.

Warren & Sproat failing, in 1827, an assignment of the mill and other property was made by Sproat, on the 5th of July (Warren having left town in the early morning of that day), to John P. Colburn, Jacob Davey, Barnabas Ellis and Harris W. Bates. The mill was run that season by H. W. Bates & Co. It was deeded, in May, 1828, by Warren, who was then in Albany, and Sproat, to William C. Kittredge, subject to a mortgage to Joel Beaman. Mr. Kittredge deeded it to his father, Dr. Abel Kittredge, of Hinsdale, Mass., in September; and he sold one-half of it back to Sproat, in October, 1829, for $3,000.

It was burned while owned by them, January 31st, 1831, and in July they sold one-third interest therein to Alonzo Safford, for $1,800, and re-built the mill. Abel Kittredge conveys his third part to his son, William C., in August, 1835, for $2,500; and by him it was sold, in December, to Sproat & Safford, for $3,100, the sale probably including stock on hand and improvements.

On the 9th of October, 1843, Mr. Sproat quit-claimed to Mr. Safford the mill and house occupied by himself, on the east of the mill; the house occupied by Charles Stratton, near the river; the place occupied by Joseph Berto, north of the river; and 20 acres of land, west

HISTORY OF FAIR HAVEN, VERMONT. **148**

of the river, which had been purchased of Isaiah Scott, in April, 1835.

Mr. Safford assigned the mill and property to Abraham Graves, in October, 1843, and it was run by him till 1850, he seeming to succeed no better with the business than others who had preceded him, although he was a man well reputed for business ability, who had accumulated property in farming. Mr. Graves quit-claimed back to Mr. Safford, in February, 1850. In May, Mr. Safford sold the whole to Albert Fuller, óf Massachusetts, and Charles A. Sweet, of Granville, N. Y., for $6,000. Mr. Fuller carried it on for Fuller & Sweet until April, 1854, when they sold to Nicholas, Daniel and George W. Hurlburt. In September, 1855, George W. deeded to Nicholas G., who deeded to Daniel, January 9th, 1857, and by Daniel Hurlburt it was deeded, the same day, to Timothy Miller.

Mr. Miller sold one undivided half, September 11th, 1858, to James P. Brown, of Hartford, by whom it was mortgaged to David D. Cole, November 1st, 1858. This mortgage was discharged, January 4th, 1860, and Betsey and William Q. Brown, as administrators of the estate of James P. Brown, deeded the same undivided half, in March, to William Miller.

149 HISTORY OF FAIR HAVEN, VERMONT.

THE GRIST MILL.

The first grist mill was built by Col. Lyon and Ager. Hawley, below the old paper mill, on the south side of the river, about 1783. We do not know how long it was run, but the grist mill on the north side of the saw mill, where it now stands, must have been built not many years afterward, as it was sold by Col. Lyon, with the saw mill, to Asa Smith and Heman Hoffman, in July, 1795, and is said to have been stripped off and re-built when owned by Solomon Cleveland, in 1797.

Pliny Adams bought out Mr. Cleveland's half interest in the mills, in April, 1798. In August, 1799, Mr. Adams sold out to Stephen Rogers, and in September, Lyon sold one-half of the grist mill to Nathaniel Dickinson. Rogers transférred his share of the grist mill to Dr. James Witherell, in January, 1803, and Dickinson conveyed his, in February, to Eliel Gilbert, who deeded it to Dr. Witherell on the same day. Witherell sold the whole to Salmon Norton, in April, 1804. Norton, in November, 1807, sold it to Joshua Quinton, selling with it the acre of land and house occupied by Richard Longshore. It was a part of this acre that was sold to John Quinton and Thomas Christie, in May, 1810, and by them afterward sold to Moses Colton.

The mill remained in the hands of Mr. Quinton

HISTORY OF FAIR HAVEN, VERMONT. 150

and his son, Joshua, Jr., until the spring of 1845, when it was sold to William C. Kittredge, Alonson Allen and Joseph Adams, Messrs. Allen and Adams deeding to Mr. Kittredge.

It was sold by Mr. Kittredge to Hezekiah and Harvey Howard, in October, 1853. On the 1st of November, 1859, Hezekiah and his wife deeded to John Balis, of Benson, all their property in Fair Haven, which included one-half of the grist mill. In April, 1860, Harvey Howard and Mr. Balis sold the grist mill, tan house and tannery to Frederick Taylor and Wellington Ketchum. The mill was afterward, in April, 1863, deeded by Mr. Balis to Mr. Ketchum. In October following, Mr. Ketchum sold one undivided half of the whole place—mill, mill house and tannery —to Jonathan Capen, by whom the mill was leased, on the 16th of November, 1866, to Nathan R. Reed, for a term of three years.

In April, 1867, Mr. Capen quit-claimed his interest to Mr. Ketchum, and he deeded the same to Henry G. Lapham, of Brooklyn, N. Y., on the same day. The old tannery was taken possession of, and re-built as a slate mill by the Union Slate Company, by whom it is now occupied as an extensive manufactory of slate mantels, billiard tables, tile, etc.

151   HISTORY OF FAIR HAVEN, VERMONT.

SAW MILLS.

The first saw mill in town was, as has been already shown, that built by Col. Matthew Lyon, on the north side of the Lower Falls, about 1783. Its history was for a number of years linked with that of the grist mill, being owned, as may be seen on a previous page, successively by Asa Smith and Heman Huffman, or Hoffman; by Col. Lyon and Dr. Simeon Smith; by Col. Lyon and Solomon Cleveland; by Col. Lyon and Pliny Adams; by Pliny Adams and Eliel Gilbert; by Eliel Gilbert and Stephen Rogers, and in September, 1799, by Eliel and Tilly Gilbert.

In November, 1802, Eliel Gilbert sold to his brother, Tilly, his half of the saw mill and one acre of land lying above it. The land and house occupied by Ebenezer Walker, Tilly sold to Salmon Norton, in September, 1804. He sold one-half of the saw mill to Isaac Cutler, in February, 1803, and bought it back of Salmon Norton, in September, 1804. He finally sold the whole to Jacob Davey, in December, 1813.

Mr. Davey sold it, together with the house and lot opposite, then occupied by John Kingsland—now Cyrus C. Whipple's—to John W., Eliab and Septimius Robinson, April 10th, 1819. The Robinsons re-deeded to Mr. Davey, in November, 1821, and Mr. Davey again sold it to his son, Albert V. Davey, in June, 1827. It was leased, August 15th, 1826, to William

HISTORY OF FAIR HAVEN, VERMONT.   152

Lusk and Abraham Sharp, till February, 1829, and sold to Albert subject to the lease. By him it was sold, September 9th, 1829, to Charles T. and William B. Colburn.

Charles Colburn sold his share to his brother, William, April 8th, 1831, and William sold one-half interest to Benjamin Warren, of Hampton, on the 11th of the same month. It was transferred by them to Apollos Smith, of West Haven, in July, 1832, and the title remained with Mr. Smith till conveyed by him to William C. Kittredge, in November, 1834. In March, 1838, Mr. Kittredge sold the mill to Cullen W. Hawkins, and Mr. Hawkins transferred it to Jacob Davey, in April, 1839, who sold it to Hezekiah and Harvey Howard, in September, 1840.

Messrs. H. & H. Howard deed it to Cullen W. Hawkins, in September, 1850, reserving water from the flume for a bark and hide mill and pump and rolling mill, built by them on the north side of the grist mill. Mr. Hawkins being killed in the mill in June, 1853, Barnabas Ellis, his administrator, sold the mill and wagon shop opposite to it, October 30th, 1854, to David H. Bristol and Harris Whipple. The mill was sold by Mr. Bristol, excepting and reserving the small "felly mill," to Dan Orms, January 30th, 1856, and Mr. Orms deeded it, in September, 1859, to the present owner, Geo. O. Kilbourn, subject to a mortgage of $285, held by Barnabas Ellis, Esq. Mr. Kilburn erected a brick building for a woolen factory, adjoining it, and the same, after being used by Messrs. E. S. Ells and Joseph Delahaunty, in 1863, for weaving soldier's jack-

153 HISTORY OF FAIR HAVEN, VERMONT.

ets, was shortly afterwards leased by Edward L. Allen, and has since been used as the manufactory of kerosene oil safes.

The second saw mill in town was erected by Gamaliel Leonard, on the falls near the State Line, in 1785. Mr. Leonard sold one-half of this mill to Jariah Lewis, in November, 1796, with the right to build a dam for said mill so high as will raise the water even with the top of a certain rock, lying in the river, about a rod from the north bank and two rods east from the head of the flume. It would seem that Mr. Lewis re-built the mill, as John Coggswell, of Whitehall, sells one-half of the same, "built by Jariah Lewis," December 31st, 1803, to James Witherell.

Dr. Witherell conveys his share, September 21st, 1807, to Joel Minor, of Middletown, and Minor, in July, 1813, sells to Mr. Leonard, the mill having been swept away by the great freshet of 1811, two years before. It was re-built by Mr. Leonard and sold, with three acres of land and the old house where Mr. Leonard had lived, to David H. Bristol, in May, 1842, Mr. Bristol taking possession, and afterward building a machine shop and a new dwelling house on the premises. It is now owned and occupied by Mr. Bristol's heirs.

The saw mill on the Upper Falls, above the iron works, was built by Stephen Holt, in the summer of 1797, for Moses Scott, of Waterford, N. Y., and James Lyon, of Fair Haven. It was a large mill, containing

HISTORY OF FAIR HAVEN, VERMONT. 154

three saw gates; one with two saws, one with one saw, and one with a gang of saws, and intended to do an extensive business, nearly all the land to the east and south being then covered with large timber, and Scott & Lyon having a nine years' lease of the lands from Col. Lyon, with the right to cut off and saw the timber.

Col. Lyon sold the mill to Josiah Norton, November 12th, 1800, subject to Scott & Lyon's lease. Mr. Norton dying, in the spring of 1803, Mr. A. W. Hyde, as guardian of Eli Norton, to whom this property was assigned, sold the same to Tilly Gilbert, in July, 1806. Mr. Gilbert now and for several years owned both the village saw mills, doing with them an extensive lumbering business. At the upper mill he sawed out as many as 4000 pine logs in a season. The lumber was sold and distributed, much of it, in southern towns, as Danby and Salem. After the opening of the Champlain canal, lumber went from the town through the canal to Lansingburgh and Troy.

The great flood, which occurred in June, 1811, and was attended with such disastrous effects generally, tore away this first double gang saw mill, and Maj. Gilbert at once set to work to build a new mill, which was only of a single gang, and was completed sometime in the winter or spring following. Mr. Gilbert sold this mill, together with a dwelling house occupied by Salem Ryder, to Jacob Davey, December 12th, 1822, and it was run by Mr. Davey until about 1833, when it was burned down and not rebuilt.

155 HISTORY OF FAIR HAVEN, VERMONT.

Joseph Sheldon, who had, in the beginning of the century, started a clover mill on his land, near the outlet of Beaver Meadow, or Marsh, which he ran in company with Dea. Asahel Munger, for several years, and which is said to have been in operation as late as 1825, or '30, erected a saw mill at the same place, in the summer of 1814, the work of building being conducted by Lanson Watkins, with whom worked Isaac Eggleston, and they both left and went off to the war. This mill is said to have been burned once, and re-built twice, or more than twice. Being conveniently located in the lumbering region, it was the center of a large and lively business in lumber, and has always been of service to the town.

About 1824, Mr. Sheldon built another mill, lower down on the stream, near where Mr. Orms' present mill stands. Eliab Briggs was the builder; but this mill ran down and was never re-built.

After Mr. Sheldon's decease, the heirs, in December, 1859, quit-claimed one undivided half of the saw mill lot, so called, consisting of 73 acres, to Joseph Sheldon, Jun., he previously owning a half of the same. He sold the saw mill and a part of the marsh above, to Dan Orms and Abram S. Taber, in January, 1860. Mr. Taber sold to Mr. Orms, in the following May, and Mr. Orms took down the saw mill and built it up again further down the stream, where it now stands.

There was a saw mill, built by Eliab Briggs, about 1817, for Olney Hawkins and Nathaniel Sanford, at the outlet of Inman Pond, above the Beaver Marsh.

HISTORY OF FAIR HAVEN, VERMONT. 156

This mill had a wheel with buckets only fourteen inches long. It was only run from March till·June, and from September till winter, but did a good business, and saved much drawing of logs. It was bought by Peter Merritt, who carried it on till he removed from town, about 1831. He sold it to Heman Stannard.

There was still another mill built, about this same year, 1817, by Dr. Ebenezer Hurd, Benjamin, Elias and Matthew Hickok, on the land of Benjamin Hickok, and near Black, or Little Pond, from which Matthew Hickok leased of Samuel Tuttle, of Poultney, the right to draw water for a mill, in May, 1816. Dr. Hurd owned two-thirds of this mill, but there did not prove to be sufficient water, and very little was ever done with it.

THE NORTON PLACE.

The place where John D. Goodwin now lives, was known in earlier days as "the Norton place." A house was built on it and occupied by·James Lyon, while his father owned it. · The place, as first sold by Col. Lyon to Josiah Norton, in September, 1799, con-

157   HISTORY OF FAIR HAVEN, VERMONT.

sisted of 10 acres, on the second division of Nathan Allen's right, and was bounded as follows: "Beginning 9 rods east 10° south of the middle of the north end of the meeting house [the old meeting house], thence running east 10° south 24 rods, in the north line of the highway, to the west line of the highway which runs towards Kelsey's; thence running north 10° east 54 1-2 rods; thence running west 10° north 30 rods; thence running south 10° west 48 1-2 rods [i. e., to the northwest corner of a six rod square piece deeded by Col. Lyon to the town]; thence running east 10° south 6 rods; thence south 10° west 6 rods, to the first named bound."

Squire Norton is reported to have built the main or front part of the house, and to have had a barn and barnyard on the west, which, in 1811, extended westward to the east line of the six rod square piece belonging to the town. He died, while resident on the place, in March, 1803, and it was occupied for a number of years by his widow, who married Moses Sheldon, Sen., of Rupert, and by his son, Salmon Norton, who died in the house, in January, 1813. In the division of the estate it was set, with other property, to the widow, the heirs retaining their right of reversion in the same.

The Congregationalist society obtained leave, about 1810, to erect their new meeting house on the southwest corner of the lot, and began drawing their materials in January, 1811. The house was raised in May following, and there does not appear to have been any deed given to the society.

HISTORY OF FAIR HAVEN, VERMONT. **158**

In September, 1816, Isaac Norton, of Benson, the youngest son and heir, having purchased ten-elevenths of the heirs' right of reversion in the widow's dower, makes a partition of all the estate with the heirs of Abigail Northrop, of Castleton, who owned the other eleventh, and this place of 10 acres is conceded to him, excepting one half acre of the same, as follows: "Beginning at a stake standing in the north line of the public Green, and ten feet east of the new meeting house; thence running north 20 rods, east 4 rods, and south 20 rods, and to the place of beginning." This half acre was sold by Almy A. Branch and J. N. Northrop, in February, 1838, to Lois Howe, and by her, in October, following, to William G. Howard, who then owned the Norton house and lot.

In April, 1831, Isaac Norton sells the place, excepting the half acre and the land occupied by the Congregational society, to Benjamin F. Langdon, of Castleton. Mr. Langdon deeds it to William B. Colburn and Benjamin Warren, April 13th, 1831. They convey it to Apollos Smith, in July, 1832, and he, in January, 1836, to Harvey Howard. Mr. Howard sells it to his nephew, William G. Howard, on the 14th of April, 1837. The place was occupied by Emmons Howard while owned by his son, William. On the 20th of August, 1842, Mr. Howard deeded a piece of land, 25 feet wide by 50 feet, to the centre school district, the land lying west of land deeded to Abram Graves, for the meeting house sheds, and extending westward to the garden of Messrs. Bullock and Cobb. He also deeded to the town, the same day, a piece 32

T

159 HISTORY OF FAIR HAVEN, VERMONT.

by 28 feet, from the northeast corner of his place, for a pound, the pound being then built thereon.

He sold his house and the nine acres of land, April 6th, 1847, to John D. Wood, and Mr. Wood occupied it until about the year 1851. In May, 1848, Mr. Wood deeded to Havillah F. Anthony one half acre on the corner where the Catholic chapel stands, the measurements being 5 rods and 3 feet across the south end, by about 12 rods northward, along the Castleton road. Mr. Anthony sold this to James Dolan, in May, 1853, and in June, Mr. Dolan deeded to Benjamin F. Gilbert a triangular piece on the corner, of 55 feet at the base, which was exchanged by Mr. Gilbert for a part of the roadway, which then ran farther to the east. Mr. Dolan afterward, in March, 1856, deeded the lot on the corner to the Rev. Z. Druon, by whom the church was built.

Mr. Wood sold to Mr. Dolan, in October and November, 1848, two half acres, north of Anthony's purchase. In March, 1850, he sold to Peter Gallipo a piece from the northeast corner of his land, 7 rods on the road by 12 rods deep, except the land belonging to the public pound. He sold to Mr. Dolan, in December, what remained between Mr. Dolan's and Mr. Gallipo's lots; and Mr. Dolan sold building lots to John Harrison, to Obadiah Eddy, and to Franklin Eddy.

Mr. Wood sold what remained of the original 10 acres of his place—then about six acres—in January, 1851, together with the brick shop, then owned by his wife, next south of the present post-office, to Rob-

HISTORY OF FAIR HAVEN, VERMONT. 160

bins Miller, of Hampton. Mr. Miller came and resided on the place, keeping a shoe store and the post-office in the brick shop, for a number of years. Mr. Miller sold a building lot to Edward W. Sheldon, back of the meeting house sheds, in June, 1860—now Philip Welcome's—and one opposite, on the east side of the street, to Mansel A. Ormsbee, in February, 1863, and this was the beginning of Center, or Carnarvon street, on which so many neat and substantial residences, and the French Catholic church, have been recently built.

He sold his house and shop to Richard E. Lloyd, February 5th, 1864, and the land on the north of his house, now covered with dwellings, to Joseph Adams, in March, 1865. Mr. Lloyd sold the house and lot to Calvin P. Austin, for Mr. Goodwin, in February, 1866, and Mr. Goodwin re-built the house, as it now stands.

THE COLTON PLACE.

The propriety of the above designation for the place now owned and occupied by William Henry Green, is derived from the fact that it was so long owned and occupied by Mr. Colton, who was, at the same time, the builder of the front, or principal part

161 HISTORY OF FAIR HAVEN, VERMONT.

of the house. The lot was first occupied, while owned by Col. Lyon, by Silas Safford, Esq., who is said to have had a public house on the ground, as early as 1787, if not three years earlier.. As we have seen, Mr. Safford removed from it to the south part of the town, in the spring of 1790, and the house was occupied, in 1795, by Jeremy Dwyer, who was a countryman of Col. Lyon, and had come from Pomfret at Lyon's solicitation. In March, 1798, and August, 1799, the place was occupied by Clement Blakesley, who worked in the mills, and Col. Lyon sold it, at this time—it consisting of one acre of land—together with one-half of the saw mill, to Eliel Gilbert. In November, 1802, Mr. Gilbert sells it to his brother, Tilly, and Tilly sells it to Salmon Norton, in September, 1804, Ebenezer Walker occupying it at the time.

Mr. Norton is said to have lived in it himself at one time, but it was occupied by Richard Longshore, in November, 1807, when Mr. Norton conveyed it to Joshua Quinton.

In May, 1810, Mr. Quinton sold to John Quinton and Thomas Christie the north half of the "one acre," they occupying the house at the time, and owning the tan yard, lying west of it. They are said to have taken down the old house and built a new one. It was occupied by John Cady, in August, 1811. They sold it to Col. Moses Colton, in September, 1813, together with four acres of land purchased by them of Beriah Rogers, lying south of the road leading to Gamaliel· Leonard's, and west of John Herring's lot.

HISTORY OF FAIR HAVEN, VERMONT. 162

In this deed they commence the bounds of the first lot, "one and one-half rods south of the southeast corner of John Herring's house-lot," thus leaving open the "highway," or lane running along the north side of this place westward to Beriah Rogers' tannery, which highway they had purchased of Isaac Cutler, in November, 1808, and which had been laid out by the selectmen on the 21st of December, following. Col. Colton erected a new house, the front, or main part of the house now occupied by Mr. Green, sometime between 1820 and 1824.

William B. Colburn, constable, took possession of the place, in April, 1833, on an execution, for Cullen C. W. Colton, the place being appraised at $1,050, subject to a mortgage to Zimri Howe, of Castleton, for $492.20. By Cullen it was deeded, in July, 1833, to Benjamin Warren. He deeded it, in February, 1834, to Heman Stannard, and by him it was sold, in November, 1838, to Simeon Cobb, who occupied it and died thereon, his administrator, Adams Dutton, selling all but the widow's third, in July, 1848, to Dr. James Sanford. On the 1st of January, 1851, Mrs. Laura S. Cobb, of Port Byron, N. Y.—whither she had removed, meantime—deeded to Dr. Sanford her right of dower in the place, and he occupied it until April, 1858, when he sold to William H. Green, of Hampton. It is now owned and occupied by William H. Green, Jr., to whom it was transferred, August 25, 1866.

BERIAH ROGERS' TANNERY.

The place where Mrs. Stow and her son, Leonard J. now reside, was, in the early part of the century, owned and occupied by Beriah Rogers, as a tannery. He had come into the town, in 1790, and worked for a time with his brother, Stephen, on the west side of the Common. In April, 1802, while resident on the ground where now Zenas C. Ellis resides, he purchased an acre of land of Josiah Norton, Esq., adjoining the garden lot at that time owned by Eliel Gilbert, and on it established a tannery. He had a number of vats, and carried on the business of tanning for customers "on shares," until about the spring of 1808, when he removed to Hampton, N. Y., and the business was continued for a time by Ansel Goodrich, who occupied Mr. Rogers' house, and was assisted by Ira Waterhouse.

In April, 1808, he sold the lot to John Quinton and Thomas Christie, of Hampton, the south line of the lot running east from the southwest corner, along the bank of the river, eight rods to the west line of the grist mill lot, then owned by Joshua Quinton. On the east line of this lot, and seemingly across Joshua Quinton's line, Messrs. Quinton & Christie erected a scythe factory, taking water for it from the flume under the grist mill, which Joshua Quinton afterwards deeds to them.

HISTORY OF FAIR HAVEN, VERMONT. **164**

In July, 1813, Quinton & Christie deed the place back to Mr. Rogers, excepting that instead of running east from the southwest corner eight rods, their boundary runs east only six rods, and then runs north 12 feet west of the scythe factory. Mr. Rogers again sells the place, in April, 1822, to Clark Davis, a wagon maker, who deeds it to Ezra Greenough, of Fair Haven, and James Greenough, of Poultney, in the August following. It was used by them in connection with the wagon maker's shop which Spencer Harvey had built over the scythe factory.

Ezra Greenough quit-claimed his interest in the lot to his brother, James, in March, 1825, and by him it was sold, in October, 1829, to Oliver Kidder. Mr. Kidder sold it to Isaac Patch and Theophilus T. Parmenter, in February, 1833. In March, Parmenter quit-claimed to Patch, and Patch sold it to David C. Sproat and Alonzo Safford. In October, 1843, Mr. Sproat deeded to Mr. Safford, the place being occupied at that time by Joseph Berto. While owned by Mr. Safford a piece was deeded to Alonson Allen and Joseph Adams from the south end of the lot, and an addition was made to it from Messrs. Allen & Adams' land on the west.

Mr. Safford sold it, in October, 1849, to Harry G. Sheldon, who then lived on the same, but it was deeded at first to William C. Kittredge, Hiram Hamilton, and Joseph Sheldon, who transferred it to Mr. Sheldon, in December, 1853. Mr. Sheldon and his wife deeded it to Israel Davey, in March, 1859, by whom the house then standing was turned around and a new house erected on the front.

THE SCYTHE FACTORY.

A building with a trip-hammer and anvil, for the manufacture of scythes, and used afterward for the manufacture of axes and hoes, was erected in the spring of 1808, by John Quinton and Thomas Christie, in company with Joshua Quinton, on, or near the spot where now the Union Slate Works stand; Messrs. Quinton and Christie buying the Beriah Rogers' tannery lot, which then ran southward to the river, and eastward 8 rods to the grist-mill lot, in April, 1808, and the building being erected across, or very near the east line of the same, adjoining the grist-mill garden.

On the 22d of July, 1813, John Quinton and Thomas Christie purchased of Tilly Gilbert, who then owned the saw-mill, the right to take water from the flume below the grist-mill, in a penstock, to their scythe factory, paying Mr. Gilbert $15.00 therefor. On the 29th of July they deeded back to Mr. Rogers the tannery lot, excepting a strip of about two rods in width along the east side where their factory stood. In September of the same year, 1813, Joshua Quinton purchased of Moses Colton, the owner of the paper-mill, the right to use water from the mill-pond for the scythe factory.

In May, 1814, Joshua Quinton quit-claimed to John Quinton and Thomas Christie, for $50, eleven square

HISTORY OF FAIR HAVEN, VERMONT. 166

rods of land, beginning at a stake in the southwest corner of a house lot then occupied by Allen Webster, about 10 feet south of the scythe factory; thence running northwardly in the west line of said lot, through the scythe factory and adjoining coal house to a stake and stones, 30 feet north of said coal house; thence eastwardly in a direct line with the northwest corner of the house occupied by Allen Webster, 2 rods; thence south-easterly to within 1 rod of the south-west corner of a house lot then lately deeded by Joshua Quinton to Tilly Gilbert; thence southerly to the south line of the first mentioned lot; thence westerly to the place of beginning, with the privilege of water from the grist-mill flume for the scythe factory. Associated with the Quintons, who had built the blacksmith shop where Henry Green now carries on business, and where they then employed several men, were John P. Colburn, Theodore Dowd, Thomas Blanchard, and Spencer Harvey. Mr. Dowd made hoes and axes and is said to have been a superior workman in cast steel. Mr. Blanchard came from Sutton, Mass., and Mr. Harvey states that he worked with him in the scythe factory about the time of the war of 1812–14. Mr. Blanchard was a noted mechanic, and invented a nail machine for Jacob Davey.

In April, 1817, Mr. Christie sold to John P. Colburn his equal undivided half of the scythe factory lot, so-called, "with the trip-hammer shop and coal house standing thereon," and in the description of the same he follows the deed of Joshua Quinton to John Quinton and himself, to the south line of the Gilbert lot;

U

167 HISTORY OF FAIR HAVEN, VERMONT.

thence runs west "to the east line of the tan yard lot; thence south to the south-east corner of the tan yard; thence west, 10 deg. south to the south-east corner of that part of said tan yard which was deeded to Beriah Rogers by the said John Quinton and Thomas Christie, in 1813."

It was made use of by Mr. Colburn for the manufacture of hoes and axes principally. Mr. Rogers sold his tan yard lot to Clark Davis, in April, 1822, and Mr. Davis sold it to Ezra and James Greenough, in August, and it was owned by one of them until 1829. During this time they occupied the scythe factory building for a wagon shop. Mr. Harvey states that he put an upper story upon it for that use, and himself ironed wagons in the lower part of the building. Mr. Greenough, who is now residing in Whitehall, N. Y., says the building was burned while owned by him, on Sunday, the fire taking in the shavings, from the pipe of one Frost, who worked for him, and who fell asleep in the shop. We hear of nothing more being done with the place until September, 1839, when Hezekiah and Harvey Howard purchased of Wm. C. Kittredge and Wm. B. Colburn, administrators to the estate of John P. Colburn, Mr. Colburn's undivided share in the scythe factory privilege, and soon after, in October, purchased of Phebe Quinton, of Hampton, Mr. Quinton's undivided half interest, paying each party $25 for the same. By them the privilege was turned to use for a bark mill and tannery, and carried on for a number of years successfully, they owning the sawmill and also the grist-mill, a portion of the time, un-

HISTORY OF FAIR HAVEN, VERMONT. 168

til the grist-mill and tannery were sold by them to Wellington Ketchum, and the old tannery was by him converted into the present Union Slate Works.

THE CLOTH DRESSING WORKS.

On the 25th of January, 1808, Jacob Davey, for $1.00 and other valuable considerations, sells to Seth Persons, of Sudbury, and Horatio Foster, of Hubbardton, two-thirds of a piece of land on the north bank of the river, west of the iron works, and adjoining the house where Abraham Sharp "now lives," for the purpose of a clothier's works solely. He also sells them, on the same day, for the consideration of $200, two-thirds of a site, with water power and privilege, under certain restrictions, for a fulling mill and dye house, to be built by the three in copartnership, on the south and east of the slitting mill. The business of fulling, coloring and dressing cloth and coloring wool appears to have been carried on by the firm of Davey, Persons & Foster, until February, 1812, when Persons sells out to Mr. Davey, for $416.67, his third interest. The business is said to have been very remunerative for some years, the price for fulling and

169 HISTORY OF FAIR HAVEN, VERMONT.

finishing cloth during the war of 1812 and '14 being fifty cents per yard.

Mr. Foster deeded back to Mr. Davey, in June, 1818, and Davey then sold to Foster the land along the river, west of the slitting mill and below the house "formerly occupied by David Brainard," with the right to take water by a penstock from his flume, for a cloth dressing establishment, when there is a sufficient supply of water so that it will not impede the motion of his mill.

Mr. Foster built a fulling mill on this ground and also the house in which Levi W. Collins now lives. This mill was burned down about 1831, and was never re-built. Mr. Foster occupied the house while he remained in town, selling it, after he had removed, in March, 1835, to Hezekiah and Harvey Howard.

Hezekiah deeded to John Balis, and Balis & Howard deeded the place to Adams & Allen, in September, 1860. They sold the barn and west part of the lot to Moseley & Pitkin, in February, 1861, and by them the barn was converted into a tin shop. In March, 1863, Adams & Allen sold the house and remaining portion of the lot to Levi W. Collins, who has raised and greatly improved the dwelling house.

HISTORY OF FAIR HAVEN, VERMONT. **170**

THE HERRING PLACE.

This place, now occupied by Mrs. William Miller, and consisting of one acre of land, was purchased by Joel Beaman, in November, 1808, of Isaac Cutler, from off the original tavern lot. It had on it a nailor's shop, or building, said to stand in the highway, near Col. Lyon's dwelling, and north of Dr. Clement Blakesley's, which had been owned by Israel Markham, in 1796, and by William Hennessy, in 1798.

It was sold by Mr. Beaman, after his removal to Poultney, to John Herring, in August, 1811. · Mr. Herring was one of the proprietors of the paper mill, and he built the front part of the dwelling house occupied by Mrs. Miller and Mrs. Bruce—hence it has been known as the "Herring house," and is so-called at the head of this chapter. Mr. Herring sold the place, together with the six acres lying to the southwest, and on the north side of the river, which were sold to Herring & Colton, by Salmon Norton, in November, 1809, to Alexander Dunehue, in October, 1813. Mr. Dunehue died the following year, and the place remained in the hands of his widow. The widow married Dr. Adin Kendrick, of Poultney, as late as 1831.

Mr. Dunehue having, in his will, bequeathed a bell for the new meeting house in Fair Haven, the claim against Mr. Dunehue's estate for the bell was finally adjusted and settled by a compromise between the town and Mr. Dunehue's heirs, and this place, together with the six acres where the marble mill stands, was quit-claimed to the town in settlement of the claim, November 4th, 1831, by Adin Kendrick, Isaac Norton, Lucinda Boland and Josiah N. Northrop.

At an adjourned meeting of the town, March 23d, 1832, it was voted "that the selectmen be authorized to sell or rent, at their discretion, the Dunehue place, now occupied by Edmund Kingsland, and if rented to cause the same to be insured against fire." On the 30th of April, Elijah Estey, Harvey Howard and Hiram Hamilton, who were the selectmen of that year, deed the whole by a perpetual lease of 999 years, to Alonzo Safford, for the sum of $800 and a yearly rental of "one peppercorn if demanded." Mr. Safford gave the town a mortgage deed of the same for the payment of $400, which remained until a few years since, when it was discharged by the selectmen. Mr. Safford occupied the place till 1844, selling the house and one acre to Mrs. Lucy Colburn, in October of that year.

By Mrs. Colburn, who had resided on it meanwhile, it was sold to Dr. B. S. Nichols, April 14th, 1860. He occupied it and sold it to Joshua Foster, of Chelsea, Vt., November 6th, 1865.

Mr. Safford sold the six acres lying on the intervale, north of the river, to Messrs. Kittredge, Allen & Adams, in March, 1845, and by them it was appropriated to the marble business.

HISTORY OF FAIR HAVEN, VERMONT. 172

SETH PERSONS' STORE.

Among the places in the village which were first sold, and built on after Col. Lyon left the town, and after the land on the east side of the present Park came into the possession of Eliel and Tilly Gilbert, the lot now occupied by the new Bank building and the drug store, then next north of and adjoining the old Hennessy or Dennis place, deserves prominent mention. It was purchased of Maj. Tilly Gilbert, by Seth Persons, December 5th, 1808, and was 4 rods wide by 20 rods deep. Mr. Persons was one of the firm of Davey, Persons & Foster, engaged in fulling and finishing cloths, and he built a store on this lot, which he had purchased of Mr. Gilbert, and also a barn.

The store was soon converted into a dwelling house, and occupied by Mrs. Anna Wells, who bought the place in the spring of 1812. In 1815 or '16, Dr. Israel Putnam, who was residing on the lot next north, built a new store on Mrs. Wells' land, which he sells to Erwin Safford, Esq., in August, 1816, and Safford, who was a son-in-law of Mrs. Wells, having purchased Putnam's place—now Dr. Wakefield's—buys Mrs. Wells' place also, in July, 1817. In July, 1819, Safford sells the two lots, each 4 rods wide by 20 rods deep, together with a distillery, near Harvey Church's tannery, to James Y. Watson.

Dr. Wakefield's place was first built on by Maj. Gilbert, who put up a house for his son-in-law, Elisha

173   HISTORY OF FAIR HAVEN, VERMONT.

Parkill, and deeded it to him, in August, 1810. It was sold by Parkill to Dr. Israel Putnam, in March, 1812, and by Putnam it was sold, as above stated, to Mr. Safford. By Mr. Watson the property was all sold, in February, 1821, to Moses Colton and Hector H. Crane. They sold it, in February, 1823, to Colton, Warren & Sproat. Mr. Colton sold to his partners, in December, 1823, and they failing in business the following summer, an assignment was made, and the property came into the hands of Abel Kittredge, of Hinsdale, Mass., and of David C. Sproat, who deeded this double lot—8 rods in width—together with the store, and the grain house on the south side of the Common, to John Jones and Worcester Morse. in December, 1829.

Messrs. Jones & Morse carried on the mercantile business together in the store, till February, 1831, when Mr. Jones sells to Mr. Morse, and removes from town. Mr. Morse deeds the grain house lot to Royal Bullock, in October, 1834, and, in December, sells the store and house to Luke Beaman, of Poultney. Mr. Beaman transformed the house into a hotel and rented it for about two years, to Ebenezer Clement, who kept it open as a public house, or hotel, having a large stable on the ground, where the drug store now stands.

Mr. Beaman sold out his store of goods to Alonson Allen, in the spring of 1836. The house which had been occupied by Mr. Clement, and was afterward occupied by James Bradshaw, and again by Jonas Reed, now of Benson, for a public house, was sold to

HISTORY OF FAIR HAVEN, VERMONT. 174

Elijah Estey, in March, 1846, by Seth J. Hitchcock, Jonathan Capen and Joseph Joslin, as commissioners for the settlement of Mr. Beaman's affairs. They also, at the same time, sold the store and store lot to William C. Kittredge. The house was taken possession of by Dr. Thomas E. and Mary F. Wakefield, to whom the same was deeded by Mr. Estey, September 19th, 1854.

Mr. Kittredge sold the old red store and lot to Increase Jones and Clark P. Hill, in December, 1847. Mr. Hill quit-claimed to Jones, in January, 1850, and in September, 1862, Mr. Jones and wife, who occupied the place as a homestead, deeded it to A. H. Stowe, including a small building used for a flour store. Mr. Stowe built the drug store and kept it till November, 1864, when he sold to Clark Smith, its present owner, who sold the old red store and ground occupied by it to the First National Bank, and greatly enlarged the drug store.

ELISHA PARKILL'S STORE.

Mr. Parkill purchased the lot for this store of Thomas Wilmot, in January, 1811, where James Miller now resides. The south line was 16 rods, the north 14 rods,

175   HISTORY OF FAIR HAVEN, VERMONT.

the west side 110 feet, and the front, along the highway, 99 feet. The store itself was first built by Maj. Tilly Gilbert, near John G. Pitkin's residence, as early as 1805 or '06, and there used by him for the sale of merchandise, Mr. Parkill and Erwin Safford acting as clerks for him, while he carried on the saw mills. It was removed by Mr. Parkill, and fitted up and used by him· for several years, being occupied afterwards for a school, by Miss Lydia Church.

In April, 1811, Mr. Safford purchased of Mr. Wilmot, another lot, adjoining Mr. Parkill's, on the northeast corner, being 32 feet in front by 76 feet deep, and on it also built a store. He sold his store and lot to Col. Joseph Watson, in January, 1814, and Parkill purchased it in October, 1815, subject to a lease to I. & H. S. Putnam, until the first of December. Mr. Parkill appears to have carried on the mercantile business in one or both of these stores, running also his distillery, on the west street, a portion of the time, till his failure, in 1824. He then deeded his store and land, in May, 1824, to William W. Fox, W. H. Leggett and Thomas Leggett, Jr., of New York, including with it, also, the 15 acres and distillery, occupied by H. H. Crane, on the west street. He sold the store building, which had been built by Safford, on the spot where James Miller's blacksmith shop now stands, to Joseph Adams, in November, 1824, and Mr. Adams removed it to the west street, making of it the house in which Charles Clyne now resides.

The Parkill store was rented by Fox & Leggetts to Sullivan Kelsey and Edward Bascom, who were sell-

HISTORY OF FAIR HAVEN, VERMONT. 176

ing goods in it in February, 1830, when Fox & Leggetts sold it to Barnabas B. Cane and Royal Bullock. There was an old cellar, Mr. Bullock states, where the Safford store stood when he bought. Mr. Bullock bought out Mr. Cane's interest, and Jacob Kingsland changed the old Parkill store into a dwelling house, in 1830 or '31, and resided in it a year or two. It was afterward occupied as a homestead by Mr. Bullock himself, who removed the wooden shop, built by him, in the fall of 1829, on Lucy Wilmot's land, on the opposite side, to the old Safford cellar, in 1831. In 1833 or '34, he removed this wooden building to the old grain house lot, which he purchased of Worcester Morse, in October, 1834—and the same, with its additions, has been recently removed, by Joseph Adams, further to the south and west—and built on the ground the brick blacksmith shop now occupied by Mr. Miller, where he worked at blacksmithing for many years.

In April, 1853, he sold the place to William H. Green, and removed with his family to Michigan. Mr. Green transferred it, three years later, to Timothy Miller, and by him and his wife it was deeded to James Miller, its present owner, in March, 1857. It has undergone various repairs and improvements, at different periods, and has lately been much improved by Mr. Miller.

177 HISTORY OF FAIR HAVEN, VERMONT.

RICHARD SUTLIFF'S PLACE.

This place, while owned by Maj. Gilbert, had a shop built on it, as early as 1810, or earlier, which report says was used at different times as a silversmith shop, a harness shop, a shoe shop, a school house and a carpenter's shop. It was sold by Mr. Gilbert, in March, 1811, to Clement Smith, whose wife was a daughter to Charles Rice, and a niece to Maj. Gilbert. They both died on this place, in 1813, and Lewis Dickinson is said to occupy it in January, 1814. It was sold, in April, 1830, by Simeon R. Smith and Catharine C. Smith, heirs to "Clem" Smith, to Dennison Willard. Mr. Willard occupied it in April, 1836, at which time he deeded it to Marcus G. Langdon, of Castleton. Mr. Langdon sold it to Richard Sutliff, its present owner, in January, 1839.

GRIFFITH O. WILLIAMS' PLACE.

This place was first sold by Maj. Gilbert, in March, 1811, to Erwin Safford, who at that time occupied the dwelling house and other buildings which had been built thereon. Mr. Safford sold it, in January, 1814,

HISTORY OF FAIR HAVEN, VERMONT. **178**

to Col. Joseph Watson, the son-in-law of Dr. Wither-ell, who had come hither from Detroit, Michigan. Col. Watson, having removed to Washington, D. C., sold the place, in December, 1832, to Nathan B. Has-well, of Burlington, by whom it was sold, in December, 1838, to Alonson Allen, Allen occupying it at the time. In February, 1839, Mr. Allen deeded·it to Dennison Willard, in exchange for the house he now occupies, on the south side of the Common. Mr. Willard sold it to James N. Kelsey, in May following, and Mr. Kelsey occupied it till December, 1846, when he sold to Elihu F. Eddy. Mr. Eddy and wife, Caroline W., convey it to Lewis D. Maranville, in March, 1859, It was purchased by Harrison Fish, in March, 1862, and occupied by him about one year. He sold it, August 26th, 1864, to Griffith O. Williams, its present owner.

JOSEPH BROWN'S CABINET SHOP.

Mr. Brown, who had previously had a shop in the old meeting house, bought a half acre of land, where Alonson Allen now resides, of Mrs. Lucy Wilmot, in August, 1823, and erected a brick house and cabinet

179 HISTORY OF FAIR HAVEN, VERMONT.

shop thereon. He sold the place, including the brick cabinet shop, benches, tools and stove, in December, 1828, retaining possession till May following, to Danforth Petty, who had worked with Mr. Brown and learned the trade of him. While occupied by Mr. Petty the building was burned, in the winter of 1830, and Petty, buying the old grain house built by Erwin Safford, just west of Mr. Adams' present dwelling house, moved it on to the knoll, eastward, about where the Baptist church is now building, and there fitted it into a cabinet shop. The building was afterwards removed and made into a dwelling house, by Ira Allen, and is the house occupied by Mrs. Allen and family.

Mr. Petty gave a deed of the place, in May, 1829, to Charlotte L. Petty, of Claremont, N. H., whom we infer to be his mother, to be held by her during her life, and then to revert to him. In November, 1830, he and she—she then residing in Fair Haven—mortgaged the house, shop and other buildings, to Barnabas Ellis and Philo Hosford. In March, 1831, they deeded the place to George W. Ware, of Fair Haven, subject to the mortgage and reserved possession till September.

Ware mortgaged it to Charlotte L. Petty. She assigned, in June, to Abraham Lowell, of Chester, Vt. The mortgage was redeemed by Elijah and Levi Beaman, of Rockingham, and discharged by Lowell, in 1835. By them it was assigned to Luke Beaman, through Jonas Gibson, in August, 1836. Mr. Beaman conveyed the place to William C. Kittredge, in January, 1837, and Mr. Kittredge sold it to Dennison Willard, in March, 1838.

HISTORY OF FAIR HAVEN, VERMONT. 180

In December, 1838, Mr. Willard sold to Mr. Kittredge the old grain store which Mr. Petty had made into a cabinet shop, with all the stone under it, and the use of the land upon which it stood, for five years, together with the privilege of erecting a stairway on the east side of the building. In February, 1839, Mr. Willard sold the place to its present owner, Alonson Allen, excepting therefrom the cabinet-maker's shop, and the use of the land on which it stood, for five years. In August, 1839, Mr. Allen purchased the cabinet-maker's shop of Mr. Kittredge, with his right in the land, Kittredge reserving a crop of turnips growing on the same.

This old grain house, alias cabinet shop, was removed by Mr. Allen in the spring of 1840, and made into a house for his brother, where the widow Allen and family now reside. It was used for a select school by Col. Artemas S. Cushman in the winter of 1838–9.

THE OLD HAT SHOP.

A building, occupied as a hat shop by Timothy Ruggles, in May, 1814, stood near the bank of the river where Lewis D. Maranville now lives, and was

181 HISTORY OF FAIR HAVEN, VERMONT.

started not long before by a son of Rev. Mr. Kent, of Benson, on land leased of Jacob Davey, for $6,00 per year. The shop and dye house were mortgaged to Allen Webster, in August, 1815.

It was sold by Joshua Quinton, in September, 1818, to Isaac Cutler, and is said to have been removed at a later period, by the sons of Duncan Cook, to a spot just north of the Fish corner, where it was occupied as a residence by Mrs. Darling, in 1837, and was afterward burned down, while occupied by Mrs. Bryant, subsequently the wife of George Mather.

DISTILLERIES.

The business of distilling spirituous liquor in the form of whiskey, from rye and corn, was extensively carried on in this town in former years. The almost universal use of whiskey made it an article of merchandise in great demand, and no store of goods was complete without it.

The difficulty and expense of transportation so far as Troy, then the principal market for grains, rendered the grain products of the country of little worth at home, and unless there could be a market and sale for them the farmer had no means of purchasing the goods

HISTORY OF FAIR HAVEN, VERMONT. 182

which the merchant might import. Accordingly distilleries, or "stills," were established, and their existence was an evidence of enterprise and business in a town.

In this town, Erwin Safford, one of its early and enterprising merchants, purchased of Isaac Cutler, or Harvey Church, in June, 1818, a piece of ground containing 12 square rods, near Mr. Church's tannery, on the side hill just back of the old parsonage, and there erected a distillery. He purchased of Mr. Church, in June, 1819, an additional piece of ground, and the use of water for his "still," and carried on the business to a moderate extent for a number of years. Of Mrs. Lucy Wilmot, he bought, in June, 1820, a small piece of ground, 24 by 30 feet, on the south side of the Common, just west of Mr. Adams' dwelling, on which he built, or had built, a grain-house. The distillery, and the store in which he traded, on the east side of the Common, he sold to James Y. Watson, in July, 1819, and Watson sold the store and distillery, in February, 1821, to Moses Colton and Hector H. Crane; Mr. Colton and Mr. Crane running the distillery built by Mr. Parkill beyond the burying ground, on the West street, one or two years, about this time, together with the Safford still, which they owned. They sold their distillery and store, and the grain-house, on the south side of the Common, in February, 1823, to Colton, Warren & Sproat. The firm of "Colton, Warren & Sproat" did a large business in distilling whiskey for several years, carrying on the store and the paper-mill at the same time. In October,

W

183   HISTORY OF FAIR HAVEN, VERMONT.

1825, they bought 4 acres of land of Horatio Foster, on the east side of the highway, south of Barnabas' Ellis', buying also at the same time of Jacob Davey, who owned the land lying next east and north, the right to use water for a "still," stipulating to pay therefor, $6,00 per year. It is highly probable that they had a distillery erected and in operation on this place at the same time they were operating the distillery on the west side of the Common. There would seem to have been some private arrangement whereby, in December, 1826, Warren and Sproat quit-claim this lot, south of Ellis', to Colton, and he quit-claims to them the paper-mill, the store, the distillery on the west side of the Common, and the grain-house, which had been deeded to Colton and Crane by James Y. Watson and Jacob Willard.

Mr. Colton sells the lot purchased of Foster, in November, 1827, to Marcus G. and Albert Langdon, of Castleton, and speaks of a distillery on the same, "recently occupied by Colton, Warren & Sproat."

The firm of Colton, Warren & Sproat carried on business until July, 1827, when the company failed and made an assignment of the store, distillery and store-house, to John P. Colburn, Jacob Davey, Barnabas Ellis and Harris W. Bates. It is said they had 2,000 bushels of grain on hand at the time of the failure. The property was afterward assigned to Barnabas Ellis, and by him deeded back, in May, 1828, to Warren & Sproat. The old Safford distillery, west of the Common, was burned down while occupied by Colton, Warren & Sproat, about the winter of 1824, and

HISTORY OF FAIR HAVEN, VERMONT.   184

Was immediately re-built, Hiram Shaw, of Hampton,
doing the work. It was occupied until the summer
of 1827, Alonzo Safford being superintendent of the
."still." The Langdons are said to have taken down
and removed the building, probably in the winter
of 1827 and '28—after their purchase of Mr. Colton—
to their land south of Mr. Ellis'. The land on which
the distillery partly stood, appears to have been covered by a mortgage deed which Mr. Cutler gave to
Col. Joseph Watson on the same day that he sold to
Mr. Safford.

The other distillery, south of the village, was run by
the Langdons for a number of years. Levi Smith and
Sidney Safford are said to have been employed in it.
A large number of hogs were annually fattened at this
distillery. Sometimes they were butchered in town ;
sometimes they were driven to Whitehall and shipped
down the lake. The work was given up in 1832, Albert Langdon selling to Marcus in February, and he
to Barnabas Ellis in November. The old "still" was
taken down, or sold by Mr. Ellis, and removed to East
Poultney.

A distillery was erected by Elisha Parkill and Hector H. Crane, about 1820, on a 15 acre lot of land
purchased by them of Tilly Gilbert, in October, 1820,
just west of the old burying ground, on the West
street. The distillery stood in the side-hill south of
the road, and Moses Colton was associated with Mr.
Crane in carrying it on in 1821. They manufactured
from 50 to 100 gallons of whiskey per day, and consumed from 20 to 40 bushels of rye and corn, at the

185 HISTORY OF FAIR HAVEN, VERMONT.

same time keeping from 30 to 40 head of cattle on
the premises. Mr. Crane sold out to Mr. Parkill for
$500, in February, 1824, and Mr. Parkill assigned the
whole, together with his store—now James Miller's
house—to Fox & Leggetts, of New York, in May, 1825,
the distillery being then occupied by Mr. Crane. The
old still house stood vacant and idle for several years.
The lot was sold at length by Messrs. Fox & Leggetts,
in November, 1830, to Joseph Warner. He sold it to
Chester Howe in May following, and Howe sold it to
Azel Willard in March, 1832. It is now owned by J.
P. Willard.

PAUPERS, AND A TOWN POOR HOUSE.

In a call for a town meeting to choose a town clerk,
made in March, 1803, after the death of Josiah Norton, Esq., we find this clause: "and to see what method
the town will take to remove Abra'm Gibbs, an old, de-
criped man, out of town, if not removed before this
meeting, and to take some method for defraying the
expense of the removal and other expense already
made in taking care of said Abraham Gibbs, by raising a tax, or otherwise, as the town shall think most
proper." The subject was not acted upon at the meet-

HISTORY OF FAIR HAVEN, VERMONT. 186

ing so called, and at another meeting, called in June, " to see what measures the town will take for the support, or removal of Ab'm Gibbs, who is now a town charge, to said town," it was "voted that the selectmen of the town still continue to provide for Ab'm Gibbs, and that they prosecute the suit now pending in Washington county concerning said Gibbs, with as much expedition as possible." It was also "voted that the selectmen should agree with some person to keep the said Gibbs by the week, not exceeding fifteen weeks, and that they have the right to move him from place to place, in the town, as often as they choose, in such a way that they get him kept by the person who will keep him the cheapest." A tax of one cent on the dollar on the list of 1802, was voted " to defray the expense arising in consequence of Abraham Gibbs being brought into this town."

A meeting was called in December, 1806, among other things "to make an appropriation to pay the town of Poultney for supporting and removing Alpheus Comstock, a pauper," and the town voted to pay the sum of $10. Poor Alpheus was a negro, and is said to have lived, previous to this time, below the grave yard, on West street. In 1812 he was in town and had two children in the public school.

At a town meeting in April, 1815, it was voted that Mrs. Hannah Rogers "continue to reside at Dea. Brainard's for the present, upon the same terms as heretofore." In March, 1816, " Thomas Richardson agreed to keep Mrs. Rogers for 8s. 6d. per week till the selectmen could do better, or get her kept cheaper."

187 HISTORY OF FAIR HAVEN, VERMONT.

'By vote of the town in October, 1815, Joel Titus was put up as a town pauper, to the lowest bidder, to find him board and lodging, and was bid off by Capt. Rood, at $2.25 per week, till next March meeting. Mrs. Rogers was also bid off by him at $2.00 per week, "if the selectmen cannot get her kept cheaper."

The only record we find of any effort to erect a town poor house is in 1817, when the article in the warning was " to take into consideration the expediency of erecting a work house, direct the mode and manner of building the same, and vote a tax to defray the expense thereof." A committee, consisting of Elisha Parkill and Moses Colton, was accordingly chosen " to confer with a committee from Poultney and Castleton concerning the building of a work house." Again in March, 1830, Tilly Gilbert, Heman Stannard and John Jones, were made a committee " to confer with any committee which may be appointed in any of the adjoining towns relative to building a poor house." That anything farther than this was ever done we do not learn.

The custom seems to have continued for many years of providing for the poor at the town meeting. Isaac Cutler was allowed $7.14, in March, 1818, "for keeping Mabby Atherton;" and in 1822 the town voted to allow Mr. Law $1.50 " for his act of humanity in bringing the Erskin girl from Granville."

A meeting of the town was called in January, 1827, and an article in the warning was, "to see if the town will take any measures to defend against an order of removal of Thomas Whitehouse from Poultney to Fair

HISTORY OF FAIR HAVEN, VERMONT. 188

Haven." The town voted to leave the subject to the discretion of the selectmen.

Polly Dwyer was "a sick person, chargeable on the town" from about 1827 to 1834. In 1832 Mr. H. Whitlock was allowed his account for keeping "the Slyter girl;" and Dr. E. Porter was allowed his account for doctoring Mrs. Erskin in 1830 and '31.

THE POUND.

In our New England town organizations the institution of the Pound is of universal and early existence, and is by no means to be overlooked. Whether it was a creature of the state, regulated by state statute, or only a police institution of the town, the thing was, and seemed to have an existence in this town, at the south-west corner of the Common, on Col. Lyon's land, as early as the year 1792, being mentioned in May of this year, in Col. Lyon's deed to Stephen Rogers. Mr. Rogers was chosen Pound Keeper, in March, 1801, an office of no mean consequence, to which the incumbent was always duly and solemnly sworn to the strict performance of his duty. Calvin Munger was chosen to the office in 1802, '03, '04, '05 and '06, but was excused and Isaac Cutler

189 HISTORY OF FAIR HAVEN, VERMONT.

appointed in 1806. The office was held by Joel Beaman, by Rufus Guilford, by Harvey Church, and others.

At an adjourned meeting, in March, 1806, Tilly Gilbert, Samuel Stannard and Silas Safford were made a committee "to fix a place to build a pound." In May the town voted a tax to build the pound, and chose Henry Ainsworth, Isaac Cutler and Curtis Kelsey a committee "to superintend the building of said pound." It was also voted "that the pound be built with cedar posts 10 feet long and at least 6 inches over at the top, and that it be boarded up with 1 1-2 inch boards, and confined on with good wrought spike, and that it be built 42 feet square."

The pound-keeper is directed and authorized by vote, April 2d, 1821, "to procure a new gate for the pound and make such repairs as are necessary."

In regular town meeting, March 1, 1824, Joel Hamilton, Elisha Parkill and David C. Sproat, were constituted a committee "to inquire into the state of the pound and the probable expense of building a new one, and to report at the adjourned meeting." The committee reported March 15th, and it was voted to build a pound, and that the select men contract for the timber, purchase a spot, and superintend the building of the pound. A lot was purchased of Mrs. Lucy Wilmot, 40 feet square, apparently where the old pound was, August 28, 1824.

At a meeting held in September, the town voted "to reconsider the vote passed in last March meeting for building a pound 40 feet square," and "to have the

HISTORY OF FAIR HAVEN, VERMONT. 190

same built 30 feet square." It was also voted "to reconsider the vote, [of which there is no record,] prescribing to the selectmen the particular materials, form, and manner of building said pound," and "that the selectmen be authorized to dispose of the materials already procured, and to proceed to build it with good, substantial cedar posts and boards or plank."

At the March meeting, 1826, sheep running at large on the public green, or in the highway, within a half mile of the meeting house, are declared liable to be impounded, and their owners to pay the lawful fee.

Frequent votes were taken in town meetings respecting the time and manner when sheep and swine should or should not run at large in the highways of the town.

In August, 1842, the pound existed on the west side of the highway leading to Castleton, in the northeast corner of Wm. G. Howard's land, and Mr. Howard then deeded a piece of 32 by 28 rods to the town as a pound.

THE PARK.

The beginning of the present public Park was made by Col. Matthew Lyon, who was, in some sense and measure, the founder of the town. He first gave to

x

191 HISTORY OF FAIR HAVEN, VERMONT.

the town, as has been already set forth, in October, 1798, "for the friendship he bore the town of Fair Haven," five pieces of land, the first being an acre for a burying ground, "the other pieces being four six rod square pieces on the four nearest corners of my land to the meeting house," . . . "so as to make the green eighteen rods square, including the highway." The highway was then six rods wide, lying in the form of a cross at right angles in front of Dan Orms' dwelling house, which was then the meeting house, and stood further to the south, thus making four corners around the meeting house which stood in the highway. Of these four six-rod-square pieces deeded by Col. Lyon, one of them takes in the ground on which the town and school house now stands, and extends up to the west side of the Congregational church; one other, the south-east square, lies south of the town house and in front of Ryland Hanger's residence, and was excepted from Col. Lyon's deed of the other land south and east of it, to Eliel Gilbert, in August, 1799. The other two, or west squares, are now built upon and occupied by the Methodist church and dwellings north and south of it. They were re-deeded or quit-claimed to the town, together with all claim to the old highway north of the meeting house, by Josiah Norton, Esq., in December, 1801, Mr. Norton having purchased of Col. Lyon the original title covering the two west squares, and they not being excepted by Col. Lyon.

In March, 1805, the town voted that the middle school district " have liberty to set a school house on

HISTORY OF FAIR HAVEN, VERMONT. **192**

the public ground near the meeting house, the spot to be established by a committee to consist of Joel Hamilton, Samuel Stannard and Silas Safford. 'The committee reported March 14th, as may be seen in the chapter on school affairs.

In April, 1805, the town " voted that the selectmen be authorized to re-lease to Tilly Gilbert all the right, title, interest, or demand, the town of Fair Haven have in, or unto, two six rod square pieces of land lying west of the meeting house, which land they hold by deed from Matthew Lyon, or Squire Norton, for the purpose of a public green, upon condition that the said Gilbert will deed to the town for the same use, all that part of the square of land lying south of the meeting house, which belongs to him, except a four rod strip from the east side of said square, and except also the house where Luther Bibbins now lives, which house he is to remove from said green, provided, nevertheless, that the town shall not be holden by anything contained in this vote unless the conditions are fulfilled on the part of said Gilbert within two years from this date."

It would seem that the conditions above stated were not fulfilled within the two years, and on the 2d Monday of March, 1809, it was again voted by the town " that the selectmen be directed to give deeds to Tilly Gilbert of some lands belonging to the town, lying near the meeting house, and to take deeds of certain lands called the Square, of Tilly Gilbert, for the use of this town." Accordingly, on the 19th of February, 1810, Salmon. Norton, Joshua Quinton, and Moses

193 HISTORY OF FAIR HAVEN, VERMONT.

Colton, selectmen of the town, deed to Mr. Gilbert the two west squares given to the town by Col. Lyon, and Maj. Gilbert, in consideration of the selectmen having deeded to him the above lands, conveys to the town the land where the Park now is, supposed to contain about 6 acres, lying west of a line running north 10° east, from a point 4 rods west of the north-east corner of Thomas Wilmot's dwelling, to the south side of the old highway running east from the meeting house. Mr. Gilbert reserves the old house standing on the above land, and occupied at the time by Isaac Cutler and Harvey Church.

The highway, which had previously to August, 1805, run past Col. Lyon's houses, northward along the extreme east brow of the village plateau, was, at that time, set further to the westward, upon what is now the Common, and we are told that, at that time, the large primitive pines were still growing where the Park now is, and we hear, too, of the great stumps which were standing on the green, and in the removal of which "bees" were made at a comparatively recent period, the free flow and use of whiskey being a not unforgotten, indispensable characteristic of such occasions. For many years thereafter, the green remained an uneven, barren sand waste, lying open to the public, traversed by vehicles in all directions, occupied here and there by piles of lumber and old iron, and diversified by a number of knolls and alternating water sinks, which in winter made fine natural skating rinks for the young folks.

About 1853, a small park was built on the north

HISTORY OF FAIR HAVEN, VERMONT. **194**

side of the Lyon tavern house, and a movement was set on foot to erect the Park on the Common, the ladies holding a fair the following winter at the tavern house, which was then occupied by Mr. Adams, and realizing some $160.00 for that purpose. A subscription was likewise made by the citizens, and a portion of the same made available toward the expense of laying out and building the fence around the Park.

A "Park Association" was organized in the spring of 1855, members thereof paying one dollar annually for the purpose of planting trees in the Park grounds. But few meetings of this Association were held. Officers were last chosen in April, 1860, and action was taken toward removing dead trees and filling their places with living ones.

Under the charter granted by the Legislature in October, 1865, the village corporation has full authority and power over the Park, side-walks, streets, &c.

VILLAGE ORGANIZATION.

The village of Fair Haven was first laid out and established Dec. 21st, 1820, under a general law of the state, by Isaac Cutler, John P. Colburn and Harvey Church, selectmen of the town at the time, as follows: "Whereas application has been made to the undersigned, selectmen of the the town of Fair Haven, to lay out and establish a village in said town agreeable to an act passed March, 1817, restraining certain animals from running at large in villages within the state, we do, therefore, lay out and bound a village in said town as follows: Beginning at the south-east corner of Barnabas Ellis', farm, (called the Wadkins place,); thence westerly on the south line of said farm, and on the south line of Enos Bristol's farm to the south-west corner thereof; thence northerly on said Bristol's, and on Tilly Gilbert's west line, till it strikes the road leading from the meeting house, in said town, to the State of New York, by way of the Rev. Mr. Cushman's; thence in a straight line until it strikes the turnpike, at the place where said turnpike and the road leading from Curtis Kelsey's westwardly, intersects; thence easterly on the north line of said road until it strikes the highway leading from Fair Haven to Castleton Mills; thence to the south-east corner of a piece of land recently sold by Curtis Kelsey to John

HISTORY OF FAIR HAVEN, VERMONT. 196

Beaman; thence in a straight line to the north-west corner of Hezekiah Whitlock's farm; thence southwardly on said Whitlock's west line to his south-west corner; thence in a direct line to the bounds begun at."

We do not learn that any other action in reference to a village, than this formal survey, was taken by the citizens of Fair Haven until the fall of 1865, when the Legislature of the state passed a charter, or act of incorporation, erecting a tract of one square mile into a corporate village, and the inhabitants of the same, at a meeting held in the hall, over Adams' store, December 4th, 1865, voted by a vote of 71 to 52, to adopt the charter, and the village has since, annually, at the meeting on the first Monday in December, elected its board of officers.

By-laws were adopted on the 21st of February, 1866, at the same place, and will be found printed in the Appendix.

THE TOWN HALL.

In a warning for a meeting of the citizens of the town to be held on the 31st day of December, 1836, for the purpose of electing trustees to take charge of the public monies, an article was inserted, "to see

197   HISTORY OF FAIR HAVEN, VERMONT.

what motion the town will take to erect a Town House." The meeting adjourned, after choosing trustees, to the 28th of January, 1837, when it was "voted to choose a committee to build a public town room over the brick school house in contemplation in the centre school district in Fair Haven, provided said district will provide the site, lay the foundation, and roof the building;" and Adams Dutton, Joseph Sheldon, Jr., and Wm. C. Kittredge were made the committee.

At the March meeting following, the voters were called on to rescind and annul the vote to build a town house, and it was rescinded.

The warning for the March meeting of 1842 had an article "to see if the town would vote something towards building a school house in the centre district for the privilege of holding town meetings therein;" but no action appears to have been taken under this head. The call was repeated in a general form in 1843, and it was "Resolved, that a committee of three be appointed to confer with the Methodist society and the centre school district to see which will accommodate the town the cheapest with a room to hold all town meetings, also moral, scientific and religious meetings, and report to the next annual town meeting." The committee were Joseph Sheldon, Jr., Joseph Adams and Samuel Wood.

The next meeting voted to hold the town meetings successively in the school houses of the four school districts.

Heman Stannard and Barnabas Ellis were chosen a

HISTORY OF FAIR HAVEN, VERMONT. 198

committee, March 2, 1846, to see what arrangements could be made towards procuring a place to be under the control of the town, in which to hold town meetings.

At the March meeting of 1855, a committee, consisting of A. Allen, I. Davey and Joseph Adams, was chosen "to estimate the expense and procure a site for a Town Hall."

This meeting was adjourned to March 28th, when it was voted to choose a committee of three "to draft a plan of a Union School and Town House, in connection with a committee of the several school districts." Ira C. Allen, Alonson Allen and Joseph Adams were chosen said committee. It was then voted that Joseph Sheldon, Jr., Sam'l Wood and C. B. Ranney be added to the committee; and it was "Resolved, That we build a Town House in connection with the districts, for union schools, not to exceed $3000." The meeting then adjourned to May 1st.

When convened again agreeably to adjournment, it was voted "to rescind the vote authorizing the building of a Town Hall." The meeting then voted to appoint "a committee of three to build a Town Hall, the cost not to exceed $1,250, including the site." Israel Davey, Alonson Allen and Hiram Hamilton were chosen said committee. It was voted to borrow from the deposit revenue fund sufficient money to build the Hall, and to pay the same on the 1st of March. The committee were instructed "to complete the Town House, ready for use, by the 1st of March next."

A meeting of the town was again called to consider

Y

199 HISTORY OF FAIR HAVEN, VERMONT.

the subject, in April, 1859, but adjourned without action.

In the March meeting of 1860 it was voted to build a Town House, and "that the U. S. deposit money be appropriated, and enough raised to make the amount $3,000." Chose I. C. Allen, I. Davey and C. Reed, building committee, and gave them discretionary power to confer and act with the Centre school district in building Town and School House in conjunction—the school district to pay one-half the expense.

• On application the selectmen called a special town meeting at S. Fish's Hotel, August 8th, to see, among other things, if the town would rescind the vote passed at the previous March meeting to build a Town House. The meeting met and adjourned.

The materials for the present Town Hall and School House having been already purchased and the contracts made, the building was erected this season, and we find that at the opening of the town meeting of March, 1861, an adjournment of thirty minutes was made, and the Inaugural Address of President Abraham Lincoln was read by H. G. Wood, Esq., as a dedication to the new hall.

BURIAL GROUNDS.

The first public burying ground in the town was laid, as we have seen, in 1785, beside what was then the principal highway through the town, a little north of the house now occupied by James Campbell, and south from John Allard's. It was located by Oliver Cleveland, Curtis Kelsey and Joel Hamilton, under a special vote of the town, taken at the March meeting of 1785, which was held at Mr. Priest's house, and is said to have had some thirty or forty graves made in it. Burials appear also to have been made in the old ground, on the south side of the west street, previous to 1798. Lyon, in his deed of an acre of land to the town for a burial ground, in October of that year, including, as he states, "the graves already made on the spot south-westerly of the meeting house."

On the 29th of January, 1819, Maj. Tilly Gilbert, for love and good will, deeds the town one acre and 60 rods of land, lying next west of land sold by him to Christopher Minot, adjoining on the east the land deeded by Col. Lyon, (or covering the same,) it being 11 rods wide by about 16 deep, reserving the right to pasture the same with sheep during his natural life, otherwise to be used exclusively for a burying ground.

In the March meeting of 1818, it was voted to raise a tax of one cent on the dollar of the list of 1817,

201   HISTORY OF FAIR HAVEN, VERMONT.

"for the purpose of surveying, cleaning and fencing the burying ground;" and "that each one shall have a right to pay his tax in such materials as may be wanted for the purpose, if paid by the first of June next, or in grain by the 15th of the same month."

At an adjourned meeting on the 13th of April, this vote was reconsidered, and it was voted "that the note of $40 against Joseph Brown, and the note of $10 against Tilly Gilbert, now in the treasury, be appropriated by the selectmen to the purpose of fencing the burying ground;" and it was further voted that the selectmen proceed to fence the burying ground, and draw on the treasurer for any expense over and above the $50. At the March meeting of 1823, it was voted that the selectmen "be directed to lot out the burying ground."

At an adjourned meeting in March, 1827, Dr. Wm. Bigelow was chosen a committee "to repair the burying ground," and a sum not exceeding ten dollars was appropriated for the purpose. The selectmen were directed at the March meeting, in 1842, "to take measures to prevent the burying yard from washing away." Great efforts were made, for several years, to stay the constant sliding down of the earth and washing away of the graves in the back part of the yard, but all to no purpose; the waste was inevitable, and while some graves were carried away into the river, others were carefully removed to a safer locality. At length the town voted, in March, 1852, to purchase 2 acres of land opposite the old ground at the price of $80 per acre, for a new cemetery, the selectmen to

HISTORY OF FAIR HAVEN, VERMONT.   202

sell off 1 acre in private individual lots, and the remaining acre to be used for a public burial ground. Alonson Allen, Joseph Sheldon, Jr., and Artemas S. Cushman were chosen as a committee to act with the selectmen in laying out the said ground.

A committee of two was chosen March 8, 1853, "to fence, grade, and pull stumps from the new grave yard, and lay out the east half into lots;" and Hiram Hamilton and Azel Willard were chosen the committee.

Again, in 1854, a committee consisting of Alonson Allen, Joseph Sheldon and Israel Davey were chosen to appoint a day and give notice when they would dispose of the lots in the east part of the cemetery, allowing the inhabitants to bid for choice.

In 1855, Jonathan Capen was appointed a special agent of the town to sell lots in the new cemetery and collect pay for those already sold. Other votes have been taken from time to time in relation to the care and improvement of the cemetery, but there is a general feeling, growing in depth and strength each year, that this cemetery is not adequate and suitable to meet the wants of the town.

A committee was chosen in the March meeting of 1868, consisting of Joseph Adams, A. H. Kidder and J. D. Wood, to look out and procure grounds for a larger and better cemetery. The committee reported in 1869, that they were unable to procure a suitable location, and they were re-appointed to act during another year. At the annual meeting in March, 1 870, a new committee, consisting of Thomas E. Wakefield,

203   HISTORY OF FAIR HAVEN, VERMONT.

Edward L. Allen and John J. Williams, was chosen to look up and purchase a site for a new cemetery.

This committee purchased, on the 8th of June, of the administrators of Israel Davey's estate, 22 acres of land lying on the south side of Davey street, along the margin of the cedar swamp, paying $3,253.50 for the same.

The question of accepting a legacy of $1000 from Mrs. Hannah H. Dyer, deceased, for the adornment of the cemeteries of the town was presented to the annual meeting in March, 1870, and a committee, consisting of Alonson Allen, Joseph Adams and Samuel W. Bailey, was chosen to examine and report at an adjourned meeting what action it was advisable for the town to take. The committee reported, May 10th, recommending the acceptance of the bequest, and a vote of thankful acknowledgement for the same—and the legacy was accepted.

MRS. DYER'S LEGACY.

Fourth.—To the town of Fair Haven, in the county of Rutland and State of Vermont, I do give and bequeath the sum of one thousand dollars, under the restrictions and in trust for the purposes following, to

HISTORY OF FAIR HAVEN, VERMONT. 204

wit: It is my will that said sum be securely invested or loaned, under the direction of the selectmen of said town for the time being, and that the interest thereof be annually collected and expended, under the direction of an agent appointed for that purpose at each annual March meeting by said town, in keeping in good repair and order the iron railing and tombstone within the same, in lot No. 2, and likewise the lot adjoining and enclosed with lot No. 2, and owned by Z. C. Ellis, in the new public burying ground in said town, wherein the remains of my late husband, Edward Dyer, are deposited, and in beautifying and adorning said two lots *especially*, and the other parts of said burying grounds by setting out and growing therein appropriate shade trees, shrubbery and evergreens.

Provided, nevertheless, and it is further my will, that unless said town of Fair Haven shall, within two years after my decease, by a vote in town meeting, duly taken and recorded, accept said legacy upon the above conditions, and thereafter use and appropriate the annual interest thereof in the manner and for the purposes above specified, then in either of such events it is my will that said sum of one thousand dollars be given to and become the property of my step-daughter, Laura D. Barnes, and her heirs forever.

Fifth.—To the First Congregational Society in said town of Fair Haven, I give and bequeath the sum of one thousand dollars, in trust, until such time as there shall be an Episcopal Church organized in said town —then said bequest to be transferred to the wardens

205 HISTORY OF FAIR HAVEN, VERMONT.

of said Episcopal Church, in trust, for the benefit of such Sabbath Schools in said town as shall exist at the time of my decease, or shall thereafter be established in connection with the Congregational, Episcopal, Methodist, or the present Welsh Church. And it is my will that the annual interest of said one thousand dollars shall be divided among such Sabbath Schools in proportion to the number of scholars regularly attending said schools during the year next preceding such division, and such division shall be annually made, by and under the direction of a committee, consisting of one member annually appointed by each of said churches, for that purpose, and the amount so divided to each school shall be invested in the purchasing of suitable books for the libraries of such school perpetually.

Before, however, such schools shall receive any benefit from the aforesaid legacy, the churches aforesaid, in said town, or some one or more of them, shall procure to be executed to my step-daughter, Harriet D. Hulett, and her heirs, a good and sufficient bond, with sureties conditioned for the faithful use of said legacy for the specific purposes above named, and in case of a failure to have the annual interest of said legacy applied and used as is above provided, that the same one thousand dollars shall be paid to the said Harriet D. Hulett and her heirs. And in case said churches should neglect, for two years after my decease, to execute such bond, or faithfully to use and apply the annual interest of said legacy, in the manner and for the purposes above specified forever, it is

HISTORY OF FAIR HAVEN, VERMONT. **206**

my will that said sum of one thousand dollars be given and paid to my said step-daughter, Harriet D. Hulett, and her heirs; Provided, none of the aforesaid churches in said Fair Haven are to have any benefit from said legacy except such as join in the execution of the aforesaid bond.

The will appoints Horace H. Dyer, of Rutland, and Zenas C. Ellis, of Fair ˚Haven, executors—and was signed by the testator, Hannah Dyer, Sept. 10th, 1866.

In a codicil to the will, made on the 16th day of October, 1868, she provides as follows: And whereas, I have also, in and by my said last will and testament, given and appropriated a certain sum of money to each of the towns of Milton and Fair Haven, in said state of Vermont, the annual interest of which is to be used and expended in improving, ornamenting and beautifying the burying grounds and cemeteries in each of said towns, as the same is specified in my said last will and testament ; and whereas, changes in such burying grounds and cemeteries may take place, either before or after my decease, I do therefore will and direct that the annual interest of the said sums of money, given as above stated to said towns of Milton and Fair Haven, shall be used and laid out in improving, beautifying and ornamenting such burying grounds and cemeteries in said towns as shall be occupied and used as public burying grounds or cemeteries, all which is to be done in accordance with the specific terms and directions contained in my said will.

I do further will and direct that whenever, if ever, the interest on said sums of money, so given as is above stated, to said towns of Milton and Fair Haven, shall not be annually used and expended in the manner and for the purposes specified in my said will, and in this codicil thereto, the said sums of money, so as above given to said towns, shall revert to and be equally distributed and divided among my heirs who may be living; that is to say, a neglect on the part of the proper authorities of either of said towns to use and expend said annual interest according to my said will and codicil, shall operate to deprive such town thus guilty of neglect, of any further use or benefit of the money so given and appropriated to such town for the purposes named above.

THE SLATE BUSINESS.

The business of quarrying slate in Western Vermont was begun in this town, by Alonson Allen and Caleb B. Ranney, in the fall of 1839, on the ledge which is nearly in front of Mr. Ranney's dwelling house, where the Boston Company is now working.

The opening was begun with a view to finding ciphering or school slates; but the material proving too hard for that purpose, the enterprise was suspended or temporarily abandoned.

HISTORY OF FAIR HAVEN, VERMONT. 208

Thomas Shaw, who had previously resided in Hoosick, N. Y., and been acquainted with the slate quarried there, examined the slate found on Scotch Hill and adjudged them too hard to be worked for any purpose. A similar opinion was expressed by a Mr. Shrives, from Hoosick, who visited the quarry in June, 1845.

In this latter year, Ira Allen and Adams Dutton made a small opening on the land of Elijah Esty, but finding nothing valuable soon quit it. Alonson Allen, however, having perfected machinery for the manufacture of ciphering slates, opened a quarry, this same year, on the land of Oliver Proctor, a little north-west of Mr. Proctor's house, from which he was able during the next three succeeding years to produce a large amount of ciphering, school slates, besides several lots of roofing slate, which were made about 1847; the first lot being taken to Whitehall, and used on a house owned by Mr. Turner, a druggist, and more recently occupied by Mr. Stowell.

The first roof covered with slate in the town, was that of the horse barn and shed of Jefferson Barnes in the south part of the town. Slate were afterwards laid on Mr. Davey's blacksmith shop and store, and in 1850, on the railroad depot.

Mr. Allen had a slate factory on the spot where the nail factory now stands, in which were finished and shipped away to market, on the average, about six hundred framed slates per day; George G. Cobb, Royal R. Stetson, Marvin Carpenter, Edward S. Bascom, David Standish, Simeon Cobb, and others, including

209 HISTORY OF FAIR HAVEN, VERMONT.

the writer of this, being employed at various times as workmen in the factory.

The production of school slates exceeding the market demand, and not proving sufficiently remunerative, it was given up by Mr. Allen in 1848, and he turned his attention once more to the quarry on Mr. Ranney's land, and to the developement of the roofing slate interest.

It was proved by the opening of various other quarries about this time, that the Taconic ledges of Western Vermont were susceptible of manufacture into roofing material. Adams Dutton and Royal Bullock, enterprising residents of Fair Haven, worked an opening and made slate at Cedar Point, on the north shore of Lake Bomoseen; and Frank W. Whitlock, a resident of Castleton, found a quarry which he worked in Castleton, a little eastward of the Fair Haven town line and in the vicinity of the present "Eagle Quarry."

Mr. Allen, leasing an acre of land of Mr. Ranney, in May, 1848, then really commenced the manufacture of roofing slate in the town. He produced about 500 squares in the year 1849. These were the purple slate. In 1850 the business received a very decided impetus by the arrival of a number of intelligent Welshmen in the town, who had been accustomed to the working of the slate quarries in Wales and in Pennsylvania. The first Welshman of whom we hear in connection with the quarries, was John Humphrey, now of New Canton, Va., who is said to have worked on the Whitlock quarry in 1849. He is said to have worked with Ira Allen at slating roofs.

HISTORY OF FAIR HAVEN, VERMONT. 210

In July, 1850, Wm. Parry, who is now a citizen of the town, John M. Jones, who afterwards resided on the Wood place, in the south part of the town, and Moses Jones, came fromNorthampton county, in Pennsylvania, and commenced to work for Mr. Allen on the Scotch Hill quarry, on the first day of August. Owen Owens and others went to work about this time on the Whitlock quarry in Castleton; and from this date the slate business has continued steadily to increase, large numbers of Welsh quarrymen, experienced in the production and manufacture of slate in the old country, coming in and contributing of their industry and labor to the wealth of the place. Mr. Allen purchased an additional acre of land of Mr. Ranney, in 1851, and continued wórking it until in 1858 he sold it to Wm. Hughes and Owen Owens.

In the early spring of 1851, Hugh W. and John J. Williams, cousins, together with four others, to wit, David S. Jones, Wm. Price, John Thomas and Wm. Pritchard, came to Fair Haven from Guilford, Vt., and began quarrying on Mr. Ranney's farm. They first leased of Mr. Ranney two and a half acres, next south of and adjoining Mr. · Allen's quarry, they to pay Mr. Ranney twenty-five cents for every square of slate, or $2,000 for the land within five years. They obtained good slate in two months from the time they commenced uncovering.

In the fall of 1851 they purchased two acres of Mr. Ranney, lying next north of Mr. Allen's quarry, on which a New York firm had worked for a short time. Having made various improvements in derricks and

211 HISTORY OF FAIR HAVEN, VERMONT.

dwellings, the Williamses sold an undivided half interest in their property to David Tillson, of Woburn, and F. L. Cushman, of Boston, Mass., and the business was carried on by them till 1857, when Tillson, having bought out Cushman, sold his interest to Asa Wilbur, of Boston.

The Williamses transferred their interest to Israel Davey and Benj. S. Nichols, in 1857. Mr. Wilbur soon after sold to Wm. Hughes, J. Nelson Proctor and Benj. Williams. Mr. Proctor sold to Hughes and Williams after one year, and the quarry was then divided, Mr. Hughes selling his portion, after a short time, to Ellis Roberts, Henry Jones, Hugh Lewis, John H. Williams and Wm. Parry. They worked their division until they sold the same to the present Boston company in 1865. Mr. Benj. Williams had made a previous purchase of Mr. Ranney of a 'strip seven and a half rods wide, extending eastward from Mr. Allen's quarry to the highway, in November 1858, from which he took out 1,200 squares of slate the first year and over 2,000 squares each year thereafter until he sold to the Boston company in 1865.

Mr. Hughes having divided with Mr. Owens, the acre purchased by them of Mr. Allen, in 1858, Mr. Owens sold his part to Messrs. Davey and Nichols, and that belonging to Hughes was sold by him, in conjunction with what he had purchased of Mr. Wilbur, to Ellis Roberts and others, from whom it passed to its present owners, the Boston company. This company purchasing Messrs. Davey and Nichols' interest, became the sole proprietors of this extensive

HISTORY OF FAIR HAVEN, VERMONT. 212

quarry, and have produced from it a large quantity of slate, the average amount produced since 1866 being 7,500 squares per year, and the quarry being now in order to produce 12,000 squares per year. John C. Smith is the present efficient superintendent.

The next largest quarry in the town is that opened by Alonson Allen, Esq., on the "Capen farm," purchased by him of Mr. Capen, in November, 1851, and now owned and worked by the "Fair Haven Marble and Marbleizing Slate Company" for the production of slabbing material for their mill. This quarry was start- by Mr. Allen about 1851, and worked a number of years for roofing slate, employing about 20 men and producing nearly 4000 squares per year, for the first six years. The slate are purple color, variegated with green, and are deemed a superior quality. Mr. Allen sold an interest in the quarry, in 1869, to Ryland Hanger, James Pottle, Ira C. Allen and M. D. Dyer, who, together with himself, compose the Fair Haven Marble and Marbleizing Slate Company, and run the quarry in connection with their extensive slate mill in the village. Besides this main quarry near the north-west corner of the Capen farm, Mr. Allen has two other valuable openings lying over the hill to the south, on this same farm ; one made by John D. Wood, about the year 1855, and yielding about 300 squares, but was abandoned on account of the water, and another more recently opened which promises to be very profitable.

A quarry was opened by Royal Bullock on land owned by him on Scotch Hill, in the fall of 1850,

213 HISTORY OF FAIR HAVEN, VERMONT.

and w● worked through the summer of 1851, and was sold by him to Messrs. Myers & Utter, of Whitehall, in the fall of 1852. It has been worked at various times, but has finally been abandoned.

In February, 1853, Asa B. Foster, of Weston, Vt., deeded the Keyes' farm, on Scotch Hill, then occupied by Mr. Keyes, and comprising 100 acres, to Asa Wilber, of Boston, and Rowland Owens, excepting one acre on the east side of the highway which he had deeded to Hugh and John J. Williams, and on which they had erected dwelling houses. A quarry was opened on this farm by Mr. Owens and John Hughes, and worked for one or two seasons. Another opening was made in 1854, and dwelling houses were erected west of the present Scotch Hill school house. This also was abandoned after one or two seasons of trial. Richard Williams is said to have worked this quarry for one season, about 1856.

The Sheldon quarry, which has proved to be a valuable vein of slate, lying on Mr. Sheldon's farm at the base of Scotch Hill, and north of Mr. Ranney's land, was opened in 1853 by Ellis Roberts, Richard Hughes and Evan E. Lloyd, to whom it was leased in August, of this year, for a term of 15 years, "if they should elect to hold the same so long," on the terms and conditions that they should pay nothing for the first 200 squares, but that they should pay 50 cents per square on every 200 squares procured thereafter, and Mr. Sheldon should draw the same to the railroad depot in Fair Haven, for one shilling per square. Ellis Lloyd, Hugh Jones and Evan Jones are said to

HISTORY OF FAIR HAVEN, VERMONT. 214

have been associated with the management and working of this quarry for a time. ' Richard H ughes sold out to Richard Roberts in June, 1854, and they were all succeeded by Evan D. Jones, who obtained a new lease of the quarry from Mr. Sheldon in February, 1859, for ten years from September 1st, 1858, on the same terms as the previous lessees had it, excepting that heiwas to pay the annual taxes. Mr. Jones took into copartnership Christopher M. Davey, of Rutland, a son of Jacob Davey, Esq., and by drifting into the hill southward, they produced a large amount of valuable slate during the last years of the lease.

The quarry known as the Lime Kiln quarry, near the town line toward West Castleton, was commenced at an early period on the land of Arnold Briggs; Mr. Briggs leasing one and one-fourth acres for the purpose, in October, 1851, to Patrick McNamara and Thomas Bulger, John Murfee and John Kelley. They were to have the property forever, so long as they should pay fifty dollars per year every three months in merchantable slate, at $3.00 per square, or $12.50 in money, as the party of the second part might elect. Patrick McNamara sold out to the others, and in May, 1853, Mr. Bulger assigned the lease to Israel Davey and Rufus C. Colburn. They assigned it to Wm. Hughes, in October, 1855, Mr. Davey having purchased of Mr. Briggs an addition to the original lease. By Mr. Hughes it was sold to Benj. F. and Robert Morris Copeland, in August, 1858, and Mr. Briggs deeds to them, in the same month, all the land connected with it which was deeded by John Billings to

215   HISTORY OF FAIR HAVEN, VERMONT.

Elihu Wright, Jr., in November, 1831. The quarry was worked by them for a few years and abandoned.

Mr. Copeland has recently purchased the Harvey lot, so-called, lying next north of this quarry, on which he has erected, in company with Benjamin Williams, a steam saw-mill, and is cutting off a large amount of valuable lumber, anticipating a valuable vein of slate on the land when the lumber is cleared away.

In December, 1851, Arnold Briggs leased to Wm. Hughes, for 99 years, 3 acres of land for a slate quarry on the lower and west side of the road, beyond, or north of Mr. Sheldon's quarry, Mr. Hughes to pay $50, the first year, and $60 each year thereafter.

Nothing further was done toward developing a quarry at this place.

On the 1st of June, 1852, Mr. Briggs leased an acre of land for a slate quarry, south of his house, and east of the highway, to James Rhine and Eben Jackson. Jackson appears to have been superseded or displaced by one John Sullivan, by whom, with Rhine, some two or three hundred squares of slate were taken out and sold to Israel Davey. Evan E. Lloyd, Ellis Lloyd, and Richard Lewis purchased Rhine and Sullivan's claim, and Henry Jones, Richard Lewis and Ellis Lloyd took a new lease of Mr. Briggs, in April, 1854, but soon abandoned the quarry after taking out about 500 squares of slate. Mr. Briggs leased the quarry again in December, 1863, to Ryland Hanger and Evan E. Lloyd, who worked it for a time in quarrying mill stock, but found the material too hard and too far away, and abandoned it.

HISTORY OF FAIR HAVEN, VERMONT. 216

In March, 1865, John J. Williams and Henry C. Nichols, purchased of John Balis, of Benson, the 130 acres of the old Appleton farm, long owned by Hezekiah and Harvey Howard, and occupied by Ralph Perkins, on Scotch Hill, and commenced the opening of a quarry on the same, southward from the quarries of the Boston company. About the same time they conveyed one-third part of the farm and quarry· to Henry G. Lapham, of Brooklyn, N. Y., and formed a co-partnership as "Williams, Nichols & Co." Mr. Nichols sold his share of the property to Mr. Williams, in July following.

On the 10th of April, 1867, Mr. Williams conveyed to Wellington Ketchum one equal undivided fourth part of the land embracing the quarry on Scotch Hill, and Mr. Ketchum conveyed to Williams one equal undivided fourth part of the property known as the grist mill, mill house and tannery, which had been owned in common by Ketchum and Capen. Mr. Williams deeded to Lapham, on the 11th of April, an additional sixth part of the farm on Scotch Hill, and he and Ketchum deeded one-half of the grist-mill and tannery premises, now converted into a slate mill, to Lapham, forming with him a co-partnership for the manufacture of slate mantles, billiards, tile, etc., under the name of "Union Slate Company." The quarry of the company on Scotch Hill not proving a feasible and profitable one, was soon abandoned; and the company, now under the efficient management of Aaron R. Vail, Esq., has obtained a supply of slate material from the valuable slate beds of C. M. Davey and Evan D. Jones,

217   HISTORY OF FAIR HAVEN, VERMONT.

in the south-west part of Castleton, and is doing an extensive and profitable business in manufacturing, furnishing employment to about 30 persons at the mill, besides some 20 more engaged by Seth N. Peck in the process of marbleizing at the same place.

The business of marbleizing slate in the town was commenced in the spring of 1859 by James Coulman and Ryland Hanger, in the building which had been erected by Messrs. Adams & Allen, in 1857, and occupied as a woolen factory by Alphonso Kilbourn, on the south side of the river opposite the marble mill. The lower, or basement room, was used by Isaac T. Milliken for the manufacture of mantel stock, and Messrs. Coulman and Hanger occupied the upper rooms, or two stories, in finishing mantles, table-tops, &c., from slate and marble. Mr. Coulman sold out to Mr. Hanger in the summer of 1862, and the business was carried on to an increased extent by Mr. Hanger, alone, for a number of years, he buying the mill of Ira C. Allen, with certain privileges of water, in the summer of 1866, and selling a fourth part of the same to James Pottle in November following.

By them the business was continued, they employing about 60 men in various departments, till the factory was burned, January 12th, 1869.

In February, a company consisting of Messrs. Hanger & Pottle, Alonson Allen, M. D. Dyer, and Ira C. Allen, was organized under the title of "The Fair Haven Marble and Marbleized Slate Company;" and the large and valuable slate quarry of Alonson Allen, on the Capen farm, so-called, was united with the mill, which was at once rebuilt and greatly enlarged.

HISTORY OF FAIR HAVEN, VERMONT. **218**

Business was resumed in the mill in April, and the company employed in the mill and quarry 115 persons during the season.

The Kearsarge Steam Slate Works, situated near the railroad depot, were erected by Simeon Allen and DeWitt Leonard, in the summer of 1868. They are now owned and run by Mr. Allen, who employs about 20 men in the manufacture of mantels, table-tops, billiards, &c.

The process of marbleizing was commenced in the second story of the building, by Patrick Burke and Simon H. Myers, in the spring of 1869. It is now carried on by Mr. Burke and A. L. Kellogg.

A quarry was opened by Norman Peck in the fall of 1868, on land leased of Otis and John W. Eddy, a little south-east from the railroad depot. Mr. Peck re-leased the quarry to Messrs. A. L. Kellogg and Wm. Parry, in the spring of 1869; Kellogg afterwards buying out Parry and selling a half interest to E. D. Humphrey. By them the quarry was re-leased to Messrs. Sheridan and Young, in the spring of 1870. The production has been mostly mill stock, used by the Kearsarge Steam Slate Works.

THE MARBLE BUSINESS.

The business of sawing marble in the town was begun in the fall of 1845, by William C. Kittredge, Alonson Allen, and Joseph Adams, under the firm name of "Kittredge, Allen & Adams;" Mr. Kittredge remaining connected with the firm only till October, 1846, after which time the business was conducted by Messrs. Allen & Adams until 1852.

The company first purchased a water-fall and mill-site of Ira Leonard, in December, 1844, on the spot where the railroad now crosses the State Line. About the same time they contracted with Wm. F. Barnes, of West Rutland, to supply them with blocks of marble for sawing, to the amount of 20,000 feet of two inch slabs for the first year, beginning October 1st, 1845, and 30,000 feet for each of the next two succeeding years.

Finding it possible to create a mill-power in the village by cutting through the peninsula, or intervale belonging to Alonzo Safford, below, and west of the paper-mill, they purchased of Mr. Safford, in March, about six acres of land and proceeded immediately to erect a dam and mill. By turning the water into a simple trench in the soft, gravelly soil, a channel was speedily made of sufficient capacity for all the water required for a mill, and about 10 feet of fall was ob-

HISTORY OF FAIR HAVEN, VERMONT. 220

tained. By the sinking of the river bed, below the mill, this fall has been increased. The first mill, with eight old-style, pendulum gangs, built by Hiram Shaw, of Hampton, was started in October, 1845. In 1851 the mill was enlarged by an addition of four gangs, and the pendulums were replaced by the more modern and improved machinery of pulleys and belts.

In March, 1845, the company obtained a lease of three acres of land, for a marble quarry, of Ebenezer Goodrich, of West Rutland; Messrs. Allen & Adams purchased the same in September, 1851, of Lorenzo and Charles Sheldon, David Morgan, and Charles H. Slason.

The opening of the quarry was begun under contract for ten years, by Wm. F. Barnes, in 1850. The marble was first made use of in the fall of 1851. Mr. Barnes worked it only about seven years, after which it was carried on by Joseph Adams and Ira C. Allen until June, 1868, when they sold it to Wm. Clement, Ferrand Parker, and E. P. Gilson.

Up to the opening of the railroad in the fall of 1849, the marble was drawn from the quarry to the mill by teams; Mr. Wm. Clement and a Mr. Gorham having a contract for the drawing for a number of years. From the mill the marble was transported by wagons to Whitehall, and there reloaded and shipped by canal to all parts of the country.

The business made a large and remunerative demand for labor, furnishing employment for about 25 men, and, notwithstanding the losses of the first two years, occasioned by the sawing of poor marble, was

221   HISTORY OF FAIR HAVEN, VERMONT.

the means of bringing into the town and distributing much wealth among the inhabitants.

The amount of marble sawed and sent away ranged from one to two hundred thousand feet a year.

In 1852, Messrs. Allen & Adams took into partnership Ira C. Allen, and united with their business the store which had been carried on by Messrs. A. & I. C. Allen, on the corner now owned by Augustus Graves, the style of the new company being Allen, Adams & Co.

In 1854, Mr. A. Allen sold his interest to Mr. Adams and Ira C. Allen, the firm then becoming Adams & Allen, and continuing as such until the fall of 1869, when Mr. Adams purchased the mill and other property in town, and the business is now carried on by Joseph Adams & Son.

THE FIRST NATIONAL BANK OF FAIR HAVEN.

Agreeably to a printed "call" for the purpose, a number of the inhabitants of Fair Haven and vicinity met at the hall of Adams & Allen on the afternoon of Wednesday, January 20th, 1864, to consider the expediency of establishing a bank in Fair Haven,

HISTORY OF FAIR HAVEN, VERMONT.

under the general banking law of the United States, approved February 25th, 1863. Hon. Alonson Allen was chosen chairman, and A. N. Adams, secretary.

A resolution being adopted in favor of the establishment of a bank in the town, on motion of B. S. Nichols, a committee of five, namely : Alonson Allen, P. W. Hyde, Joseph Adams, B. S. Nichols, and Corril Reed, was chosen to draw up a paper and circulate the same for subscriptions of stock. •The committee reported the following:

"We, the undersigned, believing that the business of Fair Haven and vicinity, requires more immediate facilities for banking accommodations, and believing that the best interests of such business would be subserved by the establishment of ·a bank under the act of Congress of Feb. 25th, 1863, to be called 'The First National Bank of Fair Haven,' Rutland County, Vt., with a capital of $100,000, with the privilege of increasing the same to $200,000, hereby subscribe and agree to take the number of shares of the capital stock of said bank, set opposite our names respectively ; said shares to be of the par value of one hundred dollars each, thirty per cent. of the said subscription to be paid to the directors within ten days after they shall be elected, and the balance agreeably to the provisions of said act."

The committee reported 160 shares subscribed, to wit ; 50 each by Joseph Adams and Ira C. Allen ; 25 each by B. S. Nichols and Allen Penfield, and 10 by Zenas C. Ellis.

At an adjourned meeting, on the 30th of January,

223 HISTORY OF FAIR HAVEN, VERMONT.

50 additional shares were subscribed, and the meeting was again adjourned to be held on the 7th of February. At this meeting, also held in Adams and Allen's hall, Hon. Merritt Clark, of Poultney, being present, and proposing to assist in forwarding the enterprize, the individuals above named, together with others, subscribed for the shares of the capital stock to the amount of $76,000; Mr. Adams taking 100; Mr. Allen 90; Mr. Nichols and Mr. Penfield each 50; Mr. Ellis 70; Joseph Sheldon 100; Merritt Clark 100; Marcilian Maynard 10; E. S. Ells 10; Norman Peck 15; C. S. Rumsey 30; Myron M. Dikeman 20; and others more or less, sufficient to insure the existence of the bank as an institution of the town.

At a meeting of the stockholders on the 18th of February, the following persons were chosen the first board of Directors: Joseph Sheldon, Zenas C. Ellis, Ira C. Allen, Joseph Adams, Pitt W. Hyde, Charles Clark, John Balis, Benjamin S. Nichols, and Chauncey S. Rumsey.

Joseph Sheldon was chosen President, Merritt Clark, cashier, and Charles Clark, teller.

The bank was opened in May, in the small building owned by Alonson Allen, on the south side of the Common, where it was kept until February, 1870, when the new bank building, on the east side of the Common being completed, the business of the bank was removed to its present place. This new building is substantially built of brick, iron and marble, two stories high, and has one of Lillie's best bank safes inside a heavy wrought iron vault, and is pronounced as secure as any bank vault in the state.

HISTORY OF FAIR HAVEN, VERMONT. 224

Samuel W. Bailey, the present cashier, succeeded Mr. Clark in October, 1865.

LITERARY AND LIBRARY SOCIETIES.

It has not been the fortune of the town to have many inhabitants of a literary education, or habit of mind. There are few eminent, or liberally educated men among the sons of the town. Yet the inhabitants have never been wholly forgetful of the benefits of intellectual culture, and while they have been liberal patrons of educational institutions, sending their sons and daughters to various academies and colleges, they have also, at several different times, founded public libraries and literary organizations.

Besides the movement made in 1799, of which mention has been made on page 124, and under which books are said to have been procured and circulated among the inhabitants, a library association was formed in the town in 1826, consisting of 100 shares, at $2,00 per share, and several hundred volumes were purchased, some of which are still in existence. Wm. C. Kittredge, John P. Colburn and John Jones, constituted the committee that made the first purchase of books, and Mr. Kittredge was the librarian who had charge of the library for the first 12 to 15 years.

225   HISTORY OF FAIR HAVEN, VERMONT.

A number of the present inhabitants were stock-holders, or share-owners, in this library, but the books being, many of them, of a too metaphysical and theological character, the interest in them was not endur-ing, and the library at length became scattered and lost. Dr. Thomas E. Wakefield was for several years the librarian.

An agricultural library of about 100 volumes, including a set of Appleton's new American Cyclopedia, was established in April, 1863, by an association of 36 shareholders, who paid each $5.00 per share. This library contains many valuable scientific books, representing the most advanced knowledge of agriculture and whatsoever concerns the farmer's avocation.

Young men's debating societies have been organized and carried on successfully through a number of seasons within the 25 years last past. A young men's "Lecture Club" was formed by ten young men of the town, in November, 1864, for the purpose of instituting a course of lyceum lectures at the town hall by some of the prominent literary and public men of the country.

The course was opened on the 10th of December by J. R. Gilmore, (Edmund Kirke,) who spoke of "Jeff. Davis and Richmond." He was followed by Col. T. W. Higginson, December 20th, on the "Freedmen of the South;" by Horace Greeley, December 27th, on "Self-Made Men;" by Rev. W. H. Milburn, January 4th, on "What a blind man saw in England;" by Prof. J. W. Fowler, January 19th, on "Social Organization;" by Rev. R. L. Herbert, January 27th, on

HISTORY OF FAIR HAVEN, VERMONT. 226

" Progress ;" by Dr. J. G. Holland, and Prof. B. Kellogg, and a poem by A. C. Wicker.

The course was not so well patronized as it was expected it would be, and the members of the " Club," among whom were Henry C. Nichols, Abraham C. Wicker, John J. Williams, Wm. Pitkin, Leonard J. Stow, Edward L. Allen, H. T. Dewey, and A. N. Adams, sustained a loss of something over $100.

Another course of lyceum lectures was instituted by a union of many of the citizens and a sale of season tickets, in the winter of 1866 and '67. In this course, lectures were given by Rev. G. H. Hepworth, Rev. W. S. Smart, Rev. J. E. Bruce, Rev. D. W. Dayton, and Hon. Samuel F. Cary.

THE ODD FELLOWS.

A lodge of the Independent Order of Odd Fellows, named " Eureka Lodge, No. 22," was instituted at Fair Haven, June 3d, 1851, consisting of ten members, into which three others were initiated and three admitted by card on the 24th of June. The lodge held its meetings in a hall fitted up by the members, in the east end of Leonard Williams' building, now Mr.

227   HISTORY OF FAIR HAVEN, VERMONT.

Graves', until 1855, when the meetings were held for about one year in the hall built by Messrs. Adams & Allen over Mr. Adams' brick store. The last member initiated, making in all 55, was in December, 1853. The Past Grands were I. C. Allen, T. E. Wakefield, Joseph Adams, M. B. Dewey, I. Jones, N. Jenne, G. W. Hurlburt, and H. M. Shaw.

The system of paying benefits, which was primarily the cause of the suspension of the order, having been abolished, an effort was made in the winter of 1869, by Grand Commissioner B. W. Dennis, a son of Royal Dennis, formerly of Fair Haven, to revive and reinstate "Eureka Lodge, No. 22," and a dispensation was obtained from the Grand Lodge for the purpose, but there has not been sufficient interest on the part of the ancient members to secure the revival of the order in the town.

THE MASONS.

The lodge of Ancient Free and Accepted Master Masons, in Fair Haven, now existing and known as "Eureka Lodge, No. 75," was begun under dispensation from the Grand Lodge, in June, 1866, holding

HISTORY OF FAIR HAVEN, VERMONT. 228

its first regular communication on June 6th, A. L. 5866. The charter was granted Jan. 10th, 1867, to 36 members of the order residing in and near Fair Haven. Simeon Allen being the first Master, Edward W. Liddell the first Senior Warden, and Hamlin T. Dewey the first Junior Warden. The number of Master Masons connected with the lodge, January 1st, 1870, was 106.

A lodge of Mark Master Masons existed in Fair Haven at a much earlier date. It was called "Morning Star Mark Lodge, No. 4," and was first convened at the lodge room of E. Ashley, in Poultney, on the 20th day of February, 1810, and of Masonry, 5810, under a charter, or warrant, from the Grand Royal Arch Chapter of the State of Vermont. Its officers were " E. Buell, W. M., Pliny Adams, S. W., and T. Wilmot, J. W." At this first meeting, Wm. Miller, then of Poultney, afterwards of Hampton, N. Y., and Joel Beaman, an early resident of Fair Haven, were among the number proposed for membership.

This lodge appears to have been the natural successor of Aurora Mark Lodge, No. 2, instituted at Poultney under a warrant from Aurora Lodge, No. 25, May 4th, 1797, the officers installed having been chosen at a meeting held at Peter B. French's hotel, in Hampton, in April, A. L. 5797, as follows: "Peter B. French, W. M., A. Murry, S. W., J. Stanley, J. W., and David Erwin, of Fair Haven, Treasurer." Ithamar Hebard was a member of this lodge, as was also Abijah Peet, of West Haven.

The meetings of the lodge were held a part of the

229   HISTORY OF FAIR HAVEN, VERMONT.

time in Hampton, and a part of the time in Poultney. A new dispensation was obtained in January, 1800, and the number of the lodge was changed, it being from this time "Aurora Mark Lodge, No. 16."

The meetings were only held occasionally, the last one being in May, 1805.

Morning Star Lodge succeeding, in February, 1810, the meetings were held at Poultney frequently, and a large number joined it, among whom were John Herring, Royal Dennis, John P. Colburn, Wm. J. Billings, and Barnabas Ellis, of Fair Haven, and Jona. Orms and Oliver Church, of West Haven.

At the meeting held on the first Monday in February, 1818, it was voted that the lodge be removed to Fair Haven, and Samuel Martin was appointed a committee to inform the G. H. Priest of the removal.

On the 16th of March, "agreeably to the dispensation of the G. H. Priest," Morning Star Mark Lodge, No. 4, convened at Fair Haven. The meetings were held in the ball room of Royal Dennis' hotel. John P. Colburn was W. M., Barnabas Ellis S. W., Thomas Christie J. W., and we find the names of members with which we are familiar, as follows: Moses Colton, M. Hickok, R. Perkins, H. H. Crane, Stephen S. Bosworth, James Y. Watson, George Warren, Elisha Parkill, Chauncey Trowbridge, D. C. Sproat, M. H Kidder, Apollos Smith, Samuel Wood, Charles Wood, J. Quinton, Jr., H. W. Bates, O. Maranville, Jacob Willard, John Beaman; and among members from other towns, Philo Hosford and Samuel P. Hooker, of Poultney, and Philip Pond, of Castleton.

HISTORY OF FAIR HAVEN, VERMONT. **230**

The lodge met several times a year at Dennis' lodge room. From January, 1823, to February, 1826, the meetings were at John Beaman's house, he having succeeded Mr. Dennis in the hotel. The last three meetings of which we have a record, were held at "J. Greenough's Inn," in November, 1827, January and March, 1828.

The lodge seems to have been very prosperous, and to have received many new members even to the last, notwithstanding many, unable to endure the storm of anti-masonic persecution which then raged, withdrew and were discharged at their own request. The lodge appears to have gone down amid the waves of an angry public prejudice.

THE GOOD TEMPLARS.

The Fair Haven Lodge, No. 92, I. O. of G. T., was chartered December 4th, 1868, and organized December 18th, in Adams' Hall, with 36 charter members; A. N. Adams being the first W. C. T., and Emma V. Chase the first W. V. T. The lodge has steadily grown in strength, interest and influence, and now numbers about 100 male members and 60 females. The chair

231   HISTORY OF FAIR HAVEN, VERMONT.

of W. C. T. has been creditably filled by Thomas E. Wakefield and John W. Eddy.

Eryri Lodge, No. 129, was chartered February 3d, 1870, Rev. R. L. Herbert being elected its first W. C. T., and Miss Louisa Williams its first W. V. T. The lodge numbers at this time, (June 1st, 1870,) 80 male members and 32 females, and is in a very flourishing condition.

The two lodges, Eryri lodge among the Welsh and Fair Haven lodge among the Americans, have received to membership in the order over 300 persons.

THE WASHINGTONIAN TEMPERANCE SOCIETY.

The great Washingtonian temperance reform was organized in Fair Haven, in 1841 and '42, with a membership of 500 persons; Joseph Adams, President, and Azel Willard, Jr., Secretary.

Members' names were engrossed on a single sheet, in double columns, and enclosed in a case with rollers and a glass front, so that any name could be readily turned to view. Finely printed pledges, or certificates of membership, were given to members. Large and

HISTORY OF FAIR HAVEN, VERMONT. 232

enthusiastic meetings were held in the meeting-house and village school-house, and men long addicted to intoxication came forward and publicly took the pledge. The fruits of the reform were visible in the sober habits and increased prosperity of the reformers.

— ◦•◦ —

THE FAIR HAVEN YOUNG MEN'S CHRISTIAN ASSOCIATION

Was organized February 4th, 1868 ; A. L. Kellogg being chosen President; R. Hanger, Vice President; James Pottle, Cor. Secretary ; F. H. Shepard, Rec. Secretary ; Rev. E. W. Brown, Treasurer ; P. A. Baker, Registrar ; and C. Reed, Isaiah Inman and Richard Lane, Directors.

The constitution provides for three classes of members, associate, active, and life members; any person of good character being privileged to become an associate member, without the right to vote or hold office, by the payment of $1.00 annually ; and persons under forty-five years of age, who are members in evangelical churches, can become active members, with exclusive right to vote and hold office, by the payment of the same sum annually. The same may become

233 HISTORY OF FAIR HAVEN, VERMONT.

life members by the payment of $10.00 at one time into the general fund.

The annual meeting is holden on the last Sunday evening in December of each year. The Association opened a reading and conference room in H. Whipple's building, over the postoffice, in the summer of 1868, and removed thence into the new and spacious room, over the First National Bank, in the fall of 1869.

THE CAMBRIAN CORNET BAND.

The Cambrian Cornet Band was organized September 28th, 1867. The members at its organization were:

Robert W. Jones,	John E. Roberts,
Robert J. Evans,	John D. Rowlands,
John R. Roberts,	John J. Evans,
John E. Edwards,	John H. Williams,
Robert P. Owens,	Edward W. Owens,
Robert J. Roberts,	John R. Hughes,
Owen W. Owens,	Owen M. Jones.

The members now are:

John W. Jones,	Robert P. Owens,
Robert J. Evans,	John E. Edwards,
John D. Rowlands,	Edward W. Owens,
Griffith G. Jones,	Griffith J. Griffiths,
Robert J. Roberts,	Edward H. Lewis,

Robert J. Evans, Secretary.

PRINTING AND PUBLISHING.

After Matthew Lyon's time, the business of printing and publishing was not carried on in Fair Haven until the year 1853. At that time, DeWitt Leonard, son of Ira Leonard, residing near the State Line, then a young lad, commenced printing for his own amusement, upon a press of his own construction. He issued several numbers of a small monthly paper called *The Banner*, in 1854 and '55, using second hand type procured from the Whitehall *Chronicle* office. Being encouraged by having several jobs given him, he ordered new type from time to time, from the founders, until in a few years he had quite a complete assortment of jobbing type. In 1856 he printed and bound for the author, Edward L. Allen, a "Slater's Guide," a table for the computation of roofing slate. This was the first book printed in town subsequent to Matthew Lyon's time. One number of a small sheet called the *Golden Sheaf* was issued in January, 1861. Business had increased so much that in November, 1861, he purchased a Gordon press, the first power press ever brought into the town. Being engaged in bookselling, he issued a small quarterly or monthly sheet, as an advertising medium, in 1856–7. In 1858–9 a variety of song books, ballads and other publications were issued from this press. In 1860, "Haynes' Sermon on

235 HISTORY OF FAIR HAVEN, VERMONT.

Universalism," and the "Constitution and By-Laws of Poultney Division, S. of T.," were among the works printed at this office. In 1862, he published a "Washington County (N. Y.) Almanac and Business Directory," with an edition of several thousand copies. This was intended to be a permanent annual publication, but the depression of business consequent upon the beginning of the war frustrated this plan.

In September, 1863, the first number of the *Fair Haven Advertiser* was issued, as an advertising medium for the merchants and business men of the town. It was circulated gratuitously, and other numbers were issued from time to time, as the demands of advertisers required, until Wm. Q. Brown purchased the office, when it was made a regular monthly publication. Its circulation was 1000 copies.

Among various other works emanating from this office was a *Quarterly Journal*, containing from 32 to 36 octavo pages, published by Ripley Female College, commenced in February, 1865, and continued until February, 1866, when Mr. Leonard sold his press to McLean and Robbins, of Rutland, and the type and other material lay unused until the July following, when Wm. Q. Brown purchased it and removed it to his dwelling house on Washington street, and adding a new Gordon press, continued the job printing business and made the *Rutland County Advertiser* a regular monthly paper. Mr. Brown, wishing to remove from the town, sold his office back to DeWitt Leonard in April, 1868, who conducted it three months, until July 1st, when he sold it to Messrs. Jones and Grose,

HISTORY OF FAIR HAVEN, VERMONT. 236

Through the efforts of the gentlemen last named, a weekly paper, styled the *People's Journal*, was started. A number of the leading business men in town assisted them in purchasing a new Taylor Cylinder press and an outfit of type and material for the newspaper. The first regular issue of this paper was dated September 5th, 1868. Its editor was Rev. P. Franklin Jones, who was also pastor of the Fair Haven Baptist church, and H. Seward Grose, Mr. Jones' son-in-law, was publisher. A part of the second story of Norman Peck's dwelling, and the second story of his new building, adjoining the drug store, were occupied as the printing office. After being connected with the paper a few months, Mr. Jones retired from the editorial chair, and Mr. Grose became editor as well as publisher.

In the summer of 1869, payments not being promptly made, the office fell into the hands of the citizens who had assisted them, by whom it was sold, in July, 1869, to DeWitt Leonard and E. H. Phelps, who continued the publication of the paper, under the firm name of Leonard and Phelps, the name of the paper having been changed to *The Fair Haven Journal*, E. H. Phelps, editor. This paper is still being published by these gentlemen, and has obtained a good circulation in Rutland and Addison counties and the neighboring towns in New York state.

MILITARY AFFAIRS.

While military affairs occupied a prominent place in the attention of the inhabitants in former years, we find but slight historical record of the early military transactions of our townsmen. In the Grand Lists of 1792 and '93, a number of persons are marked as belonging to the artillery, and others as cavalrymen, in consideration of which they were entitled to some allowance, or deduction in the Grand List. In 1802, a large number are mentioned in connection with the militia, and in consequence thereof, their lists for state taxes are $20,00 less than their lists for town taxes.

Regimental reviews seem to have been held in high esteem among the institutions of the early times, as is indicated in the specimen copy of the license for retailing liquors on the 14th, 15th and 16th of June, 1802, printed in Appendix V. Besides this review of the regiment, there was also the annual June training day with its election of company officers, inspection and drill, and its ginger-bread and molasses candy, which some of us who are yet young, hold among our boyhood remembrances, in this as in other towns. This military institution prevailed until a comparatively recent time.

In October, 1807, a meeting was called " to see if

HISTORY OF FAIR HAVEN, VERMONT. 238

the town will vote a tax to raise money to purchase ammunition to fill our magazines, as the law directs." On the 4th of November the town voted a tax of five mills on the dollar, to be collected and paid into the treasury on the 1st day of January next, to procure powder, lead, flints, &c., for the town stock of ammunition for the militia of said town." The only other record like this in the doings of the town, is a vote passed in April, 1822, " to allow Jo. Kingsland for chest for town magazine, $1.50."

In September, 1812, Salmon Norton addressed the following note to the selectmen: " Whereas I am detached for a campaign in the war, it is inconsistent for me any longer to do the duty of constable and collector for the town of Fair Haven; therefore you will accept this as my resignation, and govern yourselves accordingly."

We have no account of any others who went from Fair Haven into the war that year, but it is probable there were others, since Mr. Norton was Major in a regiment of enlisted Vermont troops, stationed at Burlington, under the command of Gen. Jonathan Orms, with whom Major Norton went out as Adjutant, but came home in January, and sickened and died. We have the list of the names of 35 men who composed the military company, and were returned as equipped for duty, in Fair Haven, in June, 1813. Of this company Peter Merritt was Captain.

In 1814 and '15, there are 42 names returned, and Moses Colton is Captain.

At the time of the battle of Plattsburgh, in Sep-

239 HISTORY OF FAIR HAVEN, VERMONT.

tember, 1814, a large company of men is said to have been enlisted in the town to go to the assistance of the American army. Moses Colton was Captain, or Colonel; Harvey Church 1st Lieutenant, and Royal Dennis 2d Lieutenant. One account is that the company was partly enlisted in the night time, and started on the way, going as far as Benson before morning. When within a few miles of Plattsburgh, a messenger with a flag of truce, came out and informed them that the battle was over, and they marched home, Elisha Parkill receiving a wad in his foot in a sham fight. Another report is that the company went as far as Whiting only, when they were met by runners informing them that the battle was fought, and there was a great division, or contention among the men on the question of advancing or retreating.

Several men from the town are said to have been in the army at Plattsburgh as substitutes, and Andrew Race was taken back by Charles Leonard, as a deserter, and was shot.

For a period of some twenty years the militia of the state was disbanded, and military parades did not occur among us.

On the breaking out of the great rebellion and civil war in 1861, the call to arms was made in our streets, and a number of our young men were enlisted. A company of cavalry volunteers was recruited in the town by DeWitt Leonard, in the summer of 1861, and was encamped for a time in barracks erected on the land of Zenas C. Ellis, north-west of his residence.

In the summer of 1862, a company was recruited

HISTORY OF FAIR HAVEN, VERMONT.

here by James T. Hyde, and encamped in barracks near Mr. Ellis'.

The town had credit with the United States Government for the following named persons as volunteer soldiers, most of them, but not all, residents of the town.

VOLUNTEERS FOR THREE YEARS, CREDITED. PREVIOUS TO CALL FOR 300,000, OCTOBER 17, 1863.

NAME.	REG.	COMP'Y.	AGE.	ENLISTED.	REMARKS.
Bonville, Adolphus	7	C	18	Jan. 7, '62	Re-enlisted Feb. 24, 1864.
Callagan, Jeremiah	11	C	29	July 25, '52	Deserted May 20, 1863.
Cantine, Geo. A.	7	C	21	Dec. 30, '61	Ser. Discharged Sept. 13, '62.
Davis. Henry	cav	H	22	Oct. 7, '61	Discharged June 18, 1862.
Dowling, Samuel	cav	H	28	Sept. 30, '61	
Gilbert, Edward	11	C	28	Aug. 11, '62	Tr. to Inv. Corps March 15, '64
Lee, Moses F.	11	C	21	Aug. 9, '62	Prom. corp. Oct. 10, '63. Mus. out June 24, '65.
Lefevre, Eli	7	C	27	Jan. 8, '62	Re-enlisted Feb. 15, '64.
Lefevre, John	7	C	21	Jan. 7, '62	" " 23, '64.
Lescarbean, Joseph	11	C	37	Aug. 11, '62	Deserted Sept. 5, 1862.
Macomber, John H.	11	C	26	Aug. 12, '62	Prom. 1st Lt. Co. L, July 11, '63
Manchester, Geo. W.	1ss	F	25	Sept. 11, '61	Discharged July 29, 1862.
Mather, Asa F.	11	C	24	Aug. 9, '62	Cor., prom. to Q. M ser. Dec. 28, '63, to 2d Lt. Co. C May 13, '65
Mather, Emmet	cav	H	21	Oct. 5, '61	1st Lt. July 6, '63.
Nichols, Henry C.	1ss	F	25	Sept. 11, '61	Discharged Oct. 31, '62.
Patch, David A.	2	B	26	June 1, '61	Prom. Corp. Oct. 22, '61. Dis. Sept. 14, '63.
Pelkey, David	11	O	33	Aug. 8, '62	Prom. Corp.
Pelkey, Joseph	7	C	20	Jan. 11, '62	Re-enlisted Feb. 26, '64.
Pelkey, Lewis	11	C	21	Aug. 9, '62	
Pocket, John	11	C	27	" 11, '62	
Proctor, Oscar C.	2ss	E	19	Oct. 8, '61	Discharged March 22, '62.
Proctor, William H.	2ss	E	21	" " "	Ser. To Inv. corps Dec. 31, '63.
Riley, Michael	7	C	25	Jan. 7, '62	Musician. Re-en. Feb. 23, '64.
Sheldon, Josephus	2	B	22	May 17, '61	Discharged April 24, 1862.
Sutliff, Emmons H.	7	C	18	Dec. 30, '61	Mustered out Aug. 30, 1864.
Smith, Albert	11	C	18	Aug. 9, '62	
Williams, Griffith	2	B	28	May 12, '61	Deserted Oct. 24, 1862.
Wood, Myron	11	C	18	Aug. 9, '62	Pro. cor. Aug. 2, '63. Ser. D'c. 28
Wood, Zebedee	7	D	18	Dec. 11, '61	Died Dec. 19, 1862.
Young, Moses	11	O	80	Aug. 8, '62	

241 HISTORY OF FAIR HAVEN, VERMONT.

CREDITS UNDER CALL OF OCTOBER 17, 1868, FOR 300,000, AND SUBSEQUENT CALLS.

NAME.	REG.	COMP'Y.	AGE.	ENLISTED.	REMARKS.
Bro, Peter	11	C	21	Dec. 12, '63	To Co. B, June 24, '65. Mustered out Aug. 25, '65.
Chase, Theodore	cav	H	21	" 7, '63	Saddler. To Co.B, June 21,'65.
Dempsey, Michael Jr.	17	I	18	Mar. 28, '64	Died March 27, '65.
Dicklow, Joseph	11	C	25	July 19, '64	Trans'd to Co. B, June 24, '65. Mustered out Aug. 25, '65.
Dicklow, Medrick	11	C	18	" " "	Trans'd to Co. B, June 24, '65. Mustered out June 29, '65.
Dicklow, Paul	11	C	19	" " "	Trans'd to Co. B, June 24, '65. Mustered out Aug. 25, '65.
Duggan, James	9	B	29	Dec. 8, '63	Died Nov. 6, '64.
Foy, Patrick	11				
Forget, George	11	C	25	" 7, '63	
Gallipo, Joseph	11	C	21	Nov. 26, '63	W'd. In gen. hos. Aug. 31,'64.
Hogan, Michael	cav	D	19	Dec. 7, '63	
Marks, Walter S.	17	I	18	April 27 '64	To vet. res. corps Oct. 11, '64. Mustered out July 14, '65.
Hawkins, Wm. C.	11	C	18	Dec. 1, 63	Died of w'ds rec'd in action. July 14, 1864.
Hooker, Edward T.	8	A			
Hunter, Robert	11				
Kelley, Eugene A.	1st	F	20	July 5, '64	Died Aug. 17, '64.
Monroe, Joseph H.	11	K	28	Dec. 9, '63	Prisoner, June 28, '64.
Pelkey, Charles	7	I			
Plumtree, John	7	I			
Preston, Henry	11	C	21	Dec. 4, '63	Sick in hos. Aug. 31, '64. Des.
Rudd, Thomas	9	B	25	" 28, "	Died January, 11, 65.
Stewart, Charles W.	54	Mas			
Woodward, Adrian T.	17	I	18	Mar. 25, '64	Mustered out June 6, '65

VOLUNTEERS FOR ONE YEAR

NAME.	REG.	COMP'Y.	AGE.	ENLISTED.	REMARKS.
Brown, Robert	54	Mas		Mar. 24 '65,	
Calvert, G. D.	11	C			
Capen, Nathan S.	11	C	24		
Dolby, Cyrus	54	Mas		Aug. 3, '64	Co. B. Must. out June 24, '65.
Granger, Nelson	7	C			
Hummerston, Henry	11	C			
Hunter, George	54	Mas			
Hunter, Samuel	54	Mas			
Manchester, Burr B.	11				
Murphy, James	7	D	18	Dec. 17, '61	Died March 29, 1864.
Ormsbee, Mansel A.	5				
Parret, Moses	7	C			
Sager, Charles W.	11	L			

HISTORY OF FAIR HAVEN, VERMONT. 242

VOLUNTEERS RE-ENLISTED, BELONGING TO 7TH REGIMENT, CO. C.

Adolphus Bonville, Eli Lefevre, John Lefevre,
Joseph Pelkey, Michael Riley,

PERSONS WHO FURNISHED SUBSTITUTES.

Charles Clark, W. B. Esty, Benj. S. Nichols.

NAVAL CREDITS.

Hiram Kilbourn, Granville C. Willey.
Not credited by name, three men.

VOLUNTEERS FOR NINE MONTHS.

Bosworth, Julius H.
Cowley, James B.
Crowley. Cornelius
Davey, Vincent C.
Foy, Patrick
Grady. Michael
Hamilton, Joel W.
Hamilton, William H.
Harrison, Charles

Humphrey, John
Humphrey Patrick
Lee, Benj. E.
Lewis, Richard
Marnes, Andrew
Maynard, English L.
O'Brien, Patrick
Perkins, Charles
Perkins, John F.

Rafferty, James
Reardon, Daniel
Roberts, Wm. S.
Rowland, John
Ware, Dallas N.
Whitlock, Hiram E.
Williams, John H.
Williams, Wm. E.
Wood, Leman

This company was enlisted in the summer of 1862 ; encamped and drilled at Castleton ; Joseph Jennings, Captain, Julius H. Bosworth, 1st Lieutenant, and Charles A. Rann, 2d Lieutenant ; mustered into the U. S. service, at Brattleboro, October 21st, as company F, of the 14th regiment of Vermont volunteers, and left the state October 22d. The regiment did service in the Army of the Potomac, in Virginia, during the winter, and took an active and honorable part in the battle of Gettysburg, in July, 1863, 1st Lieutenant Bosworth receiving a severe wound in the leg from the fragments of a shell, and Wm. H. Hamilton, who was leading another company, being mortally wounded and dying on the field.

The residue of the Fair Haven volunteers returned to their homes.

243   HISTORY OF FAIR HAVEN, VERMONT.

PERSONS WHO PAID COMMUTATION UNDER DRAFT.

Donnelly, James
Eddy, John W.
Ellis, Edgar S.
Jones, Robert W.

Kidder, Rollin M.
Lee, Wesley
Ranney, Oliver K.
Ryan, John

Sutliff, C. Wesley
Stannard, Edward J.
Taber, Abraham S.
Williams, John J.

VOLUNTEERS FOR ONE YEAR, REPORTED AFTER SEPT. 30, 1864.

Belden, Homer
Pickett, Lewis

Collins, Wm. W.
West, William A.

Maynard, English L.

All belonging to 7th Reg., Co. C, except Homer Belden, who belonged to the 5th Reg't.

PERSONS WHO SENT SUBSTITUTES.

Adams, Andrew N.
Ellis, Reuben T.

Preston, Wm.
Reed, Corril

Wicker, Abraham C.

PERSONS ENLISTED BY DE-WITT LEONARD.

Allard, Nelson, Fair Haven.
Brown, Henry W., Wells.
Burnett. Chas. F., Burlington.
Boyce, Geo. Castleton, or Poultney.
Bidwell, Edward.
Campbell, Robert G., Benson.
Combs, Nelson, Middletown.
Craig, Walton R., Putnam.
Conger, Jonas, Castle'n, or Hubbard'n.
Conger Seymour, " " "
Campbell, Fred H., Fair Haven.
Case, Chas. C., Middletown.
Carr, John W., Whitehall.
Davis, Geo. E., West Haven.
Dolphin, Wm. Middletown.
Douglass, Wm. H. H., Whitehall.
Flanders, Wallace M.
Fogerty, John J.
Grover, Wm., Middletown.
Green, Horace C., "
Gleason, Richard, Fair Haven.
Henry Joseph F.
Hamilton, Thomas, Hampton,
Henshaw, Edgar B., Middletown.

Ingram. Geo. H.
Lee, John J., Hampton.
Mallory, Geo.   "
McIllvaine, Orson, "
Maranville, Rollin C., Poultney.
Parker, Wm. H.
Parks, Robert H., Wells.
Parks, Horace M., Hydeville.
Pugh. Robert, Fair Haven.
Parris, Merritt, Middletown.
Rice Owens.
Searles, Wm. H. H., Hampton.
Stygles, James H., Brandon.
Schollar, Wm., Middletown.
Sherman, Ezra J., Clarendon.
Smith, Hubert A.
Taber Emerson, Fair Haven.
Wheeler. Geo. R
Warren, Chauncey C., Hampton.
Whiting, Abram W.
Wescott. Cyrus H., Hampton.
Warner, Geo. M.
Whiting, Joseph S.
Willey, Granville C., Lt., Fair Haven.

The above named persons were enlisted by De-Witt Leonard, for the Harlan Cavalry, at Fair Haven,

HISTORY OF FAIR HAVEN, VERMONT. **244**

in August and September, 1861. They were mustered into the "Harlan Cavalry" as Vermont Volunteers,
at Albany, September 24th, whence they went on to
Philadelphia, and were afterwards ordered to Washington and attached to the Harris Light Cavalry, under
Col. Davies, Gen. Kilpatrick being then Lieut. Col.
of the Regiment.*

Bounties paid by the town to volunteers and soldiers in the war of 1861–5, exclusive of donations
made to members of James T. Hyde's company.

```
To the 27 nine months' men and 5 others who enlisted, $60 each, $2120,00
To volunteers under the call of Oct. 1863, as follows :
          18 received $500 each,            $9,000
           2    "     300   "                  600
           2    "     100   "                  200
           1    "                              700
                                                        10,500,00
To volunteers for one year, from $300 to $800 each : total,   5,915,00
To substitutes,                                               1,383,38
To volunteers for one year reported after Sept., 1864, $400 each, 2,000,00
To volunteers re-enlisted, $100 each,                          500,00
To substitutes in 1865,                                      4,000,00

                              Total,                       $26,368,38
```

---

* Concerning this Company Mr. Leonard says : "The men were mustered
in at Albany, by Col. Sprague, U. S. A., as "Vermont Volunteers for the Harlan Cavalry," and went on to Philadelphia. The General Order from the War
Department which turned over the organization of regiments to the executives
of the different states was issued at this time, and received the next morning
after their arrival in Philadelphia. Under this order all incomplete organizations were directed to report to their respective Governors. Came back immediately, with report from Col. Harlan to Gov. Fairbanks. Reported to him
personally, and made every effort to have the men transferred to a Vermont
Regiment, (as the other Companies of the same Regiment had been transferred
by the Governors of the states from which they came,) but he neglected to act
in the matter. Meantime the men had gone on to Washington, and were attached to the Harris Light Cavalry."

SCHOOL AFFAIRS.

The town of Fair Haven was first divided into three school districts in May, 1785, as follows: The territory between "Muddy brook" and Hubbardton river constituting the First District; that south of Muddy brook the Second; and that west of Hubbardton river the Third. In September, 1788, Daniel Munger, who resided on the north and west of Muddy brook, was by vote set from the Middle to the South District, and Thomas Dickson was elected trustee for the North District; Michael Merritt for the Middle, and Col. Matthew Lyon for the South.

Tilly Gilbert, who first came to Fair Haven this season, was employed by Col. Lyon as a teacher, and it is not improbable that the old plank school house, the first in the village, was built by Col. Lyon about this time. It stood on the ground south of the old meeting house, and after the building of the new house, in 1805, was sold to Jacob Davey, who moved it to the side hill just above C. C. Whipple's present residence, where he used it for a store and office. The moving was conducted by Joel Hamilton, Esq., who went above in the building and put his hand out of the chimney hole, to give orders to the men and oxen.

HISTORY OF FAIR HAVEN, VERMONT.   246

In September, 1789, it was voted to divide the first, or middle school district, by a line east and west, near Dan Smith's house, the district so made, south of this line and north of Mud brook, to be called the fourth district.

The next record we find is of the March meeting in 1793, the year after the division of the town, when Samuel Stannard was chosen trustee for the north school district, and Dr. James Witherell for the south district; but in the following month, June, 1793, it was voted that "the south part of the town be set off for a school district, from where an east and west line strikes the fork of the road that leads to Mr. John Meåcham's." This fork of the road must have been in the vicinity of Mr. Ellis' present residence. Under Dr. Witherell, as trustee, John Brown, a young man of cultivation and refinement, from Rhode Island, and a brother-in-law of Ethan Whipple, Esq., appears to have been employed as teacher in the village district. Mr. Brown was a beautiful penman, and made the records of the town for Dr. Witherell, who was town clerk for the year 1792. Mr. Brown himself was chosen town clerk in 1793, and continued till February, 1801.

At the March meeting of 1794, it was voted "that there be a new school district established, to be called the North-East school District, and that the south-west corner of the lot of land laid out on Israel Smith's right, be the south-west corner of said school district, and that a parallel line north, 10° east, and another east, 10° south, divide said district from the other dis-

5

247   HISTORY OF FAIR HAVEN, VERMONT.

tricts." Afterwards it was voted "that the North-East school District should extend southward so far as to take in Mr. Abraham Sharp's house and improvements, and so far west as to include Asahel Munger's farm."

Thus in the second year after the division of the town, the four school districts of the present town were all in existence. Changes of boundaries were subsequently made, as we shall see, but no record of the numbering of the districts is to be found.

Of those who taught school in the village district, at an early day, besides Mr. Gilbert and Mr. Brown, already named, we are told of one Bolles, an Irishman, who, besides teaching in Fair Haven, taught also, prior to 1803, one year, near the old Episcopal church, on Hampton hill, and two years in Poultney, Rev. Dr. N. S. S. Beaman and Hon. Rollin C. Mallory, attending his schools and fitting for college under him. A man from Poultney, by the name of Cloudin, is said to have taught here, and also Charles Hawkins, Jr., prior to the year 1805. Rev. Dr. Beaman taught in the old log school house, south of the meeting house, as may be seen by his letter at the close of this part, in the winter of 1803 '04. Ethan Whipple, clerk of the district, makes return in March, 1804, that there are 52 children in the district of sufficient age to attend school. Tilly Gilbert, clerk of the district, returned the number as 44, for the years 1799 and 1800.

Elias Hickok says he taught a school one winter in the old school house on the Green, and had 97

HISTORY OF FAIR HAVEN, VERMONT. 248

scholars for six weeks. He also taught the first school in the new school house, which was built in the summer of 1805. At a town meeting, January 12, 1803, Charles McArthur was chosen a trustee for the N. E. District ; Henry Ainsworth for the South District ; James Witherell for the Middle District, and Joel Hamilton for the N. W. District, and as late as 1812 we find trustees were chosen in town meeting for the several districts as follows: In the Middle District, Tilly Gilbert ; in the South District, Eleazer Claghorn; in the N. W. District, Joel Hamilton; in the N. E. District, Charles McArthur.

At the town meeting of March 6th, 1805, it was voted "that the Middle school District in Fair Haven have liberty to set a school house on the public ground near the meeting house, the spot to be established by a committee to consist of Joel Hamilton, Sam'l Stannard and Silas Safford." This committee agreed on a report, March 14th, as follows: "We, the subscribers, being appointed a committee to fix a place for a school house near the meeting house, on the land that Col. M. Lyon deeded to the town of Fair Haven, have attended to the business of our appointment, and do now report that, in our opinion, the school house ought to be built on the east line of the six rod square piece that lies north-east of the meeting house, and that the south end of said school house ought to be set parallel with the south side of the Widow Margaret Norton's now dwelling house."

JOEL HAMILTON,
SAMUEL STANNARD, } Com.
SILAS SAFFORD,

HISTORY OF FAIR HAVEN, VERMONT.

This report, Mr. Joel Hamilton informs us in his carefully kept diary, was reconsidered on the 24th of March, the school house being located, as we elsewhere learn, a little further west, and perhaps, also north of the spot first reported. But even this did not give general satisfaction, and in November, 1811, on the 21st day, as Mr. Hamilton states it, at which time preparations were making to build the new church, the school house was moved, and probably to the place at the north-west corner of the six rod square lot, where it stood when taken down, in 1842.

This new school house was a large square building, with a steeple and belfry on the west side, or end, containing a bell, presented to the district, or town, by Christopher Minot, Esq., and the same bell which is now on the town hall and school house. The house was painted yellow without, and had an entry-way in the south-east corner, a closet in the north-east, and between them, in the east end, a semi-circular desk and raised platform. The scholars' desks were placed around the outside of the room, facing inward. Rev. Rufus S. Cushman says of this house: " The old yellow school house I remember well, whose chief external attraction was the belfry, in which hung, for a long time, the only bell in town, and the steeple, whose weather vane was a fish, the mark of many a snowball."

This house, made of wood, stood until 1842, and was the scene of many a large singing-school, scholars' exhibition, and temperance and political rally.. In the absence of any town hall it was used for meetings of

HISTORY OF FAIR HAVEN, VERMONT. 250.

every kind and name. Its place was supplied by a brick building, smaller on the ground, but of two stories in height, built a little to the eastward of the first, by Adams Dutton, Esq., in 1842. This third school house, not answering the wants of the district, was removed in 1861, and the present school building, under the town hall, was erected in the summer of 1861, the building committee, acting in conjunction with the town committee, to build a town house, being Joseph Adams, Increase Jones, and Hamilton Wescott.

It is instructive to note the analagous difficulties which attended the building of both these houses.

In the first case, a call was made in November, 1840, to see if the district would vote to build a school house, and at a legal meeting it was voted to build "a brick two story school house," and a committee was appointed to ascertain and report the probable expense. The committee consisting of Adams Dutton, Joseph Adams and Azel Willard, Jr., reported at an adjourned meeting in December, the estimated expense to be $800, and the district voted "not to except [accept] the report."

It was then voted to build a brick school house, one story high, with two rooms on the ground floor; said house to be 40x24 feet, and finished according to a plan exhibited to the meeting. Azel Willard, Jr., and John D. Stannard, were chosen a committee to build the house in the early part of the ensuing summer. It was voted " to purchase the land of William G. Howard, and build the said school house thereon, the land

251 HISTORY OF FAIR HAVEN, VERMONT.

laying west of the meeting house horse-sheds, and extending as far as Dr. Smith's east line." Other votes were taken in regard to the old house, and a tax, but no further action appears to have been made until October, 1841, when it was voted "to alter the size of the contemplated school house to 22x34 feet," and at an adjourned meeting it was voted "to rescind all former votes taken to build a school house."

Another meeting was then called, and a committee, consisting of Wm. C. Kittredge, Lucius Smith and Azel Willard, Jr., was chosen to draft a plan and report the expense of building a two story school house. The committee reported in November the estimated cost of a brick building 34x22 feet, with walls 17 feet high, at $650 34; and it was voted to accept the plan and build according to it, the house to be located "on the highest ground between the present school house and the meeting house, extending north 10 feet into Mr. Howard's land," and the committee were authorized to purchase the necessary land of Mr. Howard.

On the 20th of August, 1842, William G. Howard, who owned the land just back, or north of the old school house, deeded to the district a strip of 25 feet in width, running west from the west end of the meeting house sheds 50 feet.

Wm. C. Kittredge was chosen to superintend the building of the house, and he was authorized to let it out to the lowest bidder, not exceeding $600 and the old school house.

In the case of the last, or present school house, the call was made in March, 1860, and A. Allen, Otis

HISTORY OF FAIR HAVEN, VERMONT. 252

Eddy, and Adams Dutton, were appointed at a legal meeting, a committee to estimate and report the expense of building a school house in connection with the contemplated town hall. The committee reported through Mr. Dutton, at an adjourned meeting, that it was not advisable to build in connection with the town, and that in their opinion there was a sufficient number of scholars in the district to warrant a division of the district into two. The meeting adopted the report.

Another meeting was called in July to see if the district would build a school house in connection with the town hall. A motion to build was carried by yeas and nays, and by division of the house. A committee of five was chosen to inquire into' the expediency of maintaining the unity of the district, of supporting a graded school, and of meeting with the town in building a school house. The committee appointed were Adams Dutton, I. T. Milliken, I. C. Allen, C. C. Whipple, and Otis Eddy. The chairman of the committee made a report in favor of dividing the district; the majority reported against division, and in favor of uniting with the town to build a school building. This report was finally, after a second adjournment, adopted July 23d, and a tax was voted and a building committee appointed. A call was made for a meeting, August 29th, to rescind the vote, but no action was taken under it.

At a meeting held April 15th, 1805, it was "voted that the following in future be a division line between the Middle and South school Districts, in Fair

253 HISTORY OF FAIR HAVEN, VERMONT.

Haven : Beginning at the south-east corner of a piece of land conveyed this day by Tilly Gilbert to Salmon Norton, and is generally known by the name of the Handy lot, thence on the south line of said lot westerly to the south-west corner thereof, thence to the south-east corner of Beriah Rogers' home lot, thence on his south line westerly to his south-west corner, thence to the north-east corner of Thomas Dibble's home lot, thence following his north line to Poultney river."

In March, 1810, it was voted in town meeting that "the bounds of the North [west] school district be from the mouth of Mud brook up the east branch of said stream till it strikes the east line of Joseph Sheldon's land, thence north to the north line of the town, and thence westwardly and southerly in the line of the town to the bounds begun at."

At a meeting of the town held April 24th, 1824, the bounds of the N. E. school district were changed, and established as follows, " bounded north on the north line of Fair Haven, east on Castleton west line, west on the east line of the north school district, and south on a line drawn parallel with the original lots, as far south as the south line of the Appleton lot, where Jedediah Vaughan now lives."

We find occasional records of trustees chosen for the several districts by the town as late as 1827, in which year Oliver Kidder was chosen for the south district, and Daniel McArthur for the north-east district. At the March meeting of 1829, we find Jonathan Chandler, Benjamin F. Gilbert and Artemas S.

HISTORY OF FAIR HAVEN, VERMONT. 254

Cushman were chosen the first committee to superintend the schools. The following year the committee was re-chosen, Wm. C. Kittredge being substituted in the place of Jonathan Chandler. This committee was continued annually till 1833, Edward Lewis, Jr., serving in the place of Mr. Gilbert, in 1832.

After several unsuccessful applications for the purpose, Mr. Elias Hickok was set off to the West school District, in Castleton, March 28th, 1827, but the town refused to set off Benjamin Hickok, David Gibbs, and Samuel Smith, in the same manner.

In the March meeting of 1830, it was voted to set off to the South District so much of the Middle District as laid south of a line, "beginning on Poultney west line, and at the south-east corner of Eli Barber's farm, which is the south-east corner of a piece of land he has recently purchased of Jacob Davey; thence [running] west till it comes parallel with the east line of John P. Colburn's forty acre piece which was taken from the Durand farm; thence north 10° east, to the south line of the highway leading from Davey's works to H. Whitlock's; thence along the same westwardly to the Castleton river; thence up the same to the north line of the 1st and 2d divisions of the original right of Matthew Lyon; thence along the same, west 10° north, till it strikes the said river again; thence down the same to the State Line." At a subsequent meeting, held the 18th of March, this vote was formally rescinded.

Another meeting was called, and it was resolved in town meeting, April 12th, 1830, that the South school

255 HISTORY OF FAIR HAVEN, VERMONT.

District be bounded northerly as follows: "Beginning at the south-east corner of Eli Barber's land, on Poultney line; thence west on the line of said Barber's land to the south-west corner thereof; thence north on said Barber's west line to the south line of H. Whitlock's land; thence west on said line to the land of John P. Colburn; thence north on said Colburn's line to the highway; thence west of said highway to the bridge near the Slitting Mill; thence down Castleton river to the east line of H. & H. Howard's land; thence south to the south-east corner thereof; thence westerly on the south line of lands of Howard, Cushman, Cyrus Graves and Eli Graves, to Poultney river, providing that the inhabitants residing south of Castleton river, who have heretofore belonged to the Centre school District, shall have the right to send their children to school in said district through the ensuing summer, and have their proportion of the public money."

At a special meeting, called March 31, 1834, it was " voted that the line between the Centre school District and North-west District, dividing each from the North-east District, shall be as follows: From Castleton line, in the north line of the farm formerly owned by Benjamin Hickok, deceased; then west in the north line of said land, and in the north line of a farm formerly owned by Alanson Loveland, and in the north line of the farm now owned by Elijah Esty, and in the north line of lands occupied by Luke Warner, and in the north line of the 27 acre lot called ' the minister lot,' now Mr. Dutton's, to the east line of lands owned

HISTORY OF FAIR HAVEN, VERMONT.   256

by Tilly Gilbert; then north to the north-east corner of said Gilbert's land; then west in the north line of said Gilbert's land to Mud brook;- thence up Mud brook to Mill brook; thence up Mill brook to the Beaver Marsh; thence up the centre of Beaver Marsh to the outlet of the Upper Marsh, to the centre of the dam; from there a due north course to Benson line."

The first school house, in the South District, is said to have stood on the knoll south of Mr. Barnes', and west of the road; and it must have been built about the time the district was created, in 1793. The first record we find pertaining to the school, is a return of the number of scholars in the district from the year 1800 to the year 1807, made by Richard Beddow, Jonathan Cady, and David Brainard, as committee. The clerk's records begin in 1815, and in 1817 it was voted to take down the old chimney and provide a stove. The old chimney, saving brick sufficient for a new one, was sold to Lewis Maranville for $4.25. The fire shovel was sold to Barnabas Ellis, and the andirons to Asa Tyler. We find that one Harley Tuttle was teacher in 1815, and Obadiah French in 1816 and '17.

In May, 1830, it was voted to build a new school house, and Abner Ames, Samuel Wood, and Oliver Maranville, were chosen a committee to look up a site and report a plan for the new house. The committee reported to an adjourned meeting on the 24th of May, that they had procured a piece of land of Capt. Alonzo Safford, on the east side of the turnpike, near his north line, and would build the house of brick,

257 HISTORY OF FAIR HAVEN, VERMONT.

20x26 feet, with a woodhouse 10x14 feet. The report was accepted, and the building of the house was bid off by John P. Colburn, Esq., at $214, to be done by the middle of October. This house is yet standing on the west side of the highway, north of Mr. Kidder's. The old house was sold to Oliver Maranville for $8.50, he to move it off the land on which it stood.

A new and much improved brick school house is in process of erection at this present time—1870—on the new street recently opened by Messrs. Z. C. Ellis and Wm. L. Town, just west of Mr. Ellis' house.

ECCLESIASTICAL AFFAIRS.

The ecclesiastical action of the settlers of Fair Haven appears to have been begun in their capacity as a town organization, in the fall of 1786, when a town meeting was held at Samuel Stannard's, on the 5th day of September, Col. M. Lyon being moderator, and it was voted "*not* to divide the town into two societies;" the "societies" having the character, no doubt of "parishes," such as existed at that day under state laws in Massachusetts and Connecticut.

HISTORY OF FAIR HAVEN, VERMONT. 258

At another meeting, held at the same place, December 4th, Silas Safford, Esq., being moderator, it was voted "to hire a minister," and Thomas Dickson was chosen a committee "to treat with Benson committee how they shall proceed." A tax of two pence on the pound, on the list of 1786, was voted, and Joel Hamilton was chosen collector.

Nearly two years later a meeting was held at Philip Priest's house, September 2d, 1788, and Thomas Dickson, Dr. Simeon Smith, and Isaac Cutler, were chosen a committee to hire a minister to preach one-half the time at Matthew Lyon's, and the other half at, or near Eleazer Dudley's, and the committee are authorized to lay a tax to pay the minister. The March meeting of 1789, re-appointed the last year's committee to hire preaching.

In September, 1790, a meeting was held at the school house, near Mr. Samuel Stannard's, and these same individuals were appointed "a committee to hire preaching for the year ensuing, to the amount of £60, to be paid in grain, beef, pork or iron," and the selectmen are directed "to make a rate for the purpose, to be collected by the town collector." December 26th, 1791, it was voted "to dismiss the committee to hire preaching." We do not learn who was employed to preach to the inhabitants.

The first meeting house in the town, the same building that now constitutes Dan Orms' dwelling house, built, no doubt, mainly by Col. Lyon, though said to have been built by Deacon Daniel Munger, and which stood, at that time, in the public highway farther south

259   HISTORY OF FAIR HAVEN, VERMONT.

than now, must have been built in the year 1791, as the March meeting of 1792 was the first which was held in the meeting house. While used for a meeting house, this building was never plastered or finished, and was called by some the "Lord's barn." •

The first minister of whom we hear as hired to preach in this house, was a Rev. Mr. Farley, a young man whom Deacon Munger found in Poultney about 1803, or previously. He boarded with Maj. Tilly Gilbert while he was resident in the Lyon house, which stood on the ground of the Vermont Hotel.

A. Rev. Mr. Mills—Joseph Mills—appears to have been employed during the early part of the year 1805, preaching alternately every other Sunday in West Haven and Fair Haven. He preached his farewell discourse in West Haven, June 30th. On the 5th of July the church voted "that a call be given to Mr. Joseph Mills to take the pastoral charge of the church of Christ in Fair Haven and West Haven, and that Timothy Brainard and Asahel Munger be a committee to make out the call." But Mr. Mills did not choose to remain; and Rev. Silas Higley preached for a time in the last part of the year, and 'first part of 1806, the church voting, January 2d, that it was "expedient to give Silas Higley a call to settle as a pastor over this church and people." Paul Scott and Asahel Munger, were made a committee to present the call.

"The Church of Christ, in Fair Haven and West Haven," was formed November 15th, 1803, Rev. Dan Kent, of Benson, being moderator, and Asahel Munger, clerk. Another church was organized in West Haven, December 23d, 1816.

HISTORY OF FAIR HAVEN, VERMONT. 260

THE FIRST CONGREGATIONAL SOCIETY OF FAIR HAVEN

was organized January 2d, 1806. The first meeting being held at the school house; Asher Huggins, who resided in West Haven, was moderator, and Joel Hamilton was clerk.

Curtis Kelsey was chosen treasurer, and Timothy Brainard, Paul Scott and Calvin Munger, committee. Oren Kelsey was chosen collector, and it was "voted to give Silas Higley a call to settle as minister of the society, provided $300 can be raised for his salary.; he to have the $300 in six months after settlement, and hold it, provided he remain six years; if not, he to pay back $50 each year he falls short, and this to go back to the subscribers." Tilly Gilbert, Silas Safford and Roger Perkins were to be a committee to join the committee of the church in giving the call.

Mr. Higley did not remain, but the place was supplied by another candidate, Rufus Cushman, who had graduated from Williams College in 1805, and studied theology with Rev. Samuel Whitman, D. D. On the 18th of December, 1806, the society voted to give Mr. Cushman a call; "provided fifty pounds can be raised by subscription for his yearly salary, to preach one-half the time, and the sum of $200, as a settlement." Curtis Kelsey and Asahel Munger were appointed to extend the call on the part of the society. The church voted on the 19th to join in the call, and chose Asher Huggins, Timothy Brainard and Silas Safford, a committee to act in its behalf. Mr. Cushman was or-

261 HISTORY OF FAIR HAVEN, VERMONT.

dained and installed February 12th, 1807. The society voted, at a meeting held at Maj. Gilbert's house, January 19th, to raise $20, to defray the expense, and to request Dr. Selah Gridley to write an ode for the occasion, and Mr. Doolittle to form a tune for the same and to sing an anthem at the close, if agreeable to the Council.

On the 19th of April, 1810, application was made to Joel Hamilton, society's clerk, by Joseph Sheldon, Lewis Stone, and Tilly Gilbert "to warn a meeting of the Congregational Society to consider the propriety of building a new meeting house and to sell the old one." A vote was taken May 2d, to build a meeting house "for the use, benefit and accommodation of the First Congregational Society, in Fair Haven, to be denominated and known by the name of the First Congregational meeting house in Fair Haven," and a committee was chosen to prepare a plan and report the expense. The committee were Samuel Stannard, Tilly Gilbert, Thomas Wilmot, Jacob Davey, Moses Colton, Eleazer Claghorn, and Curtis Kelsey. This committee reported at an adjourned meeting, May 14th, that the cost of a house 53x40 feet, with 36 pews below, steeple, belfry, &c., similar to the Poultney Baptist meeting house, would be $2,400. The report of the committee was accepted, and the same committee were requested to "report at the next adjourned meeting the proper place to set said house;" to prepare a plan, and put a valuation on the pews, and they were authorized to sell the pews at public auction; "the said pews are not to

HISTORY OF FAIR HAVEN, VERMONT. 262

be sold under the said valuation, and [for] as much more as they will fetch, payable one-fourth part in cash in one year from the 1st day of September next; one other fourth part in materials, to be delivered on the spot of building by the 15th day of April next, and the residue payable in merchantable neat cattle, in three annual installments, to be delivered at the meeting house to be built, the first day of October, each year, commencing the 1st of October, 1811, or in grain, in each succeeding January."

The meeting adjourned to the 21st of May, and the committee again reported, "that they have not been able to obtain the piece of ground as yet, which seems best calculated to suit the Society to put the meeting house on; but as they still hope to obtain their wishes in this respect, have thought proper to postpone establishing the particular spot for the present, but do report, that in our opinion, it ought to be set within 20 rods either east or west from the old meeting house, and to face to the south, so that the pulpit shall be in the north end of said house."

It was voted to choose a committee of nine to superintend the building of the house, and to proceed with it as soon as the sum of $2,400 has been secured. The committee chosen were Tilly Gilbert, Samuel Stannard, Jacob Davey, Curtis Kelsey, Thomas Wilmot, Eleazer Claghorn, Joel Hamilton, Silas Safford, and Daniel Hunter.

The meeting voted that if the pews should sell for more than enough to finish the house, the committee should be authorized to apply such excess to the

263 HISTORY OF FAIR HAVEN, VERMONT.

purchase of a site, and to the purchase of a bell. There were sold 33 pews, the highest price paid being $170, by Thomas Wilmot, and the lowest $26, by Mr. Wilmot, and the total amount of sales $2,792.

A meeting in June authorized the committee to sell the remainder of the pews on the lower floor, at auction, on the first Monday in September, if not previously sold at private sale.

Joel Hamilton commenced drawing stone and timber for the house in January, 1811. The house was raised on the 10th day of May. In September a meeting was called to see if the committee should have the house painted. This meeting only directed that the committee should sell more of the pews, "or so much thereof as will raise $450, to be applied to finishing the said house." The high wind of the 20th of October blew down the steeple of the meeting house and other buildings, and the workmen were paid for replacing it.

The officers of the society, chosen at the annual meeting, December 31st, 1811, were Joel Hamilton, clerk; Curtis Kelsey, treasurer; Silas Safford and Timothy Brainard, committeemen, and Seth Persons, collector.

The house was dedicated on the 18th of June, 1812, Rev. Dr. N. S. S. Beaman preaching the dedicatory sermon, which was published. There are many now living who remember this old meeting house with its high galleries, tall pulpit, and square box pews, all made of the purest materials and ornamented in the highest style of workmanship, Elisha Scott and Lewis Stone being the principal workmen.

HISTORY OF FAIR HAVEN, VERMONT. 264

The house stood as finished, with the exception of·
a new pulpit put up in 1837 or '38, until about 1840,
when some of the timbers in the spire becoming
weak and unsafe, the spire itself was taken down by
Azel Willard, Jr., and the steeple finished with tur-
rets above the belfry, in which shape it stood until
about 1851, when the whole house was remodeled
by Charles Scott, son of Elisha Scott, and another
steeple was raised in the form in which it now stands.

Alexander Dunahue, who died in Castleton in August, 1814, had in his will bequeathed to the town of
Fair Haven "a bell, to weigh between 500 and 600,
for the use of the new meeting house in said town;
to be procured by my executor, if any estate remains
after my debts and other bequests are paid."

At a special meeting of the town, called for the
purpose, in November, 1830, Wm. C. Kittredge was
appointed an agent "on behalf of and for the town,
to attend to and take all proper and necessary measures, by law, or otherwise, to enforce and collect all
such claim or claims which such town has, or is supposed to have against the estate of Alexander Dunahue."

At another special meeting, held in June, 1831, it
was voted that the agent be authorized to compromise, settle and dischargethe claim on the Dunahue
estate, upon such terms as he shall think best; and
the selectmen were directed, in case a compromise
should be effected, "to forthwith take measures to·
procure a bell for the meeting house in Fair Haven,
weighing 600 pounds."

265 HISTORY OF FAIR HAVEN, VERMONT.

The compromise was effected by Dunahue's heirs deeding to the town in November, 1831, the house and barn and eight acres of land, which was sold by the selectmen to Alonzo Safford in April, 1832—the house where Mrs. Wm. Miller resides, and the land where the marble mill now stands.

We accordingly find in March, 1832, that Wm. C. Kittredge and Wm. B. Colburn were chosen a committee by the Congregational Society, to employ a man "to wring" the bell for the ensuing year. This bell, which was hung on a wooden yoke, and was rung with no small difficulty by the younger folk in the community, became cracked, and was removed and exchanged about 1840, by Azel Willard, Jr., for the bell which now swings in the belfry of the Congregational church.

The Rev. Mr. Cushman died February 3d, 1829. On the 22d day of April following, the church and society united in a call to Rev. Amos Drury, of West Rutland, to supply the vacancy in the pastorship occasioned by Mr. Cushman's death, and Mr. Drury accepted the call on the same day, and was installed on the 6th of May, the sermon being preached by Rev. Beriah Green, of Brandon, and the prayer of installation made by Rev. Josiah Hopkins, of New Haven. Mr. Drury's ministry continued until May, 1837.

On the 3d of August, 1838, the society instructed the standing committee to give Rev. Charles Doolittle a call to become pastor of the church and society, promising him a salary of $450, and the use of a parsonage as good as the place occupied by Mr. A. Allen.

HISTORY OF FAIR HAVEN, VERMONT. **266**

On the 31st of September, 1839, the society voted to hire Mr. Doolittle, "if he can be obtained, for the year ensuing."

The society voted, October 6th, 1840, to give Rev. Francis C. Woodworth a call to become the minister of the society, on a salary of $400, and the use of the parsonage from June previous.

Mr. Woodworth was installed over the society October 28th, 1840; dismissed on account of ill health, September 22d, 1841. He died June 5th, 1859, aged 45 years.

A committee was chosen February 10th, 1842, to hire Rev. Philo Canfield for two years, and Mr. Canfield preached in the town two or three years.

August 19th, 1844, the committee were instructed to hire the Rev. Mr. Hine "with or without a view to a settlement."

Rev. J. B. Shaw, of North Granville, N. Y., commenced supplying the pulpit in May, 1846, and received a call to settle as pastor, on a salary of $400 and the use of the parsonage, in January, 1847. He accepted the call, and was installed February 16th; Rev. Charles Walker, of Pittsford, preaching the sermon. Mr. Shaw was dismissed from his pastorship on the 13th of November, 1850, by a council called for the purpose.

The Rev. Mr. Wing preached as a candidate, in 1851. A call was given in April, 1852, to Rev. Rufus S. Cushman, of Orwell, to settle as pastor of the parish, which was declined. At the same meeting a vote was passed "to allow the church to be opened for preaching only by evangelical ministers."

267 HISTORY OF FAIR HAVEN, VERMONT.

A call was given to Rev. S. L. Herrick, of Crown Point, in October, 1852, to settle over the church and society, and Mr. Herrick became "the stated supply" of the pulpit from August, 1852, till October, 1855, when he removed with his family to Grinnell, Iowa.

Rev. Dr. Edward W. Hooker commenced preaching with the society in April, 1856, and was installed as pastor August 20th. It was voted, May 17th, to give him a salary of $500 and the use of the parsonage. He was dismissed from his charge, November 18th, 1862, and the pulpit was supplied from year to year by Rev. R. L. Herbert, of the Welsh Chapel, until the spring of 1869, he preaching one sermon on Sunday forenoon, and occasionally a discourse on Sunday evening.

The subject of providing a parsonage was first agitated at a meeting held October 7th, 1838, when a committee, consisting of A. Allen, A. H. Kidder, and O. Eddy, was chosen "to ascertain by examination, which of three places—the Colton place, the place where Mr. Drury lived, and the place where Mr. A. Allen now lives—is the best for a parsonage." The committee reported October 16th, in favor of "the place where Mr. Doolittle now lives," the same place previously occupied by Rev. Mr. Drury, and a committee was chosen to raise $800 by subscription for the purchase of the place. A. Allen, H. Hamilton, and C. W. Hawkins were chosen a committee, November 12th, to superintend repairs on the house. [For further particulars see p. 133.]

HISTORY OF FAIR HAVEN, VERMONT. **268**

METHODISM.

There were Methodists in the town at an early period. Some among the first settlers belonged to this persuasion, among whom we hear of the Ballards, Stephen Holt, and Joshua Holt, his son, in the south part of the town. Mr. Holt is said to have been very devoted to his religious exercises, and on one occasion, was praying very loud, on a dark night, under an apple tree, when two persons, Solomon Cleveland and Wales Fuller, who were passing at the time, disturbed their devotions by throwing clubs into the tree. Rev. Lorenzo Dow preached at Mr: Holt's house when he resided west of Mr. Kidder's present residence, about 1796 or '97.

Beriah Rogers is said to have had Methodist preaching at his house, he living where Mr. Z. C. Ellis now resides from 1797 to 1808. There probably were others who were favorable to some form of religion, and united with the Armenians of the time, who were then the liberal party, as opposed to the Calvinists, by whom the Methodists were, for many years, deemed heretics outside the pale of Christian recognition.

In 1827, Fair Haven formed part of a circuit with Castleton. Meetings were held once in two weeks in the school house, and the Rev. Mr. Hazleton was the preacher. He was succeeded by Rev. Joseph Ayers, by Rev. C. R. Wilkins, and by Rev. Mr. Stewart.

Fair Haven was afterward connected with East Whitehall, and was supplied for two years about

269 HISTORY OF FAIR HAVEN, VERMONT.

1838, by Rev. Albert Champlain. Rev. Joel Squiers supplied for two years, and a Rev. Mr. Cooper was supplying, assisted by Rev. Dr. Jesse T. Peck and others, from the Seminary at Poultney, when the subscription was raised to build the church about 1842 or '43.

The church was built in 1843, and the ministers who were sent here by the Troy Conference were the Rev. Mr. Graves, Rev. Matthias Ludlum, Rev. Godfrey Saxe, Rev. J. E. Bowen, Rev. Thomas Pierson, Rev. John Hasselum, Rev. David Osgood, Rev. Mr. Griffith, Rev. H. Ford, Rev. P. H. Smith, Rev. John Thompson, Rev. Hannibal H. Smith, Rev. A. Viele, and Rev. R. Fox. Rev. M. Ludlum has been stationed with the society twice. The first settled ministers were young unmarried men, and usually remained but one year. The later ones have been settled, most of them, two years each. Rev. H. H. Smith was here but one year. Rev. Mr. Fox has been with the society three years.

In 1853, the society bought land and erected a parsonage north of their church, Rev. Mr. Ford being here at the time. In 1867, under Mr. Fox's ministry, the church building was greatly enlarged and improved, and is now the largest in the place.

The society has received many accessions from people who have moved into the town, and is in a strong and flourishing condition.

HISTORY OF FAIR HAVEN, VERMONT.

WELSH RELIGIOUS MEETINGS.

Occasional religious services and preaching in the Welsh languagetook place in the town in the summer of 1851, Rev. Evan Griffiths, of Utica, and Rev. Thomas R. Jones, of Rome, N. Y., visiting the place during that season. Regular meetings were commenced at the school house early in the year 1853, Rev. Griffith Jones being the pastor. In 1857, " The Welsh Protestant Society of Fair Haven," erected a good brick church on the east side of Main street, costing about $3,500.

In the spring of 1859, Rev. G. Jones was dismissed, and removed to Cambria, Wis. Soon after his departure, a portion of the society left the church and built a new edifice on the opposite side of the street, and organized a society called " The Welsh Calvinistic Methodist." In January, 1860, Rev. R. L. Herbert, then of Utica, N. Y., accepted a call from the Fair Haven Welsh Protestant Society, and has continued the pastor of the society to the present time, 1870. The society is free from debt; has a membership of 95; an average attendance at its meetings of 170, and of 100 at the Sabbath school. Its services are conducted in the Welsh language, except one service in English on Sunday afternoons.

Of the Welsh Presbyterians, or Calvinistic Methodists, the Rev. Daniel T. Rowland, who came hither from Wisconsin, was pastor about 10 months. Rev. John Jones, from Wales, preached in Fair Haven and

271   HISTORY OF FAIR HAVEN, VERMONT.

Middle Granville alternately, about 2 years. Rev. E. W. Brown came hither from Alleghany College, Meadville, Pa., in the fall of 1865, and was pastor of the society about 3 years. He was succeeded in 1869 by Rev. Robert V. Griffiths, from Wales.

ST. MARY'S CATHOLIC CHURCH.

This church, a plain brick building, with the cross and marble tablet, standing at the north-east corner of the Green, was built in the summer of 1856, by the very Rev. Zephurin Druon, then of Rutland, to whom the lot, 88x72 feet, was deeded by James Dolan in the March preceding. It was conveyed by Zephurin Druon, in September, to Bishop Lewis Groesbraind, of Burlington.

The church was attended from Rutland by the Rev. fathers Druon and Lynch, until December, 1866, when the Rev. J. C. O'Dwyer was settled as the first resident Catholic pastor.

The foundations for a new church of very large dimensions, were laid on the west side of Washington street, sometime in 1868.

ST. LOUIS CATHOLIC CHURCH.

Rev. J. A. Boissonnault is now pastor of the church, supplying also the church at Orwell one Sunday in each month. This church was built in the fall of 1869, about $400 of the expense being raised from a Fair, holden at the town hall, and the balance by subscription.

HISTORY OF FAIR HAVEN, VERMONT. 272

THE BAPTIST CHURCH.

This society was organized December 14th, 1867, with 31 members, most of whom were from the church at Hydeville. Alonson Allen and I. N. Churchill were chosen deacons.

Meetings were first held in the chapel over Mr. Adams' store, and afterward in the town hall. Preaching was supplied for a time by Revs. L. Howard and O. Cunningham, of Rutland, and H. L. Grose, then of Ballston, N. Y. Rev. P. F. Jones became pastor of the society in June, 1868, and was dismissed after 10 months. Rev. D. Spencer became the pastor in September, 1869. The corner stone of the new church edifice, on the south side of the Common, was laid with religious ceremonies, on the afternoon of June 2d, 1870, addresses being delivered on the occasion by Revs. E. R. Sawyer, J. Freeman, W. W. Atwater, E. P. Hooker, J. Goadby, and by the pastor, Rev. D. Spencer.

The articles deposited in the corner-stone were as follows:

The articles of the Faith of the Church; the Constitution and By-Laws of the Church and Society, with the names of the Trustees and Building Committee; the name of the architect and builder; a list of the names of the subscribers towards the erection of this building; a history of the Sunday School connected with the Church, and the names of its officers; history of the Young Men's Christian Associa-

273   HISTORY OF FAIR HAVEN, VERMONT.

tion, of Fair Haven, with the names of its officers; History of Fair Haven, by A. N. Adams; Legislative Directory for 1867; Fair Haven *Journal*, Rutland *Herald*, New York *Tribune, Examiner and Chronicle, Watchman and Reflector;* collection of coins and stamps representing the currency of the country.

LETTER FROM REV. N. S. S. BEAMAN. D. D.

My Dear Sir: I taught a district school in Fair Haven in the winter of 1804, having a certificate of a Freshman's standing in Williams College, intending soon to join Middlebury College. But my knowledge of your town did not commence with my school, as my childhood was spent within 3 miles of your village, and I was 17 years old just before I commenced teaching in that place. The early inhabitants of Fair Haven I knew, as most boys know their near or more remote neighbors, the families by sight and by name, and the young folks more intimately.

I have kept no record except that of memory, and though blessed with a somewhat retentive and ready one, I can now give you only what may be reasonably expected from the hasty recollections of a man of 84 years of age.

I knew Col. Matthew Lyon, and when I was quite a small lad I was intimately acquainted with his family, especially with one of his sons, Chittenden, named, I suppose, from Governor Chittenden. We all familiarly called him "Chit." He was a bright boy, but inflammable and impulsive as a torpedo, or a witch-quill. I came very near becoming involved in an Irish row with him because I modestly declined pledging him in a "brandy smash," in modern improved

HISTORY OF FAIR HAVEN, VERMONT. 274

parlance, then called a "brandy sling," which he had paid as one of the heads of opposite parties in a game of base ball.

Of the other children of Col. Lyon I knew less than of "Chit," because we were about of the same age, he being less than one year older than myself. The family removed to Kentucky, then known as "the new State." I well remember watching the emigrant wagons as they passed through Hampton, making a fine display of their imposing white canvass, proclaiming their departure to the great unknown south-west. It was a thing to be remembered and talked about.

Col. Lyon's wife was highly spoken of, and they had one daughter famed for personal beauty and many accomplishments. My impression is that she and others died soon after arriving in Kentucky. Col. L. was a member of Congress from Vermont, and was re-elected from his new residence. He was a native of the Green Isle of the ocean, and possessed all the qualities of his race. He had talents but they were rough and unhewed from the quarry, and would have appeared more comely in the eyes of most men, if he had been subjected to the polish of the chisel.

As to Dr. Witherell, I knew him well for many years, as he was my father's family physician. He was a man of fine manly appearance, tall and well proportioned. In his profession he was considered among the first in the neighboring towns. He was agreeable in his manners, and inclined to be facetious in his visits to his patients, deeming a pleasant face one of the best potions he could possibly administer at his first visit. He was a man of considerable reading beyond his profession, and he had, as was said, several philosophical works of the French atheistical and deistical class, which were quite popular among certain politicians of that day. It has been asserted that

275   HISTORY OF FAIR HAVEN, VERMONT.

Prophet Miller, of Hampton, was in the habit of dipping into these works about the time of Mr. Madison's war with England, and that he was the expounder of Voltaire and other infidels before he engaged with Daniel and the other prophets. I record this from popular rumor and belief, and not from my own personal knowledge; but circumstances might be stated to confirm the position. That the future prophet was the pupil of the Doctor is well known.

I have said that Dr. W., while in Fair Haven, was inclined to facetiousness, and I may add to jocoseness or punning, for the purpose of confounding those who thought but little, or not at all. His associations were sometimes such as to puzzle a *philosopher* or a *fool*. I recollect he one morning came into my father's laughing heartily at the wonderment into which he had thrown a simple neighbor by saying to him: "Well, Mr. ——, it is *muggy*, *hot*, and *chilly* this morning." In analyzing the adjectives the man remained silent, and the Doctor left him at his task. He sometimes greatly amused and sometimes equally vexed his patients. He was a man of influence in his town, and I believe honored his office in Michigan as a United States Judge.

As a teacher of his children I had no other acquaintance with him than may be supposed to exist between a dignified father and a youthful pedagogue. I "boarded round," as was the custom. I was more intimate in some other houses. In this family it was *dignity* in life holding converse with youthful diffidence and reserve. In this connection I might name the family of Maj. Tilly Gilbert, who occupied the mansion once owned by Col. Matthew Lyon. Some of his children were in my school; Franklin, of your village, and Jarvis, once in the Presbyterian ministry. I felt a special interest in these lads because

HISTORY OF FAIR HAVEN, VERMONT.   276

their father had long been a special friend of my father, and he had not a little influence in getting the place for me in the Fair Haven district school. He was the most perfect gentleman, and I believe without reproach in all respects. In his house I always felt at home. I often go back to those days with great pleasure.

In this connection, with my school, I may mention the state of things in the town respecting learning and religion. The school house was just respectable and hardly that, but it was far better than the meeting house or the church. A traveler from another state is said to have asked a citizen "how far it was to the meeting house," and to have received the following reply: "The Lord has no house in Fair Haven, only an old barn which he intends to make do for the present winter." The reply was more pertinent than pious.

The school house and church stood very near their present positions, and we, teacher and scholars, passed three months without any marked disturbance; without any signal acts of tyranny on the one hand, or armed violence on the other. The names of my scholars I cannot give to any great extent.

Among the patrons of my school I may mention Mr. Munger and Mr. Dodge, a Baptist preacher, who seemed to maintain a kind of independent position in his relations. Two of his children, a son and a daughter, I well recollect. The girl was older than myself, and was the best scholar in the school, and the boy had a spice of his father's eccentricity. The lads made the fires by turns, and there had been some neglect on this subject, and we had suffered for several mornings in consequence. It was young Dodge's turn to make the fire in the morning. The preceding evening I gave strict orders to have the

277   HISTORY OF FAIR HAVEN, VERMONT.

former nuisance abated if the officer in charge had to set up all night and burn up the entire wood pile at the door. In the morning the sanctum was warm as the tropics, and little Dodge sat demurely studying his lesson in the corner.

I have spoken of the peculiarities of the elder Dodge. One anecdote used to be related in Fair Haven in that day, which may be forgotten now. The messenger of peace worked six days for his daily bread, and dispensed the gospel on the seventh. He was employed as a bloomer, [rather nailer,] in the Fair Haven Iron Works. One day a dispute took place between Elder Dodge and a fellow laborer, and after the preacher had invoked all the patience he had to his aid in vain, he threw down his tongs and straightened himself up to his full height, threw off his black coat, and said : " *Lie there, divinity*, till I do this man justice."

I heard the elder preach once in the school house, but never in the "Lord's barn," as it was then generally called, whether excluded by the elements or by church authority I am not able to say. He was a man of talents and wit. His son I met a few years since, in the town of Black Brook, in Essex county, N. Y. He is a respectable Baptist clergyman, and he very pleasantly reminded me of the incident of fire-making in the old school house in Fair Haven, in 1804—65 years ago.

     *   *   *   *   *   *

Of Mr. Cushman and his ministry I could say much, but you are no doubt well informed on these more recent events. Mr. Cushman was the much esteemed pastor of my first wife. She resided in West Haven, but was a member of the Fair Haven church. This settled minister accomplished a great and good work in your town.

Troy, N. Y., Oct. 5th, 1869.

9

PART III.

Biographical and Family Notices.

BIOGRAPHICAL AND FAMILY NOTICES.

JOSEPH ADAMS was born in Londonderry, N. H., February 1st, 1802. His ancestors were Scotch, and came to this country from the north of Ireland with the Scotch-Irish colony that settled in Londonderry in 1721. Scotch blood, with its peculiar accent and characteristics, is often prominent in the family circle. He immigrated with his parents in the fall of 1806 to Whitehall, N. Y. He married Stella Miller, a daughter of Wm. Miller, Esq., of Hampton, N. Y., Nov. 6th, 1823, and came to reside in Fair Haven in January, 1825, having purchased of Tilly Gilbert, in November previous, a piece of land on the north side of West street, adjoining the place owned by Chauncey Ward at that time, now Mr. Willard's.

To this lot he had removed in the fall of 1824, and fitted up for a dwelling house the store building which Erwin Safford had built on the place where James Miller's blacksmith shop now stands. The house is now occupied by Charles Clyne. Mr. Adams here resided and carried on his business of manufacturing boots and shoes for a number of years, having several men and apprentices in his employment meantime, among them Douglass Miller and Joseph and

282 HISTORY OF FAIR HAVEN, VERMONT.

Harris Whipple. In 1831, removing his family into a part of the old Dennis house, and selling his place on the West street, he built the brick store in the village, owned by Richard F. Lloyd, adjoining the present postoffice, then one story in height, and afterward raised to two, having in the preceding March purchased of Mrs. Lucy Wilmot a half acre of land, a part of which had been previously leased to Stephen H. Judkins, and on which Mr. Judkins then had a wagon shop standing where Mr. Whipple's house now does. In this brick store, or shop, Mr. A. carried on a large wholesale and retail business in manufacturing ladies' shoes, supplying most of the country merchants from Massachusetts to Canada line, for a number of years. He bought Mr. Judkins' shop in the fall of 1832, and fitted it up for a house, removing into it in January, 1833. He sold the place to Mr. Whipple, its present owner, in 1843, and removed to Racine, Wis. The house was burned down in the winter, and the house now standing was built by Mr. W. the following spring.

Mr. Adams returned from Wisconsin to Fair Haven in the spring of 1845, spending the preceding winter in Hampton, and entering into arrangements with Alonson Allen and Wm. C. Kittredge, for the introduction of the marble business into the town. To this business he gave his whole time and attention of its from the day inception, in felling the timber for the mill, for more than 20 years. For a number of years after its commencement the business proved unremunerative, and seemed likely, in consequence of

HISTORY OF FAIR HAVEN, VERMONT. 283

the great amount of unsound and worthless marble, and the many and large losses from bad debts, to break down in failure; but perseverance and energy saved it, and have carried it successfully through every financial crisis and strain.

Mr. Adams resided during one season after his return, where Mr. Goodwin now does, and then took possession of the place occupied at the present time by Wm. Dolan, which he had owned from 1842. In May, 1853, he purchased of John D. Stannard the old Lyon tavern house on the corner, and all the land south and west, where his own house and those of his son and daughter stand. He built his marble residence in 1860 and '61.

His son's dwelling house was built in the summer of 1861, and that of his daughter partly in 1862 and partly in 1865. His children were:

1. *Edwin R.*, b. Sept. 22, 1824; d. June 25, 1832.

2. *Oscar F.*, b. March 14, 1826; d. July 19, 1826.

3. *Ira M.*, b. May 13, 1827; d. June 9, 1833.

4. *Andrew N.*, b. Jan. 6, 1830; m. Angie M. Phelps, Aug. 1, 1855. Graduated at Cambridge Divinity School in Harvard University, July 17, 1855. Settled as pastor of the First Congregational Church in Needham, Mass., in September, 1855. Resigned in June, 1857. Became pastor of the First Universalist Society in Franklin, Mass., June 1, 1858. Resigned, and removed to Fair Haven, in the summer of 1860. Children: Alice A., Ada M., Annie E., and Stella A.

5. *Edwin S.*, b. Nov. 29, 1832; d. June 18, 1833.

6. *Helen M.*, b. June 16, 1834; m. David B. Col-

284   HISTORY OF FAIR HAVEN, VERMONT.

ton, Aug. 16, 1852. Children: Joseph E., and David B.

7. *John J.*, b. April 27, 1840·; drowned in the flume at the marble mill, Oct. 1, 1845.

8. *Joseph J.*, b. Nov. 30, 1845 ; d. Sept. 25, 1846.

THE ALLENS of this town are the children of Timothy Allen, Jr., whose father came from Woodbury, Conn., to Pawlet, in 1768. He, himself, was an early settler of Bristol, but removed to Hartford, N. Y., in 1814. His family were: 1. *Rufus*, the father of George. 2. *Richard*, the father of Ira C. 3. *Anna*, who married James Miller and settled in the north part of Fair Haven. 4. *Timothy*. 5. *Abigail*. 6. *Ira*. 7. *Barna*, a Baptist minister of Whiting and Hubbardton. 8. *Alonson*. 9. *Justus*.

IRA ALLEN, born in 1796, learned the tanner and currier's trade of a Mr. Cole, in West Granville, N. Y., and came to Fair Haven about 1817 or '18, settling in the north part of the town, near West Haven, where, in company with his brother-in-law, James Miller, he carried on his trade as a tanner and shoe-maker for some years, being engaged for two or three years previous to 1830, with Elizur Goodrich and others in the lumber business, then of considerable importance in the town. He married in 1830, Cornelia A. Smith, a daughter of Simeon Smith, and removed into the village in 1839 or '40, buying on the west side of the Common, where his widow and son, Simeon, now reside. He died on this place in 1862, leaving three children : 1. *Lucy S.*, who married Marcus B. Dewey.

HISTORY OF FAIR HAVEN, VERMONT. 285

2. *Simeon*, who is now engaged in the slate works near the depot. 3. *Elizabeth M.*, living with her mother.

ALONSON ALLEN, born in Bristol, Aug. 22, 1800; removed to Hartford, N. Y., with his father in January, 1814. When 23 years of age he kept a grocery store one year in Whitehall, near the old stone store, on the steamboat wharf. Returning to Hartford in 1824, he was employed as a clerk for Joseph Harris until the spring of 1828, when he entered into co-partnership with Mr. Harris for the term of four years, and conducted the business alone the last two years of the time. He engaged for a time in business with Mr. E. B. Doane, to whom he sold out, and spent several weeks, in company with four other persons, in the summer of 1835, traveling in central and western New York, and into Erie county, Penn. On his way back, he purchased a house and store in Conesus, Monroe county, whither he went in October following, with a stock of merchandise, leaving his family in Hartford. At the end of three months he sold out house, store, and goods, and returning to Hartford, came in March, 1836, to Fair Haven, where he purchased of Luke Beaman the store of goods which Beaman had in the old store building where the new bank now stands.

Bringing his family in April, he lived two months in the house east of the church, and then took up his residence on the place where Griffith Williams resides, purchasing the place in December, 1838, of Nathan B. Haswell, of Burlington, and exchanging it with

286 HISTORY OF FAIR HAVEN, VERMONT.

Dennison Willard, in February, 1839, for the house which he now occupies.

He kept the store and postoffice at the old stand for many years. In January, 1838, he leased the Iron Works of J. Davey, for five years, and carried them on until they were burned down, March 17th, 1842. He removed his store into the old Dennis house, on the corner, after it was remodeled by John J. Davey, in the summer of 1838, and there also kept the post-office about three years. There are few, probably, now in the town, who remember the appearance of the old Dennis tavern after it was transformed by Mr. Davey, and until taken down and rebuilt by Leonard Williams in 1845 and '46.

Removing back to the old stand during Mr. Williams' renovation, Mr. Allen again took possession of the new store on the corner, as it was when it came into the hands of its present owner, Mr. Graves, having its front to the west. Here he continued in the mercantile business under various changes, in company with his nephew, Ira C. Allen, with Joseph Adams, and again with his son Edward, until 1861.

Mr. Allen took an active interest in the development of the marble and slate business of the town, as will be seen in notices of those enterprises, and was always a prominent and influential citizen. He was never a representative of the town in the General Assembly, but was twice chosen and rechosen to serve the county in the Senate, *to wit*: in 1842 and '43, and again in 1854 and '55. He was Assistant Judge in the County Court, in 1860, '61 and '62.

HISTORY OF FAIR HAVEN, VERMONT. 287

He served the town with efficiency as selectman, in raising the town's quota of soldiers in the late civil war. He has since acted for two years as Assistant, or Deputy Assessor of Internal Revenue.

Col. Allen was proficient as a military officer, rising rapidly from the rank of a sergeant to be captain, major, lieut.-colonel and colonel of the 175th Regiment of the 10th Division of the New York State militia, a regiment composed of four companies from Hartford, two from Hebron, and one from Granville, he commanding it as colonel in 1833 and '34, when he resigned.

He first married Juliza H. Higby, of Hartford, July 19, 1829, by whom he had five children.

1. *Cornelia M.*, b. in Hartford ; m. Martin D. Dyer.

2. *Edward L.*, b. in Hartford: m. Mary Ormsbee, and is the inventor and manufacturer of "Allen's Kerosene Oil Safe."

3. *Harriet E.*, b. in Fair Haven.

4. *Douglass A.*, residing with his father.

5. *Juliza*, m. Geo. D. Spencer.

Mrs. Allen died here, April 5, 1841, and was buried in Hartford. Mr. Allen was married again in January, 1842, to Mrs. Jane G. Reed, in Granville, N. Y. She was a sister of Rev. Wm. M. Everts, of Chicago, Ill., and the widow of Rev. Alonson Reed, with whom she went to Siam as a missionary, in 1835, and where he died in 1837. She returned to America and made her home, until she was married, with her brother, Rev. Jeremiah Everts, in Elbridge, N. Y. She died January 27, 1857, and was buried in the village burying ground.

288   HISTORY OF FAIR HAVEN, VERMONT.

Col. Allen married again the third time, December 7, 1859, to Mrs. Mary E. Hurd, of Rochester.

IRA C. ALLEN, son of Richard Allen, was born in Bristol, Vt., in 1816. He came to Fair Haven in May, 1836, and was engaged as clerk in the store of his uncle, Alonson, for a number of years. He resided a short time in Whitehall in 1840, and in New York in 1844 and '45. Returning to Fair Haven, he entered into copartnership with his uncle in the store, in the spring of 1846, and became a partner in the firm of Allen, Adams & Co., in the marble business, in 1852. He purchased of W. C. Kittredge, in January, 1866, the old Minot place, dwelling and land, long occupied by Mr. K. on the west side of the Park, and erected his marble dwelling house in the summer of 1867.

He has been a representative of the town, and also a senator of the county in the State Legislature. He married Miss Mary E. Richardson, of Geneva, N. Y., a niece of Joseph Adams, in September, 1855, and has four children.

GEORGE W. ALLEN, the son of Rufus Allen, was born in Whitehall, and married Nancy Boardman, of Whitehall. He came into Fair Haven in January, 1853, bringing his family from Canajoharie, N. Y., in the spring. He has three children, Cyrus W., Juliza A., and Mary A.

PHILIP ALLEN, a carpenter and joiner from Salem, N. Y., bought Isaac Cutler's farm, on West street, in September, 1798, and resided on the same. He sold it to Paul Scott in 1802. He is said to have built a portico to the old meeting house.

HISTORY OF FAIR HAVEN, VERMONT. 289

JOSHUA ATHERTON. We find that a man of this name was in town in September, 1792, and bought 50 acres of land of Jabez Newland, northward of Mr. McArthur's, on "Scotch Hill," and that Joshua and John Atherton took the freeman's oath in town, in January, 1793. Joshua was elected tithing-man in . March, 1794. He died here September, 26, 1800; and in April, 1815, Ethiel Perkins buys an acre and a half of land of Daniel McArthur, which "the late Josiah Atherton left to his widow Abiah, now Abiah Dennison." His family were, *Polly*, who married an Alford, of Castleton; *Nancy*, who married Daniel Mc- Arthur, and a daughter, who is said to have married a man by the name of Bacon, besides two sons, *Carlisle* and *Franklin*, who went away to Pennsylvania.

HENRY AINSWORTH came from Pomfret here, in the fall of 1798, and bought Col. David Erwin's farm, consisting of 110 acres, where Asahel H. Kidder now resides. He built a large new house on the place where the small tenement house now stands, west of Mr. Kidder's residence, the main north and south road, at that time, running on the west side of the house. The house stood until taken down by Mr. Kid- der, and was occupied at various times by Silas Saf- ford, Esq., by Obadiah Eddy, R. R. Mead, A. J. Mead and others. Mr. Ainsworth bought of Stephen and Drusilla Holt, 45 acres of the original Ballard farm adjoining his on the west, in May, 1801, which he af- terward sold, in April, 1807, to his brother, Danforth Ainsworth, and Danforth sold the same in August af- ter, to Enos Wells, of Poultney. Mr. A. sold the Er-

290   HISTORY OF FAIR HAVEN, VERMONT.

win farm, originally John Meacham's, in July, 1807, to James Claghorn, of Rutland, and removed to St. Albans, where he is said to have died. We know nothing of his family.

ABNER AMES came into town from Orwell, buying in April, 1826, of James Y. Watson, his farm in the south part of the town, now Mr. Barnes'. He is said to have taken a great interest in raising and selling sheep.

His wife, Chloe, died here March 19, 1828, aged 61 years; and he had two sons, Myron and Harvey, residing with him. He sold the farm, February 10, 1831, to Philip Church, of Angelica, Alleghany county, N. Y., and removed to that place.

CONTENT ALLIS. A man of this name bought 50 acres from the west part of the Trowbridge farm, of Dr. Samuel Shaw, in December, 1799, and occupied it for about one year, redeeding it to Dr. Shaw.

PETER ALLARD was born in Boston, Mass.; removed to Sheldon, Vt., about 1775, where he married Betsey Martin. From Sheldon he came to Fair Haven in 1834, residing here about 12 years, 10 years of the time in the village, and then returning to Sheldon, where he died. His family were:

1. *Judah*, who married Camela Carr, in Fair Haven, July 3, 1836. His children are Leander, Emeline, Lucy, Nelson, Charles, Henry, Marion and Elwin. Nelson and Charles died in the army.

2. *William* married Sibel Bullock, Nov., 1829, and had three children, Amasa, Ellen and Betsey.

3. *Giles* married the widow of Joseph Brewer, and removed to Painted Post, N. Y., about 1840.

HISTORY OF FAIR HAVEN, VERMONT. 291

4. *John* married Prudence Osgood, and resides in town. His family are Francis, married to Aaron Dowd; William, married to Jennie Ward, of Rutland; Henry, married to Ellen Dikeman, of Hubbardton; Mary, married to Burr B. Manchester; Ellen, married to John A. Chase; Florence, married to Edward Fields; John and Jennie.

5. *Isaac H.*, married, for first wife, Phebe Ann Sutliff, and had three children; Hattie, married to E. Homer, and died in 1869; Katie and Emma. For his second wife he married Margaret Miller, and had one child, Abba.

He sold the place previously occupied by John Sutliff, to Wm. L. Town, and purchased the farm now occupied by him, of Jonathan Capen.

JOHN ASHLEY came here as early as 1815, from Shrewsbury, or Mt. Holly. He lived in Mr. Sheldon's neighborhood, and worked for him on the farm. He built the house where Nelson Nutting resides, and went to reside in Cuttingsville as late as 1824, or later. He had a large family whose names were *Mary, Caroline, Zerah, Harriet, Gratty, Lucius, Addison* and *Willard.*

TIMOTHY BRAINARD, known as Deacon Brainard, was from East Hartford, Conn., in August, 1787, when he purchased of Asa Tyler, of Hampton, the farm lying next south of Oliver Cleveland's between Poultney west line and Poultney river, containing 52 acres, laid out in October, 1781, to Asa Tyler, as one-half of the 2d division of Ira Allen's right, which Tyler had purchased of Col. Isaac Clark, and was the same land

292   HISTORY OF FAIR HAVEN, VERMONT.

which Josiah Squiers, of Greenfield, had improved
and been allowed by the proprietors to exempt.

Deacon Brainard lived on this place until about
1817. His wife, Jemima, was the first person in town
who died of the epidemic of 1812. She died December 5th, in her 62d year. He appears to have deeded
his place to his sons, Timothy and David, by whom
it was sold to Noah Dodge, in March, 1816. But the
Brainards are said to have occupied the farm during
the cold summer of 1816, and to have raised the only
seed corn in the town. Deacon B, died in Elizabethtown, N. Y.

Family : 1. *Timothy ;* 2. *David ;* 3. *Jemima ;*
4. *Abigail ;* 5. *John ;* 6. *Lydia ;* 7. *Charles.* These
are said to be all dead, and to have left large families—some in Michigan, some in Illinois, one in
Iowa, three in Washington, D. C., and others in New
York and Vermont.

Timothy and David removed to Elizabethtown, N.
Y. David married Roxana, daughter of Enos Wells,
and is said, in 1818, to have "formerly occupied"
the house on the south side of the road, near the slitting mill.

Jemima married a man by the name of Strickland.
She died in Vergennes, in March, 1860.

Abigail, b. Sept. 20, 1781 ; m. Oliver Cady in Fair
Haven, and had a large family. She died at Plato,
Ill., April 13, 1869, having married a Mr. Sherman,
for a second husband.

John was a hatter, and removed to Bridport, Vt.,
where he carried on a farm, and died Oct. 20, 1867,
leaving a family of six children.

HISTORY OF FAIR HAVEN, VERMONT. 293

Lydia married Chauncey Sheldon, in Fair Haven, and removed to Charlotte, Vt., where she died about 1864.

Charles died in Essex, N. Y., Feb. 29, 1868.

RICHARD BEDDOW, a soldier from Gen. Burgoyne's army, and an early settler in the town, married widow Rebecca Hosford, of Poultney, whose maiden name was Pearce, and who had a son, Ichabod Hosford. He resides on the hill east of Mr. Kidder's.

His family were:

1. *Philip.* He worked at making saddles with Barnabas Ellis, when Mr. E. occupied the old Ballard place, east of Mr. Gardiner's.

2. *Samuel*, m. Sabrina Sharp, and died in 1862, at Warsaw, N. Y.

3. *Betsey*, m. a Tuttle, a harness maker, near Troy, N. Y.

4. *Simeon*, m. Sabria Maranville, and removed to Warsaw.

5. *Lucy*, was dumb. Died in Warsaw.

6. *John*, m. a Paine.

7. *Esther*, m. John Spooner.

The family is said to be all dead.

JAMES BOWEN was a half brother to Mrs. Charles Hawkins, and came hither from Smithfield, R. I., either before or after Mr. Hawkins. He took the freeman's oath in September, 1788; was a bachelor, and boarded some years with Isaac Cutler. He owned an interest in the right of Benjamin Cutler with Charles Hawkins, selling his share to Jesse Olney. He is said to have "tended a carding machine" for Dan Smith in

294   HISTORY OF FAIR HAVEN, VERMONT.

the factory where the powder mill now is. He appears to have been living as late as November, 1807, and is said to have died at Olney Hawkins'.

JOHN BROWN, a son of Capt. Christopher Brown, and a gentleman of education, and a teacher, came hither from North Providence, R. I., in 1792, when 26 years old. His wife was Mary Whipple, daughter of Capt. Benjamin Whipple, and a sister to Ethan Whipple, whom he married in Providence, February 14, 1790. He is said to have taught school in the town. He was town clerk from 1793 to February, 1801, and during this space of time the town records were kept with great beauty and correctness of penmanship.

In May, 1793, he purchased two acres of land of Col. Lyon, on the road south of Mr. Whipple's, and there built the house in which Mr. James Campbell now lives. He afterwards added another acre of land from Mr. Whipple, and in December, 1795, he advertised in the *Fair Haven Telegraph*, his house and three acres of land for sale. He sold the place in September, 1798, to Paul Guilford, from Conway, Mass.

Meantime he had purchased, in March, 1795, of Charles Rice, 65 acres on the north side of West street, east of Olney Hawkins and west of Isaac Cutler, selling the same in October, 1797, to Nathaniel Dickinson, with the buildings standing thereon. He was keeping the public house in the village, in March, 1798, when David Mack sold it to Dr. Simeon Smith.

From Fair Haven he removed to St. Albans, in March, 1800, where he was school district clerk in

HISTORY OF FAIR HAVEN, VERMONT. 295

October, 1802. He died March 16th, 1805, being but 39 years of age, and his wife died April 11th, aged 39 years.

Their children were:

1. *Lydia*, b. in North Providence, July 5, 1790; m. Joel Beaman, of Fair Haven, in 1808, and removed to Poultney, where she survived until January, 1867.

2. *Jenks*, b. in Providence, January 17, 1792. He removed from Fair Haven to Ohio, and became a man of wealth and influence.

3. *Cyrus Augustus*, b. in Fair Haven, Oct. 30, 1794; d. Sept. 4, 1798.

4. *Abigail*, b. Jan. 2, 1797.

5. *Cyrus A.*, b. March 12, 1799; resides now in Cincinnati, O.

SHUBEL BULLOCK, b. in Baltimore, Md., in 1776; came to Fair Haven in 1798, being then 22 years of age. He was a carpenter and joiner. He married Elizabeth, the eldest daughter of Thomas Dibble, and resided several years south-west of the Cedar Swamp, where he built a bridge over Poultney river, which was called " Bullock's bridge," in 1808.

He bought one hundred acres of land of James Witherell, Esq., July 3, 1807, on the top of the hill above Col. Allen's Quarry, where he built a house, and had a large family. He sold 70 acres of this to James Hooker, in November, 1811. In the war of 1812 and '14, he enlisted as a substitute for one year, with the company that started from Fair Haven for Plattsburgh. In 1816 he left his family, and the

296 HISTORY OF FAIR HAVEN, VERMONT.

town was under the necessity of helping them.

He had two brothers, Simeon and William, younger than himself, who came to town from Utica, N. Y. He died in the town, February 13th, 1848, in his 72d year. His wife died since 1862, when with her daughter Caroline, at St. Clair, Mich.

His family were:

1. *Alfred.* He first married Polly Williams, of West Haven; is now living with his second wife in Fair Haven.

2. *Pamelia*, m. Darius Jones, of Dresdén; now in Smith Creek, Mich.

3. *Cordelia*, m. John Jones, of Dresden, and afterward David Standish, and resided in town.

4. *Royal*, b. Dec. 11, 1805.

5. *Polly*, m. Chas. Stratton, in West Haven; resided in Fair Haven for a number of years; now at Barnard's Bay, N. Y.

6. *Thomas*, m. Zuba Plummer, of West Haven; resides at Port Huron, Mich.

7. *Esther*, m. H. Nelson Parke, of Whitehall; has 4 children.

8. *Shubel*, removed to St. Clair, Mich., and married.

9 and 10. *Betsey* and *George*, twins. Betsey m. Geo. Sartwell, of Whitehall, and died near Burlington. George died at an early age.

11. *Caroline*, m. Geo. Plummer, of St. Clair, Mich.

ROYAL BULLOCK, second son of Shubel, was apprenticed by the selectmen of the town, to learn the blacksmith's trade with John P. Colburn, in the spring of 1818, and went to live with Mr. Colburn, then just

HISTORY OF FAIR HAVEN, VERMONT. **297**

married and resided in the old place where Thomas Hughes resides. In 1826, upon attaining his majority, he went to Troy and worked for a time. Returning to Fair Haven, he drove a four horse stage, and carried the mail from Fair Haven to Shoreham, in the winter of 1828 and '29, for Messrs. Cushman & Stevens, boarding at the time at Mrs. Wilmot's hotel. In the fall of 1829, he built a blacksmith shop on the east side of the street, a little south from the present site of the Vermont Hotel. In February, 1830, he bought, in company with Barnabas B. Cane, the old store and land opposite his shop, which had been owned by Elisha Parkill. There was an old cellar where Erwin Safford's store had stood, and where James Miller's shop now is, at that time. Mr. Bullock removed his shop from the east side of the street to this cellar and made it into a house, in which his sister Esther kept house for him for a time. Jacob Kingsland, having married, about this time finished the old Parkill store into a dwelling house, and occupied it for a short time. It was occupied by Samuel Warren Guilford, who died there in February, 1832. Mr. Bullock then employed Miss Harriet Spratt to take charge of the house for him, and married her in the summer. He moved the north house to the south side of the Common, and erected the present brick shop in its place, in 1833.

He sold his place to Wm. H. Green, in the spring of 1853, and removed to Concord, Mich., in May, where he now owns a good farm.

His family are:

1. *Mary*, m. Wm. Spratt, in Concord, Mich.

298   HISTORY OF FAIR HAVEN, VERMONT.

2. *Martha*, m. Isaac N. Smalley, a son of David Smalley, who removed from Hampton, N. Y., to Concord, Mich.

3. *George*, m. Alice Bartholomew ; is a blacksmith, and resides in Jonesville, Mich. He was in the battle of Bull Run, and afterward enlisted as captain for three years, and became provost marshal at Nashville, Tenn., for a year and a half.

4. *Olla*, and 5. *Henry*.

SIMEON BULLOCK married Rebecca Littlefield. He resided, in 1811, where Otis Eddy does. He had a horse and was pressed into the service, with his team, in the war of 1812 and '14. He died in Concord, Mich., in 1864.

Family :

1. *Sibel*, m. William Allard, a son of Peter Allard. Has a daughter, Ellen, in town.

2. *Jedediah L.*, d. April 16, 1834, aged 21 years.

3. *Christopher M.*, d. Jan. 8, 1836, aged 18 years.

4. *Dudley*, resides at Vermontville, Mich.

5. *Simeon*, b. Feb. 26, 1816, m. Betsey Cobb, Sept. 17, 1837 ; d. March 1, 1858, aged 37 years. His children are, Charles W., deceased; Harriet E., deceased; Julia A., Albert C., and Sarah F.

6. *Jane*, m. a Howell ; resides in Concord, Mich.

7. *Caroline*, is a widow in Parma, Mich.

8. *John*, was blown up in a mine in California and died.

WILLIAM BULLOCK, brother to Shubel and Simeon, married Emily Dibble and removed to Dresden, N. Y., and thence to Kendall, N. Y. He died in Canada. His widow remains in Kendall.

HISTORY OF FAIR HAVEN, VERMONT. 299

SAMUEL BIBBINS, who married Deborah Cleveland, and resided in Hampton, on the spot where Charles J. Inman now does, in 1789, is said to have been a resident of Fair Haven, in 1809. His son Luther was resident in the old house which stood on the Common, in April, 1805, and his daughter, Alvira, married Albert, a son of Oliver Cleveland.

CLEMENT BLAKESLEY resided in the house which stood where Henry Green now lives, in 1798 and '99. He was called "Doctor," but seems to have worked for Col. Lyon, in the mills, rather than to have practiced medicine.

JABIN BOSWORTH was here and took the freeman's oath in 1803. His father was miller in the grist-mill at Whitehall, and died there. His mother married Eliada Orton, near the lake, in West Haven, and they removed on to the place in Fair Haven, now occupied by Hiram Briggs. Jabin was a shoemaker. He married Betsey Brevort, a sister to Henry Brevort, then of West Haven, now of Addison, and resided where Arthur Blennerhasset now resides. We only hear of two children, *Josephus* and *Edna*. He removed to Hebron, N. Y., and thence to Olin, N. Y.

STEPHEN S. BOSWORTH, brother of Jabin, was also a shoemaker and worked at one time with his brother. He is said to have lived where R. W. Sutliff now resides and on the hill above the present railroad crossing of the Poultney road.

In his family were *William*, *Chapin*, *Carr*, and others. He was present at the meeting of the Masonic fraternity in the old Dennis ball-room, in January,

300   HISTORY OF FAIR HAVEN, VERMONT.

1828, and the order made a donation to his family the same season. He went west and died soon afterward.

JOEL BEAMAN, a brother to Luke Beaman, came to Fair Haven from Leominster, Mass., in the spring of 1805, and engaged with John Herring and Moses Colton in the paper making business, hiring the paper mill, which was then owned by Alexander Dunahue, of Castleton, and running it until the March following, when it was burned, and Messrs. Herring, Colton & Beaman divided their paper on hand, Mr. Beaman selling his in Montreal, and Herring and Colton taking theirs to Troy or Albany.

Buying out Mr. Dunahue after the fire, they immediately set to work to erect a new mill, which was run by them in company till April, 1811. Mr. B. then sold to his partners, having removed to Poultney, and there opened a public house at the West village. He is said to have boarded with Isaac Cutler, and in November, 1808, he purchased of Mr. Cutler an acre of land and house where Mrs. Wm. Miller resides, the south-east corner said to be 1 1-2 rods from the house of Quinton and Christie, then occupied by John Cady. This he sold in August, 1811, to John Herring. Mr. Beaman married, in 1808, Lydia, the oldest child of John Brown, Esq. He died in Poultney, March 20th, 1846, leaving a large family, who were:

1. *George H.*, formerly editor of the *Rutland Herald*, now residing at Centre Rutland.

2. *Mary L.*, deceased.

HISTORY OF FAIR HAVEN, VERMONT. 301

3. *Minerva L.*, m. R. C. Mallory.

4. *Mary*, deceased.

5. *Joel D.*, deceased.

6. *John B.*, lawyer in Poultney.

7. *Jencks*, graduated at West Point, and died in 1846, on his way home from the Mexican war.

8. *Cullen C.*, keeps public house in Poultney.

9. *Caroline L.*, resident in. Poultney.

10. *Charles H.*, deceased.

11. *Jane*, resides in Poultney.

12. *Frances H.*, resides in Poultney.

JOHN BEAMAN, originally from Massachusetts, came hither from Rutland, where he had married Sally Russel. He was a silversmith by trade, and owned and occupied a shop standing near where the office built by Col. Allen now stands, in 1817, after Mr. Wilmot's death. He is said to have had a shop, at a later period, near where Richard W. Sutliff's tailor shop now is. It was a new shop in 1811. He was keeping the tavern house of Mrs. Lucy Wilmot in 1816 and '17, and in the cold summer of 1816 he raised 30 bushels of potatoes from a peck of seed, planted by him in the garden, then west of the hotel barns, a harvest which was considered note worthy for the year.

It is said that James Olds, who worked for Beaman, and one Clarke, were taken up for stealing silver ware from Beaman's shop. Olds got clear, but Clarke went to States prison.

In 1819 and '20, Beaman kept a public house in Bridport, and in August, 1820, bought about 80 acres

12

302 HISTORY OF FAIR HAVEN, VERMONT.

of land of Curtis Kelsey, Jr., lying west of Mr. Esty's farm, and removed on to the same. He sold this place to Olney Hawkins, December 2, 1826, and in March, 1827, the place being then occupied by John Parkill, Hawkins sold it to Joseph Warner, of Chelsea, Vt.

He was constable here in 1823 and '24, and kept the Dennis tavern after Mr. Dennis' departure from town in 1823. At the great celebration of the Fourth of July, 1825, he furnished the public dinner on the ground near Mr. Sutliff's shop.

A man of intemperate habits, he died a drunkard in West Troy, N. Y., whither he had removed.

He was married in Massachusetts; came from Rutland here, and his children were, *Henry*, *Martha*, *Mary* and *Harriet*.

LUKE BEAMAN, a brother to Joel, and ten years younger, came from Leominster, Mass., to Poultney, in the fall of 1816, bringing his wife, Betsey Gibson, in the winter, and marrying her in Chester, on the way, January 17, 1817. He was engaged for about 20 years in manufacturing combs in the building which was long used for a depot, and lately removed. In December, 1834, he bought the store and dwelling of Worcester Morse, in Fair Haven, and removed hither in the following spring, carrying on the mercantile business at the old stand, recently removed to give place to the new bank building, and remodeling the house in which Dr. Wakefield now lives, into a hotel, in 1836. In the fall of this year he bought the house now occupied by Col. Allen, and occupied it until the next year, when he sold it to Wm. C. Kittredge, and moved into the house which had been owned and occupied for a long time by Joshua Quinton, now owned by Thomas Hughes.

The Wakefield house was used as a hotel by Ebenezer Clement, about two years, and passed into the hands of Wm. C. Kittredge.

Mrs. Beaman died August 17, 1844. He removed to Port Kent, N. Y., in 1847, and afterwards resided at Mooer's Junction.

His family were:

1. *Mary*, m. James Bradshaw, who now resides in Hydeville.

2. *Betsey*, became the second wife of James Bradshaw.

3. *Martha L.*, m. Chauncey G. Fish.

4. *Augustus*, became a printer and died in New York in 1853.

5. *Jonas*, m. Jennie Cummings, and resides in New York.

6. *Sylvester*, d. Jan. 7, 1853, aged 21 years.

7. *Hoit*, m. Louisa Mather.

8. *Harriet R.*, d. March 20, 1840.

DAVID BRISTOL removed from Newtown, Conn., to Salem, N. Y., directly after the close of the Revolution, and came thence to Fair Haven in 1807, buying, May 12th, of Thomas and Rhoda Dibble, about 50 acres of land which had been Mr. Dibble's home farm, and was the 3d or 60 acre division of Oliver Cleveland's right, except about 10 acres sold to Shubel Bullock by the heirs of Oliver Cleveland. This farm

304 HISTORY OF FAIR HAVEN, VERMONT.

laid along the banks of Poultney river, to the south
and west of Mr. J. W. Esty's present dwelling house,
and is now owned by Mr. Esty. Mr. Bristol and his
wife Abiah, deeded 20 acres of this place, including
one-third of the building, to their eldest son, Enos,
March 14, 1811. They had also deeded him 4 acres
of it from the south-east corner, and running to the
river. Salmon·Norton had deeded to Abiah the 10
acres which Shubel Bullock owned. April 23, 1822,
David deeds to Hiram, his second son, the undivided
half of the 50 acres which he then owned. Enos had
previously, in November, 1820, sold his 20 acres to
Beriah Rogers, both residing in Hampton, and Rogers
had deeded it, April 1, 1822, to Hiram, reserving a
square of 95 rods from the north-east corner, and 17
acres westward to the river, to Abiah Bristol.

April 10, 1823, David and Abiah both quit-claim
the whole 60 acres to Hiram.

June 14, 1830, Hiram, then of Hampton, sells the
60 acres to Barnabas Ellis. Hiram had bought of
Josiah Goodrich, February 4, 1828, 25 acres, and this
he also sold to Mr. Ellis, April 4, 1831.

Mr. David Bristol married Abiah Peck. He died
in Whitehall, N. Y., October, 1833 or '34., at 73
years of age. She died in Illinois aged 84 years.

Their children were *Enos*, *Polly*, *Hiram*, *Oliver*
and *Harvey*.

Polly married Stephen Ransom, of Salem, and continued to reside there.

Hiram married Sarah Spink, of Whitehall, N. Y.,
a sister of Isaac Spink. He removed hence to Gen-

HISTORY OF FAIR HAVEN, VERMONT.   305

essee county, N. Y., and thence to Napierville, Ill.
He now lives in Aurora, Ill. He has had four children, of whom Ira and Ann were born in town. Ira
is dead; Ann resides in Illinois. George and Sarah
were born in western New York, and reside in Kane
county, Ill.

· Oliver married a Peck, in Cambridge, N. Y.; removed to western New York about 1830, and thence
to Batavia, Ill., where he was extensively and successfully engaged in the manufacture of fanning mills.
He died, February, 1867, leaving a third wife, but
having no heirs his property was divided between his
wife and his other relatives.

Harvey, b. in 1803, was a blacksmith by trade.
He married a Hotchkiss, of East Whitehall, and removed to Batavia, Ill., in company with others from
Whitehall, in 1836, where he bought a section of 640
acres of land, and was prospering in the manufacture
of an improved plow, when he died in 1843, leaving
five children, three of whom are now living in Batavia; one son, David, and two daughters; one of whom
married a Buck, and one a Wright.

Enos Bristol, eldest son of David, came from Salem
with his father in 1807. Besides the land which he
held with his parents, he purchased, January 5, 1809,
of Beriah Rogers, of Hampton, 56 acres on the south
side of the Whitehall road, where Wm. L. Town
now resides, and this became his home place for many
years. He sold it, January 26, 1831, to Stephen
Ransom, of Salem, N. Y., by whom it was sold, January 19, 1835, to John Sutliff.

306   HISTORY OF FAIR HAVEN, VERMONT.

Mr. Bristol was married in Salem, to Miss Susan Hinckley, of Wellington, Conn., and his family were:

1. *David Hinckley*, b. June 7, 1804, in Salem and continued for his life a resident of this town. Died Aug. 27, 1869.

2. *Ann*, who married John W. Eddy, and now lives in Cambridge, N. Y. They have one son, Albert.

3. *Betsey*, who married Daniel Rice, of Cambridge, N. Y., and has 4 children, Delia, Mary Jane, Marcus and Charles.

4. *Albert Gallatin*, who married Sophia Tafft, and resides in Whitehall, N. Y. He has had 3 children; Charles and Lillie are living.

5. *James Clark*, deceased.

6. *Phebe Ann*, who married Charles Porter, Cambridge, N. Y.

Mrs. Bristol died April 29, 1827, aged 45, and Mr. B. married the widow of Richard Hawkins the next fall. He died Aug., 1833, aged 56; was buried in Detroit, Mich.

DAVID H. BRISTOL, eldest son of Enos, was married to Lucy Hawkins, eldest daughter of Charles Hawkins, Feb. 22, 1832.

Their family are:

1. Martha A.

2. Sarah Jane, m. David Mahon; m. for her second husband, Andrew Sperbeck, of Poughkeepsie.

3. Susan C., m. Charles Carter, in Poughkeepsie, N. Y.; d. July 12, 1870, aged 30 years.

4. Edwin R., m. Emerancy Town, youngest daughter of Wm. Town.

HISTORY OF FAIR HAVEN, VERMONT. 307

5. Mariam Emeroy.

6. Cullen.

JACOB BARNES, a soldier for seven years in the Revolutionary War, and drawing an annual pension of $96.00 while he lived, came from Woodbury, Conn., in the spring of 1806, spending the summer with his son-in-law, Noah Tuttle, of Castleton. He came into town in the autumn, and resided, during the winter, with his son-in-law, Samuel Smith, who had bought the farm now owned and occupied by D. P. Wescott, of Dr. Samuel Shaw, of Castleton, the previous spring. In April, 1807, Mr. Smith deeded Barnes 15 acres on the flat toward Mr. Esty's, on which he built a house, and Mr. Barnes resided there till he died, January 27, 1821, aged 76 years. The place was deeded by Artemas Branch, July 17, 1826, to the widow and heirs of Silas Hawkins, and conveyed back to Alvin and Eli Smith, the sons of Samuel Smith, in May, 1832, by Roswell C. Hawkins and Happylona, his wife. Mr. Barnes' wife, Rebecca Crowell, was born on the ocean. They were married in Milford, Conn. She died in town in the summer of 1822, aged 77 years, and both were buried in the old village burial ground, which is now caved off into the river.

Their family, born in Connecticut, were:

1. *Hannah*, b. Sept. 12, 1766, in Waterbury, Conn.; m. Ayers Tuttle, and removed to Tioga county, Pa.

2. *Mary*, b. Sept. 13, 1769; m. Samuel Smith.

3. *Rebecca*, b. Dec. 20, 1774; m. Noah Tuttle and settled in Castleton. Has a son in Rutland.

308   HISTORY OF FAIR HAVEN, VERMONT.

4. *Sarah*, b. April 8, 1777; m. Samuel Atkins in Pennsylvania.

5. *Lydia*, b. October 5, 1779; m. Uriel Curtis, and removed to Phillipstown, Pa.

6. *Clarissa*, b. March 17, 1782; m. to Artemas Branch, by Rev. R. Cushman, of Fair Haven, Dec. 27, 1807.

7. *Eli Y.*, b. Sept. 14, 1784; removed to Pennsylvania; now resides in Lockport, N. Y.

JEFFERSON BARNES, b. in Rutland, July 21, 1801, m. Laura Dyer, April 14, 1824, and died on his place in Fair Haven, Oct. 3, 1861. He purchased the farm where his son now resides, south of Mr. Kidder's, of Erastus Hulett, of Wethersfield, in Nov. 1836, and moved on to it with his family, in March, 1837. The wagon shed, built by Mr. Barnes, on the west side of the road, in 1847, was the first building roofed with slate in the town. Mr. Barnes' house was burned, and rebuilt soon after.

Family:

1. *Harriet M.*, b. Feb. 22, 1825; m. J. P. Sheldon, April 15, 1842; d. Sept. 11, 1846.

2. *Edward Dyer*, b. Jan. 8, 1827; m. Juliza Eddy, Aug. 20, 1867.

3. *Myron D.*, b. June 22, 1830, m. Caroline Bryant, Jan. 27, 1859.

4. *Geo. Palmer*, b. Sept. 14, 1833.

5. *Delia E.*, b, Nov. 12, 1836; d. Oct. 1, 1841.

6. *Charles J.*, b. in Fair Haven, July 18, 1844; d. April 13, 1846.

HISTORY OF FAIR HAVEN, VERMONT. 309

THOMAS BLANCHARD, from Sutton, Mass., took the freeman's oath here in September, 1809. He was a noted mechanic, and is said to have worked for Mr. Davey in the iron works, and for John P. Colburn in the scythe factory, where Spencer Harvey states that he worked as an apprentice with Blanchard in making axes and hoes. It is related that while he worked for Mr. Davey, he invented a nail machine, Mr. D. finding materials and boarding him, he to own one-half of the machine. He started an imperfect model, and a great number of people went to see its operation. Returning to Massachusetts, he afterwards sent Mr. Davey the model of a machine, on which he obtained a patent. At a later period he worked in the armory of the U. S., at Springfield, Mass., and there invented a machine for turning gun stocks.

AMOS BRONSON was a resident of Fair Haven, and chosen a tithingman, in March, 1801. He was a carpenter and joiner, and married Amy Durand, a daughter of Jeremiah Durand. He went away to Batavia, N. Y., about 1805, and died in Pennsylvania.

JOHN BRONSON is said to have come from Granville, N. Y., and to have been a brother-in-law of Andrew McFarland for whom he was clerk in a store as late as 1804. He was here and took the freeman's oath in September, 1794.

HARRY BRONSON, a lawyer from Richmond, studied with Judge Daniel Chipman, of Middlebury, and came here about 1822, residing about two years, and practicing his profession. He is said to have occupied an office previously occupied by Dr. Hurd, near where

310　　HISTORY OF FAIR HAVEN, VERMONT.

R. E. Lloyd's store stands. He married a daughter of Squire Coleman, of West Haven.

WM. J. BILLINGS, a hatter, came from Greenfield, Mass., to West Haven, in 1810. He resided with his daughter, Mrs. Joseph Sheldon, in Fair Haven, after 1834, and died December 30, 1850.

Family:

1. *Mary P.*, m. Joseph Sheldon.

2. *William J.*, resides in West Haven.

3. *John*, m. Betsey Butterfield. In Oct., 1829, he and his brother Hiram purchased the old Perkins farm, containing 200 acres, of Hiram Bates. He occupied it, and sold it in April, 1835, to Oliver and Jonathan N. Proctor. He now resides in New Jersey.

4. *Hiram*, m. Camela Kidder, daughter of Oliver Kidder, Dec. 5, 1832. He was a blacksmith and formerly resident in town; removed to Castleton where he died about 1860.

5. *Avery*, is a harness maker in Ferrisburg, Vt.

HARRIS W. BATES came from Benson about 1816 or '18, and worked in the paper mill. He married Nancy Phelps, a sister of Geo. Warren's wife. He removed to Troy, N. Y., about 1828, and is said to have been a man of excellent character.

ELIAB BRIGGS, a mechanic and mill-wright, m. Catherine Paine; bought the Paul Guilford place, where James Campbell resides, in April, 1816, and made additional purchases of Tilly Gilbert and Ethan Whipple. He sold the whole, consisting of 14 acres, to Heman Stannard, in April, 1826, and removed to Benson, and thence to Michigan, where he remained

HISTORY OF FAIR HAVEN, VERMONT. 311

until 1868, when he returned to Fair Haven, and died "on the town," while boarding with Stephen Ward, in Hubbardton. He built a saw-mill at the outlet of Inman Pond, about 1817, for Olney Hawkins and Nathaniel Sanford.

HIRAM BRIGGS, b. in West Castleton, then "Screwdriver," February 23, 1806, is a nephew to Eliab Briggs, and a present citizen of the town. He married Susan Shattuck, of West Castleton, August 26, 1828, and removed to "the Shirland place," near Mt. Hamilton, in the north part of Fair Haven, in the November following. Since which time he has continued to reside on the same farm, "working on his land by day and making boots and shoes by night; has never become wealthy, but has always paid his debts promptly, and has succeeded in laying up a trifle from year to year."

He has had three sons and five daughters, grown to adult age:

1. *Hiram Franklin*, the eldest son, a marble finisher by trade; d. in Brattleboro, aged 29 years.

2. *Charles Horace*, a harness maker; d. in Luzerne, N. Y., at the age of 30.

3. *James Tilly*, the youngest son, served two years in the union army as a member of the First Vermont Cavalry; lost his health, returned home and died at the age of 22 years. Three of the daughters died, their ages ranging from 16 to 22 years.

Martha Jane and *Hattie*, still live.

ARNOLD BRIGGS, JR., resident on Scotch Hill; came from Benson about 1833. He first purchased, of

312   HISTORY OF FAIR HAVEN, VERMONT.

Elizur Goodrich, in April 1831, with his brother Amasa, of Benson, one undivided half, of the place on which he resides—a part of the original Charles McArthur farm—owned by Abraham Sharp, Jr., In March, 1832, they bought of Heman Stannard the other undivided half. Mr. Briggs has made additional purchases to the farm, and must now have upwards of 200 acres.

He married Adaline, daughter of Oliver Proctor, in Benson. They have one son, *Arnold Wilson*, who is now in Texas.

DR. CHARLES BACKUS studied medicine with Dr. Theodore Woodward, and graduated in 1821. He came to Fair Haven and opened a store in the west end of the old Quinton house, about 1824, Wm. Dennis, now of Cambridge, Mass., being his clerk.

He removed from Fair Haven to West Troy, N. Y., taking with him a store ready framed. He left Troy and practiced medicine for a time in Rochester, N. Y., but removed thence to Granville Corners, N. Y., in 1839, where he followed his profession.

He came back to Fair Haven in 1842, bringing a reputation for much skill and knowledge in medical practice, but followed by his cherished enemy, intemperance, by which his usefulness was destroyed and he was at last slain.

He occupied the old Quinton house, his four daughters keeping house for him, and had his office in a room in the old Dennis hotel after it had undergone transmutation at the hands of John Jacob Davey. Dr. Backus removed to Hydeville in 1846, and died

HISTORY OF FAIR HAVEN, VERMONT. 313

at Castleton Corners in the fall of 1852, being buried at Castleton by the Masonic Fraternity, of which he was a member.

He married a Miss Smith, of Sudbury, and she is said to have been a woman of talent and spirit, who yearned for a better life. She died in 1841, at Granville, N. Y. The daughters were *Frances*, *Mary*, *Charlotte*, and *Ann*, of whom Frances only survives, and resides in St. Paul, Minn.

Dr. WM. BIGELOW was bôrn in Middletown, Nov. 9, 1791. He studied medicine with Dr. Ezra Clark, of Middletown, and received an honorary degree from Castleton Medical College. He married Miss Dorinda Brewster, of Middletown, in October, 1815, and came to Fair Haven to reside this same month, occupying the house next south of Maj. Tilly Gilbert's, and practicing his profession. In December, 1823, he purchased of Maj. Gilbert the old meeting house, which had been transformed into a dwelling house and cabinet shop by Joseph Brown, and made it his home till the fall of 1828, when he removed to Bennington, and sold his place in the June following, to Dr. Edward Lewis, his successor.

He resided in Bennington until 1858, when his health gave out, obliging him to abandon the practice of his profession. He served as state senator from Bennington county one term. Removing to Springfield, Mass., in 1858, he remained there with his son, Edmund, until his death, April 20, 1863. His widow still survives him.

314 HISTORY OF FAIR HAVEN, VERMONT.

Their children are:

1. *Olive Stone*, b. in Fair Haven Oct. 6, 1816. She married Dr. Dewey H. Robinson, of Bennington, April 12, 1838, and has three sons living. Dr. R. died in May, 1848: she resides with her sister Loraine, in Troy, N. Y.

2. *Emma Loraine*, b. in Fair Haven, Aug. 24, 1818. She married John N. Squires, of Bennington, Jan. 12, 1841, and of their five sons and one daughter, four sons are living.

3. *Edmund*, b. in Fair Haven, Feb. 14, 1821; m. Lucy Camp, of Troy, N. Y., Sept. 13, 1847.

He now resides in Springfield, Mass., where he is a manufacturer of a soda and syrup apparatus. He has one son.

4. *Ellen*, b. in Fair Haven, Sept. 11, 1823; d. Oct. 14, 1834, in Bennington, Vt.

5. *William Henry*, b. in Fair Haven, Feb. 6, 1826; d. in Bennington, April 20, 1846.

6. *George Warren*, b. in Fair Haven, Sept. 21, 1828. He now resides in Boston, Mass.

7. *Mary Sophia*, b. in Bennington, Vt., May 16, 1832; m. Samuel B. Sanford, of New York, in July, 1858; and now resides in Troy, N. Y.; has one daughter.

ELI BARBER removed with his family from Montgomery, Vt., to Benson, and came thence to Fair Haven in June, 1826, and purchased a farm of Elisha Parkill, where Jeremiah Durand had first settled, now owned by Col. A. Allen. He sold it, together with the land now occupied by I. H. Allard, west of the

HISTORY OF FAIR HAVEN, VERMONT. 315

village, which he had purchased of Tilly Gilbert, to Jonathan Capen, in 1833, and removed to Poultney, where he died. His family were, *Heman*, now resident in Benson; *Lyman*, *Edmund*, *George*, who died in Iowa, *Spafford*, who died in Poultney, and *Lucinda*, who married Marcus Bliss, of Castleton.

JOSEPH BREWER, an Irishman, highly respected, worked in the iron works. He purchased of Abel and Nancy Woods, in July, 1827, 31 acres of land on the plain, where Patrick Starr now resides, then adjoining Josiah Goodrich's farm on the east, and there built the house which Mr. Starr has lately moved from the south side of the highway. He married Fidelia White, a sister to Mrs. Walter Rogers, who, after his demise, about 1830, married Giles Allard, and re. moved to Painted Post, N. Y.

WILLIAM BRADY was admitted to the freeman's oath, in town, in September, 1827. He was brought up from boyhood by Timothy Goodrich. He married a daughter of Capt. Sanford, of West Haven, worked at lumbering, and was dissipated. Has a son who is a photograph artist in New York.

WILLIAM BARRY, an old man who worked in the paper mill; lived on the hill, near where John E. Maynard does about 1834. He was here eight or ten years.

JOSEPH BERTO is said to have come from Canada to Hampton, N. Y., whence he came to Fair Haven about 1839. He resided a part of the time while resident in town, where Mrs. Stow now does. He carried on Judge Kittredge's farm, and also worked

316   HISTORY OF FAIR HAVEN, VERMONT.

in the paper mill. He removed to Spring Vale, Wis., where he died in 1867. His family reside near Ripon, Wis.

MICHAEL BURNS came from Queens county, Ireland, to Fair Haven in 1836, and worked in the Iron works 19 years. In 1855 he bought the old Maranville farm in the south part of the town, of Reuben T. Ellis —then about 72 acres—and resided on the same till the spring of 1860, when, having sold the farm the previous year to Thomas Bulger, he removed to the old Parker farm, in Hampton, N. Y., where he now resides. His wife was Bridget Sheppard. They have no family.

. ARTHUR BLENERHASSETT came from Clare county, Ireland, in 1848, and resided at different times near Otis Hamilton's and Joseph Sheldon's. He purchased the place formerly owned by James Miller, in the north part of the town, in 1861, and now resides thereon. He married Susan Hill, and the family are:

1. *Robert.*
2. *Eliza*, m. Geo. Shepardson.
3. *Mary Ann*, b. in town; m. John Harrison.
4. *Rollin A.*
5. *William Henry.*

OLIVER CLEVELAND was born in Rhode Island. He is reported to have come into Hampton from Killingworth, Conn., probably in 1777. He had a cousin, Soloman, who also settled in Hampton, and afterward resided in Fair Haven. He married Azubah Smith, a sister of James Smith, a Revolutionary soldier. He died September 5, 1803, in his 70th year.

HISTORY OF FAIR HAVEN, VERMONT. 317

She survived till August 20, 1823, when she died at the house of Lewis Maranville, Sen.

Family:

1. *Sarah*, b. Nov. 15, 1756; m. Isaac Race.
2. *Azubah*, b. April 16, 1759; m. Benjamin Parmenter.
3. *Josiah*, b. March 23, 1764.
4. *Rhoda*, b. Aug. 18, 1764; m. Thomas Dibble.
5. *Ann*, b. Feb. 28, 1766; m. John Lewis.
6. *Esther*, b. Aug. 8, 1770; m. James Sharp.
7. *Albert*, b. June 19, 1772.
8. *James*, b. Dec. 6, 1774.
9. *Lydia*, b. March 31, 1775; m. Lewis Maranville.
10. *Sabria*, b. Dec. 16, 1779; d. March 12, 1796, and was buried in Hampton, N. Y.

JOSIAH CLEVELAND married Chloe Spoor, of Hampton, and resided on the south part of the farm which had been improved by his father, where Chauncey Wood now resides. He sold this place about 1817, and removed to Hampton Flat, where he died May 26, 1824.

His first wife died in Fair Haven, September 13, 1808, in her 40th year. By her he had 11 children, as follows:

1. *Olive*, b. Aug. 9, 1785. She first married Ira Durand, but left him and married Elijah Vaughn, Sept. 26, 1810.
2. *Oliver*, b. Aug. 14, 1787; m. Anna Ball, of Schuylerville, N. Y. He was three times married, and died in Ashtabula county, Ohio, in Nov., 1868.
3. *Betsey*, b. Oct. 1, 1789; m. William Higgins, of Benson.

14

318 HISTORY OF FAIR HAVEN, VERMONT.

4. *Laura*, b. Aug. 27, 1791; m. Joel Barber, of Benson.

5 *Nicholas*, b. June 26. 1793; m. Sally Morris; resided in Warsaw, N. Y.; d. in Dec. 1868.

6. *Lucy*, b. Dec. 5, 1795; m. Elijah Merritt, of Benson.

7. *Lucinda*, b. Jan, 20, 1798; m. Horace Knapp, of Benson.

8. *Charlotte*, b. April 6, 1800 : first m. Nathan Filley, and is now the second wife of Horace Knapp.

9. *Royal*, b. Sept. 4, 1802; m. Mary Warren, of Sandy Hill, N. Y.; resided in Conneaut, Ohio.

10. *Bulina*, b. June 4, 1805; m. Ezra Morgan, of Hampton, N. Y.

11. *Cyrus*, b. Sept. 4, 1807; resides in Conneaut, Ohio.

Mr. Cleveland married Deborah Spoor, of Hampton, Dec. 8, 1810, for his second wife, and by her had two daughters.

12. *Chloe*, b. Nov. 18, 1811. She married Reuben Sherwood, of Benson.

13. *Mary*, who died at an early age.

He married the third time to Betsey Roberts, of Poultney, and had one son.

14. *John*, b. Nov. 2, 1820. He now resides in Iowa.

ALBERT CLEVELAND, second son to Oliver Cleveland, married Alvira Bibbins, daughter to Samuel, and sister to Luther Bibbins, of Hampton. He sold out his portion of his father's farm in the fall of 1813, and removed to Pennsylvania. In 1854 he was living with his wife near Portage, N. Y. Both died previously to

HISTORY OF FAIR HAVEN, VERMONT. 319

1860. Their family were,

1. *Salmon*, who died in Pennsylvania.
2. *Sabria*, deceased.
3. *Calvin*, resides in Avon, N. Y.
4. *Annis*.
5. *Polly*, m. first a Hovey, and second Elijah White.
6. *Harry*, resides in Nunda, N. Y.
7. *Elisha*.
8. *Eliza*.
9. *Deborah*.

JAMES CLEVELAND, third son to Oliver, married, first, Charity Way, of Hampton. She died in Fair Haven about 1811, on the old Ballard place, west from Mr. Kidder's. He was married the second time to a widow Maynard, who resided in the South School district. He is said to have been noted for trading horses, and resided, as late as 1828 or '29, on the Beddow place. He removed to Western New York, Wayne county, where he died as late as 1863 or '64.

Of his family we hear of *Amaziah*, *Avery*, *Satira*, *Leonard*, *James*, and perhaps *Nelson* and *Charity*.

Avery is said to have married and died in Warsaw, N. Y., and James to be now resident in western New York.

Leonard went to Convis, Mich., where he had a fine, valuable farm of 250 acres. He died in Albion, Mich., in Feb., 1868. His widow removed to Marshall, where a son and daughter also reside.

SOLOMON CLEVELAND, a son of Enoch Cleveland, of Hampton, and cousin of Oliver Cleveland, of Fair Haven, and an intimate friend of Col. Matthew Lyon,

320   HISTORY OF FAIR HAVEN, VERMONT.

was for a time resident in this town. He came from Canaan, Conn., to Hampton, then known as " Greenfield," and thought to be in Vermont, with others of his father's family, in the summer of 1777, before the battle of Hubbardton, and was one who went, at the call, to meet the English in the battle of Bennington.

In May, 1786, there was surveyed to him 4 3-4 acres of land in Fair Haven, on the fourth division of the right of Oliver Cleveland ; the land joining on to Oliver Cleveland's north-west corner, and lying along the river not far from Enoch Cleveland's house.

Enoch Cleveland buys of John Smith, of Poultney. in Sept., 1787, 4 3-4 acres of undivided land on the first division of the right of Wm. Seymour, and this lot is re-surveyed to him on the same day. On the 1st of Sept., 1788, Enoch, "for, and in consideration of the natural good will I bear toward my beloved son Solomon," deeds the lot to Solomon, and he, in November, conveys it to Col. M. Lyon.

He seems to have been in Fair Haven, and taken the freeman's oath here in July, 1791. In August, 1796, he is said to be a resident of Hampton, when he buys of Col. Lyon one equal half of the saw-mill and grist-mill, on the lower falls, and 17 1-2 acres of land near where Z. C. Ellis resides, and removes into town with his family.

He rebuilt the mills, Jonathan Orms working as his chief mill-wright, and built a house on the lot south of the paper mill. He sold his share of the mills and the land, in April, 1798, to Pliny Adams of Hampton, taking in exchange a farm in East Poultney, to which he removed.

HISTORY OF FAIR HAVEN, VERMONT. 321

He was married in Canaan, Conn., to Martha Rathbone, and had eight children, *Almeda, Solomon, Enoch, Patty, Abigail, Samuel, Lydia,* and *Fassett.*

Of these, Samuel, born in 1792, and now residing with his daughter, Mrs. James T. Freeman, of Hydeville, well remembers many of the incidents of his boyhood in Fair Haven, and to him the writer is indebted for several interesting facts.

Solomon Cleveland, Sen., died in Diana, Lewis county, N. Y., in the year 1844, aged 89.

Isaac Cutler, who has been mentioned as coming into town in the spring of 1785, and settling on West street, where he opened a public house, having sold his farm in the fall of 1798, to Philip Allen, of Salem, N. Y., must have come into the village to reside soon afterward, and may have made his home with his brother-in-law, Nathaniel Dickinson, who kept the public house of the village. Mr. Cutler purchased the house and about 10 acres of land of Dr. Simeon Smith, of West Haven, February 5, 1803, and sold the same to Thomas Wilmot, of Poultney, September 18, 1809. In February, 1810, he appears to have lived in a part of the old house which stood on the Common, Harvey Church occupying the other part. On March 7, he bought of Rufus Guilford about 12 acres on the west side of the village, the same on which Stephen Rogers had his tannery, and the lot where Owen Owens now lives, long occupied as a parsonage.

On this place he built, and occupied, while he remained in town, the house in which Mr. Owens lives. He sold to Harvey Church, in April, 1812, the house

332 HISTORY OF FAIR HAVEN, VERMONT.

which Church then occupied, together with the tan house, built by Stephen Rogers, and one acre and twenty-three rods of land, the house being the same which is owned and occupied by Wm. Dolan.

Mr. Cutler deeded his home place of 10 acres, running back to the river, to James Watson, formerly of Fair Haven, in June, 1818, reserving the privilege of living on the same. He removed to West Haven in the spring of 1827, and resided on the ground where Mr. Nathaniel Fish now lives, until his death, which occurred in November, 1832, when he was 86 years old. He was buried in the old grave yard above the house of Seth Hunt.

He had been a soldier in the Revolutionary war. He was married first to Susanna Watson. She died February 21, 1824, in her 69th year.

On the 20th of August following, he married the widow of Samuel Kenyon, of West Haven, whose maiden name was Elizabeth Adams. He left no family. He was a prominent and influential man in the town, largely connected with its public and business affairs. Being a justice of the peace, he was universally known and designated as "Squire Cutler."

THE CADY FAMILY. There were a number of brothers of this name among the early residents of Fair Haven and vicinity. They were all the sons of one John Cady, was was born in Killingworth, Conn. Dec. 9, 1736, and died in Westport, N.Y., in February, 1824. His wife's name was Hannah Miles. She was born June 17, 1736, and died at Westport, December 25, 1823. Their children were Benjamin,

HISTORY OF FAIR HAVEN, VERMONT. 323

Jonathan, John, Zeruah, Adin, Hannah, Calvin, Thomas, Rebecca, Sarah and Oliver. Of these,

JONATHAN CADY, b. May 19, 1760, is said to have resided, at one time, on Hampton hills. He was school committee in South district in 1807. He was a soldier in the war of the Revolution; was stationed for a time at Fort Ticonderoga, and was present at the surrender of Gen. Burgoyne. He lived to be 92 years old, walking to the village of Westport, five miles and back, only a few days before his death, which occurred in Westport, September, 20, 1852.

· JOHN CADY, b. June 7, 1762; came from Reading to Fair Haven in 1803, remaining here until 1813, He is said to have built a house in the woods, east of where John Moore now lives, perhaps where Charles Hawkins afterward resided, but sold the place to Maj. Tilly Gilbert as early as 1807, and removed into the grist-mill house, where he lived in 1808. He is after this said to have lived eastward from the iron works, where Otis Eddy now lives. He left Fair Haven in 1813, and died in Wirt, Alleghany county, N. Y., in 1845, in his 83d year. He married first a Clark, and afterwards a Sherwin. He had four sons and five daughters:

Benjamin, who went to Canaan, Conn., where he died.

Adin, who was fife major in the 11th Regiment in the war of 1812, and died in the army. Adin is said to have been wounded in the battle of Lundy's Lane, and brought into Buffalo, where the physician pronounced him in a fair way to recover; but upon the

324   HISTORY OF FAIR HAVEN, VERMONT.

removal of the hospital patients from the city at the threatened attack of the British, he was exposed, took cold, and died in the hospital.

Lucinda, who died in Fair Haven.

Hannah, b. 1795, who is living in Illinois.

Lewis, who now resides in Whalonsburg, N. Y.

Clark C., who resides in Middlebury, Vt.

Eliza, and *Zeruah* who died and were buried in Fair Haven, and *Eliza*, the youngest, who now resides in Alleghany county, N. Y.

ADIN CADY, b. December 16, 1766, "a genial, good man," came with his wife from Reading, and appears to have taken the freeman's oath here in 1810, but resided afterwards in Poultney, where he died in March, 1848. He had a daughter *Caroline* who married deacon Daniel Whitcomb, of Poultney, and a daughter *Eunice*, who married a Mr. St. John, of Poultney.

OLIVER CADY, b. September 20, 1781, came into town from Reading in 1803, and took the freeman's oath here at the freeman's meeting in September of that year. He is mentioned as leader of the choir of the Congregational society in 1804. He married, October 12, 1805, Abigail Brainard, called also "Nabby," or "Mabby" Brainard, a daughter of Deacon Timothy Brainard, of this town. Both were very fond of music, and communicated the musical talent to their children. They are said to have lived over the river, in Mr. Richard's neighborhood, in 1811. They resided in Orwell in 1813, and either while there, or previously, he went out as drum major with

HISTORY OF FAIR HAVEN, VERMONT. 325

a company which started to join the American army at Plattsburgh, (probably the company from Fair Haven,) but too late to take part in the battle. From Orwell they seem to have gone to West Rutland to reside, in 1815, being dismissed, at their request, from the Congregational church in Fair Haven, in August of that year, and recommended to the church in West Rutland. From West Rutland they removed to Westport, N. Y., in the fall of 1819, where Mr. Cady died, April 30, 1841. She lived until April of the present year, when she died at 82 years of age, at Plato, Ill. She was a woman of great energy and executive talent, "active and playful as a child up to the very day of her death," and "talked of her death as cheerfully as if it were only a pleasant journey."

Mr. Cady suffered from poor health the last years of his life, so that while "honest and thoroughly upright," "despising a mean act," he lost his property and left his family in debt. This indebtedness was paid by his widow, with the help of her youngest son, Chauncey M., who worked out on a farm, at $10 per month, for two seasons after the father's demise. Of such stuff was his family made.

The children were:

1. *Clara*, b. July 22, 1806, in Fair Haven; now Mrs. Geo. Skinner, of Wadham's Mills, in Westport, N. Y.

2. *Charlotte*, b. Oct. 30, 1807, at Fair Haven; now widow of Orrin Skinner, Plato, Ill.

3. *Calvin Brainard*, b. July 11, 1809, at Fair Haven; a graduate of Middlebury College, and Congregational minister at Alburgh Spa., Vt.

15

326   HISTORY OF FAIR HAVEN, VERMONT.

4. *Charles Thomas*, b. May 18, 1811, at Fair Haven ; now in Detroit, and former member of the Michigan Legislature.

5. *Cornelius Sidney*, b. in Orwell, Feb. 28, 1813 ; is a graduate of Oberlin College and Theological Seminary, and a Congregational minister at Evanston, Ill., near Chicago.

6. *Chester Oliver*, b. in West Rutland, March 3, 1817; d. at Cooperstown, N. Y., March 22, 1844.

7. *Chauncey Marvin*, b. in Westport, N. Y., May 16, 1824; fitted himself for college at Oberlin; engaged in a clerkship in Michigan; taught music and assisted to found Olivet College, in Eaton county, Mich., and graduating from Michigan University in 1851, went to New York and engaged with W. B. Bradbury in musical labors, being editor of the *New York Musical Review*, until, in 1856, he removed to Chicago, and has been engaged with Geo. F. Root, in the publication and sale of music, under the firm name of "Root & Cady," since December, 1858.

8. *Caroline Matilda*, b. in Bridport, Vt. ; d. at Elizabethtown, N. Y., Aug. 22, 1832.

HARVEY CHURCH, a nephew to Oliver Church, of West Haven, was here and took the freeman's oath in September, 1803. He was a shoemaker, and worked for Calvin Munger, in a small shop built by Stephen Rogers, where Mrs. Ira Allen now resides.

He married Lucy Orton, a step-sister of Jabin and Stephen S. Bosworth, and was living, in February, 1810, in a part of the old printing office on the Common. He appears to have removed in the spring into

HISTORY OF FAIR HAVEN, VERMONT. 327

Parkill's house, where Dr. Wakefield now lives, where he resided in August, but removed not long after to the house now occupied by Wm. Dolan, buying in April, 1812, of Isaac Cutler, the house, shop, and tanyard—about one acre and twenty-three rods—which had been owned by Munger at his decease in 1806. This place was deeded by him, August 24, 1827, to Francis S. Hemmenway, of Shoreham, and Church, failing in business, went away to Wisconsin about 1831.

He had four daughters, the three oldest of whom were *Betsey, Adeline, and Lucy.*

. LYDIA CHURCH, a widow from Massachusetts, whose maiden name was Babcock, and who was married to Ethan Whipple, in December, 1815, had a family who came to Fair Haven, as follows:

1. *Sophronia*, m. a Smith, of Massachusetts.

2. *Betsey*, m. Joel Hickock; d. in town about 1838.

3. *Lydia*, m. a Mr. Todd, and resides in Rockville, Ill.

4. *Sylvanus*, was engaged in the salt business at Syracuse; d. in Whitehall and was buried in Fair Haven.

5. *Lucinda*, m. Florus Meacham; is now dead.

6. *Harvey*, who married and resides in Troy, N. Y., where he has been engaged in the lumber trade.

MOSES COLTON came hither from Sutton, Mass., in 1805, and hired the paper mill, in company with Joel Beaman and John Herring, of Alexander Dunahue, for one year. In March, 1806, the mill was burned,

328 HISTORY OF FAIR HAVEN, VERMONT.

and Herring, Colton and Beaman, bought the premises, the same month, and rebuilt the mill immediately. In March, 1813, Mr. Colton bought Herring's half interest in the same, they together having previously bought out Beaman's interest, in April, 1811.

In April, Mr. Colton sells one-half the mill to Geo. Warren. In January, 1819, he sells the other half to David C. Sproat, but appears to have retained an interest in the business till 1826.

Mr. Colton was chosen constable and collector here in March, 1806; was one of the selectmen in 1809; was captain of the militia in 1814, and afterwards chosen colonel.

In September, 1813, he purchased of John Quinton and Thos. Christie, the premises where Henry Green resides, on which he built the front, or main part of the house now standing.

He deeded this place to his son, Cullen C. W. Colton, who sold it to Benjamin Warren, in July, 1833.

Col. Colton leased of Mrs. Lucy Wilmot, Aug. 11th, 1829, the Lyon tavern house, for five years, she agreeing that no tavern should be kept on the Dennis stand, then owned by her and occupied by James Greenough. At the expiration of this lease, in 1834, Col. Colton removed with his family to Lafayette, Ind., where he resided as late as 1851, when last heard from.

He first married Miss Betsey Waters, from Massachusetts. She died June 10th, 1824, in her 42d year, leaving two children.

1. *Cullen C. W.*, b. Nov. 11, 1809. He became a clerk with Peter Myers, of Whitehall, N. Y. He re-

HISTORY OF FAIR HAVEN, VERMONT. 329

moved to Lafayette, Ind., where he now resides and has a family. He is President of the Wabash Canal Company.

2. *Elizabeth Adeline*, b. July 5, 1811; m. Elkinah Mason, a son of John M. Mason, of Castleton.

Col. Colton married, for his second wife, his first wife's sister, Lydia Adeline Waters.

THOMAS CHRISTIE was born on the St. John's river, in New Brunswick, March 11, 1773; learned the trade of ship-carpenter, and when about 35 years of age took up his residence in Fair Haven, Vt., entering into partnership with his uncle, John Quinton, in a store and scythe factory, about 1808.

He was elected to several town offices, and the *Vermont Register* for 1817 contains his name as Representative in the State Legislature, or Assembly, for Rutland county, [Fair Haven.] His politics were of the Jeffersonian school, and he continued all his life a conservative member of the Democratic party. His health failing, he was obliged to close out his business in Fair Haven, about the year 1822, and seek a change of climate. After spending a winter in Georgia he purchased a farm in the town of Batavia, N. Y. After remaining some twenty years on this farm he sold out and removed to Darien, Genesee county, N. Y., having purchased another farm, in the spring of 1843, where he remained until his death, which occurred August 7, 1848. He had suffered most of his life from weak lungs, but the disease which proved fatal was erysipelas.

His reputation as a man of strict integrity and high

330 HISTORY OF FAIR HAVEN, VERMONT.

toned morality was unexcelled, and few men better deserved the name of "gentleman" in its most liberal sense. He was never known to have an enemy.

His remains were subsequently removed from their resting place in Darien, to the beautiful cemetery of Elmwood, near Detroit, to which latter place his widow and two sons removed in 1849, and where they still remain. He was married in 1823, to Mary Kendrick, of Hanover, N. H., a sister of Dr. Kendrick, of Poultney, who survives him at the age of 77. The eldest son, *James A. Christie*, is book-keeper and clerk in the boiler works of Desotell & Hutton. The youngest, *Thos. S. Christie*, is one of the firm of Hodge & Christie, iron founders and machinists.

JOHN PEABODY COLBURN, b. in St. Johns, N. B., November 25, 1787 ; came with his father's family from Frederickton, N. B., to Vermont, in July, 1808.

The family settled at first in West Castleton, where the father was engaged with Joshua Quinton in a saw-mill. John P. settled in Fair Haven. The family afterward resided in Benson and in Fair Haven. They removed to Perry, Wyoming county, N. Y.

Mr. Colburn worked at his trade as a blacksmith, with Mr. John Quinton, in the shop where Henry Green now works, for several years. At the time of the battle of Plattsburgh he is said to have been one of the military company from Fair Haven and vicinity, that went out, but returned without reaching the scene of war.

He was chosen one of the listers and constable and collector of the town, in March, 1816, and continued

HISTORY OF FAIR HAVEN, VERMONT. 331

in the latter office for several years. In the spring of 1817, he bought of Thomas Christie one-half of the scythe factory, standing on the ground of the Union Slate Works, and in company with John Quinton, carried on the factory and the blacksmith shop for a time. Thomas Blanchard, a celebrated mechanic of those days, is said to have worked for Mr. Colburn manufacturing axes and hoes. A number of young men, about this time, worked for Mr. Colburn, and learned the blacksmith trade of him, among them Wait Arms, of Castleton, Spencer Harvey, Royal Bullock, and Charles T. Colburn.

In March, 1822, he purchased of Jacob Davey a piece of land south of the paper mill, and built thereon the elegant brick dwelling house, now standing near the railroad. He entered into a plan with Jacob Davey and James Y. Watson, about 1825, to erect a furnace at the head of East Bay, and went so far as to build the stack just below Carver's Falls. In 1829 he was interested in the business of grinding manganese at Mr. Davey's works.

He was an active member of the Masonic Fraternity, and had the symbols of the order wrought into his dwelling house, as may be seen to this day. In politics he was an active member of the Republican party, which then existed, and came to be an Assistant Judge in the county court, which post he held at the time of his death, December 8, 1831.

He first married a sister of Royal Dennis, Miss Betsey Dennis, of Hardwick, Mass., in 1818, and went to keeping house in April, in the house long after-

332 HISTORY OF FAIR HAVEN, VERMONT.

ward known as the " Quinton house," now owned by Thomas Hughes. She died September 9, 1822, leaving him two children, *Moses* and *Betsey Dennis*.

He married Miss Lucy Davey, in July, 1824, of whom he had five children. Mrs. Colburn is still living, and a resident of Fair Haven.

Family:

1. *Moses*, is a graduate of Vermont University and of the Andover Theological Seminary. He was for some years a settled minister in South Dedham, Mass. He is now preaching in Waukegan, Ill.

2. *Betsey Dennis*, resides with her brother.

3. *John P.*, b. in 1826; studied law in Burlington, Vt.; removed to Iowa City, Iowa, where he was admitted to the bar, and immediately afterward died, Dec. 10th, 1853.

4. *Susan*, m. Rev. A. H. Bailey, and resides in Sheldon, Vt.

5. *Rufus C.*, resides in Fair Haven.

6. *Albert Vincent*, b. July 8, 1830. He entered the Military Academy at West Point, in June, 1851, was graduated and appointed second lieutenant in the 1st U. S. Cavalry, under Col. Sumner, in 1855. He was first stationed at Jefferson Barracks, Mo., and afterwards at Leavenworth, and on the Plains.

He was promoted to be 1st lieut. of his regiment in the early part of 1861. The same year he was promoted to be captain, and again to be major in the Adjutant General's Department, U. S. Army, and finally was appointed to be lieutenant-colonel and aide-de-camp in the U. S. volunteer service, which position

HISTORY OF FAIR HAVEN, VERMONT. 333

he held at the time of his death, June 17, 1863. His remains were brought from St. Louis to Fair Haven, and were buried in the village burying ground from the residence of his uncle, Israel Davey, Esq.

7. *Lucy*, the youngest child of Mr. Colburn, married C. T. Jenkins, of Bayport, Hernando county, Fla., where she now resides.

GEORGE COLBURN was employed in the service of Messrs. Colton, Warren & Sproat, for several years, about 1825, after which he went to Syracuse, N. Y., where he subsequently died.

CHARLES T. COLBURN commenced work with his brother, John P., at blacksmithing, in Fair Haven, January 1, 1823, and remained in the same until his brother's demise in December, 1831. He married Miss Olivia Moulton, a granddaughter of Silas Safford, Esq., at Pittsford, where he now resides.

WILLIAM B. COLBURN, a younger brother of John P., George and Charles T., was born in Frederickton, N. B., October 20, 1803, and came with the family to Vermont, in 1808. He was clerk in the store of Messrs. Colton, Warren & Sproat, for two or three years, about 1825 and '27. He went into company with Edmund Kingsland, succeeding Messrs. Colton, Warren and Sproat in the mercantile business, in the old red store, on the east side of the Common, about 1827 or '28. He purchased the saw-mill adjoining the grist-mill, in company with his brother Charles, in the fall of 1829.

In the spring of 1831, Benjamin Warren, of Hampton, became associated with him in place of his

334 HISTORY OF FAIR HAVEN, VERMONT.

brother, and they sold the mill to Apollos Smith, or Alpheus Smith, of West Haven, and also the Norton house and lot north of the Common, about 1832. Messrs. Colburn & Warren carried on the carriage making business together, while running the saw-mill.

Mr. Colburn was in the lumber business at West Castleton, running the saw-mill there. He afterward removed to Castleton, and held the office of deputy sheriff for several years. He also represented the town of Castleton in the General Assembly for two years. He kept the public house at the " Corners," a number of years previous to 1854, when he removed to Grant county, Wisconsin. During the civil war he was military store keeper at St. Louis. After the war he removed to Detroit, Mich., where he resided with his children, and died September 20, 1869, aged 66 years, having suffered much for two years previously. from what was supposed to be a cancer in the stomach.

He married Miss Betsey Hawkins, daughter of Charles Hawkins, 2d, about 1825, and his family are:

1. *George;* 2. *Cullen;* 3. *Mason;* 4. *Charles;* 5. *Henry;* 6. *Elizabeth.*

George, Cullen and Elizabeth reside in' Detroit, Mich. Mason is in the tanning and leather business at Factory Point, Vt., and Henry resides in Cincinnati, Ohio.

Rev. RUFUS CUSHMAN, the first settled minister in Fair Haven, was born in Goshen, Mass., September 18, 1777. He graduated at Williams College in 1805, and studied theology with Rev. Samuel Whitman, D. D. He was ordained and installed as pastor of the

HISTORY OF FAIR HAVEN, VERMONT. 335

Congregational church and society in Fair Haven, February 12, 1807. Mr. Cushman purchased of Paul Scott, April 19, 1808, a little more than 20 acres of land, lying on the south side of West street—the same now owned and occupied by John P. Sheldon—and here made his permanent home while he lived. In April, 1826, he purchased of Samuel W. Guilford, an addition of 50 acres to his farm—30 acres south of the highway and 20 acres on the north of it.

On the 12th of October, 1813, at a meeting called for the purpose, the town voted to give, grant and confirm, release and forever quit-claim to Mr. Cushman, his heirs, &c., "all the lands of the first settled minister's right which belong to the town," and then voted that "if the Rev. Mr. Cushman shall think proper to give the town the sum of $500 as compensation for the minister's lands, the town do agree to take a mortgage of his farm, where he now lives, as security for the payment of the said sum of $500, to be paid at the time when he ceases to be the minister of Fair Haven, without any interest for the same."

At another meeting, held Nov. 1, the town voted "to accept a clear deed of Rev. Mr. Cushman's farm as a consideration for the minister's lands, instead of a mortgage, as previously voted, and furthermore to lease the farm to the Rev. Mr. Cushman, his heirs and assigns, for the term of 999 years, free of rent during the time that he continues his ministry in Fair Haven, and from and after that time, he to pay a yearly rent of $30, to be laid out for the support of the Gospel, under the direction of the inhabitants."

336 HISTORY OF FAIR HAVEN, VERMONT.

On the 29th of May, 1820, the selectmen were authorized and directed to deed the farm to Mr. Cushman, free and clear of all incumbrance, except that he, Mr. Cushman, is to covenant, and agree to continue his ministerial labors is said town, as heretofore, during the full term of 20 years from and after his first settlement, for the consideration of his being hereafter paid an annual salary of $300, and provided, in case of his removal by death, that the farm is to be deeded to his heirs the same as though it had been deeded free of encumbrance.

Owing to the smallness of his salary, Mr. Cushman used to take students into his family. He fitted several for college. The people used to turn out and help him gather in his hay and draw his wood.

He married Theodosia Stone, who was also born in Goshen, and is said to have assisted him with means to complete his studies for the ministry. She died at her son Artemas', in Fair Haven, June 10, 1844, aged 65 years.

They had seven children, only five of whom lived to mature age.

1. *Artemas Stone*, b. December 28, 1807; m. Phebe S. Davey, daughter of Jacob Davey, Nov. 10, 1836, and now lives in Jackson, Mich., whither he removed in 1854. He was for several years a teacher in town, and afterwards associated with Israel Davey in the iron business. His family are, Harriet, Jane, and Charlotte.

2. *Wealthy Stone*, b. June 23, 1813; m. Rev. Wm. C. Dennison, of Castleton, Oct. 16, 1832. She died

HISTORY OF FAIR HAVEN, VERMONT. 337

at Dexter, Mich., Oct. 12, 1844, leaving one child only living.

3. *Rufus Spalding*, b. Aug. 31, 1815; m. Sarah F. Gibson, of Sandy Hill, N. Y., August 10, 1845, and has three children; Delia N.,. Allerton E., and Sarah O. He graduated at Middlebury College, in Aug., 1837; was installed as pastor of the Congregational church in Orwell, in Dec., 1843, and resigned his charge and removed to Manchester in May, 1862, where he now resides as pastor of the Congregational church.

4. *Electa Lyman*, b. May 2, 1817; m. Amasa W. Flagg, of Hubbardton, Sept. 12, 1842. She died Aug., 1855, at Castleton. Her children are Rufus C., Sarah, and James.

5. *Jerusha Almira*, b. Oct. 23, 1823; m. Pliny F. Cheever, of Castleton, Sept. 10, 1851. Her children are Caroline E., Jane, Harriet C., and Edward.

Mr. Cushman died February 3, 1829. His successor, Rev. Amos Drury, writes concerning him as follows: "He lived greatly beloved by the people of his charge, and in the high esteem of all who knew him, and died universally lamented by all his acquaintance. As a humble token of their high respect for his worth, his people erected a plain, neat marble slab, with a suitable inscription to mark the place of his interment." His son Rufus, describing his character for the Cushman genealogy, says of him: "He was a good, plain Puritan man, distinguished for solid rather than brilliant qualities. He was sedate, firm, persevering in his labors, not remarkable for force or

348 HISTORY OF FAIR HAVEN, VERMONT.

energy, or power of imagination. He was a worker and was willing to work on in the cause of his Master whose service he loved, and whose life he aimed to imitate. His theology was of the old Pilgrim stamp; his life was pure, kind, peaceful. He·did what he could to bring sinners to repentance and to embrace the truth as it is in Jesus, to promote and diffuse love to God and man."

"He was temperate in all his habits, never used tobacco or alcoholic spirits was one of·the first; ministers in the region to favor the temperance reformation. His last sickness was a malignant epidemic fever. He was prostrated by apoplexy. His last words were, "Lord Jesus receive my spirit." "He was fond of music; was a fine base singer; could read and sing any ordinary tune at sight."

From his diary we have the following extracts: "Lord's Day, June 27, 1813. The past week has been a season of anxiety, peril, sorrow, and joy-to us. But the Lord has carried us through them all. I long to live in the Lord always, for His arm is full of strength. He never disappoints those who put their trust in Him. Eternal praise is due Him."

"Lord's Day, July 4, 1813. The day of American Independence. God was pleased to deliver this nation from the oppression of a foreign yoke, and make us a free people. He has granted us privileges which have not been enjoyed by any other people on the globe. But what return have we made for his loving kindness and tender mercy? He has nourished and brought us up as children, but we have rebelled

HISTORY OF FAIR HAVEN, VERMONT. 339

against him. He has not cut us off as our sins deserve, though He has sent judgments upon us—the sword to slay, the pestilence to destroy, and the fear of famine. Well may the Saviour weep over us as he did over Jerusalem."

"July 10. My soul is distressed for the youth of this place. They appear to think of nothing but diversion and carnal amusements."

"Lord's Day, Aug. 1. Have been contemplating for some time upon the importance of the Redeemer's being a person in whom unbounded confidence can be placed both by God and man, in order to be a successful mediator between them. He is such a being! We need not fear! He is every way qualified to fill the important station of mediator, and fulfill the trust imposed upon him by his Father and our Father. Hence then the importance of faith, trust in his mercy, compliance with its conditions."

ELIJAH COLEMAN, a nephew of Dr. James Witherell, took the freeman's oath here in September, 1803. He studied medicine with Dr. Witherell, and went away in 1808.

AMOS CLARK, of Whitehall, in December, 1804, came and lived on Scotch Hill. He worked at coaling for Jacob Davey, until June, 1813, when he purchased 20 acres of land, lying north and east from Harmon Sheldon's now residence, and there built and resided for some years. His wife's name was Betsey. He also had a daughter Betsey, and a son Joseph, who taught singing, and afterward became an' Episcopal clergyman. He is said to have removed to Skaneateles, N. Y., and to have died in the West.

340 HISTORY OF FAIR HAVEN, VERMONT.

Moses Clark resided in the house built by John Ashley in Mr. Sheldon's neighborhood. He sold the place to Nelson Nutting, in September, 1850. His daughter married a Mr. Cheeseman.

James Claghorn, of Rutland, bought of Henry Ainsworth, in July, 1807, the Erwin farm of 110 acres, now owned by Mr. Kidder, and on the same day sold to his brother, Eleazer Claghorn, also of Rutland, one undivided half of the same.

They occupied the farm together. Eleazer died here, August 3, 1812, in the 42d year of his age, and in May, 1814, his wife, Hannah, and Joel Hamilton, as administrators of his estate, deeded his half of the farm to Silas Safford. On the same day Mr. Hamilton conveyed to Mr. Safford the other, or James Claghorn's part, he having purchased it in March, of Ebenezer Mussey and Wm. Alvord, of Rutland, to whom it had been willed by James Claghorn.

Eleazer had a daughter *Lucy*, born in town, December 27, 1808, and a son *Eleazer J. H.*, born December 20, 1810. He is said to have had a son *Charles* and a son *Horace*. Mrs. Claghorn took a letter of dismission of the Congregational church and recommendation to the church in Castleton, May 22, 1825.

Jonathan Chamberlain erected a distillery about where the nail factory now is, for the purpose of making essences of birch, wintergreen, peppermint, &c., and finally made cider brandy. The distillery was burned about 1812. In March of the same year, according to the school report, Mr. Chamberlain had

HISTORY OF FAIR HAVEN, VERMONT.   341

seven children in the Middle School District. He is said to have had a son *Thomas* and one by the name of *Jonas*, who was a school teacher.

DUNCAN COOK, a Scotchman and a tailor, is said to have been taken a prisoner by Gen. Burgoyne in the Irish rebellion, and to have come to America in 1798. He was in town as early as 1806 or '08, and lived two or three years in the old house which stood on the common. In the winter of 1835, he occupied the house owned by Mr. Keating, which is now standing just north of J. H. Williams' store, known in more recent times as the old, widow Ranney house. He was intemperate in his habits, and is said to have become crazy and gone off, after which his wife married Nathan H. Darling, and resided, in 1837, and later, in the old hat shop, which had been moved by one of her sons to the spot just west of Mr. Stephen Fish's residence, and which was afterwards occupied by widow Bryant, and was finally burned down. The sons were, *Solon H.*, who married Sarah S. Cobb, and *Roland*, who died at the West.

JACOB COBB was born in Taunton, Mass., October 28, 1778. He married, in January, 1801, Mary Crossman, who was born in Norwalk, Conn., October 3, 1781, and soon afterward removed to Londonderry, Vt., whence he came to Fair Haven, about 1809 or '10. He first resided on the plain, east of Mr. Moore's for a period of nine years, where he employed a number of men in making nails from the nail rods furnished by Jacob Davey, and transported from the works on horseback, and for the making of which Mr. Davey paid 5 cents per pound.

342   HISTORY OF FAIR HAVEN, VERMONT.

Mr. Cobb spent one year in Pawlet and then moved on to 'the place where Otis Eddy resides, having a shop there, and making nails with his four boys, for several years subsequent to 1818. He removed to the house which had been occupied by Mr. Kingsland and others, on the top of the hill south of the paper mill, where he died April 4, 1832, aged 54 years. His wife survived until April, 1844.

Their family were:

1. *Mercy*, b. in Londonderry, April 8, 1802, and died in town July 5, 1865, aged 63.

2. *Simeon*, b. in Londonderry, April 1st, 1804; m. Pamelia Maranville, July 16, 1826; d. Aug. 5, 1847, aged 43 years. His family were:

1. *Caroline*; 2. *Ira*; 3. *Ellen*; 4. *Martha*.

These removed to Warsaw, N. Y., where Ira married Lydia Maranville, and Ellen married Vivalda Ely, and Martha died. By his second wife, Laura Mudget, he had 3 children, who, with their mother, reside in Cold Water, Mich.

3. *Barnum*, b. in Londonderry, Oct. 19, 1806; d. July 25, 1849, aged 41 years.

4. *Jacob*, b. in Londonderry, Dec. 29, 1808; d. Aug. 1870.

5. *Gilbert*, b. in Fair Haven, June 2, 1811; d. July 25, 1811.

6. *Sarah Smith*, b. in Fair Haven, July 30, 1812; m. Solon H. Cook, June 8, 1834. He died Oct. 30, 1842, aged 31 years, and she married Dan Orms, Dec. 20, 1852. She died Oct. 25, 1865, aged 63 years. Her daughter, Marion, married Geo. A. Cahtine, and now resides in Rome, N. Y.

HISTORY OF FAIR HAVEN, VERMONT. 343

7. *Betsey*, b. Jan. 19, 1816; m. Simeon Bullock, Sept. 17, 1837. She now resides with her children in town.

8. *Mary*, b. May 5, 1820; m. Hiram Clark, Dec. 31, 1843. He resides at Newark, N. Y. She died Oct. 8, 1849, aged 29 years.

9. *George Gilbert*, b. June 20, 1822; m. Mary Ann Kelly, in July, 1850. She is deceased.

SIRENUS COBB, a bloomer, worked for Col. Lyon; had a son *Sirenus*, who went to Eddyville, Ky., and a son *Reuben*, who removed to Chittenden after his father's death. He was warned out of town in 1809.

PETER COON, b. in Canada, of Dutch parents, was in the British army prior to 1812, but deserted and came to Fair Haven. He was a cooper by trade and built a shop near his house, on Mr. Gilbert's land, north of the village, and nearly opposite Geo. Allen's, where he worked. He married a French wife, whose father's name was Wm. Bell. They were simple folk. Mr. Coon had a number of children, among whom were *Joe*, *Eliza*, *Amanda*, *Fred*, and *Peter*. At the March meeting, in 1833, the town voted to appropriate a sufficient sum of money to remove Mr. Coon and family, including Mrs. Bell, to the western part of the state of New York. They removed to Steuben county.

Dr. WILLIAM CATON was a surgeon in the U. S. Navy, and attached to Com. McDonough's fleet on Lake Champlain, in the time of the war of 1812 and '14. The fleet was stationed at Whitehall during one winter, and Dr. Caton boarded at Thomas Ranney's, who kept a public house in North Whitehall, whence he came to reside on Scotch Hill, in Fair Haven.

344 HISTORY OF FAIR HAVEN, VERMONT.

He drew a pension of $25,00 per year, and boarded at Daniel McArthur's, where he died about 1820. He gave to Philena Ranney, in July, 1819, the house and a four acre lot where Arnold Briggs now lives, which Miss Ranney sold to Abraham Sharp.

HECTOR H. CRANE, said to have been a grandson of Daniel Hunter who resided on West street in 1813, and to have come hither from Ira, was first a clerk for Elisha Parkill. He bought 2 acres of land north of the village, of Silas Holden, in January, 1819. In October, 1820, he bought 15 acres of land of Tilly Gilbert, in company with Mr. Parkill, with whom also he erected a still on the lower side of the road, west of the old burying ground.

He continued to carry on the distillery with Mr. Parkill until February, 1824, when he sold out to Parkill, and removed to Vergennes. While here he married Caroline Smith, the eldest daughter of Clement Smith. They had 5 children, of whom all are dead but one. Mr. Crane removed from Vergennes to Albany, N. Y., where he kept the Eagle Hotel, and died, his wife keeping the house awhile after his death.

CEPHAS CARPENTER came into town from Ira, in 1821. He purchased the home farm of Olney Hawkins on West street, in May of that year, adding to it 60 acres, in July of the following year, by purchase of Jacob Willard.

He quitclaimed to his son, Lyman, in April, 1828; Lyman deeding, in 1830, to Chester Howe. He was twice married. His first wife's name was Phebe Collins; his second, Mehitable Ormsbee. By the first he had eight children; by the last three.

HISTORY OF FAIR HAVEN, VERMONT. 345

He died at his place on West street, February 26, 1829, aged 75 years, and was buried in the old village burying ground.

His family were:

1. *Ira*, m. in Castleton, and removed to Athens, Ohio, where he died, leaving a family of sons and daughters.

2. *Cephas*, m. in Ira and removed to Athens, Ohio. Has no children.

3. *Polly*, m. Simeon Guilford.

4. *Phebe*, m. first James Hunter, of Ira, and afterwards a Mr. Storrs, of Moriah, N. Y.; has a son in Ohio, and a daughter who married Dr. Samuel Lowe.

5. *Rosman*, m. Richard Tilliston, and has a family in Moriah, N. Y.

6. *Lucy*, m. a Mr. Lovell, and went to Western N. Y.

7. *Betsey*, m. Russell Fish, of Ira.

8. *Benoni*, b. May 30, 1797, m. Julia Sheldon, daughter of Joseph Sheldon, Esq., in Jan. 1826, and removed to Moriah, N. Y., where he died in the following Nov., leaving one son, Benoni G., who is in the business of life insurance in New York.

9. *Lyman*, m. Susan Newton, of Ira. He resided with his father on the home farm. . He was engaged with Gilbert Leonard from 1830 to 1837, in the business of woolen manufacturing at the State Line. He removed to Illinois and died there. He had a daughter Angeline, who married Dr. Hubbard, of Whitehall, and two sons, Sylvester, who died in Kansas, and Henry, who now resides in Ira.

346 HISTORY OF FAIR HAVEN, VERMONT.

10. *Marvin*, b. 1800, m. Laura Perkins, of Castleton. She died in March, 1867. He was killed while coupling cars at the Fair Haven depot, Sept. 26., 1852. His family were : Cephas V., now resident in town ; Isabella, residing with her brother, and John M., who died Sept. 8, 1858, aged 17 years.

11. *Hannah*, m. Simeon Willard.

DAVID CULVER, a miller, came hither from Shoreham as early as 1828, and resided in the grist-mill house for several years afterwards. He removed to Hydeville, and then came back to Fair Haven and resided for a time in Barnabas Ellis' old harness shop, on the east side of the highway, opposite Mr. Ellis' dwelling house, where Mrs. Culver died. He had three daughters, *Ann*, *Eliza*, and *Alice*. Eliza married Joseph Whipple, and removed to Mansfield, Tioga county, Penn., whither Mr. Culver also went and there died.

JONATHAN CAPEN, b. in Vassalboro, Maine, May 10, 1804, removed thence to Pittsford, Vt., in 1815, where he resided until 1822, and removed to Keeseville, N. Y. From Keeseville he came to Fair Haven, in May, 1829, having, in company with Edmund and Jacob D. Kingsland, purchased of Jacob Davey a half interest in the iron works. Messrs. Kingslands and Capen ran the works two years, making $500 apiece the first six months, and losing what they had made during the next six months. In the spring of 1831, Jacob D. Kingsland and Mr. Capen sold out to Edmund Kingsland, and he sold out to Mr. Davey in the spring of 1832 and removed to Keeseville.

HISTORY OF FAIR HAVEN, VERMONT. 347

Mr. Capen then rented the works for one year, and made $1,000 in running them. In December, 1833, he bought of Eli Barber the farm where Col Allen's slate quarry is, and 60 acres now owned by I. H. Allard, west of the village, removing on to the farm in the spring of 1834, and residing there until 1845.

He sold the farm to Col. A. Allen, Nov. 7, 1851, and in November, 1852, purchased of H. & H. Howard, the old McWithey farm on West street, consisting then, of 90 acres. He sold 70 acres, lying north of the river, to Oliver P. Ranney, March 25, 1858. In April, 1866, he sold the remaining 20 acres, and the 60 acre lot of Eli Barber, lying south of the river, to Isaac H. Allard ; Mr. Allard having sold his place south of the highway to Wm. L. Town. Mr. C. sold his home place in the village to Mr. R. Hanger, in the fall of 1866, and removed to Hampton Flat in the following spring. He removed to Poultney in the spring of 1869, where he now resides.

He first married Miss Emoroy S. Blanchard, of West Rutland, in January, 1831. She died December 15, 1850, and he afterward, in March, 1854, married Mrs. Mary C. June, of Poultney. His family by his first wife were :

1. *Eliza Stuart.*

2. *Flavia Caroline*, m. Albert E. Hall, in May, 1865, and died in six weeks afterward in Alabama, whither they had removed.

3. *Theophilus*, d. aged 4 years.

4. *Emeroy B.*, m. Solomon P. Gidings, and resides in West Rutland.

348   HISTORY OF FAIR HAVEN, VERMONT.

5. *Lucy Maria*, b. in 1849.

JONATHAN CHANDLER, a physician in copartnership with Dr. Lewis, in 1830, and '31, was from Massachusetts, and returned thither. He was reported to have been engaged to marry Martha Gilbert.

JAMES CAMPBELL married Eliza Holden in Queen's county, Ireland, and came to Fair Haven in 1836. He bought a piece of land of Wm. Frazier, in 1837, near Chauncey Goodrich's. In 1848 he purchased of Miss Kelsey the place where he now resides, north of the village, the place on which John Brown originally settled. His family are:

1. *Kate;* 2. *Mary;* 3. *Eliza;* 4. *Lucy;* 5. *Margaret;* 6. *Julia*, (m. to David McBride;) 7. *John;* 8. *Thomas;* 9. *Sarah;* 10. *Mattie;* 11. *James.*

JEREMIAH DURAND was the first settler on the hill farm now owned by Col. A. Allen, eastward from his slate quarry. He came into town in company with Israel Trowbridge, from Derby, Conn., in the autumn of 1780. He had married for his first wife, in Derby, November 12, 1772, Hannah Trowbridge, a daughter of Israel Trowbridge. She died in 1777, leaving one infant child, *Hannah*, whom he committed to the care and keeping of his wife's sister, Abigail Trowbridge, and who afterwards became the wife of Olney Hawkins.

Upon his wife's demise he enlisted in the Revolutionary War, and probably remained in the army until 1780, when he came to Fair Haven. His second wife's name was Sarah Andrus, by whom he had six hilcdren. He died in 1798, and his widow was mar-

HISTORY OF FAIR HAVEN, VERMONT. 349

ried to Lewis Wilkinson, of Benson, June 22, 1806, by Isaac Cutler, Justice of the Peace.

His family were:

1. *Hannah*, b. Jan. 6, 1776, and the only child of his first wife. She married Olney Hawkins.

2. *Sarah*, who married John Gorham, of Batavia, N. Y., and went thither about 1824.

3. *Ira*, who first married Olive Cleveland, the eldest child of Josiah Cleveland, but left her, and married, May 10, 1808, Susanna Lewis. He afterward married Rebecca Dennison, by whom he had a daughter *Welthy*, who became the wife of Seneca McArthur, and a son *David*, who lives in Crown Point, N. Y. He died at Crown Point in 1864, aged 82 years.

4. *Patty* b. July, 1783; m. Benj. Lewis, of Poultney, and afterward a Mr. Cramton. She is now living. Her children are *Laura*, *Clark*, *K*,, and *Paulina*.

5. *Amy*, who married Amos Bronson, a carpenter and joiner, in Fair Haven. They removed to Batavia, N. Y., about 1805, and died somewhere in Pennsylvania.

6. *Nancy*, who married Ashley Root, of Benson.

7. *Rhoda*, who married Ira Carpenter, of Benson, and now resides in Le Roy, N. Y., where she has three daughters.

NATHANIEL DICKINSON came into town from Massachusetts, as early as 1790. He built a store near Dr. Witherell's, on West street. In June, 1795, he was keeping Col. Lyon's tavern, and kept it for several years afterward. He was constable in 1802, and is

350   HISTORY OF FAIR HAVEN, VERMONT.

said to have lived in a part of the old Hennessy house in 1804, and to have been afflicted with paralysis. He resided in West Haven, near Dr. Smith's, in 1809, and died there in July, 1811. His funeral was held at the church on the 14th of July. His wife was Sally Gilbert, only sister of Tilly Gilbert. She died December 16, 1810, aged 42 years.

LEWIS DICKINSON, a bloomer, was in town in 1802; built a forge with Salmon Norton; resided, in 1814, where Richard W. Sutliff now does.

NATHAN DURKEE, called "Durgee" by the old inhabitants, was a bachelor from Pomfret, Vt., and came here as early as 1792 or '93. He professed to have studied medicine, and was called "Doctor." In 1798 he had "a small assortment of English and India goods, at the corner opposite Brown's tavern," which he advertised "for cash, country produce, or ashes." He was "a wicked old man," says one, and boarded at the Lyon tavern where he died, his brother John, from Pomfret, taking care of him in his last sickness.

JEREMIAH DWYER came to Fair Haven from Pomfret, Vt., through the influence of Col. Lyon, about 1793. He was a countryman of Lyon's, and lived, in 1795, where Henry Green now does. In December, 1695, he was postrider from the printing office, in Fair Haven, through Castleton, Hubbardton, Sudbury, Whiting and Cornwall, to Middlebury Falls.

Family:

1. *Jeremiah Howard*, who was a Baptist minister, and removed to Whitehall, where he married a Miss Harlow. He is said to have been involved in the con-

HISTORY OF FAIR HAVEN, VERMONT. 351

spiracy to blow up Squire Cook's office in Poultney, and to have fled the state in consequence. He had two sons who were ministers.

2. *Polly.* In 1827, we find Polly named as "a sick person, chargeable on the town," and from that time till about 1834, she is the subject of many amusing records on the town books. In 1828 it was voted in March meeting "that Polly be put up at vendue"— rather cruel for a land of freedom, but the intent was good—"to be taken by the lowest bidder and comfortably provided for as to victuals, clothing, doctoring and every other expense, for one. year." "Owen Kelsey, bid her off at $100."

In 1830 she was bid off by Daniel McArthur at $93. She was struck off in 1833 to David Perkins at $92.

3. *James.*

4. *Fanny*, b. 1781; m. Orren Kelsey, in 1800; d. Feb. 26, 1869.

5. *Hannah.*

6. *John.*

7. *Patrick.*

8. *William.*

EBER DENNISON was assessed in the lists of 1804, '06 and '08, and is said to have resided in the south district, near the east side of the Cedar Swamp. His daughter, *Rebecca*, married Ira Durand, and he had a son who was resident in Castleton a few years since.

THOMAS DIBBLE, a noted horse farrier and cattle doctor, came from Nobletown, N. Y., and married Rhoda, a daughter of Oliver Cleveland. He resided

352 HISTORY OF FAIR HAVEN, VERMONT.

west of the Cedar Swamp, and near the river, previous to 1807, at which time he purchased the farm which had been settled by Jeremiah Durand, now owned by Col. A. Allen, and resided on it until 1817. He sold it to Elisha Parkill, and removed to West Haven, where he and his wife both died.

Family:

1. *Elizabeth*, m. Shubel Bullock.

2. *Harry*, m. Clara Priest, daughter of Noah Priest. He removed to Parma, Orleans county, N. Y., where his wife died, and he removed to Ohio.

3. *Emily*, m..Wm. Bullock, brother to Shubel Bullock.

4. *Dolly*, m. Fox Kelly, of West Haven.

5. *Fanny*, m. Col. Lemon Barnes, who now resides in Whitehall, N. Y.

JAMES DOWNEY. "James Downe" took the freeman's oath in the town, September, 1791, and we hear that a man of this name lived where Cyrus C. Whipple now does, working for Col. Lyon in the forge, and that he had several song, among them one Lysander "Downie," who drew a prize of $10,000 in a lottery, went away and educated himself, and then purchased a military commission in the British army in Canada, and became commander of the English fleet that fought against Commodore McDonough in the war of 1812 and '14. We cannot verify the story and give it for what it is worth.

We find that James Downey, Jr., of Granville, N. Y., in December, 1792, purchased of Daniel Arnold, a fourth of the Leonard forge, in the town, selling it

HISTORY OF FAIR HAVEN, VERMONT. 353

again in June, 1798, to Samuel Atwood, and that Charles Downey, or "Downie," took the freeman's oath here in March, 1793.

ELDER JORDAN DODGE was a Baptist preacher, resident here in 1804, and is said to have been really the first settled minister of the town. He preached in the school-house and in private houses, and a portion of the time at the church in Hampton. In common with many others, and in•keeping with the custom of the day, he was warned out of town, with his family, in May, 1804. He lived, at one time, on the south side of West street, beyond the old burying ground; at another, and perhaps later period, on the north side of the street, running past the iron works, then called "Johnny-cake Lane," having a shop on the rocks above the iron works, where he is said to have worked at his trade of nail-making. Dr. Beaman represents him as a bloomer, working in the forge during the week, and preaching on Sunday. He was a man of excitable temper, eccentric, naturally talented, and witty. Numerous anecdotes and stories are told concerning him, all similarly characteristic.

It is related that, as he had some trouble in the church, the church taking him to discipline for some violence on his part, he felt himself persecuted, and remarked that an apple tree which held many clubs in its branches was clubbed on account of the superior quality of its fruit, when one hearing it, replied that sometimes trees were clubbed because of great hornets' nests contained in them. Dr. Beaman refers to two of his children, and relates another anecdote

354 HISTORY OF FAIR HAVEN, VERMONT.

quite in keeping with the above, to which the reader's attention is referred in another part of this volume.

The following epitaph is handed down by tradition as written by Elder Dodge:

> " Here lies old Dodge, who dodged all good,
>   But never dodged evil ;
> He dodged all he could,
>   But never dodged the devil."

NOAH DODGE, who was a farmer in the south part of the town, from March, 1816, to 1831, resided from 1803 to 1815 in Glover, Vt. He married Rebecca Cameron, of Barre. He removed to Rutland in 1815, and in the spring of 1816 bought the farm of Timothy Brainard, south of Charles Wood's and came into the place to reside. He sold the farm of 50 acres to his son Arnold, in April, 1831, and went away to Columbus, Ohio, afterward removing to Illinois, where he died in 1852.

Arnold sold the farm, said to be sixty acres, to Nelson R. Norton of Poultney, in September, 1832. Norton sold it to Hezekiah Howard the following spring ; Howard sold it to Stephen Beach, of Castleton, in July, and Beach sold it to Lyman Sherwood, in March, 1837.

Mr. Dodge's family, all born in Glover, were ;

1. *Rebecca*, first married Samuel G. Trowbridge, from Massachusetts, and afterward Alfred Ward, of Hampton ; now resides in Poultney.

2. *Arnold*, m. a sister to Ebenezer Gould of Hampton. He resides in Illinois.

8. *Mandana*; she first married Nelson Hyde; is now the wife of Ira M. Clarke, of Poultney.

HISTORY OF FAIR HAVEN, VERMONT. 355

4. *Calista*, m. Martin Hyde, of Poultney; is now dead.

JACOB DAVEY, for many years the most prominent and active business man of Fair Haven, was born in Boonton, N. J., November 12, 1771. His family, consisting of his mother and sister, afterwards resided in Morristown, N. J., He married Miss Phebe Dey, on the 8th of December, 1795, and resided in Dover, N. J., where their first three children were born, and the second one died.

He removed with his family to Vergennes, Vt., in the spring of 1800, where Lucy, afterward Mrs. Colburn, was born in October, 1801. Delia, now Mrs. Stowe, was born in Ferrisburgh, in March, 1803, and Mr. Davey is said to have spent one year in Bridport.

He came to Fair Haven in the spring of 1804, to superintend the iron works for Dan Smith, and brought his family hither in the fall. He first resided for several years in the house, at the foot of the hill, where Cyrus C. Whipple now resides, and had an office, or store, on the hill above the house. He bought the works of Mr. Smith, together with about six acres of land, extending along the river westward to the, turnpike, and covering the spot on which he afterward built, and where the family has so long resided, in October, 1807; at the same time taking a lease for seven years, with the privilege of purchasing, of the 300 acres of land owned by Mr. Smith in connection with the works, lying on the east and south, beyond the river. This land he purchased in June, 1812.

356 HISTORY OF FAIR HAVEN, VERMONT.

Mr. Davey's business transactions were extensiv and prove him to have been a man of remarkable capacity and enterprise. Besides carrying on his forge and rolling mill, he was engaged with Messrs. Parsons & Foster in fulling and finishing cloths during the time of the war of 1812. He was one of the building committee of the new meeting-house; he erected his own new and large dwelling house in 1815, moving into it in October, and when his works were burned in November, he at once rebuilt them, and erected numerous other dwelling houses for the use of his men. He owned and ran the saw-mill on the Lower Falls, and afterward bought the saw-mill on the rocks above his works, together with a house near the bridge, which had been occupied by Salem Ryder just previous to 1822. He dealt extensively in real estate, and was one of the selectmen of the town in 1813, '14 and '15. Though not a member of the church, he was an active member of the Congregational Society, and contributed liberally to the support of public institutions. He was a Federalist in his politics, and in the time of the war, belonged to the Washingtonian Benevolent Society, a political organization, supported by the Federalists.

His great fault was intemperance, which made him, like many others of his neighbors, a frequent visitor at the public inn and stores, where Mr. Davey was behind hand with none in merry wit and the humorous joke. Instances are remembered and related, which we will not here repeat, of his quickness in *repartee*. He appreciated the benefits of education

HISTORY OF FAIR HAVEN, VERMONT. 357

and gave his children more than common facilities for self-culture.

He died at his home, October 15, 1843. His wife died the 19th of January, 1856.

His family were:

1. *Mary Ann*, b. in Dover, N. J., Oct. 13, 1796. She married Alanson Mitchell, June 4, 1818, and had 5 children: Lucy Jane, who married James T. Phelps and resides in Chelsea, Mass; Jacob, now in Florida ; Phebe, who married C. M. Willard, Esq., and now resides in Castleton ; Daniel, deceased; and Mary Ann, who married Clarence C. Hard.

2. *James Dey*, b. Feb. 5, 1798 ; d. Dec. 8, 1799.

3. *Albert Vincent*, b. in Dover, N. J., Oct. 24, 1799 ; m. Lucinda Smalley, June 6, 1834; has one son, Vincent C., and now resides in town.

4. *Lucy*, b. in Vergennes, Oct. 20, 1801; m. John P. Colburn, Esq., July 6, 1824.

5. *Delia Hoagland*, b. in Ferrisburgh, March 21, 1803 ; m. Leonard Stow, of Elizabethtown, N. Y., Jan. 19, 1830, and now resides in town with her children, Leonard J. and Delia.

6. *Caroline*, b. in Fair Haven, March 16, 1805 ; m. Dr. Edward Lewis, Dec. 16, 1825.

7. *Jane Eliza*, b. in Fair Haven, Nov. 23, 1806 ; m. Alpheus J. Smith, Feb. 26, 1830. They had 3 children, a daughter, Vincent and William.

8. *Phebe Loraine*, b. in Fair Haven, March 26, 1809 ; m. Artemas S. Cushman, Nov. 10, 1836.

9. *John Jacob*, b. in Fair Haven, April 3, 1811. He purchased the old Dennis tavern house, in Feb.

358   HISTORY OF FAIR HAVEN, VERMONT.

1838, and spent the year in repairing and altering the same for a store and offices. He afterwards went away, and is said to have been a portrait painter in Spain, several years since.

10. *Israel*, b. in Fair Haven, May 28, 1813 ; m. Harriet Kilbourn, daughter of Alphonso Kilbourn, then of Hydeville, Nov. 12, 1856. He was engaged for some years in the mercantile business with Mr. James Adams, of Castleton. At his father's decease he came to Fair Haven as administrator of the estate, and remained in the town as proprietor of the iron works until his death, which took place after a very brief illness, at his house, Aug. 14, 1869. His family are John C., deceased; Hattie K., Israel, Anna and Mary.

11. *Christopher M.*, b. in Fair Haven, Aug. 1, 1815 ; m. Narcissa B., daughter of Hon. Myron Clark, late of Manchester, in June, 1834. He was a graduate of the University of Vermont, in the class of 1841, and was engaged in trade in Burlington for a number of years. He was a short time connected with the Western Vermont Railroad as receiver. He died very suddenly at his residence in Rutland, on the evening of April 8, 1870, having but just returned from Fair Haven, whither he had been during the day, and where he had been for several years previously engaged in the slate quarrying business. His family were Jane Eliza, the wife of Henry W. Cheney, of Rutland, and Henry Clark, who graduated at Williams College, in 1869.

12. *Chalon F.*, b. in Fair Haven, Aug. 28, 1817, and

HISTORY OF FAIR HAVEN, VERMONT. 359

was married to Georgiana H. Vernon, Dec. 23, 1843. He resided several years in Burlington, where he was liberally educated at the University, and has latterly been associated with the life insurance business in New York city.

ROYAL DENNIS was born in Hardwick, Mass., and came thence to Fair Haven in 1807. He married Susan Watson, a sister of James Y. Watson, who was born in Brookfield, Mass., and who died in Rockland, Me. Mr. Dennis kept the old Lyon tavern, owned by Cutler, one year, and in May, 1809, bought of Alexander Dunahue the old Hennessy store, where Mr. Graves' store now stands, and about an acre and a half of land, and by building an addition eastward, over the old highway, and putting on a new front with balconies on the west, facing the new highway, he converted it into a large and commodious hotel, which was kept by him, and was widely known throughout the country as the Dennis Tavern.

Mr. Dennis became involved by signing for Dr. Ebenezer Hurd, and was obliged to make over his place, March 15, 1822, to his brother, Samuel Dennis, of Boston, by whom it was afterward sold, through John P. Colburn, attorney, to Lucy Wilmot, in August, 1829.

Mr. Dennis removed from Fair Haven to Hartford, N. Y., in 1823, and there died in 1830. He was captain of the militia in 1819, and went in a subordinate office, within a few miles of Plattsburg, at the time of the war in 1812. His family were:

1. *Bowman W.*, who was born July 4, 1805, and

360   HISTORY OF FAIR HAVEN, VERMONT.

worked with Jacob Willard, at masonry, until 1826. He now resides in Byron, Mich., and is an eminent, highly active and beloved member of the Odd Fellow's Fraternity.

2. *William W.*, who now resides in Cambridge, Mass.

3. *Polly*, married William Barber, of Pontiac, Mich.

4. *Elizabeth*, m. S. G. Hidden, of Concord, Mass., and died in Boston, Feb., 1869.

5. *George R.*, resides in Fentonville, Mich.

6. *James Y.*, resides in Rochester, N. Y.

7. *Selah Gridley*, is in Hallowell, Me.

ALEXANDER DUNAHUE, whose parents came originally from Ireland, and died in Castleton, was a peddler, and acquired considerable property. He married in Fair Haven, sometime prior to 1804, Miss Rebecca Norton, youngest daughter of Josiah Norton, Esq., and resided on the plain a little eastward from Hydeville, where he died, August 19, 1814, aged 43 years. He was an eccentric person, and requested that he might be buried under an apple tree, nigh his house, so that his ghost might appear to Mr. Loveland's boys, who had troubled him by stealing his apples. He was at first buried on his place, but afterward was removed to the old burial ground in Fair Haven, where a large flat tablet has for many years stood over his grave.

From his will he appears to have had brothers and sisters, *Daniel, William, Katy* Jewett, *Hannah* Sargent, and *Betsey*.

He owned, for a short time, in the spring of 1804,

HISTORY OF FAIR HAVEN, VERMONT. 361

the two south fires in the forge, which Lyon had sold to Wm. Hennessy. He bought the paper mill of his brother-in-law, Salmon Norton, in July, 1804, selling it in March, 1806, to John Herring, Moses Colton and Joel Beaman.

In April, 1807, he bought of Mr. Norton the old Meacham store and land adjoining, which he sold to Royal Dennis, in May, 1809, and which Mr. Dennis constructed into a tavern.

In October, 1813, he purchased of John Herring the house and lot of six acres, lying toward the river, where the marble mill now is. These were afterward deeded to the town by Dr. Adin Kendrick and wife, of Poultney, (Mr. Dunahue's widow having married Dr. Kendrick,) in consideration of a clause in Mr. Dunahue's will, giving to the Congregational society in Fair Haven, "a bell, to weigh between 500 and 600 lbs., for the use of the new meeting-house."

Shortly before his death, on the 1st day of August, he deeded to the town 60 rods of ground, lying "south and south-west of the dwelling house of Royal Dennis," it being a piece five rods wide by twelve rods long, east and west, which had been left off from the south part of the twelve rod square piece sold by Col. Lyon to Mr. Hennessy, in 1794, and which Hennessy had sold to Elijah G. Galusha for $50. Dunahue had bought it in August, 1803, of Galusha, then of Eddyville, Ky., for $8,00, and he deeds it to the town "to be used for a public green only, which is expressly understood in this contract."

This land was, formerly, all south and west of Mr.

362 HISTORY OF FAIR HAVEN, VERMONT.

Graves' store, its south-east corner being six rods N. 10° E. from the north-east corner of the old Lyon tavern.

It is told of Mr. Dunahue that he was quite given to sharp retorts, and that shortly previous to his last sickness he was sitting by the stove in Mr. Dennis' bar-room, with his boots off, to warm his feet, when the Rev. Mr. Cushman entered, and perceiving signs of illness in Mr. Dunahue's face, said to him: "Friend, you look as though you were not going to stay with us long." "No," he replied, "I am not—only long enough to warm my feet." The incivility of the remark troubled his conscience, and in his last sickness he sent for Mr. Cushman to come and see him, and in his will bequeathed a bell to Mr. Cushman's church, which, alas! Mr. Cushman did not live to see. The bell was, however, at last obtained, about the year 1831.

He was in the Revolutionary War, and at Ticonderoga with the American forces when Gen. Burgoyne came up the lake.

DAVID DOBBIN, a Scotchman, and a cousin of James Miller, came hither from Argyle, N. Y., about 1821, and with Mr. Miller and Ira Allen, formed the firm of "Miller, Allen & Dobbin," and did business as tanners and curriers, and boot and shoe manufacturers, for a number of years, in the north part of the town. He went from Fair Haven to Ireland, and married while there, returning hither after an absence of about two years, with his wife, and afterward removed to Argyle as late as 1831 or '32.

HISTORY OF FAIR HAVEN, VERMONT. 363

He had two daughters, born in town; had three children by an earlier wife, in Argyle, namely: *John, Mary* and *Betsey.*

NATHAN H. DARLING was here, residing on West street, in 1825, and made brick on the river bank, near where Mr. Hanger's slate factory now stands, in 1831. He married the wife of Duncan Cook, and lived on the corner, west of Mr. Fish's, as late as 1837. He is said to have made brick, also, a little south-west of John P. Sheldon's, near the river, and in two other places in the town, namely: opposite Adams Dutton's present residence, north of the village; and on the east side of the Munger road, where Francis Pósey has recently worked a brick-yard.

REV. AMOS DRURY was born in Pittsford, Vt., December 18, 1792. He was the eldest of nine children of Deacon Calvin and Azubah (Harwood) Drury. His father, Calvin, was born in Temple, Mass., May 8, 1765, and was the son of Ebenezer, born in Shrewsbury, Mass., January 19, 1734. His mother was the daughter of Rev. E. Harwood, the first pastor of the Congregational church, Pittsford, Vt.

While a child he was hopefully converted, and united with the church in his native town when only eight years of age. He had no literary education except from the common school and academy; worked on his father's farm till of age. Then to gratify his father's choice, studied medicine with the physician of his native town, and attended one course of lectures at the Medical Institute, Castleton, Vt. His own desire had been to become a minister, and

364 HISTORY OF FAIR HAVEN, VERMONT.

before completing his medical studies he changed his purpose in that direction. Studied theology with Rev. E. H. Dorman, of Georgia, Vt., and Rev. Josiah Hopkins, D. D., of New Haven, Vt., teaching district and singing schools at intervals to defray his expenses. He was licensed to preach in the fall of 1818, by the Addison Association, and first settled as a pastor of the Congregational church in West Rutland, Vt., as successor of Rev. Lemuel Haynes, (the colored minister,) June 4, 1819, Rev. Josiah Hopkins, D. D., preaching the sermon. Here he continued until after the breaking out of the anti-Masonic excitement occasioned by the murder of Morgan. Being himself a Free Mason, his connection with the order was attacked, and he was dismissed at his own request, April 22, 1829. Without a Sabbath's interval he went to Fair Haven, where he was installed pastor, May 6, 1829, Rev. Beriah Green, of Brandon, preaching the sermon. From Fair Haven he was dismissed in May, 1837, and again without a Sabbath's interval, began preaching at Westhampton, Mass., having declined a call to Windsor, Vt. He was installed pastor of the Congregational church, at Westhampton, June 29, 1837, Rev. Harley Goodwin, of New Haven, Conn., preaching the sermon. He died while on a visit to friends at Pittsford, Vt., July 22, 1841, in his 49th year. His disease was pronounced by Dr. Perkins, of Castleton Medical Institute, to be yellow fever, as nearly as the climate would admit of. His farewell sermon, at West Rutland, was published; also one or two sermons, or ad-

HISTORY OF FAIR HAVEN, VERMONT. 365

dresses, delivered before the order of Free Masons. He received the honorary degree of M. A. from Middlebury College, in 1824. February 7th, 1820, he was married to Sarah P. Swift, of Fairfax, Vt., who survived him twenty-three years.

He had six children, three of whom died in infancy. Their names were :

1. *Amos K.*, b. July 12, 1821 ; now a farmer residing in Greensboro, Vt.

2. *George B.*, b. April 24, 1823 ; now a mill-wright in Northampton, Mass.

3. *Sarah A.*, b. Dec. 28, 1825 ; now wife of Royal B. Rice, of Williamsburgh, Mass.

4. and 5. *Horace* and *Henry*, (twins,) b. April 27, 1828 ; d. Sept. 8, and 9, 1828.

6. *Horace Henry*, b. Sept. 25, 1829 ; d. April, 19, 1833.

Rev. Willard Child, D. D., preached his funeral sermon, at Pittsford, from Matt. 25, 23 : "His Lord said unto him, well done," &c. The last sermon he wrote he did not live to preach. It was prepared for the Communion Sabbath after he should return from his visit to Vermont. It was read to his people by Rev. Mr. Wiley, at the first communion service after his death. The last benediction which he pronounced to his own people, was Num, 6, 24 to 26 : "The Lord bless thee, and keep thee," &c.

Mr. Drury is characterized as " not a great sermonizer, but an impressive preacher ;" a man of "very solemn deportment in the pulpit, and more than usually gifted in prayer ; of deep feelings and warm attach-

366   HISTORY OF FAIR HAVEN, VERMONT.

ments; faithful and self-sacrificing." A man "of more
than ordinary ability and success; possessing great
knowledge of human nature, and a large stock of common sense; of jovial disposition, generous nature; always governed by Christian principle; firm in family
government; could not tolerate trifling or duplicity;
a good pastor, who knew familiarly every one; a good
nurse in the sick room," and these traits constantly
tested, for his wife was always an invalid. His salary
was always small, and he was always pecuniarily em-
barrassed until the last two years of his life.

[The above was written by Rev. A. W. Wild.]

REV. CHARLES DOOLITTLE was settled as pastor over
the Congregational society of Fair Haven, in August,
1838, but remained only one or two years, removing
hence to Middle Granville, N. Y., where he remained
and preached for several years. He received the degree of M. A. from Middlebury College in 1841.

ADAMS DUTTON, b. in 1793; carried on a brick-yard
in Rutland at an early day; married Salome Bixby, of
Mt. Holly, and resided in Castleton in 1831, whence
he came to Fair Haven in the spring, buying of Ethan
Whipple, in June, his home farm—now Mr. John Allard's—where he commenced the manufacture of brick,
the same season, in a yard near Muddy brook.

He sold this place to Seth J. Hitchcock, on the 1st
of May, 1843, retaining possession until the 1st of
April, 1844; and on the same day bought Mr. Hitchcock's place in the village, where the Vermont Hotel
now stands. He resided on this place, engaging meanwhile in the manufacture of slate pencils by new and

HISTORY OF FAIR HAVEN, VERMONT. 367

original machinery, and also in quarrying slate in company with Royal Bullock, on Cedar Point, in Castleton, until the summer of 1851, when, selling his place in April to Israel Davey, he purchased of Burleigh Davis, in July, his present homestead of about 50 acres, and 10 acres of woodland on the hill south of H. Hamilton's.

His family are:

1. *Mary*, m. J. D. Smead; is now residing in Hydeville.

2. *William, A.*, m. Amelia Kathan, of Dummerston, Vt.

3. *Joseph*, m. Adda Wright, of Pawlet; resides in Castleton.

4. Eliza, m. Seymour Wilson.

5. *Lucy Jane*, m. Carlos L. Gorham.

6. *Daniel*, m. Minnie Smith, of Keene, N. H.

BURLEIGH DAVIS was originally from Rutland, where he married Lucy Keyes, the daughter of James Keyes. He resided in West Haven, in February, 1838, at which time he purchased of John Martin, of Fair Haven, 37 1-2 acres of land which Martin had purchased of Luke Beaman, and on which he was then residing; the same is now occupied by Adams Dutton. In October of the same year, he purchased of Lois Howe, about 12 1-2 acres more on the west. Mr. Davis resided on this place for a number of years, and also occupied the farm owned by Messrs. H. & H. Howard, on West street. His wife died here, May 3, 1851. He sold his place to Mr. Dutton in July, 1851. He afterward married Mrs. Mary, widow of

368   HISTORY OF FAIR HAVEN, VERMONT.

Thomas Ranney, and resided on her place, where J. H. Williams' store now is.

He died, at the West, February 1st, 1865, and was brought back to Fair Haven and buried.

His family by his first wife were:

Jane, Henry, James, Abigail, Horace, Mary, and *Frank.*

JOHN W. DEWEY, b. in Royalton, Vt., in 1794; m. Sarah Hamlin in 1823; d. November, 1862. He came to Fair Haven to reside, in 1838, having previously resided ten years in Hubbardton, and two years in Castleton. He built a house adjoining the old burying ground, on the east, where his widow and family still reside. '

His children are:

1. *Julia H.,* b. in 1825; m. in 1846, to Geo. W. Hurlburt, and have two children, Edward C., and Frank W.

2. *Marcus B.,* b. in 1830; m. Lucy S. Allen, in 1853.

3. *Hamlin T.,* b. 1840; resides with his mother.

4. *Ellen F.,* b. 1836; d. 1837.

ELI and AMBROSE EVARTS; see p. 45.

COL. DAVID ERWIN; see p. 65.

ELINUS ELLIS was here and took the freeman's oath in 1809.

BARNABAS ELLIS, the son of Barnabas Ellis and Elizabeth Spencer, and the seventh of ten children, was born January 1st, 1785. He married Belinda Kidder, and established himself, for a time, in the harness making business in Weathersfield, Vt. He re-

HISTORY OF FAIR HAVEN, VERMONT. **369**

moved from Weathersfield to Lempster, N. H., and thence to Hampton, N. Y., in the fall of 1813. While there he purchased of Anna Wells, in Fair Haven, Nov. 22, 1813, the Ballard, or Holt farm, in the south part of the town, paying therefor $1,000. He moved on to the farm in the following spring, and ever after continued a leading and influential citizen of the town, until his death, May 9th, 1860. His wife died March 12, 1855, aged 67 years. In May, 1818, he purchased of Lanson Watkins the farm on which his son, Zenas C., now resides, and removed to the same, building the brick house thereon standing, about 1828, or '29, and having a harness and saddle shop in the orchard, on the east side of the highway, in which he carried on his trade for many years. He was a highly esteemed and useful citizen.

Family:

1. *George W.*, b. in Weathersfield,- Oct. 19, 1809; m. Mary Swallow, May 26, 1834; d. in Windsor, July 12, 1842.

2. *Eunice V.*, b. in Weathersfield, Sept. 22, 1811; m. A. W. Flagg, Oct. 22, 1856; resides in Castleton.

3. *Abner C.*, b. in Hampton, N. Y., Dec. 17, 1813; resides in Sandwich, C. W.; has two children.

4. *Hiram B.*, b. in Fair Haven, Jan. 13, 1816; m. Olivia Ladd; d. in Greenfield, Ill.; left two children.

5. *William H.*, b. June 6, 1818; m. Maria Wooley; resides in Greenfield, Ill., and has four children.

6. *Zenas C.*, b. July 25, 1820; m. Sarah B. Dyer, Sept. 13, 1847; resides in Fair Haven; has four children, George W., Edward D., Horace B., and Zenas H.

370 HISTORY OF FAIR HAVEN, VERMONT.

7. *Caroline B.*, b. Feb. 13, 1824 ; d. Jan. 13, 1845.

8. *Reuben T.*, b. Dec. 27, 1827 ; m. Mary A. Ranney, Feb. 12, 1856 ; children, Charles R., and John A.

9. *Mary B.*, b. April 4, 1830 : m. Wm. Henry Northrop, and resides in Castleton.

JONATHAN EGGLESTON was here as early as 1810. He is said to have taken the shop where John Manning made wooden ware, over the iron works, after Manning left it, about 1816, and there manufactured screws.

ISAAC EGGLESTON, brother to Jonathan, was a carpenter, who stuttered in his speech. He worked for Enos Bristol, on his house, in 1811. In 1814, he worked with Lanson Watkins on Joseph Sheldon's saw-mill, and, with Watkins and others, left to go to the war.

ELIJAH ESTY came here from Natick, Mass., in the spring of 1825, having previously, while stopping in Rutland, purchased of Harry Spalding, of Middletown, April 1, 1822, the Kelsey farm, of 185 acres, in Fair Haven, on which he now lives. The first year after purchasing, he leased the place to Mr. Spalding ; the the second and third years, to his brother-in-law, Capt. Stephen Daniel, of Rutland.

He married Fanny Bacon, who was sister to Deacon Griggs' wife, of Centre Rutland. She died April 19, 1860, aged 70 years.

His children are:

1. *Elbridge G.*, m. Mrs. Betsey Andrus. She died April, 1868.

2. *William B.*, m. Miss Mary Aborn.

3. *John W.*, m. Miss Sarah Hawley.

HISTORY OF FAIR HAVEN, VERMONT. 381

OBADIAH EDDY was born in Taunton, Mass. He married Fanny Lyon, of Woodford, Vt., and came to Fair Haven from Arlington, about 1832, having purchased of Alonzo Safford, in conjunction with his son, John W., in May, of the previous year, the farm on which Mr. Kidder now resides. He lived on the farm and worked a portion of the time in the forge. He sold the farm, in July, 1839, to Abner and Rowley R. Mead, of Rutland, and purchased of Lyman Sherwood in the following January, the Brainard, or Dodge farm, south of Chauncey Wood's. He sold this farm in Oct., 1852, to Samuel D. Jones, reserving the use of it till the following April. In June, 1853, he purchased a building lot of James Dolan, in the village, and built the house in which William Parry resides.

He removed to Marquette, Mich., to reside with his sons, in the spring of 1859, where he died in September, 1862. His wife survived till April 30, 1869.

Family :

1. *Otis.*

2. *John W.*, who married Ann Bristol, and removed to Cambridge, N. Y., in the fall of 1841, where he still resides and has a son named Albert.

3. *Norman E.*, m. Caroline Clement, in Woodford, Vt. He resided at Sutherland Falls, about 1835, and removed to Marquette, Mich. His children are Emily, Ellen, Alvin, Lucy and Henry.

4. *Elihu Faxon*, m. Caroline Whipple, and removed to Marquette, Mich. He has two daughters, Viola and Ellen, Viola being married to a Mr. Hall, of Green Bay.

372   HISTORY OF FAIR HAVEN, VERMONT.

5. *Benj. Franklin*, m. first Mary Andrus, by whom he has one son, Eugene. His second wife was Loraine B. Hickok, by whom his children are Izora and Harrison T. She died in Aug., 1867, and he married again in Wisconsin.

6. *Cullen C.*, m. and resides at Marquette, Mich., whither the family nearly all went to engage in the business of making iron.

OTIS EDDY, son of Obadiah, was born in Bennington, Vt., and came from Arlington to Fair Haven, in March, 1824, to work in the forge, or iron bloomary, for Jacob Davey. He was engaged for many years in this occupation, working for Alonson Allen when he leased the works, as late as 1840. He purchased the land, whereon he resides, of Abraham Sharp and Harris W. Bates, in 1826, and in August, 1827, purchased 6 acres and 95 rods more, of Jacob Davey next west of his own, and of the house wherein Jacob Cobb had previously resided.

He married Sophia Kidder, Sept. 27, 1827.

Family:

1. *John W.*, m. Adeline Hitchcock, of West Haven, and has one daughter, Jennie.

2. *Mary C.*, m. George Fleeman.

3. *Juliza S.*, m. Edward D. Barnes.

HORATIO FOSTER was "of Hubbardton," in the winter of 1808; came to Fair Haven the following spring, and engaged with Jacob Davey and Seth Persons, in a clothier's works, near the iron works. He continued in this business, either with Mr. Davey, or alone, for about twenty years. He built the house now oc--

HISTORY OF FAIR HAVEN, VERMONT. 373.

cupied by Lewis W. Collins, residing there in 1832.

In March, 1835, he resided in Sheldon, Genesee, Co., N. Y., and then sold his home place, in Fair Haven, to Hezekiah and Harvey Howard. He married a daughter of Samuel Pettee, who resided with him. His children were *George*, *Gilbert*, and *Melissa*.

STEPHEN FISH, b. in 1787, a nephew of Joel Hamilton, came from Uxbridge, Mass., to reside with his uncle, Mr. Hamilton, of this town, about 1810. He was admitted to the freeman's oath here in September, 1811, and married Chloe Narrimore, a sister to Benj. Narrimore, September 30, 1811. She came from Goshen, Mass.

Mr. Fish removed to West Haven, where he carried on the Minot farm, until 1827, residing, meantime, at the foot of the long hill, on the old turnpike, and being keeper of the turnpike gate. He purchased, in September, 1819, in company with Heman Stannard, 100 acres, where Otis Hamilton now resides, then the Everts farm.

He bought out Mr. Stannard's share, in September, 1821, and continued to carry on the farm while residing in West Haven. He removed and took up his residence on the place, in the spring of 1827. In May, 1835, he sold his farm, then containing 142 acres, to Otis Hamilton, and removed in the fall, to the place on the corner, west of Mr. Esty's, purchased, October 12th, of John Warner, where he continued to reside until his death, which occurred December 3, 1849.

His family were:

21

374 HISTORY OF FAIR HAVEN, VERMONT.

1. *Nathaniel*, b. May, 1813; m. Dorcas Kenyon. Their children are Newell, Samuel, Chloe and Martha.

2. *Rebecca Miriam*, b. Sept. 1814, was married to Cyrus C. Whipple.

3. *Lydia Hamilton*, b. March, 1817; m. Cullen W. Hawkins.

4. *Erastus Parsons*, b. Jan. 1819; d. Sept. 29, 1838.

5. *Susanna Hunt*, born Sept. 2, 1821; d. Dec. 13, 1827.

6. *Sarah Richardson*, b. Nov., 1822; d. Jan. 1, 1828.

7. *Chauncey G.*, b. Oct. 11, 1824; m. Martha L. Beaman, daughter of Luke Beaman, Esq., formerly of this town. They have two children, Hattie and Libbie.

Mr. Fish's wife died Jan. 23, 1828, and he married the second time, in Oct., 1829, to Lavina Hitchcock, of West Haven, who survived him, and died Jan. 21, 1866.

TIMOTHY GOODRICH, from Woodbury, Conn., came hither in 1784, and settled on the east half of the first division lot of Asa Dudley's right, where Joseph Sheldon now resides. He married Kezia Hines, whose sister, Eunice, married Gen. Jonathan Orms.

His family were:

1. *Wait*, or *Waitstill*. 2. *Timothy*, who died in southern Ohio. 3. *Chauncey*. 4. *Elizur*. He also had a daughter, *Sally Kezia*, who died in 1812, at about 10 years of age. Mrs. G. died Oct. 10, 1803, in her 43d year.

HISTORY OF FAIR HAVEN, VERMONT. 375

Mr. Goodrich married, for a second wife, widow Rebecca Steele, whose father was a Mr. Stoddard, of Bethlehem, Conn., whither Mr. Goodrich went and resided for a while, about 1818. He died in town, February 17, 1829, in his 73d year, the same month in which Rev. Rufus Cushman died. His wife, Rebecca, died one week afterward, February 23, aged 70 years. In August, 1818, while resident in Bethlehem, he deeded to Chauncey the north part of the first division of Ebenezer Frisbee's right, on which Chauncey then lived, he having purchased the same, together with a lot of 59 acres lying on Mt. Hamilton, of Joel Hamilton, in March, 1801. The home place fell into the possession of Elizur, who occupied it for a time. At his decease it was sold to Mr. Sheldon, its present owner.

CHAUNCEY GOODRICH resided and died on the farm now owned and occupied by John D. Wood. He first married Deborah Orton, a sister of Mrs. Harvey Church. She died in about one year, November 14, 1811, in the 22d year of her age. He next married Polly Narrimore. She died August 23, 1825.

Their children were:

1. *Alanson*, who is resident in Michigan.

2. *Sally*, m. Benj. Smith, of Whitehall. Their children, now resident in Fair Haven, are, John C., Mary A., Cordelia M., Chauncey S., and William L. Mr. Smith died February 1, 1859, and Mrs. S. married Charles Hancock, of Concord, Mich., in 1870.

3. *Mary Ann*, m. Samuel Adams, of West Haven.

4. *Levi*, m. Rebecca Adams, of West Haven; is now in Concord, Mich.

376   HISTORY OF FAIR HAVEN, VERMONT.

5. *Welthy*, m. Judson R. Harlow, of Whitehall.

By a third wife, Polly Spratt, he. had one son, Chauncey, who is now resident in Concord, Mich. She died May 10, 1827, in her 34th year.

He was married a fourth time, to Phebe Spratt, a sister of Polly, who survives him at this time, and resides with her daughter, Polly, at Castleton Corners. Her children were *Polly* and *William*. William is in Chicago.

Mr. Goodrich died Sept. 20, 1856, aged 68 years.

ELIZUR GOODRICH first married Betsey, a daughter of Elisha Kilborn, of Hampton, in January, 1817. She died August 11, 1822, in her 25th year. He next married Sally Richardson, a daughter of Thomas Richardson, and niece of Mrs. Joel Hamilton. She died September 27, 1833, aged 34 years.

His children were, by his first wife:

1. *Altha*, b. Aug., 1817 ; m. Otis Hamilton.

By his second wife:

2. *Betsey Ann*, m. Samuel D. Williams, now resident in Hydeville, Vt.

3. *Mary Jane*, m. Rev. A. B. Lyon; d. at Mr. Hamilton's, Dec. 3d, 1866, aged 37 years.

4. *Elizur*, now a resident of the West.

Mr. Goodrich was largely engaged; at one time, in the lumbering business in Fair Haven. He owned and ran boats on the Champlain Canal, and removed to Whitehall, where he died, September 27, 1834, aged 42 years.

ASA GOODRICH resided near Orms' mill, in West Haven, at an early day. We hear of three sons:

HISTORY OF FAIR HAVEN, VERMONT. 377

1. *Erastus*, who is mentioned on page 104, as an apprentice of Gen. Orms, and who took the freeman's oath in the town, in Sept., 1803.

2. *Ansel*, who was a tanner and currier, and carried on the old Beriah Roger's tannery, in town, after Rogers left, about 1808. He occupied Roger's house, where Zenas C. Ellis resides, and had his house burnt. He married Luna Bosworth, and removed from Fair Haven to Chazy, N. Y.

3. *Alvin*, who was drowned at 7 years of age, near Carver's Falls, about 1799.

JOSIAH GOODRICH, whose father, Josiah, kept tavern in Benson, in the time of the war of 1812, was a shoemaker, and resided on the farm now owned and occpied by J. W. Esty, as early as 1818. He sold the place to Barnabas Ellis, subsequent to 1830, and went away to the West.

THE GILBERTS were the descendants of Thomas and Jemima Gilbert, of Brookfield, Mass.

Thomas was the son of Thomas and Martha Gilbert, and was born in Brookfield, in 1723.

His wife, Jemima, was the widow Cutler, of Brookfield, and had a family before she married Mr. Gilbert, as follows:

Gen. *John* Cutler, who came to Fair Haven, and died here, Aug. 21, 1821, aged 70 years.

Isaac Cutler, Esq., a prominent early inhabitant of Fair Haven.

Abigail, who married Charles Rice, and died in West Haven, June 16, 1820, in her 66th year, and *Catherine*, who married Dr. Simeon Smith, and after-

378   HISTORY OF FAIR HAVEN, VERMONT.

ward Christopher Minot, Esq., of Boston, and died in West Haven, in 1833.

By Mr. Gilbert her family were:

1. *Eliel*, b. April 10, 1766; resided in Brookfield.
2. *Tilly*, b. Nov. 10, 1771; came to Fair Haven.
3. *Sally*, b. Jan. 23, 1769; m. Nathaniel Dickinson and died in Fair Haven, Dec. 16, 1810, aged **41** years.

Upon Mr. Gilbert's decease, she came to Fair Haven and resided with her son Isaac. In Aug, 1807, she bought a farm of 42 acres, on Scotch Hill, of her son, John Cutler, and sold it to John Snell, in Jan., 1811, she residing in West Haven.

TILLY GILBERT, known in former days as "Major Gilbert," came to town, as has been noted on page 72, in the spring of 1788, and was employed by Col. Lyon, to teach school. Though never enjoying the advantages of more than two months at school himself, he was yet a very good scholar and competent teacher, and wrote finely and correctly, as the town records, kept by him for so many years, abundantly evince.

After studying medicine with Drs. Hull and Witherell, and taking the freeman's oath, in town, in the summer of 1791, he went into mercantile business in Benson, and then into the manufacturing of iron in Orwell.

Returning to Fair Haven, in 1799, (see p. 117,) he entered actively and extensively into business, opening a store of merchandise, and also supplying the inhabitants with their drugs and medicines from

HISTORY OF FAIR HAVEN, VERMONT. 379

his house, where the Vermont Hotel now is. He owned a half interest with his brother, Eliel, in the lower saw-mill, until November, 1802, when he bought out his brother's share, together with the 264 acres of land Eliel had purchased of Col. Lyon. He bought the saw-mill, on the Upper Falls, above the iron works, in the summer of 1806. He sold the lower mill to Jacob Davey, in December, 1813, and the upper mill, in December, 1822.

He built the house in which his son, Benjamin F., now resides, in 1814.

He was chosen town clerk in April, 1803, to fill the vacancy caused by the sudden death of Josiah Norton, and was re-elected to the office every year thereafter, while he remained in town, except the time from 1809 to 1813, when Ethan Whipple was clerk.

He removed to West Haven—to the old Minot house, so-called, in 1832 or '33, where he remained retired from active duties till his death, which occurred at West Haven, September 5th, 1850, when he was 79 years of age. Interesting anecdotes, illustrative of his life and character, are told of him, many of which will, no doubt, be made public by his son, Jarvis J.

He married Patty La Barron, in Benson, February 12, 1793. She died in West Haven, November 28, 1852, aged 80 years. Their family were:

1. *Sally Maria*, b. in Benson, Feb. 24, 1794; m. Elisha Parkill, August 13, 1815. Mr. P. died in 1827, and she married Ebenezer W. Dewey, Oct. 9, 1834, and removed to Flint, Mich.

380   HISTORY OF FAIR HAVEN, VERMONT.

2. *Benjamin Franklin*, b. Sept. 11, 1797; m. Emeline Bullard, from Shrewsbury, and has a family of four children: Tilly, m. to Frances Proctor; Emeline, Julia Ann, m. to D. K. Graves, and Benjamin Franklin. He 'succeeded his father as town clerk in 1832, and held the office nearly every year till 1859. No other person living remembers so well the early affairs and history of the town.

3. *James Jarvis*, b. March 13, 1800 ; m. Mary Ruggles, of Castleton, daughter of John Ruggles, and had two children, Martha LaBarron, who m. Joseph Pomeroy, and resides in Burlingame, Kan., and Tilly, who resides in Flint, Mich.

He married Sarah C. Beach, a second wife, Nov., 1827, and had eight children; Mary R., m. Mansel A. Ormsbee ; Jarvis ; Sarah E., m. Alonzo Noyes; B. Franklin, enlisted in the army at Flint, Mich., and died at Nashville, Tenn. ; Harriet A., m. Palmer E. Paine; Guy R., resides in Sioux City, Iowa; John Q. A., and Edward J.

He entered Middlebury College in 1816, but left after two years, and went with his brother, Benjamin F., to Virginia as a teacher, returning after one year and studying theology with Rev. Amos Drury, then of West Rutland. He was licensed to preach as a Congregational minister by a council of ministers held in Fair Haven; preached for a time in Hartford, N. Y.; went thence to Chesterfield, N. Y., and was settled nine or ten years in Brumantown, N. Y. He preached in West Haven for two years, about 1841, and was afterwards settled in West Dorset, and did missionary

HISTORY OF FAIR HAVEN, VERMONT. 381

labor also in Sunderland and Arlington, returning to West Haven to reside after his father's decease.

4. *Wm. Sidney S.*, b. April 19, 1802; died March 21, 1810.

5. *Alexander Hamilton*, b. Nov. 28, 1804, d. Dec. 22, 1804.

6. *Martha W.*, b. April 11, 1809, m. Hiram K. Hunt, of West Haven. Family, Helen and Gilbert.

7. *Mary L.*, b. Dec. 11, 1812, m. Edw. W. Andrus, a minister from Connecticut, and who now resides near Martinsburg, *Va. Family: Watson, Warren, Mary, Samuel, Molly, Thomas.

8. *Harriet Ashley*. Drowned, in January, 1834, in Hoosic river.

PAUL GUILFORD, Sen., came to Fair Haven from Conway, Mass., in the fall of 1798, buying, Sept. 17, of John Brown, the house and three acres of land which Brown had occupied and advertised for sale in the Fair Haven paper—now Mr. James Campbell's. One tradition is that while in Massachusetts his wife left him, and went to reside among the Quakers, while according to another account, he came away from Conway to get rid of her. He married Deborah Bundy, in Fair Haven, and is said to have dropped down dead in the corn-field. He died June 20, 1811. His widow deeded the place to Paul and Simeon, as administrators, in Dec. 1811. He had four sons, *Paul, Simeon, Rufus,* and *Silas.*

PAUL GUILFORD, Jr., came to town in the winter of 1807, purchasing in January of that year, of Tilly Gilbert, the Russell Smith farm, on West street, and

382   HISTORY OF FAIR HAVEN, VERMONT.

settling on the same, where he carried on the harness business, and died January 20th, 1813. The place was sold by Simeon Guilford, of Ira, in June, 1814, to Samuel Warren Guilford, subject to the widow's dower.

Mr. Guilford married Mary Warren, in Conway, Mass. She removed to Benson after his demise, where she married a Mr. Merritt, and afterward Mr. Stephen Sherwood. She removed to Palmer, Mich., and there died, in November, 1837, aged 72 years.

Mr. Guilford's family were :

1. *Lovisa*, b. in 1786; m. Abner Bigelow, by whom she had two sons, William and Alanson. She died in 1825.

2. *Philinda*, b. in 1790; m. in Fair Haven, May 29, 1810, to Lemuel C. Nims, of Manlius, N. Y., and had 5 children.

3. *Asenath*, b. in 1793; m. Henry Wells, of Camillus, N. Y. She had three children.

4. *Samuel Warren*, b. in 1793; m. Sarah Myra Whipple, daughter of Ethan Whipple, Esq., in Jan., 1814.

He died where James Miller now lives, Feb. 9, 1832, aged 38 years, leaving two children, Amy, b. July 13, 1816, who married Edward S. Bascom, Oct. 20, 1841, and now resides in Whitehall, N. Y., and Samuel Warren, Jr., b. Nov. 20, 1822, who married Emeline M. Trowbridge, of Pittsford, and now resides in Rutland.

5. *William*, b. 1794; died young.

6. *Chester*, b. 1796; died young.

7. *Rufus*, b. 1800; m. Maria Jerome, in 1822; resides in Castleton, N. Y.

HISTORY OF FAIR HAVEN, VERMONT. 383

8. *Alvin*, b. 1806; m. Louisa Ford; resides in Camillus, N. Y.

9. *Mary Matilda*, b. 1808; m. Edward S. Bascom, in 1828, and died in Somerset, Mich., March 26, 1841, leaving one son, Rollin Eugene, who resides in Whitehall, N. Y.

SIMEON GUILFORD married Mary Carpenter, a daughter of Cephas Carpenter, of Ira, and resided for a time in Ira; was there in 1814, and afterward removed to Fair Haven, whence he removed to Moriah, N. Y., about 1831. His wife died in Moriah. They had a daughter, *Sophronia*, who married Ransom Nichols, and now resides in Crown Point, N. Y. They buried, in Fair Haven, a son, *Ransom Marlow*, July 19, 1822, aged 13 years, and a daughter *Mary Viola*, Aug. 5, 1822, aged 8 years. They had a daughter, *Phebe*, and now have a son, *Ransom Marlow*, born about 1824, residing in Chicago.

RUFUS GUILFORD, a physician, resided on the Calvin Munger place—now Wm. Dolan's—and purchased it in February, 1809, of Tilly Gilbert and Rebecca S. Munger, administrators of Calvin Munger's estate. He sold the place, then consisting of about 12 acres, in March, 1810, to Isaac Cutler, for $1,000, which was an advance of $300 from what he paid for it. He is said to have removed to North Granville, N. Y., and there practiced medicine, and died, leaving some of the family residing there. His children's names were, *Maria, Harriet, Jane, Gordon*, and *Robinson*.

SILAS GUILFORD, m. Sylvia Miller, of Hampton, N. Y., January, 15, 1803, and had 14 children. He

384 HISTORY OF FAIR HAVEN, VERMONT.

resided in Fair Haven, and Hampton, until about 1824, when he removed to Dresden, N. Y., and thence went to New Haven, Oswego county, N. Y., in 1838, where he died in 1848. She died March 10, 1858, aged 71 years.

Family:

1. *Franklin*, b. Jan 3, 1804; resides in Owasso, Mich.

2. *Paulina,* b. Sept. 1, 1805; m. Mr. Wetherbee, and resides in Dresden, N. Y.

3. *William M.*, b. April 17, 1807; is a teacher in Louisiana; formerly in Andover, Vt., and Joliet, Mich.

4. *Silas*, b. Jan 20, 1809; deceased.

5. *Nelson*, b. March 24, 1811; is in Fremont, Mich.

6. *Amy M.*, b. Jan. 3, 1813; m. Isaac Nelson, and resides in Fremont, Mich.

7. *Erwin C.*, b. Sept. 14, 1814; is in Eaton county, Mich.

8. *Arza L.*, b. Jan. 11, 1817; deceased.

9. *Lois A.*, b. Dec. 11, 1820; m. Alva Bronson, now a widow in Toledo, Ohio.

10. *Ransom M.* b. June 11, 1822.

11. *Thomas S.* b. May 8, 1824; is in St. Charles, Saginaw county, Mich.

12. *Walden W.*, b. in 1827; resides in Fremont, Mich.

13. *Hiram S.*, b. March 1, 1829; resides in St. Charles, Mich.

14. *Oscar A.*, b. 1831; resides in Castalia, Ohio.

CYRUS GRAVES, b. in Spencertown, Mass., in 1768, m. Roxana Rose, of Rhode Island, and removed to

HISTORY OF FAIR HAVEN, VERMONT. ·385

Rupert, Vt., about 1790. He removed to Fair Haven from Rupert, April 1, 1825, with his wife and their four unmarried children, viz: Orpah and Ruth, Eli and Joel, leaving Nathan and Abram on the old homestead in Rupert, and Allen, the elder brother, in India. He bought of Jacob Willard the old Isaac Cutler farm, on West street, on which he settled.

Mrs. Graves died of consumption, July 2d, 1825, aged 57. Mr. G. was afterwards married to Mrs. Mehitable Alden, of Dorset, with whom he lived until his death. He died March 10, 1844, aged 76 years. Mrs. Graves still lives and resides in Sandwich, Ill.

The eldest son of the family, *Nathan*, was born in Rupert, where he has lived to a good old age, (84 at the present time,) on the same place where he was born—an unusual thing in this time of change. He has four children.

Allen was born in Rupert; m. Mary Lee; was educated at Middlebury College, studied theology at Andover, Mass., and was sent as a missionary to the Mahrattas, by the Am. B. C. F. M., in the year, 1817, where he lived and labored thirty years. He effected a translation of the whole Bible into the Mahratta language, which is the version now used. His widow outlived him about twenty years, remaining with the people among whom her husband had labored to promulgate the Gospel. In 1833, Allen and wife visited America. On their return to India, *Orpah* accompanied them as a teacher. She was there married to the Rev. D. O. Allen. She only survived the climate one year.

386   HISTORY OF FAIR HAVEN, VERMONT.

Abram was born at Rupert, Vt., July 15, 1797. He married Zilpha Rose, of Milford, Otsego county, N. Y., Nov. 6, 1823; remained in Rupert ten years; there had five children; lost two of them in infancy; moved to Fair Haven in 1833; resided here nineteen years; had four children; here five died in childhood, leaving him but two, Cyrus Spencer, and Cornelia Ann. He represented the town in the State Legislature four years; moved to Warrensburg, N. Y., in 1852, resided there five years; moved to Greenfield, Ga., in 1857; resided there two years.

His son, Cyrus S. Graves, married Jennie L. Mc-Donald, of Warren county, N. Y., and moved to Ga. with his father. They moved to Thomasville, Ga., in 1859, where Cornelia Ann married E. O. Thompson, of Macon, Ga.

Cyrus S. died in 1862, at Calhoun, Ga., aged 31 years.

Abram died in 1865, at Thomasville, Ga., aged 68 years.

Zilpha died in 1869, at Thomasville, Ga., aged 64 years.

Cyrus S. had three children; one died in Thomasville, Ga., in 1861. His widow moved with her two remaining children to Courtland county, N. Y., where she still lives. Cornelia Ann resides at Thomasville, Ga., with her husband. She has four children.

Eli was born in Rupert, in 1803. Married Naomi Whedon, of Washington county, N. Y., in 1829. He studied theology at Auburn, N. Y., and was licensed and ordained by the Rutland Association as

HISTORY OF FAIR HAVEN, VERMONT. 387

an evangelist, Aug. 27, 1837. He labored as stated supply for various churches in southern Georgia and Florida. He had two children, Samuel and Mary Ruth, who are both married and living in southern Georgia. Eli died July 16, 1866, of typhoid fever, at Quitman, Brooks co., Ga., aged 63. Naomi died in March, 1869, of heart disease, at the same place, aged 61.

Ruth was born in Rupert, in 1807. Although a cripple from childhood, she obtained a good education and always employed herself for the good of those about her, particularly the children and youth. Always an example of everything that was lovely and of good report. She spent several years of the latter part of her life at the south, and died in Lee county, Ga., Sept. 15, 1868, aged 61.

Joel S. was educated at Middlebury College, graduated, and went first to Florida, as a minister. He afterward settled in Georgia. He married Eunice —— and has seven children. He was a unionist in the time of the late war, and fled with his family from the rebels, who had threatened several times to hang him. Overtaken by them he was robbed of all he had, but succeeded in reaching New York, and went thence to Illinois, where he remained till the fall of 1868, and then returned to St. Mary's, Ga., where he now preaches every Sabbath when he is able, to a small congregation.

JAMES GREENOUGH came from Lebanon, N. H., to Fair Haven about 1818, and here married Pluma Kidder, a daughter of Oliver Kidder. He was a wheel-

388   HISTORY OF FAIR HAVEN, VERMONT.

wright, and carried on his trade over the old scythe factory for a number of years. He kept the old Dennis tavern for two years, 1828 and '29, and then removed to Whitehall, N. Y., where he now lives, and has two sons, *Myron* and *Henry*.

-EZRA GREENOUGH, a brother of James, married Caroline Orms, and worked with his brother. He now resides in Brockport, N. Y., and has a son, *Charles*, who has been a· constructor of railroads in South America.

STEPHEN HOLT, one of the earliest settlers in the south part of the town, on the old Ballard farm, married Drusilla Ballard. He resided in 1804 where J. W. Esty now does, and removed about 1808 to the place where Hezekiah Bosworth afterward built and resided, in Hampton, N. Y. He had a son, *Joshua*, who was a reckless boy and who married his cousin, Tersey Wilder, March 24, 1811. See p. 20.

BENONI HURLBURT. See p. 26.

ABEL HAWLEY, who came to Fair Haven to reside with his son Ager, and his daughter, Clarinda Safford, was the grandson of Samuel Hawley, who came from England to Stafford, Conn., in 1666. His father's name was Ephraim, who had ten sons and two daughters. Of these, Abel, Gideon, Jehiel and Josiah settled in Arlington. Abel's children by his first wife were Peter, Mary, James, Ager and Abel. By his second·wife, Bethiah Curtis, his children were Sarah, Esther, Prudence and Clarinda.

Mr. H. was a familiar friend of Col. Ethan Allen, and, it is said, was the only person who could safely

HISTORY OF FAIR HAVEN, VERMONT. 389

reprove him for profanity. He resided with Mrs. Safford, and died here, Oct. 16, 1797, aged 77 years. His tomb stone is yet standing, having been removed with Mr. Safford's, to the new grave yard, on the north side of West street.

AGER HAWLEY, son of Abel, came with Silas Safford, from Arlington, in the year 1782, and built the first grist mill in town, in 1783. See p. 36. He resided about 19 rods south from the bridge over the river, and died there, in Dec. 1784. He was buried in the old burial ground, near Mr. Whipple's, in the north part of the town. His widow married Derrick Carner, of Hampton, and removed to Underhill, Vt., where they both died.

His family were:

1. *Isaac ;* died at 18 years of age.

2. *Asa*, b. Jan. 5, 1771, and was bound out to Ira Allen at 14.

3. *Silas*, b. 1776. He learned the tanner's trade, in Granville, N. Y., removed to Auburn and thence to Rochester, where he started the first pail and sash factory and built the first Presbyterian church, and hired the first minister. He died in Rochester, in 1857.

4. *Moses.*

5. *Bethiah*, m. Justus Narrimore, of Hampton, and removed to Underhill, Vt.

ASA HAWLEY, who was miller in the town when a boy, in 1785, and again in 1812 and '13, m. Clara Brooks, of Hampton, Feb. 19, 1794. He resided in Pawlet in 1806, but afterward in Whitehall.

390 HISTORY OF FAIR HAVEN, VERMONT.

His family were:

Sally, Betsey, Abigail, Asa, Silas, Charlotte, and Harvey.

Of these, Harvey was born in Fair Haven, June. 19, 1812. Asa, born in Pawlet, Jan. 12, 1806 ; lives in Whitehall, N. Y. He m. Miss Freelove Spink, sister to Isaac Spink, and has 3 children, Rev. Chipman R., Sarah, who m. J. W. Esty, and Mary.

Silas, b. in Whitehall, Aug. 8, 1809 ; m. Henrietta Morris, of Hampton, and has one son, Morris C. He resides in Colton, St. Lawrence county, N. Y.

MOSES HOLMES. See p. 56.

JOEL HAMILTON, the youngest son of Ezra Hamilton, came here from Brookfield, Mass., in 1783. He resided, during the greatest part of the time he lived in the town, where his nephew, Hiram, now does, and died there, June 5, 1826. He was chosen constable of the town, in March, 1785, and continued in the office till 1793, when he was succeeded by Charles Rice. He was also deputy sheriff of Rutland county for a number of years. See p. 39. He married Jerusha Walker, from Brookfield, Mass., who survived him, and married Squire Demming, of Castleton, dying in September, 1839.

Mr. Hamilton had no family. His father died in Hampton, on the Flat, beyond Mr. Richard's, February 25th, 1810, in his 77th year. His brothers and sisters were, Jesse, Rachel, Rufus, Lydia, Mary Ann, and Israel. His wife's sister married Thomas Richardson, who came from Brookfield and resided in Fair Haven.

HISTORY OF FAIR HAVEN, VERMONT. 391

HIRAM HAMILTON, son of Rufus, of Brookfield, Mass., came to town in 1823, to live with his uncle, Joel, and upon his uncle's death succeeded to the possession of the farm on which he now resides. He married Abigail Clapp, daughter of Joshua Clapp, formerly of Greenfield, Mass. She died in April, 1842, and he afterward married Martha Spratt.

His family, by his first wife, were:

1. *Mary*, the wife of John J. Williams.
2. *Joel W.*
3. *Sarah*, who m. Wm. Pitkin.

OTIS HAMILTON, b. in Brookfield, Mass.; came to Fair Haven in the spring of 1829; bought the farm on which he still resides, of Stephen Fish, in April, 1835. He married Altha Goodrich, May 28, 1835.

His family are:

1. *Charlotte*, m. Henry Franklin.
2. *Rufus*, m. Carrie A. Gates.
3. *Juliza A.*, m. James T. Phelps, and resides in Chelsea, Mass.

CHARLES HAWKINS, Sen., was born in 1736; came to Fair Haven from Smithfield, R. I., with his family, in the summer of 1786, and settled on the land on which he continued to reside while he lived, in the west part of the town, near Poultney river. See page 63. He died in town, March 31, 1810, in his 75th year.

His wife's maiden name was Sarah Olney, and she had a brother Byron Olney, and a half-brother, James Bowen, who resided in the town. She survived Mr. Hawkins, and married Michael Merritt, December 13,

392   HISTORY OF FAIR HAVEN, VERMONT.

1810. She died April 24, 1815, in her 73d year.

Mr. Hawkins' family was as follows:

1. *Jabez*, who was a privateersman during the Revolutionary war, and was three times taken a prisoner. He died of consumption, at his father's, in Fair Haven, August 13, 1795, in his 35th year, and was buried in the old village burying ground.

2. *Abigail*, b. in Rhode Island; m. Ethan Whipple, Nov. 30, 1788, in Fair Haven, and died Feb. 12, 1813, in her 39th year.

3. *Olney*, b. Sept. 1767 ; m. Hannah Durand.

4. *Amy*, b. in 1770 ; married Dr. James Witherell, in Fair Haven, Nov. 11, 1790.

5. *Charles*, Jr., m. Sarah Bates.

6. *Richard*, m. Sylvia Dilano, of Pittsfield, Mass. He died in town, in 1827 or '28, and his widow married Enos Bristol. The children were, Sidney, d. in Detroit ; Harriet, m. a Clyne, in Hampton ; George d. at Suspension Bridge, N. Y.

OLNEY HAWKINS, son of Charles, married Hannah Durand, and resided, for a time, on a part of the Trowbridge farm, which is now owned by David P. Wescott. In January, 1797, he bought a piece of land on the corner of the old road, leading from West street to Mr. Stannard's, and in the summer of 1802 he purchased 35 acres, running down to the river, of Judge James Witherell. He lived on this place and carried on the blacksmith business until he sold his home farm to Mr. Carpenter, in the summer of 1821. See p. 79. For one year thereafter he occupied the Everts place—now Otis Hamilton's—but bought his

HISTORY OF FAIR HAVEN, VERMONT. 393

father's old homestead in 1822, and rebuilt the house and occupied it until May, 1827, when he removed with his family to Superior, in Washtenaw county, Mich., where he died, November 12, 1827, aged 60 years.

His wife died in March, 1848, in the village of Dicksboro', in the same town, aged 72 years.

Their family, born in Fair Haven, were as follows:

1. *Daniel*, d. in the army, near Plattsburgh, in 1813, not then 21 years old.

2. *Abigail*, d. July 17, 1822, in her 26th year.

3. *Amy*, d. in Ann Arbor, Mich., in 1851, in her 53d year.

4. *Jabez*, m. Sarah, daughter of Dr. Ebenezer Hurd, and now resides in Sumner, Gratiot county, Elm Hall P. O., Mich., and has two daughters living.

5. *Olney*, a lawyer in Ann Arbor, has four daughters; three of them married.

6. *Jane*, lives in Saginaw with a daughter of her brother Jabez.

7. *Jackson*, resides in the town of Ann Arbor; has three sons and a daughter. The eldest son died in the late war, at Vicksburg.

8. *Winfield Scott*, d. at Dicksboro', Feb. 27, 1848.

CHARLES HAWKINS, Jr., b. 1775; m. Sarah Bates. He was constable in 1807, and resided on West street. He resided, after 1822, in the house which had been occupied by Harvey Johnson, on the road eastward from John Moore's. He died at Castleton Corners, December 31, 1848, aged 73 years. Mrs. H. died April 16, 1849, aged 60 years.

394 HISTORY OF FAIR HAVEN, VERMONT.

Their family were:

1. *Lucy*, b. May, 1808; m. David H. Bristol.

2. *Betsey*, m. Wm. B. Colburn, about 1825.

3. *Cullen W.*, m. Lydia H. Fish, and had four children, Warren, Farnham, William C., and Sarah.

He was a wheelwright in town, and owned the sawmill in the village, where he was killed by the saw, June 11, 1853.

William C., was a member of Co. C., 1st Artillery, Vt. Vols.; was wounded near Petersburg, Va., June 23, 1864, and died at Willett's Point Hospital, Long Island, July 14, 1864, aged 17 years. His remains were afterwards brought to Fair Haven, and interred in the village cemetery.

4. *Nancy*, m. James Barney, and died at Lancaster, Wis.

5. *Sylvia*, m. Harris Whipple.

6. *James* and *Amy*, twins. Amy married Joseph Bates, and resides in Lansing, Iowa. James married Eveline Harlow, of Whitehall, and resides in Lancaster, Wis.

DR. STEPHEN HALL; see p. 70.

FREDERICK HILL; see pp. 76 and 121.

WILLIAM HENNESSEY; see p. 106.

HEMAN HUFFMAN; see p. 107.

BENJAMIN HICKOK was born in Castleton; resided in Hubbardton at the time of the battle, in Sept., 1777, and was taken prisoner by a party of Indians and tories on Sunday morning while at breakfast. He removed to Fair Haven in the spring of 1804, buying 52 acres of land of Levi Trowbridge, adjoining Cas-

HISTORY OF FAIR HAVEN, VERMONT. 395

tleton town line, east of D. P. Wescott's present residence. It is in part now owned by Mr. Wescott. The house stood south of the highway. He was chosen a surveyor of highways here, in March, 1805, and one of the selectmen in 1806. He died here, March 21, 1825, aged 83 years. His family were:

1. *Matthew*, who was a resident here in March, 1804, and married Lucy Stevens.

2. *Benjamin*, died in Benson.

3. *Nancy*, m. John Mears, of Milton, Vt. Their family were James, Nancy, Rebecca, Daniel, John, Elias, Milo, Mary, and Clarissa.

4. *Elias*, d. in Hubbardton.

5. *Elias*, 2d, m. Betsey Whipple, of Fair Haven.

6. *Mary*, b. Dec. 16, 1785; m. David Gibbs, of Benson.

MATTHEW HICKOK resided in the large two story dwelling built by him, which stands just over or on the town line, towards Hydeville. In May, 1816, he leased of Samuel Tuttle, of Poultney, the privilege of using water from "Black Pond," for a saw mill for 20 years, and in May, 1817, he had built a saw mill in company with Ebenezer Hurd, Benjamin and Elias Hickok, on the land of Benjamin Hickok. He removed to Illinois, and afterward to Madison, Ashtabula county, O., where he died.

His family were:

1. *Welthy*, m. Elijah Remington, of Castleton.

2. *Robert S.*; resides in Madison, O.

3. *Hiram.*

4. *Sally*, or Sarah, m. Hail Mason, of Castleton, and removed to Illinois.

396 HISTORY OF FAIR HAVEN, VERMONT.

ELIAS HICKOK, b. December 9, 1780; m. **Betsey Whipple**, daughter of Ethan Whipple, July 16, 1807. He came to town in 1802, and taught school in the old log school house, which stood on the Common, during the winter of 1804, and '05, and had 97 scholars for six weeks. In the winter of 1805 and '06, he taught the first school in the new school house, which was built in 1805, situated a little back of the present school and town house. He is still living with his children.

Family:

1. *Mary Ann*, b. Aug. 13, 1808; m. Stephen Babcock, of Poultney, now residing in town. Their children are Cornelius L., Francis R., George C., and Mary P.

2. *Nancy Maria*, b. Jan. 15, 1810; m. Sidney L. Merritt; now residing in Cuba, N. Y.

3. *Betsey Maria*, b. May 15, 1812; m. Rollin C. King, of Benson; both are now dead.

4. *Abigail W.*, m. Rev. Wm. C. Mitchell, in Illinois, whither she had gone as a teacher, and died in the town of Waterloo.

5. *Sarah A.*, m. Gilman Emerson, of Dummerston, Vt. Both are dead.

6. *Giles G.*, m. Amelia ———, at Mineral Point, Wis.

7. *Loraine R.*, m. B. Frank Eddy, and died Aug. 15, 1867, leaving two children, Izora and Harrison T.

8. *Ethan B.*, d. early.

9. *Helen M.*, m. C. C. Wetsell, and resides in Amsterdam, N. Y.

HISTORY OF FAIR HAVEN, VERMONT. 397

10. *Harrison T.*, m. Alice Hall, of Saratoga Springs, and is now in Amsterdam.

Mr. Hickok is said to have had a small store of goods, obtained by way of an uncle, in Lansingburg, N. Y., at his house south and east of Mr. Wescott's now residence, previously to the war of 1812. He built the house which now stands east of Mr. Wescott's and north of the highway.

JOHN HERRING, paper maker, came hither from Sutton, Mass., in 1805, and engaged with Moses Colton and Joel Beaman in paper manufacturing. In 1811 he bought the place which Mrs. Miller has lately sold to Richard E. Lloyd, and erected thereon the house now standing. He sold the same, in Oct. 1813, to Alexander Dunahue. He married Sally Brevort, of West Haven, and had three children in the public school in March, 1812. He removed hence to West Rutland, keeping a public house there for a time, and thence went to Marcellus, N. Y., where he is said to have built a paper mill. He had a brother Absalom, who worked with him while here.

DR. EBENEZER HURD came hither from Sandgate, in 1809, buying of Dr. Witherell, in July, his home place in the village, on the present site of the Vermont Hotel, making it his home and practicing his profession for ten years. He had a brother, Gildersleeves, and a sister, Azubah, who died here, Jan. 20, 1813, aged 23 years. He married Maria Betsey Witherell, daughter of Dr. Witherell, at her father's, in Poultney, in 1814. He removed to Detroit in 1819, where he had a very extensive and successful practice. He died in Chicago and was buried in Detroit, in 1869.

398 HISTORY OF FAIR HAVEN, VERMONT.

His family were:

1. *James Cullen*, d. in Detroit, aged 9 years.

2. *Sarah*, m. Jabez Hawkins, son of Olney Hawkins, and resides at Elm Hall, Mich.

3. *Elijah*, d. in Fair Haven.

4. *Mary*, m. a son of Gov. Leverett Woodbridge, in Detroit; d. in 1865.

5. *Elizabeth*, m. Geo. Hoffman, in Detroit; now resides in New York, where he is engaged in the insurance business.

6. *Charles L.*, educated for a lawyer, at Ann Arbor, but died before he commenced practice.

7. *Benzina W.*, d. in 1848.

8. *James Cullen*, 2d., died.

BENJAMIN HASKINS came hither from Sandgate, about 1811, and bought 42 acres of land of John Snell, on' Scotch Hill, in December, 1812. He was in the Revolutionary War eight years. He then married his cousin, Molly Haskins, in Rochester, Mass., and settled there, where three of his children were born. Removing thence to Conway, Mass., about 1790, where four more of his children were born; he remained here till 1799, when he came to Arlington, and lived five years, and from there to Sandgate, and thence to Fair Haven. From Fair Haven he went to Trenton, N. Y., where he died. His wife died September 8, 1859, at 96 years of age.

Their family were:

1. *Sylvia*, m. Joseph Freeman, of Salem, N. Y. He came to Fair Haven and resided for a year or two, then went to Cambridge, N. Y., where he died. She

HISTORY OF FAIR HAVEN, VERMONT. 399

removed to Salt Point, married again and died there.

2. *David*, b. 1785; m. in Poultney, and removed to Rome, N. Y., where he had a family of nine children.

3. *Phineas*, m. and lived in Essex, N. Y., where he died in Dec. 1865.

4. *Lydia*, b. 1790, in Conway, Mass., married Russell Miller, in Arlington; now lives in Benson.

5. *Polly*, d. when 25 years of age.

6. *Benjamin*, d. at 9 years of age.

7. *Jeremiah Ballard*, b. in Conway before 1799; was named from a Methodist minister of that name who had preached in Conway. He died at 22 years of age.

8. *Lyman*, d. at 5 years of age.

9. *Fanny*, married at the West and died there.

10. *Betsey*, b. 1809, in Sandgate.

JOSEPH HASKINS; see p. 27.

JAMES HARRINGTON, a judge of the county court, came hither from Ira, and bought the farm of Judge Witherell, on West street, in August, 1808. His brother, Theophilus, was famous for his decision in the case of the slave brought before him for return to slavery, demanding a bill of sale from the Almighty as authority for such rendition, and so holding Vermont forever true to freedom. Judge Harrington sold his farm in Fair Haven, in March, 1810, to Daniel Hunter, and returned to Ira.

DANIEL HUNTER, bought of Judge Harrington, on West street, in March, 1810, and had a family resident thereon. He had a son *Daniel* and a daughter *Betsey*.

400   HISTORY OF FAIR HAVEN, VERMONT.

He sold his farm to David Rood, in February, 1813, and is said to have died previous to 1816.

SILAS HOLDEN, an unmarried man from Connecticut, resided here with Lewis Stone, and was admitted to the freeman's oath in 1814. He owned land north of the village, which he sold to Hector H. Crane, in 1819. He removed to the West.

SAMUEL HOWARD, b. August 28, 1794; came to Fair Haven from Londonderry, Vt., with his mother's brother, Jacob Cobb, while a boy, in 1809 or '11, and worked for Mr. Cobb at nail-making. He went to Springfield, Mass., and worked for a time, and then back to Londonderry, where he set up the blacksmith business, and married Marinda Brown, November 7, 1821. She was born November 28, 1802, and died in Fair Haven, January 27, 1865, aged 62 years. He came again to Fair Haven soon after his marriage, and remained in the town till his death, April 29, 1868.

His family are:

1. *Lucinda*, b. March 1, 1824; m. Newton Jenne, March 7, 1847. Mr. Jenne was a wheel-wright, resident in town, and died Nov. 16, 1863, leaving a son, Myron.

2. *Caroline Loraine*, b. May 29, 1826; m. James E. Williams, of Hydeville, and since his decease Roswell R. Lewis.

3. *Samuel C.*, b. June 21, 1829; m. Ann Bramble, and now resides in Brandon.

4. *Norman E.*, b. Oct. 17, 1831; m. Mary Harrison.

5. *Susan J.*, b. Dec. 22, 1834; m. John G. Pitkin.

HISTORY OF FAIR HAVEN, VERMONT. 401

6. *William L.*, b. Sept. 11, 1837.

7. *George W.*, b. Feb. 22, 1840; d. Oct. 29, 1860.

8. *Harriet J.*, deceased.

9. *Myron E.*, b. Feb. 24, 1844.

EBENEZER HOWARD, a younger brother of Samuel, came hither also in company with J. Cobb, and learned nail-making. He is said to have married a daughter of Sirenus Cobb, and to have removed to Wisconsin, where he has left a family.

HEZEKIAH AND HARVEY HOWARD, brothers, came from Reading to Benson, in 1818, buying, in November, of Lewis Stone, in Fair Haven, the place on West street, where O. P. Ranney resides, 43 acres on the south side of the street, and about 14 acres on the north side. They came to reside on the farm in February, 1819, and soon established a tannery in the hollow, on the south side of the street, where they carried on the business with success until about 1838, when they removed to the village, (having bought the dwelling house of Horatio Foster in 1835,) and established their tanning works just below the grist mill, buying, in the fall of 1839, the site and water privilege of the old scythe factory for the purpose. They afterward owned both the saw mill and grist mill, and carried on the tannery. Hezekiah sold all his interest in the property to John Balis, of Benson, in Nov., 1859. He first married Ruth Stanley. She died April 24, 1857, in her 73d year. He afterward married the widow of Joseph Sheldon, who survives him. He died in 1859, aged 79 years. They buried a daughter, *Lucy*, their only child, in 1829, aged 17 years.

402   HISTORY OF FAIR HAVEN, VERMONT.

Harvey was born in March, 1789, in Reading, Vt., and was never married. He resides with John Balis, in Benson.

EMMONS HOWARD, the eldest son of William Howard, and brother to Hezekiah and Harvey, was born in Pomfret, Conn., and removed when a boy, with the family, to Reading, Vt., of which they were among the first settlers. He removed from Reading to Sharon, residing there twelve years, and thence came to Fair Haven, in Sept., 1823. He first lived where Otis Eddy now does for a year, then occupied the place north of the village, afterwards owned by Stephen Fish, for two years, and resided twelve years in the house which stood a little east from where John Moore now resides. His son, William, bought the place where Mr. Goodwin resides, in the spring of 1837, and he removed thither about the same time. He moved from Fair Haven to Stratton, Vt., in 1842 or '43, where he died, in Aug., 1851. His wife was Betsey Goddard, of Reading. She died in Stratton, in 1855.

Family:

1. *William G.*, b. in Reading. He resided in Fair Haven a number of years previously to 1842, when he married Rhoda Wyman, in Rockingham, Vt. He died in Springfield. His widow married and resides in Londonderry.

2. *Mary*, resides in Royalton.

3. *Rhoda*, d. here in 1839.

4. *Betsey Maria*, resides in Royalton.

5. *Laura*, m. Richard W. Sutliff.

HISTORY OF FAIR HAVEN, VERMONT. 403

6. *Adeline H.*, resides in Royalton.

7. *Hollis E.*, resides in Royalton.

JACOB (?) HIBBARD resided in the Minot house, previous to 1824. His widow resided in the south district about 1827, and the daughters on West street in 1828 and '9, where they carried on the tailoring business. *Lucretia* m. a Mr. Saxe, and died soon after. *Ruth* married a Dr. Morse. *Ebenezer* died in town. We hear of *Jacob, Almira* or *Alvira, Bradley*, and *Sally.*

SETH J. HITCHCOCK, b. in Farmington, Conn., April 15, 1784, m. Hepsey Blinn, of Great Barrington, Mass. He came to Fair Haven on the first of April, 1841, having previously resided in West Haven. He was a teacher for many years, and a music master. He died on his place, north of the village—now John Allard's —Feb. 27, 1852. His wife died two days before, and both were buried at the same time.

Their children were:

1. *William A.*, a physician who settled in Shoreham and there died.

2. *Jane J.*, who first married a Palmer and had three daughters. She is now the wife of Stephen Murrell, of Hartford, N. Y.

ISAIAH INMAN. See p. 74.

EZEKIEL JONES, father of Dennis Jones who was for many years President of the Whitehall Bank, took the freeman's oath in town in Sept., 1788, and was assessed in the grand list in 1789 and 1793. He worked in the iron works, and as late as 1805 he resided in a log house on Scotch Hill, and his son, Dennis, attended school in the village.

404 HISTORY OF FAIR HAVEN, VERMONT.

JOHN JONES, the first Welshman whom we hear of in town, came hither from Poultney about 1826, and entered into the mercantile business where the Bank now is, in company with Worcester Morse. He married Huldah Miller or Millard, of Ballston, N. Y.; sold out to Mr. Morse and removed to Rochester, N. Y., where he died.

STEPHEN·H. JUDKINS had a wagon shop about 1829 and '30, where Harris Whipple's house now stands. He was in partnership for a time with James Greenough, and sold his shop to Joseph Adams, who made it into a dwelling house.

GURDON JOHNSON, originally from Guilford, Conn., came into Fair Haven from Granville, N. Y., about 1802. He was a fuller and clothier, and had a fulling mill near the river, south of Gen. Orms' saw mill. He purchased of Gen. Orms, in August, 1802, between three and four acres of land in Fair Haven, laying at the foot of the old Dry Falls, which he mortgaged to Samuel Johnson, of Guilford, Conn. He was driven out of his house by the great freshet of July, 1811, and removed his residence.

To an account against Enoch Wright for dressing cloth, beginning in April, 1805, and dated at Fair Haven, March 19, 1806, he appends these amusing lines:

> " The above account, if you will pay in wheat
> I and my family will eat :
> But if you don't, I'll tell you what,
> I and my family must go to pot ;
> But if you pay in wheat at large,
> I and my family will you discharge."

He died in 1812. His family were:·

HISTORY OF FAIR HAVEN, VERMONT. 405

1. *Clarissa Fidelia*, who married Samuel Francis, a hatter, in West Haven. She died Nov. 5, 1805, in her 24th year, and was buried in the grave-yard above Gen. Orms' dwelling house.

2. *Gurdon Collins*, who married Louisa Lee, a daughter of Deacon Lee, of Poultney. He sold the home place, in Jan. 1813, to Gen. Orms, and removed to Skaneateles, N. Y. His children have been educated at Kenyon College, O., and are said to be highly respected and influential people.

3. *Vacton*, removed to parts unknown.

4. *Esther* was a poetess, and stories were told in former years of her hermit-like haunt in one of the ancient "pot-holes" at the foot of the Dry Falls, whither she was accustomed to retire to court or indulge the visitations of the Muses. She married Corfil White, and removed to Skaneateles, N. Y., and is said to reside now in the town of Aurora, N. Y.

5. *Brainard*, m. Susan McPherson, of Lenox, Mass., and removed to Chazy, N. Y., about 1820. He now resides in Plattsburgh; has a daughter there and a son in Oregon.

6. *Statyria*, d. about 1811, when about 14 or 15 years old.

THOMAS JAMES, m. Mary White, and had a family of 13 children, in Norfolk, Eng. He migrated to America with his family about 1838, residing for a year in Montreal, where he served as a soldier for a time, and then came to Fair Haven, and resided near Otis Hamilton's. He was resident a number of years in West Haven, and died in Fair Haven, May 15, 1867, aged 76 years. His wife died in June, 1860.

25

406 HISTORY OF FAIR HAVEN, VERMONT.

Family :

1. *Sally*, d. in Montreal.

2. *John*, m. and resides in Castleton.

3. *Mary Ann*, m. George Leggett. now resident at Independence, Iowa.

4. *William*, resides in Oregon.

5. *Elizabeth*, m. Thomas King.

6 and 7. *Samuel* and *Eliza*, twins. Samuel m. Hannah Town, and has a family in town. Eliza became the second wife of Thomas King and resides in Saratoga, N. Y.

8. *Thomas*, is a maimed soldier of the late war, resident in Pennsylvania.

9. *Emily*, deceased.

10. *David* was blown up and killed at the Powder Mill, in 1856.

CURTIS KELSEY, Sen., came into town in 1782, from Woodbury, Conn., settling on the farm where Elijah Esty now resides. See p. 34. He had married Submitty Parsons, the daughter of a highly respectable citizen of Killingworth, Conn., and had five children, all born in Killingworth.

1. *Parsons*, b. Oct., 1768, m. Lucinda Ames, of Rutland, in 1793, and settled in West Haven, where he died of consumption in 1822, when 54 years of age. His family were Chauncey, Lyman, Katy, Guy, Caroline, Curtis and Calvin.

2. *Orren*, b. April, 1770.

3. *Lovisa*, m. Joel Spaulding, of Rutland, and had two sons, Alonzo and Harry.

4. *Lyman*, d. here, in 1796.

HISTORY OF FAIR HAVEN, VERMONT. 407

5. *Curtis, Jr.*, b. in Killingworth, in 1779, and was three years old when the family came to Fair Haven.

Mr. Kelsey was one of the first farmers and wealthiest inhabitants of the town previous to 1800. He deeded his farm to his grandson, Harry Spaulding, of Danby, in 1821, whither he removed, and died in March, 1827, aged 87 years. His wife died in April, 1828.

ORREN KELSEY, son of Curtis, m. Fanny Dwyer, of Fair Haven, in 1800. He continued to reside in the town, and died here in Feb. 1847. Mrs. K. died Feb. 25, 1869. He was a post-rider from Fair Haven to Ferrisburgh in 1795, carrying the Fair Haven papers and mail to towns along the route. In after years he was constable in the town, and often pleaded suits in law before justice's courts with success.

His family were:

1. *Mitty M.*, m. Levi Smith, May 14, 1829. Died in 1839, at 37 years of age, leaving two children, Harris and Sally Maria. Mr. S. was foreman for A. & M. G. Langdon, in the distillery, 1828–32. He now resides at Kalamazoo, Mich.

2. *James N.*, m. Jane Long. She died April, 1849, and he died of consumption, May 27, 1855. He was constable for many years. He has left four children living, Francis, Thaddeus, Don and Albert.

3. *Fanny*, first married Eli Drake, and is now the widow of Sheldon Doane, in Benson. Their children are, Louisa, Sally, and Olive.

4. *Olive M.*, now living with her sister in Castleton.

5. *Lovisa*, m. Henry Whitlock and resides in Castleton. Their family are, Charles, Fanny Ann, Delia Abba, and Miles H. 6. *Sally*, deceased.

408 HISTORY OF FAIR HAVEN, VERMONT.

CURTIS KELSEY, Jr., m. Betsey Sperry, of Castleton. His family were:

1. *Polly.*
2. *Sullivan*, now residing in Corunna, Mich.
3. *Adeline.*
4. *Charlotte.*
5. *Orson.*
6. *Leland.*
7. *Marcus W.*, resided at Pontiac, Mich., and died there.
8. *Francis.*

JOHN KINGSLAND married Lucy Davey, only sister of Jacob Davey, in New Jersey, and must have come into town about the time, or not long after Mr. Davey came. In May, 1810, he buys of Daniel Hunter a house and lot on the south side of the road, next beyond Paul Scott's place, the house being then occupied by Silas Shirtliff. He buys of Hunter another house lot on the north side of the road, in November, which he sells to David Rood, in Oct., 1813.

In May, 1814, he deeds his home place to Jacob Davey. He had a large family. In 1819 he lived on the place where C. C. Whipple now lives. At a subsequent period he occupied the one-story red house standing on the hill south of the railroad.

His family were:

1. *Mary*, m. Rodman Brown, and removed to Keeseville, N. Y. Brown built the first rolling mill at Keeseville.
2. *Jane*, m. a Mr. Field. He died in Keeseville.
3. *Sarah*, resides with her brother Edmund.

HISTORY OF FAIR HAVEN, VERMONT. 409

4. *Edmund*, m. Susan Watson, a daughter of James Y. Watson, and removed to Keeseville, engaging there in an extensive business in iron and nails.

5. *Jacob D.*, m. Lucy L. Lewis, Feb. 24, 1830, a sister of Dr. Edward Lewis. He was at one time associated with Wm. B. Colburn in the mercantile business in town, and afterward with his brother, Edmund, and Jonathan Capen in making iron and nails, at Mr. Davey's works, but removed to Keeseville, and continued for some years to make iron and nails. He is now residing in Burlington. He has a son, Abraham, in Chicago, and two daughters in Burlington.

6. *Phebe*, m. a Mr. Farnham, of Keeseville.

7. *Nelson*, resides in Keeseville.

8. *William*, is in Pennsylvania.

9. *Abraham*, lately in Washington, D. C.

10. *Lucy Ann*, m. a Mr. Baber, and is now in Keeseville.

11. *Martha*, and two others, who are now deceased.

Mr. K. went back to New Jersey, where he died, his wife going to Keeseville to reside with Edmund, where she died about 1856.

OLIVER KIDDER came from Weathersfield, in March, 1813, stopping at first for a few months on the Hampton side of the river. On the 20th of March he purchased of David Rood, of Fair Haven, 42 acres and 137 rods of land, on the Fair Haven bank of the Poultney river, adjoining widow Wells' farm on the west, it being a part of the original Ballard farm which had been sold off by Solomon Wilder on the 21st of January, 1809, to his cousin, Solomon Wilder, of Brat-

410   HISTORY OF FAIR HAVEN, VERMONT.

tleboro, and purchased by Mr. Rood in February of the same year. He subsequently purchased, Sept. 2d, 1815, of John White, of Whitehall, the balance of the Wilder farm, said to be about 40 acres, running westward to the river, Mr. White holding it by virtue of a mortgage deed given him by Wilder, Feb. 20, 1798. and this place, where Chas. W. Gardiner now resides, together with lands on the Hampton side of the river, became Mr. Kidder's home place, where he remained until his demise, April 27, 1857, aged 84 years.

Mr. Kidder was married in Weathersfield, to Phebe Hulett, a sister of Mason Hulett, Esq., from Belchertown, Mass. She died in Fair Haven, Oct. 22, 1857. also aged 84 years.

Their family were as follows:

1. *E'liza*, b. Dec. 5, 1797, m. Charles Wood, of Hampton, Nov. 30, 1817, a brother of Samuel Wood, Sen., Esq. He died here in February, 1832, in his 40th year. Their children are Chauncey and Phebe.

2. *Mark H.*, b. Jan. 1, 1799, m. Rachel Clemens, in Essex, N. Y. Children's names are Edward, Julia, Noble and Rachel.

3. *Pluma*, b. Nov. 11, 1800, m. James Greenough, now of Whitehall, N. Y.

4. *Lavonia*, b. Aug. 19, 1802, m. Charles Cheney. of Willsboro', N. Y., and had four children, Julia, Henry, Ellen and Arthur.

5. *George M.*, b. Aug. 13, 1804, m. Elizabeth Cutler, of Highgate, by whom he had four children, Kate, George, Warren and Myron. He was married a second time to Caroline Ketchum, of Sudbury, by whom

HISTORY OF FAIR HAVEN, VERMONT. 411

he has two children, DeWitt and Henry. He resides now in Swanton.

6. *Sophia*, b. Aug. 30, 1806, m. Otis Eddy, a resident of this town, Sept. 27, 1827.

7. *Camela*, b. March 30, 1808, m. Hiram Billings, Dec. 5, 1832, a former resident of this town, who died in Castleton, about 1860.

8. *Philena*, b. Jan. 23, 1811, m. Franklin Griswold, of Castleton. She died Aug. 25, 1859. Her children were Frances, Sarah and George.

9. *Asahel H.*, b. Jan. 23, 1813, who is at this time, and has been for many years, one of our town's most prosperous and successful farmers, and a leading and highly respected citizen. He married Lucy Pepper, of Highgate, and has four children, Rollin, Elizabeth, Albert and Katy.

WILLIAM C. KITTREDGE, son of Dr. Abel Kittredge and Eunice Chamberlain, was born in Dalton, Berkshire co., Mass., Feb. 23, 1800. He graduated at Williams College, in 1821, and studied law with Hon. E. H. Mills and Hón. Lewis Strong, of Northampton. He went to Kentucky and resided a year, where he was admitted to the bar in 1823, afterwards spending six months in the office of Hon. Jona. Sloan, of Ravenna, O.

He came to Fair Haven in the fall of 1824, and was admitted to the Rutland county bar in December. He boarded for a time at Mrs. Wilmot's hotel, and had his office on the north side of the hotel, up stairs. In Aug., 1827, he bought of Catherine Minot the house and seven acres of land, on which he so long

412   HISTORY OF FAIR HAVEN, VERMONT.

resided, on the west side of the Common. He had an office at one time south of his house, afterwards near the north-east corner of his house. The same is now a dwelling house north of Dr. Carpenter's, and near the Welsh Calvinistic church. He built an office which he occupied for a number of years prior to 1866, on the north side of 'his house. He owned for many years a large farm, lying beyond the river eastward and south of the iron works, where the railroad and depot now are, which he purchased of Jacob Davey, and which is now partly in Mr. Eddy's farm. In Jan., 1866, he sold his home place on the west side of the Park to Ira C. Allen, and built in the summer following the house now occupied by his family. He died ere he had fully completed his new residence, at Rutland, June 11, 1869, being on his way to Bennington in the discharge of official duties as U. S. Assessor of Internal Revenue, which office he held at the time of his death. He had been thrown from his sleigh the winter preceding, and received a fracture of one of his limbs, from which he had suffered much and was but just recovering.

Judge Kittredge was a man widely known and respected in the community and the state, being a lawyer of ability and prominence, and always before the public. For eight years he represented the town in the legislature, and was county senator two years; was two years speaker of the House of Representatives, five years state's attorney, six years judge of the county court, one year judge of the circuit court, one year Lieut. Governor and President of the Senate,

HISTORY OF FAIR HAVEN, VERMONT. 413

and for nearly seven years Assessor of Internal Revenue. He filled these places with honor and to the acceptance of his fellow men, because his eminent abilities and high moral and religious character fitted him to be thus called of his fellow men, without any obtrusive officiousness, or office seeking on his part. He was active in the cause of temperance, filling several prominent offices in this work, and was at one time lecturer on medical jurisprudence in Castleton Medical College.

Says one who knew him: "In politics Judge Kittredge was a Whig; in religion a Congregationalist; in manners elaborately polite and courteous; in conversation affluent, affable and animated; in stature, tall and stately; he was ever the advocate of the conservative and moral."

On the 30th of May, 1866, he wrote to a friend: "I relinquished the practice of law nearly four years since, having outlived a whole generation of my brethren of the bar in this county, many of whom were my very kind friends, and whose memory I cherish with sincere, and I may say affectionate regard. I now recall to mind the names of thirty lawyers, members of the bar of Rutland county, who have deceased since I had the honor of being admitted to its privileges—many of whom were strong men, able lawyers, and eloquent orators—kind, intelligent associates. Their course is finished, their race is run, and I am one of a few, very few, lingering upon the verge almost of the vast ocean, which I, as they have done, must pass—soon pass, from the present, to the great life to come."

26

414   HISTORY OF FAIR HAVEN, VERMONT.

Judge Kittredge was married three times; the first time, in October, 1827, soon after purchasing the place which he made his home in Fair Haven, to Sally Maria Hatch, daughter of Jonathan Hatch, Esq., of Troy, N. Y.; the second, in September, 1831, to Harriet Newell Adams, daughter of James Adams, Esq., of Castleton, and in 1838, to Mrs. Charlotte Button, daughter of Daniel Pomeroy, and widow of Nathan Button, of Brandon. She survives, together with Mr. Kittredge's four children, *Frances; Harriet Elizabeth; Charlotte Pomeroy;* and *William C.* Six other children died under two years of age, and one, *Mary Chamberlain*, died July 8, 1856, aged 10 years and 11 months. Frances married Nicholas G. Hurlburt, and now resides in Greenfield, Dade county, Mo. Harriet E. married Dr. Enoch E. Johnson. He died in Salisbury, Vt., and is buried in Fair Haven. Charlotte P., married Henry G. Sturtevant, and now resides in St. Louis, Mo. Wm. C. occupies the home place with his mother, and is Assistant Assessor of Internal Revenue.

OLIVER KITTREDGE, a physician, who died in Salem, Mass., married Mary Hamilton, a sister of Hiram and Otis Hamilton, and she, being over 80 years old, is now a resident of Fair Haven, living with her daughter, Mrs. Caleb B. Ranney.

Her family are: .

1. *Jacob.* He was a sea captain, and never married. He came to Fair Haven from Salem, Mass., and bought land with his brother-in-law, Mr. Ranney, on Scotch Hill, in Nov., 1835, making a division in April,

HISTORY OF FAIR HAVEN, VERMONT. **415**

1838. He had 100 acres south of Mr. Ranney's, which he sold in March, 1840, to James and Albert Keyes, of Rutland. He went away in 1841, to Illinois, and died in the town of Oxville, Ill.

2. *Charlotte*, m. C. B. Ranney.

3. *Anson*.

4. *Samuel*, removed from Salem to Dayton, O.

5. *Oliver*, removed from Salem to Dayton, O.

6. *Mary*.

7. *Sarah E.*, m. John P. Sheldon.

JOHN KEATING, a tailor, was here in September, 1827, when he purchased of Tilly Gilbert a half acre of land from the north end of Gilbert's orchard, and there built a house and shop. In May, 1832, he purchased of Horatio Foster 12 acres and a half, called "the Roberts lot," lying on the plain north of the village. In January, in 1835, Keating and his wife Hannah, were in Monroe, Mich., and then sold to Thomas Clark, of Poultney, the half-acre lot, at that time occupied by Duncan Cook, and the 12 acre lot on the plain. The lots were both sold by Mr. Clark, in April, to William B. Colburn.

ALPHONSO KILBOURN, b. in Poultney, in 1801; m. Harriet Johnson, of Poultney, in 1823, and resided successively in Milton, Enosburg, Shoreham and Hydeville. He came to Fair Haven to reside, in 1857, building the house now owned and occupied by Corril Reed, and a cloth factory where the Fair Haven Marbleizing Works now stand. He died in October, 1865.

His family are:

416   HISTORY OF FAIR HAVEN, VERMONT.

1. *George O.*, b. in Enosburg in 1824; m. **Mary** L. McLean, in California; has two children, and now resides in Salisbury, Conn.

2. *Maria*, b. in Berkshire; m. Hon. P. W. Hyde, of Hydeville.

3. *Mary*, b. in Enosburg; m. Henry C. Gleason, of Shrewsbury, Vt.

4. *Harriet*, b. in Enosburg; m. Israel Davey.

5. *Hiram*, b. in Georgia.

6. *Jennie E.*, b. in Milton; m. Darius P. Schuler, of Amsterdam, N. Y.; d. in July, 1866, leaving two children.

JONATHAN LYNDE; see p. 22.

COL. MATTHEW LYON. Most prominent among the early settlers of Fair Haven was Matthew Lyon, a native of .Ireland, who came to this country a poor boy, at 13 years of age, and was bound out, in Connecticut, on his arrival, to pay the cost of his passage, the indenture of his apprenticeship being afterwards transferred, or sold to a second party for a yoke of steers, an incident which led to many a homely joke, as well as bitter taunt, in after times, and furnished Lyon with his favorite oath : " By the bulls that bought me!"

From Connecticut Lyon found his way to Vermont, then a new country without organization, lying in dispute between New Hampshire and New York. He had married for his wife a Miss Hosford, by whom he had four children, *Anna, James, Pamelia*, and *Laurin*. She dying, he married as a second wife the widow Beulah Galusha, a daughter of Col. Thomas Chittenden, afterwards Governor of Vermont, in whose em-

HISTORY OF FAIR HAVEN, VERMONT. 417

ployment he had been. By her he had four children, *Chittenden, Minerva, Matthew,* and *Noah.*

He is said to have begun his residence in Arlington, in company with Col. Chittenden and Capt. John Fassett, Jr., in the autumn after the battle of Bennington, each taking possession of the confiscated houses of tories; but Lyon was in the state at least the year before, for in the summer of 1776, when about 30 years of age, he held a lieutenant's commission in a company of soldiers stationed at Jericho, under the command of Capt. Fassett. The company refused to serve in view of their extreme and unsupported position, and Lyon was accused of influencing the soldiers to desert, but always denied it, and cast the blame on Fassett and the other officers. Lyon made the report to Gen. Gates, at Ticonderoga, and with the other officers was arrested, tried by court martial, and cashiered for cowardice.

Lyon was afterwards, in July, 1777, restored by Gen. Schuyler, and appointed a paymaster; and, although the affair damaged his military reputation, causing him to be nick-named "the Knight of the Wooden Sword" in his subsequent fierce political conflicts, yet as a civilian and political leader, it did not materially lessen his influence. He became a captain and a colonel in the state militia, and served the state in its contests with tories and " Yorkers."

He was deputy secretary to Gov. Chittenden and his council, and was, even before this time, and until 1780, clerk of the court of confiscation, which had been set up at Arlington after the battle of Benning-

418   HISTORY OF FAIR HAVEN, VERMONT.

ton, by the Council of Safety, and through whose authority Chittenden, Fassett, and Lyon had taken possession of the houses of the leading tories. This court had everything its own way, and when a few years afterward Lyon was called upon to deliver up the record of its proceedings, he utterly refused to do so.

Lyon was chosen Representative from Arlington, in 1779, and the succeeding years until 1782, in which position he served the state on several important committees.

While in the General Assembly, convened at Manchester, in October, 1779, he became one of the original proprietors, or grantees named in the charter for the township of Fair Haven. He must have visited the town himself the following year. See p. 35.

In November, 1782, he bought of Elijah Galusha, his step-son, whose name is also among the original proprietors of the town, the right to nearly 400 acres on Scotch Hill. This he sold in July, 1783, while still resident in Arlington, to Charles McArthur, of Nobel, or Nobletown, N. Y., who had married a daughter of Gov. Chittenden, and sister to Col. Lyon's wife. He removed to Fair Haven, with his family, in the year 1783, having already established the saw-mill and grist-mill in the town.

He first resided near the north end of the bridge which crossed the river just above the grist-mill, subsequently building and residing on the site of the old tavern stand on the hill, and at a later period, on the site of Mr. Knights' present tavern. He commenced the erection of the forge and iron works, in the sum-

HISTORY OF FAIR HAVEN, VERMONT. 419

mer of 1785, and of the paper-mill not long after, thus making himself the father of the town, and causing it to be called and known far and wide, for many years, as "Lyon's Works."

In 1786 he was one of the assistant judges of the Rutland county court. He was one of the selectmen in 1788, 1790, and 1791, and appears to have given his attention principally to his own affairs, and those of the town, until the admission of the state into the Union, in March, 1791. From this time to the close of the century, he became politically prominent in the canvass of his district as a Republican or Democratic Representative to Congress, contending in every election as "the representative of the commercial, agricultural, and manufacturing interests, in preference to any of their law characters." See p. 96. At the first election, in August, 1791, Lyon had 597 votes to Israel Smith 513, and Isaac Tichenor 473. On the second trial, in September, Tichenor withdrew, and Smith was elected by a majority of 391 over Lyon. Another election took place in January, 1793, but no choice was made, Lyon receiving in Fair Haven and four adjoining towns, 355 of the 376 votes polled. Smith was re-elected in March, and again in February, 1795, Lyon and Smith being the only candidates, and receiving, the former 1,783, the latter 1,804, a majority of 21 for Smith.

In 1796, Lyon succeeded in getting the election, and took his seat in Congress in November, 1797. He began his career in Congress by a long speech against the custom then in vogue of replying to the

420   HISTORY OF FAIR HAVEN, VERMONT.

President's Message, and asked to be excused from attendance upon the personal presentation of the reply by members of Congress. He was excused at the first session, but when he renewed the motion at the second session it was voted down. In January, 1798, Lyon became involved in a personal fray with Hon. Roger Griswold, of Connecticut, on the floor of Congress. Griswold interrupted Lyon with an allusion to the wooden sword, which, it had been said, Lyon had received on the occasion of his being cashiered at Ticonderoga, and Lyon resented the insult by spitting in his face, whereupon Griswold drew up his fist and proposed to take his satisfaction on the spot, but was prevented by his colleague, Mr. Dana.

This had occurred while the House was not in orderly session, and Lyon plead that he was unaware of having violated the rules, but a resolution to expel him therefor having been considered in committee, and pressed to a vote, in February, failed of the requisite two-thirds majority. Griswold, however, dissatisfied with the result, took up the matter on the 20th, after the fashion of Preston S. Brooks, in our own time, and the members were obliged to interfere and separate the combatants. A motion to expel them both was lost.

Alluding to the first part of this affray, in an address to his constituents, written on the 14th of February, Lyon says: "Perhaps some will say I did not take the right method with him. We do not always possess the power of judging calmly what is the best

HISTORY OF FAIR HAVEN, VERMONT. 421

mode of resenting an unpardonable insult. Had I borne it patiently I should have been bandied about in all the newspapers on the continent which · are supported by British money and federal patronage, as a mean poltroon. The district which sent me would have been scandalized."

Lyon was a violent hater of the Federalist administration party, and gave utterance to many a stinging diatribe against it, yet nothing more severe than has been uttered a thousand times with impunity in later years. But the famous "Alien and Sedition Law," as it was called, by which aliens might be banished and enemies punished, had just gone into effect, July, 1798, and under this law Lyon was accused, indicted, and brought to trial at the October term of· the U. S. Circuit Court, held at Rutland. The charge against him was that of using "scurrilous, scandalous, malicious, and defamatory language" concerning the President, founded on these words, published in the *Vermont Journal*, at Windsor, on the last of July, but written in June, fourteen days *before* the passage of the law:

" But, whenever I shall, on the part of the Executive, see every consideration of public welfare swallowed up in a continual grasp for power, in an unbounded thirst for ridiculous pomp, foolish adulation, or selfish avarice; when I shall behold men of real merit daily turned out of office, for no other cause but independency of spirit; when I shall see men of firmness, merit, years, abilities and experience, discarded in their applications for office for fear they possess that

27

422 HISTORY OF FAIR HAVEN, VERMONT.

independence, and men of meanness preferred, for the ease with which they take up and advocate opinions, the consequences of which they know but little of; when I shall see the sacred name of religion employed as a state engine to make mankind hate and persecute each other, I shall not be their humble advocate."

It was also alleged against him that he had "maliciously" procured the publication of a letter from France which reflected somewhat severely on the government. Lyon plead his own case before the jury, but the charge of the judge was strongly against him, and he expected little mercy from the jury, who returned a verdict for the government. He was sentenced to four months imprisonment, and to pay a fine of $1,000 with the costs of prosecution.

The marshal and his assistants were persons who were particularly unfriendly and obnoxious to him. He expected to be imprisoned in the jail at Rutland, but the marshal resided at Vergennes, and insisted that he should go to that place, parading through the most populous part of the town, [city,] as they passed to the jail. He was there closely confined, and for some time was not allowed the means of writing to his friends. At length a stove was sent to him by his friends from Fair Haven, and he was made as comfortable as possible for the winter. Gen. Clark and another brother-in-law were admitted to see him.

He stated to the court, on the occasion of his trial, that his property had been estimated by him to be worth $20,000, but he had made over the productive

HISTORY OF FAIR HAVEN, VERMONT. 423

part of it to secure persons.who were bound for him, and he did not think he could raise $200 in cash.

In the election which had taken place in September, there was no choice, but at the second trial, about the time or soon after his imprisonment, Lyon was re-elected by 500 majority.

He was only saved from a re-arrest at the expiration of his term of imprisonment, February, 1799, by immediately proclaiming himself on his way to Philadelphia as a member of Congress. He was escorted in great triumph, by a procession of his friends, under the American flag, through many of the towns of the state, stopping at Bennington, where he was formally addressed and *feted*. An effort was made to expel him from Congress, but without success.

Upon the expiration of his second term in Congress, Lyon removed to Kentucky, where he engaged. extensively in business, and again became a member of Congress. See pp. 111 and 112. He had a contract to furnish vessels for the government, delivered at New Orleans, during the war of 1812, but failing to get them there in time, suffered loss, and was obliged to make an assignment of his property, his son Chittenden being the assignee, and himself advancing largely to pay his father's obligations.

Lyon petitioned Congress, in 1820, for remuneration for his fine and imprisonment under the Sedition Laws. The committee reported in his favor, but Congress failed to pass the bill, until as late as 1833 restitution was made to his heirs.

He obtained an appointment as government agent

424 HISTORY OF FAIR HAVEN, VERMONT.

among the Indians in Arkansas, in 1820, and proceeding thither, was chosen the first delegate to Congress from Arkansas, but died before taking his seat, on the 1st of August, 1822, near Little Rock.

Enough has been said of his character in previous pages of this book. See p. 104 and following. Of his family it is interesting to learn what we can, and the following letter written by his son, Chittenden, while a member of Congress, at Washington, April 5, 1828, and addressed to Hon. James Witherell, gives desirable information, and will be read by many persons with interest:

DEAR SIR :—Your esteemed favor of the 17th ult. was received this morning, and letter contained therein handed to Col. Watson.

It gives me great pleasure to receive this attention from the long and much valued friend of my lamented father, and brings to my mind the scenes of my childhood. I well recollect you and your family, and regret to learn that so many of them have, like my own connection, "gone the way of all flesh." You enquire after my mother. She is no more ; she survived my father about 18 months, worn down with grief and affliction for the misfortune and death of her husband and two children in less than two years ; but she found consolation and resignation in religion. She had been for the last twelve years of her somewhat eventful life an exemplary member of the Methodist Episcopal Church, and died in full hope and faith of sleeping in the arms of her God. My eldest half-brother, James Lyon, died in South Carolina about four years since, poor. My eldest half-sister, Ann Messenger, and her family, reside in Illinois near Belleville. Her husband is in comfortable circumstances, and very respectable. Sister Pamelia resides in the same state ; her husband, Dr. Geo. Cadwell, died some two years since, leaving seven unmarried daughters, and no son, (his only one having died some years before him,) in moderate circumstances. My half-brother, Elijah G. Galusha, resides in Kentucky, near me. He married the daughter of Mr. Throop, and is a poor farmer. My eldest own sister, Minerva, resides in Beavertown, Penn. Her husband, Dr. Catlett, late surgeon in the U. S. Army, died a little more than three years ago, in moderate circumstances. My sister, Aurellia, died about nine months before my father, leaving two

HISTORY OF FAIR HAVEN, VERMONT.

orphan children. Her husband, Dr. H. Skinner, died about two years before her, and left a pretty little estate for their children. My brother Matthew, lives within two miles of my residence, (Eddyville, Ky.,) and is doing very well. in fact getting rich, for he minds the main chance and dabbles but little in politics, but is a candidate for Elector on the Jackson ticket. My sister Eliza Ann, born in Kentucky, resides also in the state of Illinois. She married a worthy man, but poor, and moved to that state about one year ago. My youngest brother, Giles, also born in Kentucky, and who lived with my mother, died in the 20th year of his age, about five months before my mother.

Of those who went with or followed my father, besides our family, G. D. Cobb, who married Modena Clark, resides at Eddyville; has a large and respectable family, but is reduced in his circumstances in consequence of losing a valuable farm, which was taken by a prior claim after a long law suit, which he had highly improved. Capt. Throop has been dead many years; he died as he lived, poor. His wife, second daughter, and youngest son went to her brother, Samuel Vail, at Baton Rouge, La., and are all dead. His eldest son, John, resides at Eddyville, a vagabond. His daughter, Betsy, is a widow. Samuel C. Clark resides with G. D. Cobb; is poor, and has lost one leg, amputated close up to the body; and last, old General Whitehouse, who you no doubt recollect followed my father to Kentucky, and survived both my father and mother, and several of the younger branches of the family, and died about eighteen months since, having been a charge on my hands for many years.

In answering your enquiries I have necessarily been led into a long, and to you, somewhat uninteresting letter, while a long speech was making upon the Tariff bill, which is still under consideration in the House of Representatives.

I have had a severe indisposition since my arrival here, which confined me near a month, but I am now perfectly recovered. I have had the misfortune to lose my wife since I left home. She died on the 4th of February, and has left me a family of five young children, the eldest 10 years, the youngest 3 months and 4 days.

Please present my respects to your good lady.

Very respectfully your obedient servant,

CHITTENDEN LYON.

Hon. James Witherell.

Chittenden Lyon is said to have been a man of excellent capacity. He died in 1842, leaving a son named Matthew S., now a resident of Evansville, Ind., and another, Thompson A., of the firm of "Roe and Lyon," insurance agents at Louisville, Ky.; a daughter, who is the widow Mary O'Harn, of Eddyville, and another daughter who married W. B. Machen, of Eddyville, and died in 1852.

Matthew Lyon, Jr., died at Eddyville, in 1847, and left two sons, Gen. H. B. Lyon, and Matthew M. Lyon, together with one daughter, resident all of them at Eddyville. Mention is made of a daughter of Matthew Lyon, Sen., Eliza by name, who married John Roe, and removed to northern Illinois.

JAMES LYON has been mentioned on p. 96 as one of the publishers of *The Farmer's Library*, in 1793, and on p. 110 as the publisher of the *Scourge of Aristocracy*. *The Farmer's Library* appeared to have been started by him at Rutland, in the spring of 1793, and afterwards to have been removed to Fair Haven and merged with the *Gazette*. As we learn from the letter of his brother, published above, James Lyon died in South Carolina, about 1824.

JOHN LYON was in town and worked in the iron works in the year 1808. He owned a share of the forge with Mr. Davey, in 1812, and bought land of Mr. Davey, in or near the Cedar Swamp. He died in the village, where Col. Matthew Lyon had resided, February 3, 1813, aged 51 years; and his son *Stephen* and wife Jemima, sold off the property and removed to Hanover, N. Y., in the autumn of the same year.

GAMALIEL. LEONARD, the son of Gamaliel Leonard, was born in Raynham, Mass., May 31, 1757. He was a descendant of James Leonard, who landed in this

HISTORY OF FAIR HAVEN, VERMONT.

country from the west part of England, about 20 years after the landing of the Pilgrims, and who erected the first forge in this country, on the banks of the Taunton river.

He was a soldier in the Revolutionary War, being nine months at Boston on the first call, and afterwards went to the defence of Ticonderoga. He worked two years in the Lenox furnace, and from Lenox, or Pittsfield, removed in company with one Fuller, to Greenfield, N. Y., now known as Hampton Hills, in the year 1785, residing on what was at one time known as the Gould farm, for about a year, making a pitch, meantime, and erecting a saw-mill on the Fair Haven side of the Poultney river, on land which he bought of Heman Barlow, in January, 1786. See p. 62. He removed into town in the spring of 1786, and took up his residence where he so long remained and died, near the State Line. In company with Elias Stevens and Daniel Arnold, of Hampton, he built a forge below his saw-mill, in 1788, and is said to have been interested in a forge in New Haven or Salisbury. He was one of the board of selectmen, in 1811. He was married to Anna Witherell, a cousin of Dr. James Witherell, in Norton, Mass., February 17, 1783. He died in Fair Haven, August 7, 1827, and was buried in Low Hampton. His wife was born in Norton, Mass., Nov. 27, 1758. She died in Fair Haven, April 23, 1830, and was also buried in Low Hampton.

Family:

1. *A son*, b. June 22, 1784; d. July 8, 1784, and was buried in Lee, Mass.

2, *Anna*, b. in Greenfield, N. Y., Aug. 24, 1785 ; m. in Fair Haven, to Isaac Matthews, of Whitehall, N. Y.; d. Dec. 12, 1819, leaving four children, Salmon L., who was a minister, and died abroad; Vincent, now in Warsaw, N. Y.; Laura A., and George, who resides in Dubuque, Iowa. Mr. M. married again. in Granville, N. Y., and removed to Warsaw, N. Y., where he died.

3. *Charles*, b. in Fair Haven, June 1, 1787 ; m. Betsey Colburn, a sister of John P. Colburn, Esq., and at her decease, another sister. He is said to have been engaged with Mr. Colburn for two or three years about 1810, in making scythes, near where Mrs. Wm. Miller resides. He was a carpenter and joiner by trade, and in April, 1814, lived in the house built by John Herring. He was one who went out as a soldier in the War of 1812 and '14, and is said to have received a bounty of $100 for returning Andrew Race for desertion. He removed to Perry, Genesee county, N. Y., where he kept a hotel for many years, and was in the woolen manufacturing business. He died.in Portage, N. Y., Sept. 22, 1854. He had three children, John, Catherine, and Eugene, by his first wife, and one named Betsey, by his second. John m. Julia Inman, of Hampton, N. Y., and removed to Perry, N. Y., and thence to Plymouth, Ind., where he died. Catherine m. a Mr. Lowe. She now lives with her daughter in Centralia, Ill. Eugene married, and resides in Kentucky. Betsey died in Whitehall, and is buried in Low Hampton, N. Y.

4. *Ira*, b. May 24, 1789 ; m. Anna Haskell, in Blandford, Mass. He worked at the carpenter's trade

in his early life, and also made chairs at his father's place. In 1812 he was in Genesee county, N. Y., where he owned and cultivated some land for a year or two, after which he returned and purchased the old homestead which he owned until his death, Nov. 2, 1865. He represented the town in the Legislature for several years, and held other town offices. His wife was born in Blandford, Mass., Oct. 20, 1795. She died in Fair Haven, May 20, 1856. Their children are David H., now residing in Hampton; DeWitt, the publisher of the *Fair Haven Journal*, and Helen A., who married Welcom Manchester and resides in Low Hampton.

5. *Katy*, b. Aug. 19, 1791; d. July 1, 1804.

6. *David H.*, b. June 4, 1793; d. Nov. 20, 1816.

7. *Gilbert*, b. Jan. 20, 1795; m. Terzah Ashley, daughter of Leonard Ashley, of Hampton, N. Y. He is said to have carried on a small furnace near Mr. Davey's works, between 1812 and '20, and the woolen factory in Hampton, in company with Lyman Carpenter afterwards. Failing in the business crisis of 1837, he removed to Egg Harbor, N. J., where he died, Feb. 23, 1849, and his wife six days afterwards. His family were George, who died at 13 years of age, James, Henry, two daughters, and Gilbert. When last heard from only one daughter and Gilbert were living, and resided in Philadelphia, Pa.

8. *George*, b. Sept. 13, 1797; d. Dec. 14, 1816.

9. *Joshua*, b. Aug. 13, 1800; went to Genesee county, N. Y., where he married, lost his wife and married again, his second wife being Lucy Wilder,

of Warsaw, N. Y. She died in Mooretown, C. W., Sept. 22, 1864, and was buried in St. Clair, Mich. Their son, James W., when last heard from was in Paducah, Ky.

EDWARD LINKFIELD is spoken of as a resident, who took the freeman's oath here in March, 1793, and was warned out of town in October, 1814.

DR. EDWARD LEWIS, a son of Edward Lewis, of Hampton, N. Y., commenced the practice of medicine in Benson; married Caroline Davey, a daughter of Jacob Davey, Esq., of this town, Dec. 16, 1825, and came to Fair Haven to reside, in 1829, taking the place of Dr. Wm. Bigelow, who had removed to Bennington. In June he buys of Dr. Bigelow the house and lot in which Lewis then lived, the same that Dan Orms now owns, adjoining the town hall and school house.

Dr. Lewis left here in the summer of 1834, selling his place to Dr. Lucius Smith, and followed his father's family and others to Jackson, Mich. He died in Jackson, January 1, 1867. His wife died October 6, 1848.

Their family were;

1. *Edward P.*, d. May 30, 1833.
2. *Mary*, b. July 29, 1831; deceased.
3. *Willard C.*, b. June 28, 1833; lives in Jackson.
4. *Caroline*, b. May 23, 1838; now in Jackson.
5. *Lucy D.*, b. Aug. 19, 1837; now in Jackson.
6. *Edward C.*, b. Nov. 30, 1838; deceased.
7. *Charles*, resides in Jackson.
8. *Israel*, died in Michigan.

HISTORY OF FAIR HAVEN, VERMONT. 431

TREAT LOVELAND, and his wife, Betsey, of Castleton, in April, 1810, purchased of Ralph and Mary Carver, the land which the Carvers had inherited from Israel Trowbridge's estate, north and west of D. P. Wescott's present residence, then adjoining Curtis Kelsey's farm, and on which a dwelling house was standing less than 25 years since. • They had two sons, *Alanson* and *Truman*. Alanson m. Sophia Orms, daughter of Gen. Jonathan Orms, in 1815, and resided on the home farm.

Alanson and Sophia deeded 77 acres of the place, in June 1827, to Eliel Bond, of Castleton. They had two sons, Ransom and Cornelius, who are resident in Ohio. Alanson and wife died in Ashtabula'county, Ohio.

JOHN MEACHAM, SEN., mentioned on p. 18 as one of the first settlers, married Sarah Hall, in Williamstown, Mass., and had a family of ten children ; the first three of them born in Williamstown :

1. *Sarah*, b. Dec. 7, 1773 . m. Alvin Fuller, in Fair Haven, and removed west.

2. *John*, b. Feb. 24, 1776.

3. *Rhoda*, b. Jan. 28, 1778.; m. Daniel Baldwin, in Pawlet.

4. *Esther*, b. April 23, 1780, in Fair Haven ; *is said* to have been the first child born in town ; m. Thomas Pickett, in Galway, N. Y.

5. *Jacob*, b. June 22, 1782 ; m. in Pawlet ; d. at the West.

6. *Joel*, b. April 2, 1784.

7. *James*, b. March 12, 1786.

8. *Eliza*, b. Nov. 23, 1788 ; m. Perley Ainsworth, in Pamelia, N. Y., and removed to Castleton, Vt., about 1830.

9. *Isaac*, b. Nov. 15, 1790.

10. *Rebecca*, b. July 19, 1793.

JOHN MEACHAM, JR., was a poor boy, in Fair Haven, but rose by his own energy and effort to be a merchant in the town, in 1804, when about 28 years of age, and removing hence to Castleton in 1805, continued in the mercantile business there, acquiring quite a fortune, and becoming Probate Judge for the district of Fair Haven, which office he held at the time of his death. He married Mary Langdon, in 1806, and had one child, *Clarissa*, now the wife of Hiram Ainsworth, Esq. of Castleton.

MICHAEL MERRITT came into town in the summer of 1780, from Killingworth, Conn. See p. 30. He was born in 1738 ; married in Killingworth, to his first wife, Lucy, by whom he had the following children, all born in Connecticut:

1. *Bartholomew*, b. Jan. 7, 1762 ; removed to Benson, where he lived and died.

2. *Michael*, b. Nov. 14, 1763 ; first married Miss Sally Olney, and afterward a widow Parsons ; resided in Benson, and had four children: Sally, m. a Higgins ; Michael P., d. in Granville, N. Y.; Eli, m. Caroline Remington, and has five children living in Ohio ; Bogardus, m. Cynthia Nolen, and lives in Cuba, N. Y.

3. *Martin*, b. July 26, 1765 ; removed to Canada.

4. *Ansel*, b. March 20, 1767 ; m. Betsey Stannard,

HISTORY OF FAIR HAVEN, VERMONT. **433**

daughter of Samuel Stannard, Esq.; removed to St. Lawrence county, N. Y.

5. *Jemima*, b. Jan. 26, 1769 ; m. Henry Cramer, of Benson, who died leaving her a widow.

6. *James*, b. Nov. 18, 1770; m. Esther Downs, a sister of Simeon Downs, of West Haven; d. in Granville, N. Y.

7. *Nathaniel*, b. Sept. 20, 1772; m. a Miss Hurd, from Sandgate.

8. *Lucy*, b. Sept. 8, 1774; m. Russell Smith, and upon his decease married Wm. Hawkins, and is said to have married the third time.

9. *Lydia*, b. May 5, 1776 ; m. Uriah Lewis.

10. *Peter*, b. April 23, 1778; m. Polly Ann Mallory, whose father was from Connecticut; she d. June 15, 1810, aged 25 years, and he married Ruth Hurd, a sister of Dr. Ebenezer Hurd, for his second wife, Nov. 25, 1810. She died in 1844, at Royal Oak, Mich. He died at Angelica, N. Y., in 1861.

11. *Rebecca*, b. March 30, 1780 ; m. Salmon Norton, Esq., of this town.

Mr. Merritt's first wife died in town, Sept. 15, 1810, in her 74th year, and he married Sarah Hawkins, the widow of Charles Hawkins, Esq., on the 13th of December following. He died Aug. 18, 1815, in his 78th year, and was buried in the old village grave yard.

PETER MERRITT, had five children, by his first wife :

1. *Noble*, b. in 1802 ; m. Betsey Bates, in 1826; has three children, now in California.

2. *Minerva*, b. in 1804; m. Nathaniel C. Ranney, who now lives in Iowa.

3. *Sidney*, b. 1806; m. Nancy M. Hickok, Feb. 9, 1830, a daughter of Elias Hickok, Esq.; had seven children, of whom six are living, and most of them reside in Cuba, N. Y.

4. *Alanson*, b. 1808; m. Harriet Erle; is a physician at South Bend, Ind.; has three children living.

5. *Polly Ann*, b. 1810; m. Walter Loomis, and resides at New Hudson, N. Y. She has had four children, and has but one living.

Mr. Merritt's children by his second wife, Ruth Hurd, are:

1. *Burgina*, b. 1811; m. Robert 'S. Peasley, and resides in Wisconsin, but has no children.

2. *Simeon*, b. in 1813; has been married twice; resides now in Wisconsin, and has one child.

3. *Lucy*, b. in 1816; m. a Mr. Chapin of South Bend, Ind., and died there in 1858, leaving no children.

SIMEON McWITHEY m. Sarah Vandozer. See p. 25. In November, 1821, she is said to be lately of Brutus, Cayuga county, N. Y., and deceased, Wm. Barnes being her administrator. Of their children we hear only of *James, David, Isaac*, and *Levi*. James and David took the freeman's oath in July, 1791.

In April, 1795, Isaac purchased of Philip Priest and Asa Smith, a farm of 60 acres on Scotch Hill, now owned by the Union Slate Co., and resided there a few years, selling the place to Tilly Gilbert, in October, 1800. He married, some say Kate Sharp, others say Loraine Church, and is said to have died on Scotch Hill. His children were Simeon, Hulda, Elsie and Almira.

HISTORY OF FAIR HAVEN, VERMONT. 445

DANIEL MUNGER came from Litchfield, Conn., in the summer of 1783, settled on what is known as the "Munger road." See p. 42. He was a deacon in the church, and had the reputation of being very rigidly religious. He died Feb. 10, 1805, in his 80th year. He had a brother Eli.

His family were:

1. *Asahel*, b. June 3, 1770; m. Lydia Boland, Jan. 22, 1795.

2. *Elizabeth*, m. Joseph Snow.

3. *Hannah*, m. Stephen Rogers.

4. *Calvin*, b. 1776; m. Rebecca S. Hemenway, of Shoreham.

5. *Phebe*, m. Abijah Warren.

ASAHEL MUNGER's family:

1. *Phebe*, b. Nov. 12, 1796; m. Cullen W. S. Warren.

2. *Amanda*, b. July 28, 1799.

3. *Delight*, b. Jan. 28, 1801; d. March 16, 1805.

4. *Eunice*, b. May 25, 1803; d. April 20, 1808.

5. *Asahel*, b. Sept. 29, 1805; went to Oregon as a missionary.

6. *Calvin*; went to Rochester, N. Y.

7. *Daniel*, b. Oct. 9, 1812; m. Caroline M. Kerr, of White Pigeon, Mich., in 1841. She died in 1853. He died Aug. 18, 1863, in Detroit, Mich., where he was the editor of a city paper, and where two of his six children, Louis and Louisa, alone survive him, and reside.

8. *William*, resides at Hillsdale, Mich.

Asahel Munger removed with his family to Mich.

436 HISTORY OF FAIR HAVEN, VERMONT.

in 1817, having sold his farm to Dr. Ebenezer Hurd, Oct. 11, 1816.

· CALVIN MUNGER, son of Daniel, learned the shoemaker's trade of Stephen Rogers, and bought out Rogers' house, shop and tannery, on the west side of the Common, March 31, 1801. He died April 17, 1806, in his 31 year, and his wife removed to Shoreham. They had two sons: one of them, Sendol Barnes Munger, born here Oct. 5, 1802; was educated at Middlebury College, and went to India as a missionary in 1834.

REUBEN MUNGER, JR. See p. 43.

CHARLES McARTHUR, SEN. See pp. 44 and 45. He first married a daughter of Gov. Chittenden, and sister of Col. Lyon's second wife. By her he had three sons, John, Daniel, and Allen.

1. *John* worked at printing for James Lyon.

2. *Daniel*, m. Nancy Atherton, a daughter of Joshua Atherton, and his children were Delinda, Nancy, Alphonso, Avery, and Louisa.

Nancy m. James McOmber. Alphonso wrote his name "Francis A." Avery m. Maryette Tomlinson, of Castleton, and removed to Michigan.

3. *Allen*, went away to Pennsylvania, but came back here and died previous to 1821. His children were, Cyrus, who resided in Columbia, Pennsylvania, in 1828; John B., who sold his place to Arnold Briggs, Aug 1, 1835; Elvira who married Jeff. Sherman, of Rutland, Tioga county, Penn., and Charles, who also resided in Rutland, Penn., in 1835.

By his second wife, Rebecca Stanton, Mr. McArthur had seven children :

4. *Charles*, went to Missouri, and afterward, in 1835, resided in Arkansas.

5. *Clintha*, m. Elisha Vaughn.

6. *Harvey*, is said to have injured himself bringing potatoes out of the cellar, and to have bled at the lungs till so weak that he fell from his horse and died.

7. *Bradford G.*, removed to Michigan.

8. *Alexander,* m. Sally Gaines, of Castleton, a sister of Mrs. Ralph Perkins, and removed to Michigan.

9. *Minerva*, m. Elihu Wright.

10. *Seneca*, learned the cabinet-maker's trade of Joseph Brown between 1818 and '20; married Wealthy Durand, daughter of Ira Durand, of Hampton, and died near Rochester, N. Y. His widow is said to be living.

JEHIEL MITCHELL. ~See p. 74.

ISRAEL AND DAN MARKHAM, brothers, were resident here and took the freeman's oath in July, 1791. Israel was a blacksmith and had a shop in the highway near Col. Lyon's house, in March, 1796. See p. 107.

LEWIS D. MARANVILLE. See p. 119.

Family :

1. *Lucinda*, not married; removed to Warsaw, N. Y.

2. *Oliver*, not married; removed to Warsaw, N. Y.

3. *Sabria*, m. Simeon Beddow, Feb. 20, 1823; removed to Warsaw, N. Y.

4. *Stephen*, resides in Warsaw, N. Y.

438   HISTORY OF FAIR HAVEN, VERMONT.

5. *Pamelia*, m. Simeon Cobb; d. in town.

6. *Lewis D.*, b. 1809; m. Laura Ann Kimball; resides in town.

7. *Lydia*, m. and resides in Arcade, N. Y.

8. *Christie*, resides in Warsaw, N. Y.

9. *Charity*, d. at 17 years of age; was buried on the old homestead.

ANDREW McFARLAND, known as "Captain McFarland," came to Fair Haven from Hampton, N. Y., and and had a store of goods in the old Boyle and White store, about 1804, succeeding Mr. Gilbert in the office of postmaster, also, about the same time. Failing in business, his uncle, Joshua Quinton, took charge of his goods and debts, in 1806.

He was "deputy custom house officer" in 1809 and '10, and is reported to have made a noted seizure of some $2,000 worth of smuggled dry goods at Granville, N. Y.; the goods having been purchased - with butter, in Canada, for Elisha Parkill, and being at the time *in transitu* for the South, Joel Hamilton and Eleazer Claghorn conveying them in a clandestine manner, in their wagons, and pretending they had wheat.

From Fair Haven Mr. McFarland went into the army, in 1812, and was stationed at Sackett's Harbor as captain of a company of cavalry. He moved his family to Sackett's Harbor, in 1816, and was there keeping a large public house, in 1818, afterwards removing to Ohio. He married Sally Bronson, of Granville, N. Y., whose brother, John—see p. 309—was clerk for him in 1804. He had a son *Quinton*, and a daughter *Eliza Ann*.

CHRISTOPHER MINOT, cashier of a bank in Boston, married for his second wife, Catherine Cutler, widow of Dr. Simeon Smith, of West Haven, about 1805, and came to West Haven to reside, buying, in October, 1805, a strip of land in Fair Haven, where Ira C. Allen's new marble dwelling house now stands. This strip of land was but three rods wide by eighteen deep, and he subsequently, in 1811, added to it by two further purchases, and erected the large building thereon which was for many years, and recently, the home of Judge Kittredge. The building was constructed for a place of resort and musical entertainment, and made use of as such. Mrs. Charles Rice resided in it during the war of 1812 and '14. Mr. Allen has lately moved it to West street.

On the completion of the new school house in Fair Haven, in 1806, Mr. Minot presented the town, or district, with a bell for the same, and the bell still swings in the belfry of the town hall and village school house, bearing the inscription: "1806. G. Holbrook, Brookfield. Presented by C. Minot, Fair Haven."

Mr. M. died in West Haven, August, 22, 1824, in his 71st year, and his widow sold the place in Fair Haven, then consisting of seven acres, to William C. Kittredge, August 6, 1827. She died March 30, 1833, aged 72 years.

Mr. Minot's family, by his first wife, were: *Sarah C.* m. John Thomas, a sea captain, who came to West Haven and opened a store; *Elizabeth*, m. Thomas Swan, of Roxbury, Mass.; *Mehitable*, m. first a Richards, afterwards Patrick Johnson, of Whitehall, N. Y., and *George R.*, and *Frank*.

440 HISTORY OF FAIR HAVEN, VERMONT.

COLLINS MILLS occupied a house, built in 1809 by John Herring, on the top of the hill, west from the paper mill. He had three children in the public schools, in 1812. He was a paper-maker, and resided here as late as 1831.

JOHN MANNING was here in March, 1812, and had three children in the public school. He was warned out of town this same month. He lived somewhere between Mr. O. P. Ranney's and Mr. James Campbell's. His wife, Polly, died March 18, 1814, in her 31st year, and he was married to Olive Filley, July 4, 1815, by Isaac Cutler, justice of the peace. He manufactured wooden ware and dishes in a factory on the rocks, over the iron works, as late as 1816, and afterwards went west.

RUSSELL MILLER, b. in Arlington, and there married Lydia Haskins, about 1809, going thence to Chateaugay, N. Y., and remaining until 1815, when he removed to Fair Haven, living, in 1818 and '19, on the plain east of Mr. Moore's present residence. He moved to Benson in 1833, where he has since remained. He has had a family of seven children, all of whom are dead but three. *Russell*, his eldest and only son, went to Georgia as a teacher, in 1840, and there gained a reputation in the practice of law, but died of consumption in 1846.

JAMES MILLER, b. in 1781, in the county of Antrim, Ireland; came to Argyle, N. Y., in 1799, where he married Catherine Batey, about 1804 or '05, and after two years removed into the town of Whitehall. He had two children born in Argyle: *Martha*, June 8,

HISTORY OF FAIR HAVEN, VERMONT. **441**

1805, and *David*, July 6, 1806, and four born in Whitehall, *Nancy*, *John*, *Ann C.*, and *Catherine*, born April 22, 1813. Losing his wife at this time, he removed to Argyle, and while at work at his trade of shoemaking for Timothy Allen, of Hartford, married Mr. Allen's eldest daughter, Anna, sister of Ira and Alonson Allen.

Their first child was:

1. *William*, b. in Hartford, Sept. 6, 1817; was drowned in the river west of Otis Hamilton's residence, about 1827.

They removed to Fair Haven, in February, 1818, locating in the north part of the town near the well-known Apollos Smith tavern. Here the remainder of Mr. Miller's family were born:

2. *Timothy*, b. March 19, 1819; m. Susan Brown, of Hartford. They have one daughter Betsey A., m. Seth N. Peck.

3. *Abigail A.*, b. Feb. 1, 1821; d. about 1865.

4. *John*, b. Nov. 12, 1822; m. Betsey Martin; d. in 1858.

5. *Margaret*, m. I. H. Allard.

6. *James*, m. Ann Dowd; d. Sept. 21, 1870, aged 46 years, leaving five children, Frederick, Mary, Edward, John, and George.

7. *Justus*, first married Eliza Brayton, of Hartford, N. Y., and had two children, George and Frank; m. Elizabeth Bockus for his second wife, and they now reside in Troy, N. Y.

8. *William*, m. Mary Shaw, in Bradford, Vt., and after her death, Mary Foster, of Chelsea, Vt. He

442 HISTORY OF FAIR HAVEN, VERMONT.

died of consumption at Austin, Minnesota, Jan. 5, 1869, and was buried in Chicago. His children, by his second wife, are Willie and Lulu.

Mr. Miller was the senior partner in the firm of Miller, Allen & Dobbin, in which Ira Allen and David Dobbin were associated with him in tanning and currying leather, and manufacturing boots and shoes. They were also for a time in the lumber business. In February, 1824, they purchased of Chauncey Goodrich 10 1-2 acres of land, with privilege of dam to raise water for a bark-mill. Mr. Miller went into the business of boating on the Champlain canal, also, with Elizur Goodrich. They ran a line of passenger dayboats between Troy and Whitehall, in 1835 and '36; but the enterprise miscarried and was given up.

Robbins Miller, son of Wm. Miller, of Hampton, N. Y., located in Fair Haven, in 1851. See pp. 159 and '60. He removed to Pontiac, Mich., in 1863. He married Mary Barber, of Addison, and has two children, *Mary E.* and *William.*

Sylvanus Morton was resident in town in November, 1826, when he purchased 5 acres of land and a dwelling—now J. P. Willard's—of Nathaniel Hart, of Castleton. His wife was Lucy Stanley, a sister of Mrs. Hezekiah Howard. He died early in the year 1829, leaving a son, *David,* and daughter, *Rebecca,* the wife of George Gardner, both residing in Reading, and another daughter, *Huldah,* the wife of Jirzy Hammond, of Windsor. They deeded the 5 acres on West street to Lucy. In January, 1832, Harvey Howard, administrator, sold the same to Azel Willard.

HISTORY OF FAIR HAVEN, VERMONT. 443

Mrs. Morton married a Perkins, and lived and died in Benson.

WORCESTER MORSE, b. in Poultney; m. Caroline Farnham, a sister of Wm. L. Farnham, Esq., came to Fair Haven in August, 1828, and engaged in the mercantile business in company with John Jones, in the old stand where the new bank building now is. They bought the store and the house where Dr. Wakefield resides, together with a large grain store on the south side of the Common, of Wm. C. Kittredge and David C. Sproat, in December, 1829. Jones sold out to Morse in February, 1831. Morse sold the *lot* on which the grain store stood, to Royal Bullock, in October, 1834. He sold the store of goods, and dwelling house to Luke Beaman, of Poultney, in December, 1834. He removed with his family to Vermontville, Mich., leaving Poultney in May, 1836; but not finding the new country satisfactory, returned to Madison, Ohio, and settled. He now resides in New Oregon, Howard county, Iowa. His family were four children: *Ellen*, living with her father; *Laura*, married in Ohio, and now a widow; *Charles*, married in Beloit, Wis.; removed to Pennsylvania and died, and *George*, b. in Ohio; now in Iowa.

JOHN MOORE, b. in Killinchy, Ireland, in January, 1794; came into Fair Haven in 1851, having resided some 17 years previously in West Haven. He purchased his home place of James N. Kelsey. He married Elizabeth Shenks, and his first four children were born in Killilagh, Ireland:

1. *John*, b. in 1824; d. in West Haven, in Sept. 1870. His wife was Eunice Needham, and he has left seven children living.

2. *James*, was lost in the Golden Gate, on his way home from California.

3. *Thomas*, d. in Fair Haven.

4. *Robert*, d. in June, 1832, on the passage from Ireland.

5. *William*, b. in Canada; d. in DeKalb, Ill.

6. *Louisa*, b. in West Haven ; resides at home.

7. *Jane*, m. Oliver K. Ranney ; d. in 1868.

8. *Lydia*, deceased.

9. *Betsey*, m. O. K. Ranney, and now resides in Pacific City, Iowa.

JABEZ NEWLAND. See p. 77.

JOSIAH NORTON, ESQ., who is mentioned on pp. 115 and 116, as having bought out the paper mill and much of Col. Lyon's interests in the town, in the year 1800, was born October 12, 1747. He removed from Berlin, Conn., to Castleton, in 1797, and died in Fair Haven, March 26, 1803, aged 55 years. He was buried in Castleton. His first wife, Rebecca Cogswell, died January 14, 1797, aged 42 years. By her he had seven children : *Lucinda, Abigail, Salmon, Burke Eli, Rebecca, Erastus* and *Isaac*. He married, for his second wife, widow Margaret Cole, who survived him, and afterward married Moses Sheldon, of Rupert. Concerning his children, Lucinda, b. in Berlin, Conn., in 1774, m. Samuel Couch, who died March 1, 1801. She afterwards m. a Mr. Boland, who died in the war of 1812 and '14. She died in Castleton, March 1, 1848. Abigail, m. Ira Northrup. She died in Castleton, Feb. 11, 1808, and left three children, Alma, Rebecca and Josiah. Burke

HISTORY OF FAIR HAVEN, VERMONT. 445

Eli married Miss Joan Cramer, of West Haven, Jan. 19, 1811. He died Dec. 26, 1812, aged 27 years, leaving two children, Josiah and Julius. Josiah died in Wisconsin, Julius now lives in Benson. Mrs. Norton, wife of Burke E., died March 7, 1838, aged 50 years. Rebecca m. Alexander Dunahue, and afterwards Dr. A. Kendrick, of East Poultney. She died about 1840. Erastus died in the war of 1812 and '14. Isaac m. Mrs. Adams, of Hampton, N. Y. He died in Benson, about 1853, leaving four children, Willard, Mary, Henry and Louisa.

SALMON NORTON, ESQ., eldest son of Josiah Norton, born in Berlin, Conn., in 1782; upon his father's death, in March, 1803, succeeded to the possession of the paper mill and lands adjoining. He was chosen constable and collector in 1805 and '06, and selectman in 1809. He was chosen constable again in March, 1812, but resigned his office in Sept., as he says, "he is detached for a campaign in the war." He enlisted as adjutant under Gen. Orms, and went to Burlington, where he was stationed under Gen. Williams. His family were living at this time in the house formerly owned by his father, east from the church. He came home on a visit in the winter, was taken suddenly sick. Dr. Hurd bled him, and he died January 7, 1813, in the 32d year of his age. He married, about 1802, Rebecca, a daughter of Michael Merritt. They had a son, 1. *Josiah*, born March 23, 1803, who died early. Their other children were, 2. *Salmon Cogswell*, b. Jan. 24, 1805; m. Philena Ranney, and removed to Marcellus, N. Y., where he died.

446　　HISTORY OF FAIR HAVEN, VERMONT.

3. *Lucy Maria*, b. June 1, 1807; m. Salmon Richards, of Poultney.

4. *Glorvina Emily*, b. Nov. 19, 1809; m. a man by the name of Keeler.

5. *Josiah*, b. July 4, 1813.

Mr. Norton's widow is said to have married John W. Robinson, a poor man, called "long John."

BYRON OLNEY. See p. 391. In June, 1795, Jesse Olney bought of James Bowen 52 acres of the first division of Benjamin Cutler's right on Mt. Hamilton, and leased the same to Nedabiah Olney for life. Nedabiah sold it to James Witherell, March 5, 1798, with the house and barn, occupied by him. We hear of Ezekiel Olney and Davis Olney.

ELIADA ORTON married widow Bosworth, of Whitehall, and removed from West Haven to the north part of Fair Haven, early in the present century. Of his children we hear of *Arena*, who married Giles Hurd, or Hard; *Deborah*, who married Chauncey Goodrich, and died Nov. 14, 1811, in her 22d year; *Amasa*, *Uriah*, and *Lucy*. Lucy married Harvey Church.

Mr. Orton's wife, Luna, died April 9th, 1822, aged 68 years, and he is said to have given up his farm to Mr. Church, and to have lived with him in the village till he dropped down dead in the street, April 16, 1823, aged 75 years.

GEN. JONATHAN ORMS, a carpenter and mill-wright, came from Northampton, Mass., about 1788, stopping a short time in Pittsfield, Vt., on his way. He was engaged for Dr. Simeon Smith in building a forge on the west side of the falls, which he afterward owned,

HISTORY OF FAIR HAVEN, VERMONT.

and on which he built the saw-mill and grist-mill, so long known as "Orms' Mills."

He worked for Solomon Cleveland, on Lyon's Mills, in 1796. He married Eunice Hines, at the house of Mr. Timothy Goodrich, about 1790, and settled in the West Haven part of the town, on the ground where Seth Hunt now resides. He afterward resided for a number of years, on the south side of the highway, in Fair Haven, and was chosen to fill town offices in 1803 and '04. He built the two-story dwelling, now occupied by Mr. Hunt, in 1804, and removed into it in the fall.

He was General-in-Chief of all the militia in Vermont, in the time of the last war with Great Britain, and had his headquarters at Burlington.

His wife, Eunice, died in West Haven, March 27, 1824, aged 55 years, and was buried in the cemetery just above and north of his house. He married again to widow Gaines, whose maiden name was Annah Doyle. She died January 14, 1837, in her 67th year. He married for his third wife, widow Lura Weston, a daughter of Ebenezer Lyman, and sister of Hiram and Eleazur Lyman. She survives him and resides at the West.

He removed to Castleton Corners in 1842, and died there August 8, 1850, aged 86 years. He was buried beside his first wife, in West Haven.

His family by his first wife, were:

1. *Pamelia*, b. in 1792; resides with her brother in Whitehall, N. Y.

2. *Allen*, resides in Northampton, Iowa.

3. *Sophia*, m. Alanson Loveland.

4. *Alanson*, deceased at three years of age.

5. *Betsey*, m. John Ransom, of Poultney, and they reside in Cleveland, O., where they have three children.

6. *Caroline*, m. Ezra Greenough.

7. *Dan*, b. in Fair Haven, Feb. 13, 1804.

8. *Jonathan*, resides in Whitehall, N. Y.

9. *Cornelius*, resides in Jamestown, N. Y.

DAN ORMS, a native of Fair Haven, first married Amelia Gaines, a daughter of his father's second wife. She died March 13, 1849, aged 40 years. Mr. Orms resided for some years in Hampton, N. Y., and carried on the woolen factory opposite his father's mills, where the powder works now are. He came to Fair Haven, and married Mrs. Sarah S. Cook, the widow of Solon Cook, in 1852, and purchased a half interest in the place he now owns and occupies, of Simeon Bullock's estate, in 1853. He purchased Joseph Sheldon's saw-mill, at the outlet of Beaver marsh, in January, 1860. His children are *Myron*, who is now living in St. John, Mich., and *Fanny*, who married A. H. Barber.

DAVID PUNDERSON. See p. 57.

BENJAMIN PARMENTER was one of the earliest settlers of the town, and built a house near the Cedar Swamp. He married Azubah, the second daughter of Oliver Cleveland. He is said to have resided at one time on the knoll east of the railroad depot, where Mr. Kittredge's dwelling now stands. He had a daughter, *Ann*, who married a Plummer, and one, *Polly*, who died at Harvey Church's.

HISTORY OF FAIR HAVEN, VERMONT. 449

PHILIP PRIEST came hither from Killingworth, Conn., in 1780. See p. 31.

His family were:

1. *Trubey*, b. Feb. 4, 1763, in Connecticut; m. Elijah Tryon, of West Haven, Feb. 21, 1786. Their children were Dela F., William, Betsey, Elijah, Cynthia, Samuel W., Jason, Mariah, Matilda.

2. *Betsey*, m. Asa Smith prior to 1796.

3. *Noah*, b. about 1780; was first m. to Nabby Cleveland, youngest daughter of Enoch, a sister of Solomon Cleveland, of Hampton, N. Y. His second wife was a Spoor; and his eldest child, Clara, m. Harry Dibble. He had a son Chauncey, one named Erastus, and a daughter named Trubey. He was an active politician on the Federalist side, a pettifoger, and a noted anti-Mason. He is said to have gone to western New York and there died.

4. *Abi*, m. Timothy Martin, and removed to Chateaugay, N. Y., where he died, and she married Gideon Knowles.

5. *Diana*, m. James Dada.

6. *Charity*, m. Hamilton Bolles. She has a daughter living in Whitehall.

7. *Elizabeth*, mentioned as the 5th daughter in Mr. Priest's will.

8. *Merritt*, is said to have removed to southern Ohio and died there.

9. *Zadock*, of whom we can only learn that he was a Methodist minister in southern New York, or Pennsylvania, and has left a record of his life among the Methodists.

450 HISTORY OF FAIR HAVEN, VERMONT.

10. *Polly*, married a Mr. Hall and had two sons who were Methodist preachers.

11. *Sally*, m. Benj. Emmons, and died in Chateaugay, N. Y.

12. *Aaron*, b. in Fair Haven, March 27, 1784; resided for a time in Benson, where he engaged in mercantile and lumber business, and whence he started to go to Fort Edward to purchase an anchor, in 1808, or '10, but put up at a tavern near Comstock's Landing over night, and was never afterward heard from.

ETHIEL PERKINS came from Derby, Conn., about 1795—See p. 120—settling in the spring of 1799 on the place recently owned by Oliver Proctor, on Scotch Hill. He is said to have been a soldier in the Revolutionary war, and to have been in the battle of Bunker Hill. His wife's name was Esther Fox. He died here in Feb., 1826.

His family were, *Joseph*, *David*, *Hannah* and *Roger*. Joseph and David remained in Connecticut. Hannah and Roger came to Vermont, and Hannah married Joseph Tuttle, of Castleton.

ROGER PERKINS married Betsey Candy, of Oxford, Conn., and had a family of twelve children :

1. *Candy*, d. in Michigan, in 1863.

2. *Esther*, d. in Castleton,

3. *Fairy*, m. John Snell, who came hither from Addison, and removed to Enosburg. Their children were John and Delight.

4. *Charles*, was a shoemaker ; went to New Boston, and died in 1840, leaving one child.

5. *Ralph*, resides in town.

HISTORY OF FAIR HAVEN, VERMONT. 451

6. *Nancy*, never married, and died at Dr. Smith's, in West Haven.

7. *Hiram*, m. a Russell, of Castleton.

8. *Riley*, was drowned at Whitehall.

9. *Emmet*, died in London, C. W.

10. *Harris*, removed to London, C. W., where he now resides.

11. *Caleb*, resides in London, C. W.

12. *Betsey*, m. John Gaines of Castleton, and removed to Michigan about 1839.

Roger Perkins died in London, C. W. His wife died here, April 15, 1834, aged 63 years.

RALPH PERKINS, son of Roger, married Polly Gaines, of Castleton.

His family are:

1. *Laura*.

2. *George*, m. widow Coroline Gault, and resides in Castleton.

3. *James G.*, m. Louisa Kenson.

4. *Polly Ann*, m. Nathan Ager, from Keene, N. H., now residing in Castleton.

5. *Emeline*, m. Wm. Perry.

6. *Maryette*, m. Romeo Proctor.

7. *Sarah D.*, m. Richard Lewis.

8. *Charles*, m. Betsey Davis.

9. *John*, m. Laura Andrews.

10. *Lucy*, deceased.

11. *Ralph*, m. Jane Cook.

12. *Ellen*, m. Lucian Haight.

ELISHA PARKILL came hither from Benson, about 1806, to serve as clerk for Tilly Gilbert, in a store near where John G. Pitkin now resides. He took the freeman's oath in 1809. Buying Mr. Gilbert out in the store, he carried on the mercantile business in company with Erwin Safford for a time. In August, 1810, he bought of Mr. Gilbert the lot and house which Gilbert had built for him, standing where Dr. Wakefield now lives. This he sold to Dr. Israel Putnam, in March 1812. He purchased a lot of Thomas Wilmot, in January, 1811, and removed his store to the same—now James Miller's dwelling house, below the blacksmith shop. He afterward owned the store built by Safford, where the blacksmith shop now stands, and was a prominent business man of the town, owning several farms and running a distillery on West street, in company with Hector H. Crane, until about 1824, when he became insolvent. He married Sally Maria, eldest daughter of Tilly Gilbert, August 13, 1815, and died at his residence, where Wm. Dolan now resides, July 3d, 1827, aged only 42 years. His widow afterward married Ebenezer W. Dewey, and removed to Flint, Mich.

JOHN PARKILL, brother of Elisha, came hither, also from Benson, and resided on his brother's farm in the east part of the town, about 1817. He resided at the corner, now Mr. Fish's, north of the village, in March, 1827. He removed to the West and died, and his widow, Diadama, came back to Whitehall, where she married a Mr. Jillson.

SETH PERSONS, mentioned on p. 168, as of Sudbury, in Jan., 1808, was engaged here with Messrs. Davey and Foster in cloth dressing for a number of years.

HISTORY OF FAIR HAVEN, VERMONT. 453

He also had a store on the east side of the Common. See p. 172.

ABEL PARKER, from Hampton, N. Y.—see p. 17—was resident on West. street, in the old Isaac Cutler house, lately removed by Mr. Wescott, in 1813, and had a cider mill there as late as 1816. His daughter married Hon. Zimri Howe.

DR. ISRAEL PUTNAM, b. March 25, 1785, was the son of Eleazer Porter Putnam, and Rebecca Putnam, of Corinth, Vt., and was a practicing physician and surgeon in the town, as early as 1811. In May of this year, on the 20th inst., he married Charlotte, daughter of Silas Safford, Esq., and in March following resided where Dr. Thomas E. Wakefield now does, and also purchased the place of Elisha Parkill. At the close of the war he rebuilt the store on Anna Wells' lot, adjoining his own, and opened a store of goods, but sold his place soon after, in August, 1816, to his brother-in-law, Erwin Safford, and removed to Hartford, N. Y., in 1817. He died December 10, 1835.

His family were:

Betsey S., Israel S., Charlotte 'S., Silas S. 1st., Harriet N., Lafayette, Silas S. 2d., Samuel P., and *Fannie Loraine.*

He had a brother, Smith Putnam, who kept a store for a time where the old blacksmith shop now stands, opposite Knight's Hotel.

Silas Safford Putnam, 2d, b. May 31, 1822, in Hartford, N. Y., and Fannie L., b. May 12, 1825, are the only living children of Dr. Putnam. Silas S. is the inventor of the celebrated Curtain Fixture which bears his name, and of the "Patent Forged Horse Nails." He resides in Neponset, Mass. Fannie Loraine married J. B. Stockman, and resides in Roxbury, Boston.

DANFORTH PETTY came to Fair Haven from Claremont, N. H. He learned the cabinet maker's trade with Joseph Brown, whose shop and house, now Col. Allen's homestead, he purchased in December, 1828, with all the benches, tools, &c. The building was burned, while owned by him, in the winter of .1830, and he purchased the old grain house, built by Erwin Safford, just west of Joseph Adams' present dwelling house, and removed it to the knoll where the Baptist church is now building. and used it there for a shop. He sold the place to George W. Ware, and removed in the fall of 1831, first to Chester, and soon after to Detroit, where he engaged for a time in keeping the American Hotel. He now lives with his sons in Pontiac, Mich.

He first married Anna Hosford, daughter of Philo Hosford, of Poultney, and had two sons, *Courtland* and *George.*

His wife died in Detroit, and he married Mrs. Jane Ann Sproat, a niece of David C. Sproat. His three sons, Courtland, George and William, are now in the stove and tin business, in Pontiac, Mich.

OLIVER PROCTER removed from Townsend, Mass., to Benson, about 1823. In the spring of 1835 he came to Fair Haven, and purchased, with his son, Nelson, the Daniel McArthur home farm, and the old Perkins

HISTORY OF FAIR HAVEN, VERMONT. 455

place, on Scotch Hill. He married Sarah Drake, of Lanesboro, Mass., and had five children. His wife died about 1822, and he afterwards married Polly Barber. He died January 11, 1868.

His family are:

1. *Ruth*, b. Nov. 14, 1803; m. Arnold Briggs.

2. *Diantha*, b. Jan. 4, 1805; m. a Mr. Olmstead, of Benson, and moved to Potsdam, N. Y.

3. *Jonathan Nelson*, b. Feb. 17, 1808; m. Betsey Briggs, sister of Arnold Briggs, and has six children: Sarah, wife of Almon J. Gibbs, of Benson; William H., residing in Coldwater, Mich.; Oliver, residing in Nebraska; Oscar V.; Lawrence N., m. Charlotte Wood; residing in Benson, and Frances, who m. Tilly Gilbert.

4. *Wilson*, b. Jan. 14, 1810; m. Pamelia Russegue; resides at Castleton Corners.

5. *Romeo*, b. Sept. 3, 1816; m. Maryette Perkins.

JOSIAH QUINTON, SEN., originally of New Hampshire, came hither from Whitehall, N. Y., now Hampton—where his brother John resided, and his sister, who had married a McFarland—about 1806, bringing with him a famous horse. He was subsequently the owner of the grist-mill, and died at his house—now · Thomas Hughes'—March 2d, 1829, leaving two sons, *Joshua, Jr.* and *George*. Joshua, Jr. came to town at the close of the war, in 1815, then about 19 years of age, and wearing his sailor's dress which he had worn in the privateering service during the war. He married Sally Watson, a daughter of Benj. Watson, March 29, 1818, and had a son, John, who learned the shoemaker's trade of Joseph Adams, and moved

456 HISTORY OF FAIR HAVEN, VERMONT.

away to Perry, N. Y., prior to 1840. A younger son
and daughter went away with him to Walpole, N. H.,
in 1846. George Quinton married Ann Bush, of
West Haven, and was engaged in trade at that place.

JOHN QUINTON, a brother of Joshua, was in town in
1810, and with Thomas Christie bought and built
where Henry Green now resides. He was a blacksmith, and was in company with John P. Colburn, as
late as 1818. He subsequently moved back to Hampton, and married Phebe Miller, in 1823. He died on
his place—now Wm. S. Miller's—in 1829. She survived till July, 1863.

CHARLES RICE. See p. 60.

STEPHEN ROGERS, mentioned on page 61, m. Hannah Munger, daughter of deacon Daniel Munger,
February 12, 1789. His family were three children :
Lucy, m. Joseph Davis, of Castleton; *Stephen*, m. a
Palmer, and became a Congregational minister at one
time settled in Claremont, N. H.; and *Lorenzo* who
has a family and resides in Westport, N. Y.

AMBROSE ROGERS, brother of Stephen, came from
Branford, Conn., soon after Stephen. He was a tailor
and resided where Hiram Briggs now does. He married Sally Bullard, January 10, 1799, and had five
children, three of them born in Fair Haven.

He removed to Newport, near Syracuse, N. Y.,
subsequent to 1806, where he died. His family were
Lucia, Alpheus, Beulah, Alonzo and *Ambrose.* The
two latter are said to be in business in Syracuse,
N. Y.

BERIAH ROGERS—see p. 77—m. Miss Achsah Rob-

HISTORY OF FAIR HAVEN, VERMONT. 457

erts, of Queensbury, N. Y., December, 20, 1798. She was a daughter of Capt. Ezekiel Roberts, a hero of the Revolution, and died· in December, 1832, having had ten children. Mr. R. afterward married widow Hannah Burhans, of Bethlehem, N. Y. His first three children were born in Fair Haven : 1. *Lemuel R.*, b. March 7, 1800. 2. *Frances*, b. Jan. 1, 1802 ; d. Aug. 25, 1804. 3. *Hiram*, b. Dec. 20, 1803. 4. *Frances* 2d, m. a Mr. Boody and resides in Johnsburg, N. Y. 5. *Elsie*, m. Lucius Palmer ; resides in St. Lawrence county N. Y. 6. *Drusilla*, m. a Mr. Pangborn; is a widow in Whitehall, N. Y. 7. *Beriah.* 8. *Jerusha.* 9. *Harriet.* 10. *Lucy.*

Mr. Rogers sold his farm in Hampton to Satterlee Miller, about 1847, and removed to Whitehall, where he died in Feb. 1851.

JARED ROGERS, b. in Dec., 1777, followed his · brothers to Fair Haven in the fall of 1792. He here married Olivia Buck. He removed to Hampton in 1803, where he remained till his death, Oct. 24, 1861.

His family were: 1. *Jared*, b. in Fair Haven. 2. *Grove.* 3. *Eli.* 4. *Rachel J.* 5. *Mary.* 6. *Ebenezer.* 7. *Lydia.* 8. *Lucy.*

SETH ROGERS occupied a house in 1809, south of Z. C. Ellis' present residence, and on the east side of the road. He had a son, *Walter*, who married Eliza White, a sister of Charles White, of Whitehall, N. Y., and had a family resident on West street as late as 1835. He moved away to Salina, N. Y.

ANDREW RACE—see p. 47—is said to have come hither from Hoosick, N. Y. He was a cooper.

458 HISTORY OF FAIR HAVEN, VERMONT.

ISAAC RACE, came from Nobletown, Dutchess co., N. Y., to Hampton, in 1779, and afterwards moved into Fair Haven. He married Sarah, daughter of Oliver Cleveland, and had eight children: 1. *Sarah*, or *Sally*, m. Joseph Benjamin, Dec. 30, 1804; d. in Hampton, April 10, 1869, aged 93. 2. *Clarissa*, m. Spencer Scott. 3. *Rhoda*, m. Nathaniel Howard. 4. *Elijah*. 5. *Russell*. 6. *Peter*, was shot in the army, at Plattsburg, N. Y. 7. *Catherine*. 8. *Samuel*.. Isaac Race died March, 1811.

SALEM RYDER, an old sailor; had a half brother, Zerah; came from Connecticut to Salem, N. Y., and thence to Fair Haven about 1810 or '11. He ran the saw mill on the upper falls, above the iron works, and occupied Mr. Davey's house, near the mill, in 1822.

CAPT. DAVID ROOD, came from Salem, N. Y., to Hampton, in the year 1806, settling just over the river from where Chas. W. Gardiner now resides. In February, 1809, he bought 42 acres of the Ballard farm, or east part of the Wilder place, in Fair Haven. This he sold to Oliver Kidder, in March, 1813. In February, 1813, he purchased of Daniel Hunter the old Dr. Witherell farm, on West street in Fair Haven—now H. Wescott's—and removed to the same. His sons, David and Cyrus, were in the military company here in June, 1813, and he is mentioned as one of the grand jurors and highway surveyors in March, 1815. He sold the farm in Sept., 1816, to Jacob Willard, and removed soon after to Weathersfield, Genesee co., N. Y., now in Wyoming co., where he died in 1830. He married Sarah Rogers, and had a family of seven children:

HISTORY OF FAIR HAVEN, VERMONT. 459

1. *Lydia*, m. Ormus Doolittle, of Hampton, N. Y., and removed to Genesee county.

2. *Lucy*, m. Cornelius Spurr, while living in Fair Haven. They removed to Covington and thence to Alexander, Genesee co., N. Y. She died in 1860. He visited Fair Haven in 1869.

3. *David, Jr.*, m. Sally Frasure; d. in Jamesville, N. Y.

4. *Sally*, m. Reuben Doolittle, brother to Ormus; was married at same time as Lydia. He died in Weathersfield, N. Y. She resides with her son, ex-senator Doolittle, of Racine, Wis.

5. *Cyrus*, m. Susan Pettengill, of Warsaw, N. Y., and now lives in Iowa.

6. *Eli*, m. Eliza Tanner, of Warsaw, N. Y.; afterward Emeline Monroe; now lives in Weathersfield.

7. *James*, m. Calista Robinson, of Erie co., N. Y. He died in 1856.

TIMOTHY RUGGLES was a hatter and had a shop near the river, south of Cyrus C. Whipple's, in 1814. He came from Hartford, N. Y., and removed thence, where he died.

JOHN RUGGLES, a mason, came from Poultney and resided for a time on West street, removing thence to Castleton, where Rev. James Jarvis Gilbert married his daughter.

NATHAN RANNEY came from Bethlehem, Conn., to Whitehall, N. Y., to the place where John Orms now resides, in 1802, and moved his family in 1804. He removed to Fair Haven in the spring of 1817, and occupied the Munger farm, on the departure of the

Mungers to the West, for two years, after which he resided on Scotch hill until his death, Jan. 12, 1831, aged 79 years.

His first wife's name was Ruth Cole, by whom he had nine children. She died in Whitehall, in 1816, and he married the widow of Charles McArthur, of Scotch hill, about 1819.

His family were:

1. *Phebe*, first m. Abel Foster, and afterward Aaron Smith, of Whitehall.

2. *Thomas S.*, m. Mary Martin, of Enosburg, kept tavern for some years on the old Wm. Wright place, in Whitehall, and removed to Enosburg in 1823, where he died about 1834, his family subsequently making their abode in Fair Haven, and his widow marrying Burleigh Davis.

Thomas' family were, Mary, Oliver Perry, Helen, Edwin, Althea, Nathaniel, and Betsey.

3. *Ruth*, b. in Connecticut, in 1790, and died in Whitehall, in June, 1866.

4. *Martha*, m. Levi Reed, of Granville, N. Y., Jan. 16, 1818, and soon after removed to Moriah, where she remained until Oct., 1854, when Mr. Reed came to Fair Haven, and Mrs. Reed died here, April, 1869. Her family were, Fayette, Corril, Nathan R., Helen, and Edgar.

5. *Elizabeth*, d. in Whitehall, in 1868.

6. *Nathan*, enlisted in the war of 1812, at 16 years of age, and did efficient service, refusing offered promotion. He went to St. Louis, Mo., where he married Amelia Jane Shackford, and is one of the leading and

highly respected citizens of St. Louis. His children are, Jane, Julia, Maria, Anna, Ella, Howard and Gertrude.

7. *Philena*, m. Salmon Norton, Jr., and removed to Marcellus, N. Y., whence, on the decease of Mr. Norton, she removed to Angelica, and afterward to reside with her daughter Ellen, at Morenci, Mich., where she died. Her children were Mary and Ellen.

8. *Nathaniel C.*, m. Minerva Merritt, a daughter of Peter Merritt, Esq., of this town, and removed to Angelica, N. Y., about 1831. He removed from Angelica to Marshall, Iowa, about 1861 or '62. His children are Harrison and Harriet, Julius and Julia, a duet of twins.

9. *Caleb B.*, m. Charlotte Kittredge, and is one of our oldest and most respected fellow-citizens. His childrens' names are, Mary A., and Oliver Kittredge. Mary married Reuben T. Ellis, and resides in town. Oliver first married Jennie Moore who died in 1868, at her home on Scotch hill. He next married his first wife's sister, Betsey Moore, and now resides in Pacific City, Iowa.

REV. SEPTIMIUS ROBINSON. Rev. Rufus S. Cushman says, "the first male school teacher I can recollect was Septimius Robinson, who studied theology with my father." We find that he taught school in the town in 1819 and '20, giving Tilly Gilbert a receipt in full for his two years' service. He was born in Poultney, July 27, 1790, and passed his youth in Dorset. He was the son of Eliab and Lucy (Richardson) Robinson, parish of Scotland, Conn., and was a descendant of the

Puritan John Robinson in the fifth or sixth generation.

In the spring of 1819 he purchased of Jacob Davey, in company with John W. and Eliab Robinson, the saw-mill adjoining the grist-mill, in the town, and they resided where Cyrus C. Whipple now does. John W. married the widow of Salmon Norton. He himself had married, in Sept. 1813, Lucy Stoddard, of Pawlet. After studying theology with Rev. Mr. Cushman and being licensed to preach, he went to Underhill, Vt., where he was settled and ordained in March, 1824. He was afterward settled in Morrisville, Vt., where he died in 1860. His first wife died at Milton, Vt., April 21, 1834, aged 45 years—and he married Semantha Washburn, of Montpelier, Vt., Jan. 6, 1835, who survives him. He had five children by his first marriage and three by the second. A son, Wm. Albert, is pastor of the Congregational church at Barton, Vt.

[We are indebted to the Rev. A. W. Wild for most of the above facts.]

CORRIL REED, b. in Moriah, N. Y., Dec. 14, 1823, m. Marcia A. Bridges, of Deerfield, Mass., in June, 1848, and came to Fair Haven in the spring of 1849. He succeeded Azel Willard, Jr., in the store on the premises now occupied by R. E. Lloyd, but sold out his dry goods in 1855 and engaged in the flour trade. He is now town clerk, and has held the office for several years. He has one son, Rollin C., b. Jan. 14, 1856.

ABRAHAM SHARP, SEN. See pp. 22, 24. He m. Jemima Vandozer, and his family were:

1. *Abraham*, m. Diadama Watson, near Bennington,

HISTORY OF FAIR HAVEN, VERMONT. 463

and had two sons: Robert, b. Feb. 28, 1794, is now a town charge; and, Abraham, who first m. the widow of Jacob Willard, and was married a second time in Moriah, N. Y., whence he removed to Michigan and died.

Upon his wife's death, Abraham 2d married Sibyl Childs, of Granville, N. Y., by whom he had four sons and three daughters, Isaac, John, Simeon, Chauncey, Switty, Harriet and Minerva. Isaac married an Angell, of Castleton, removed to Schroon, N. Y., and thence to Ohio. John married in Schroon. Simeon was a shoemaker. Chauncey was a carpenter and joiner. All went to Ohio.

2. *James*, m. Esther Cleveland.

3. *Dreese* went West when young.

4. *Stephen* went to Colchester, Vt., studied law in Burlington, and married a Munson, of Colchester.

5. *John*, d. at Fort Miller, N. Y.

6. *Hannah*, m. Abraham Utter, a potter, who had a shop at an early day near the corner of the road leading to Castleton.

7. *Polly*, m. Luther Corbin on Scotch hill.

8. *Speedy*, m. John Leech.

9. *Kate*, m. Isaac McWithey.

10. *Nelly*, m. John Blighton, a Dutchman, who worked with Abraham Utter.

11. *Jemima.*

Abraham Sharp 3d owned the farm on Scotch hill which is now owned in part by Arnold Briggs and by Joseph Sheldon, and was largely engaged at one time in the lumber trade, but failed in business about 1828, leasing his farm on Scotch hill, including the crops, in July of that year, to John D. Stannard, Gilman Stannard, Russell H. Cook, Simeon Barber and Isaac H. Smith.

THOMAS STONNAGE is said to have cleared up the land now owned by Mr. Eddy, south east from the depot.

SILAS SAFFORD was born in Norwich, Conn., Sept. 11, 1757. He enlisted in the Continental army in 1778, and was a sergeant. He was taken sick after nine months and went home on furlough. When convalescent he hired a German whom he met in the streets of Norwich to go as his substitute in the army. He married Clarinda Hawley, of Arlington, Vt., Dec., 1780, and came to Fair Haven in 1782—being the first known settler in the present village. See p. 35. He was chosen the first justice of the peace of the town and held the office for forty years, much of the time doing most of the justice's business. He died May 12, 1832, aged 74 years. His wife died Aug. 17, 1847, aged 82 years. Both are buried in town.

His family were:

1. *Olivia*, b. in Arlington, Oct. 29, 1781; m. Abel Moulton, of Castleton, and had one son and five daughters, one of whom married Charles T. Colburn, Esq., now of Pittsford.

2. *Russell*, b. in Fair Haven, Jan. 23, 1784; d. Jan. 26, 1786, and was buried in the old and first burial ground of the town, on the old road between James Campbell's and John Allard's.

3. *Erwin*, b. Jan. 27, 1786; m. Lucia Wells, a

HISTORY OF FAIR HAVEN, VERMONT. 465

daughter of Enos Wells, of Poultney, May 15, 1810, and had three sons, George, Henry and Satterlee. He was for some years an active business man in the place. In March, 1811, he bought the house and lot where Griffith Williams now owns, on the east side of the Park. This he sold to Jos. Watson, lately of Detroit, in Jan., 1814. In April, 1811, he bought a store lot of Thomas Wilmot, where James Miller's blacksmith shop now stands, which he sold to Elisha Parkill, in Oct., 1815. He appears to have resided in Middletown in 1816, buying in Aug., of Dr. Israel Putnam, the store which Putnam had lately rebuilt on Anna Wells' land, a few rods north of Royal Dennis' inn, and the house and lot where Dr. Wakefield resides. In July, 1817, he bought of Anna Wells, then of Lyons, N. Y.,*the land on which the store stood. He sold both lots, with the store and a distillery erected by him near Harvey Church's tannery—back of Owen Owens' dwelling house—in July, 1819, to James Y. Watson, and removed to Bennington. He died in Philadelphia, in March, 1855.

4. *Clarinda*, b. Jan. 1, 1788; d. May 27.

5. *Clarinda* and *Lydia*, twins, b. Feb. 18, 1789. Lydia died Feb. 25, and was buried near Ethan Whipple's, in the old burial ground. Clarinda married Col. Stone, of Charlotte, and had two sons, Silas and Reuben. Silas is in Cleveland, O., and Reuben is in New York. She died in Jan., 1818.

6. *Silas, Jr.*, was educated at Middlebury and Yale Colleges—taught school here in 1810 or '11—was first rector of Episcopal church in Middlebury. He died

of consumption, in New Jersey, on his way to the Southern States, in Dec., 1816.

7. *Charlotte*, m. Dr. Israel Putnam, May 20, 1811; d. in Feb., 1862.

8. *Aurilla*, died of measles.

9. *Alonzo*, b. March, 1798; m. Mrs. C. B. Howard, of Orwell, and remained for many years in the town, owning his father's farm in the south part of the town from 1825 to 1831. He purchased a third interest in the paper mill in 1829, and leased the house where Mrs. Wm. Miller lately resided—now Mr. Lloyd's—of the selectmen, in 1832, and occupied it until about 1844, when he sold out and removed to Kalamazoo, Mich., where he now lives

10. *Harry*, b. Aug. 1, 1800—removed to Bennington in 1820, where.he married Lydia Norton, and remained 18 years, removing thence to Philadelphia and engaging in the coal trade. He visited Fair Haven in the fall of 1868, and returning home, died soon after, leaving one son and three daughters.

11. *Fanny*, b. 1802; d. Aug. 21, 1822.

12. *Sidney*, b. Dec. 26, 1805; m. Mary Gordon, of Michigan; resided for a time in California; is now in Kalamazoo, Mich.—was employed here by A. & M. G. Langdon in the distillery, in 1828–'32.

13. *Frank*, b. Aug. 19, 1808; m. Mary F. Rogers, of Boston, and now resides in Boston. He visited Fair Haven in 1869, on his way from Michigan where he had been resident for some years.

SAMUEL STANNARD, b. in Killingworth, Conn., in 1749, came to Fair Haven in March, 1783. See p. 41.

He married Jemima Wilcox, who was born in 1746, and died June 25, 1834, aged 88 years. He died April 8, 1815, in his 67th year.

Family:

1. *Betsey*, m. Ansel Merritt, and moved to Potsdam, N. Y.—had a daughter, Charlotte, who married a Mr. Post, in Hopkinton, N. Y.

2. *Daniel*, m. for his first wife Mary Davidson, of Fair Haven, and had four children, Gilman, Charles, Charlotte, and John D. He removed to Schroon, N. Y., where he married for his second wife Sophia Goodwin, and had seven children, Mary, Harriet, Chauncey, Burton, Samuel, Harris, and Joseph. He died in Schroon, Aug. 15, 1860, aged 83 years.

3. *Charlotte*, m. Bohan Sheppard and resided for a time in West Haven, removing to Norfolk, St. Lawrence co., N. Y. Their family were, Julia Eliza, m. a Mr. Childs; Chauncey; Fanny, m. Mr. Farwell, of Oswego, N. Y.; Betsey; George; Bohan; Charles, resides in Ogdensburgh, N. Y.; Edward, and Charlotte.

4. *Samuel*, m. Rebecca Petty, resides in Georgia, Vt. His family are, Heman, of Colchester; Ami, who removed to the west; Laban, now in Fairfax, Vt.; Betsey, deceased; Sarah, at the West; Benjamin; Samuel, of Georgia; General George J. Stannard, of St. Albans; Charlotte; Daniel; and Lucas, a lawyer in Minnesota.

5. *Heman*, b. in Killingworth, Conn., Dec. 27, 1780, d. May 16, 1863; came to Fair Haven when three years old, m. Minerva Smith, daughter of Samuel Smith, of Fair Haven. Family: Betsey, m. Almon

Bartholomew, of Whitehall, N. Y.; Eliza, m. Satterlee Miller; Julia, m. Edmund Kirtland, of Granville, N. Y.; Mary; Heman, m. Maria Kirtland; Edward, m. Mary Childs, and Charlotte.

JOHN D. STANNARD, son of Daniel, was clerk for Mrs. Wilmot in the tavern for a number of years, and at length purchased the tavern stand and kept it himself. He married Maria Eaton, of Castleton, and removed to Geddysburg, N. Y. His children are, Charles H., George and Isadore.

DR. SIMEON SMITH. See p. 69.

ASA SMITH. See p. 107.

DAN SMITH, b Jan. 28, 1759, in Suffield, Conn.; came from Sharon, Conn., to West Haven, then Fair Haven, at an early day. He resided in close proximity to the town line, and was more or less intimately associated with the business and interests of the town for several years. He was a nephew of Dr. Simeon Smith, and must have come into town as early as the Doctor himself, being chosen one of the listers here at the March meeting of 1788. In the summer of 1801 he leased the iron works in our village, of Edward Douse, of Dedham, Mass.; purchased them in July, 1803, and sold them to Jacob Davey, Oct. 1, 1807. He had a forge and nail factory, also, on the falls in West Haven, built during the war of 1812 and '14, and made nails on the Fair Haven side of the road, opposite the old Smith tavern, now Wood's. He early—about 1804—built the house which is now owned and occupied by Wm. Preston, considered, in its day, one of the finest in the whole country.

HISTORY OF FAIR HAVEN, VERMONT. 469·

He had five children: *Betsey*, m. a man by the name of Doolittle; *Lucy*, m. Moses Strong, Esq., of Rutland; *Loraine*, m. Dr. N. S. S. Beaman, of Troy, N. Y.; *William H.*, went to Vergennes, where he died; and *John D.*

He removed to Panton, where he died, Feb. 15, 1833.

APOLLOS SMITH, SEN., a brother of Dan Smith, came from Sharon, Conn., to Troy, N. Y., and thence to West Haven about 1787 or '90, opening there the famous "Smith Tavern," kept for so many years by his son, Apollos. He was born in Suffield, Conn., December 5, 1756; m. Anna Gay, December 3, 1778, and died February 25, 1810, aged 53 years. His children were: *Augustus, Apollos, Simeon, Horace, Augustus 2d, Cornelia, Henry G.*, and *James*.

APOLLOS SMITH, JR., m. Delia Jewett, of Sharon, Conn., and came to West Haven. His children were: 1. *Alpheus*, m. Jane Davey, and had two sons, Vincent and William; 2. *William L. G.*, who graduated at Middlebury College, and is now a practicing lawyer in Buffalo, N. Y.

SIMEON SMITH, 3d son of Apollos, Sen., was born January 20, 1783; m. Susan C. Babcock, in Lenox, Mass., came to Vermont, and took up his residence on the Fair Haven side of the highway, nearly opposite the house where Wm. Preston now lives, and died in town, December 6, 1830, aged 47 years. His wife died May 9, 1840, aged 51 years.

His family are:

1. *Cornelia Ann*, m. Ira Allen

2. *Horace S.*, m. Caroline Spratt.

3. *Benjamin B.*, m. Sally K. Goodrich.

4. *Samuel St. J.*, d. Jan. 29, 1836.

5. *Susan Elizabeth*, d. Sept. 20, 1839.

6. *Lucy*, d. Jan. 16, 1820.

7. *Apollos S.*, m. Mary Burns, and now resides in Nebraska.

8. *William C.*, removed to Burlington, Mich.

9. *Susan R.*, m. Ira Mansfield.

10. *Augustus*, now in Wilmington, Mich.

RUSSELL SMITH, a carpenter, who came into town from West Haven, about 1795, and bought lands of McWithey and Cutler—see p. 118—erecting a house on the same, the house now standing east of John P. Sheldon's, married Lucy Merritt, 2d daughter of Michael Merritt. He died March 19, 1797, in his 30th year, leaving three children, *Olive, Sally* and *Lydia*. His widow married Wm. Hawkins. Olive married Oliver Warren; Sally married Russell Cramer.

CAPT. CLEMENT SMITH, usually called "Clem," was a brother of Russell. He married Mary, a daughter of Charles Rice. She was niece to Maj. Tilly Gilbert. He bought of Maj. Gilbert, in March, 1811, the place where Richard W. Sutliff, now resides. His wife died April 9, 1813, aged 33 years. He died October 22, 1813, aged 40 years.

His family were:

1. *Caroline*, m. Hector H. Crane.

2. *Simeon R.*, m. Feb. 23, 1830, Eliza Ann Hitchcock.

3. *Catherine C.*, the 1st wife of Benj. Narrimore. She died Oct. 16, 1840, aged 35 years.

4. *Christopher M.*, d. leaving no family.

SIMEON R. SMITH, son of Clement, married Eliza Ann Hitchcock, and had three children:

1. *Mary Eliza Ann*, b. Nov., 1830; d. April 16, 1847, at C. C. Whipple's.

2 and 3. *Simeon Russell*, and *Christopher M.*, twins; b. Jan. 23, 1832. Simeon Russell d. Aug. 18, 1833, and Christopher M., a physician, at Mifflinville, Pa., Aug. 22, 1856.

The father died Aug. 8, 1832, in West Haven, aged 28 years; the mother Aug. 4, 1833, aged 21 years.

SAMUEL SMITH came hither from Woodbury, Conn., about 1803. In April, 1806, he bought of Dr. Samuel Shaw, of Castleton, 140 or 150 acres which had been occupied for a time by Jacob Slyter and Content Allis, and is now owned and occupied by D. P. Wescott. Slyter continued in the house till the following spring. Mr. Smith built a new house on the place. He sold the whole farm in April, 1835, to Preserved Fish, of Ira, for $2,800, and went away to Chicago, Ill.

He first married Abigail Judson, and had two childred, *Isaac* and *Minerva.* Isaac did not come to Vermont. Minerva married Heman Stannard. He next married Mary Barnes, a daughter of Jacob Barnes, and by her had three children, *Alvin, Rebecca*, and *Eli.*

Alvin went to Chicago in September, 1834, and died there four weeks afterward. Rebecca, b. 1804 m. John Dennison, of Castleton. She died at the West. Eli now resides in Iowa.

DR. LUCIUS SMITH, m. a daughter of John Conant, Esq., of Brandon, and came thence to Fair Haven, buying the place now occupied by Dan Orms, of Dr. Edward Lewis, in October, 1834, and practicing medicine in town till 1842, when he sold his place to Simeon Cobb, and Simeon Bullock, and returned to Brandon, where he died in about a year afterward. His wife, who was sickly while resident here, recovered, and became the wife of a Baptist clergyman now in California.

JUDAH P. SPOONER. See pp. 96 and 97.

JOSEPH SHELDON, son of Joseph Sheldon, of Dorset, b. in 1776; came to Fair Haven in 1798, he being then 22 years old. See p. 119. He married Diadama Preston, of Poultney, about the year 1800, and settled on the lands owned by his father, in the north part of the town, buying of his father, May 24, 1804, the 1st and 4th divisions of Jonas Galusha's right, his father having purchased the whole right of Benjamin Sheldon, of Suffield, Conn., in January, 1799. In December, 1806, he bought out the interests of his father's heirs, Oliver Sheldon, of Burlington, Israel Sheldon, Ruth, Lydia and Ann, all of Dorset.

He dwelt on this place, engaged in farming and an extensive lumber business, and rearing his large family, until 1840, when having purchased the Cushman farm of the heirs of Rev. Mr. Cushman, in the previous August, he removed and took up his residence until his decease, on the place where his son, John P., now lives, leaving to Harmon the home farm.

His wife died June 29, 1846, and he was married again the following year to Rachel Preston, a sister of his first wife.

His children by his first wife were:

1. *Julia*, b. in 1801; m. Benoni Carpenter, Jan., 1826, and removed to Moriah, N. Y. Mr. C. died leaving one son, Benoni G., and she afterward, in 1845, m. Lanson Day, of Granville, N. Y., where she now resides.

2. *Joseph*, b. Dec. 27, 1802; m. Mary P. Billings, in Feb., 1829, and both are now living in town. They have had five children: Mary C., d. Jan. 15, 1843; Emily B., d. Jan. 9, 1846; Phebe P., m. Samuel W. Bailey, now resident in town; Susan, m. Edwin H. Gibson, and resides at North White Creek, N. Y., and Emeline, d. May 5, 1846.

3. *Harmon*, b. in 1804; m. Angeline Maynard, and has two sons, Joseph K. and Leander H.

4. *Emeline*, b. 1806; m. John Russegue, of Benson, Nov. 24, 1831.

5. *Asaph*, b. 1809; d. in 1832.

6. *Betsey Eliza*, b. 1812; m. Henry Russegue, June 4, 1835, and now lives in Benson. Their children are, Jane, John Henry, James, Amelia, Joseph S., and French.

7. *John P.*, b. 1819; m. Harriet M. Barnes, April 15, 1842; she d. four years after, Sept., 1846, and he m. Sarah Eliza Kittredge, in Oct., 1848. His family are George A., Herbert K. and Frederick B.

8. *Louisa L.*, b. 1821; m. Dr. F. Root, of Hampton, N. Y., and is living in East Hamilton, N. Y.

Capt. Joseph Sheldon ran a boat through the Champlain Canal from the time he was 21 years old until the year 1836. For ten years afterward he ran his boat from Whitehall to New York, through the canal and river.

In 1835 he bought of Chauncey Goodrich the place on which he now resides, it belonging to the estate of Elizur Goodrich. Mr. S. engaged extensively, after 1846, in farming and sheep raising, obtaining a large reputation for the value of his stock, which have proved a lucrative source of profit. He has also worked a valuable quarry of slate on his Scotch Hill farm. He has been for a number of years President of the First National Bank, of which his son-in-law, S. W. Bailey, is Cashier.

MOSES SHELDON, JR., of Rupert, Vt., whose father married widow Margaret Norton, was tenant of the Erwin farm, belonging to the Norton estate—now J. W. Esty's—as early as April, 1809. He occupied it in 1812 and '14; held a lease of it from Isaac Norton, of Benson, for three years from July 1st, 1819, and sold the lease in March, 1820, to Joseph Perry. Perry sold it in May to Josiah Goodrich, reserving a crop of wheat and the use of the house and garden for one year. Sheldon was intemperate, and died of delirium tremens. His wife was an Eastman, of Rupert; and of his children, *Calvin* m. a Babbitt, of Castleton; *Sarah* m. Benjamin Warren; *Julia* m. Wait Arms; and *Moses* was a cripple, or dwarf, said to have been made so by the use of calomel. He was bound out by the authorities of the town to John Keating to learn the tailor's trade. He afterward went to Dorset and became the owner of a good farm.

HARRY G. SHELDON, b. July 1, 1807; came from

HISTORY OF FAIR HAVEN, VERMONT. 475

Sheldon, Vt., to work for Mr. Davey, about 1826; m. Fanny Marshall about 1832; d. July 16, 1860. His wife died in 1865.

Family: *Edward W;. Betsey J.*, d. Sept. 24, 1853, aged 18; *Caroline* m. Frank Dockam, deceased; *Harry*, d. a prisoner in the late war; *Christopher*, now resident in Springfield, Mass.; *Josephus*, dead.

BENJAMIN STEVENS, m. Naomi Atherton; was a resident north of the village, and south of Ethan Whipple's in 1798, and 1800, having purchased an acre of land of Col. M. Lyon, in Sept., 1798.

JOSHUA STEVENS resided, in 1820, in the house built by John Herring on the top of the hill, west from the paper mill. It had been occupied by Collins Mills, in 1809. Daniel Kites lived in it in 1826, and Stevens again in 1835. Mr. Stevens had a son *John*, who removed to Massachusetts, and a son *Jonathan*, who was a wheelwright in town, and who removed to Castleton, where he died, leaving a family.

JACOB SLYTER, called "Slaughter," was a Dutchman, from Poultney, who in June, 1800, bought 100 acres of land of Dr. Samuel Shaw, of Castleton. See p. 121. He deeded it back to Shaw in 1805. Several amusing stories are told of him, among them one that he sold a wild cat to Herring and others, who ate it for a coon.

PAUL SCOTT came from Granville, N. Y., in the spring of 1802, and bought the Cutler farm on West street, of Philip Allen. He sold 20 acres to Rev. Mr. Cushman, in 1808. He worked with his borther, Elisha, and Lewis Stone, building the new meeting house in 1811. His daughter, *Perley L.*, married Chauncey Ward. He removed to Poultney, where his brother, Elisha, resided, about 1814.

LEWIS STONE was in town in 1803. He married in Granville, N. Y. He bought the McWithey farm, on West street, in 1812, selling it to the Howards, in November, 1818, and removing to Ashtabula, Ohio.

SILAS SHIRTLIFF, a tailor, lived and worked on West street, where Hamilton Wescott's house now stands. He sold his house in January, 1806, to Dr. James Witherell, for $86, Witherell owning the land.

JOHN SNELL, a blacksmith, came here from Addison, Vt., and worked for Jacob Davey, and for John P. Colburn. In January, 1811, he purchased of Jemima Gilbert, of West Haven, 42 acres of land next south of Charles McArthur's, on Scotch Hill, and lived on the same, selling it in December, 1812, to Benjamin Haskins, and removing to Enosburg, where he died in 1863. He married Fairy Perkins, a daughter of Roger Perkins, and left two children, *John* and *Delight.*

DAVID C. SPROAT, b. in Albany, N. Y., August 9, 1794; m. Sarah Kittredge, at Dalton, Mass., February 1st, 1819, and moved to Fair Haven in May of the same year. Mr. Sproat had purchased an interest in the paper-mill, in January, 1819, in company with George Warren, and continued his connection with the business until his removal from the town.

In February, 1825, he purchased an acre of land of Jacob Davey, east from the paper-mill, and built thereon the two-story dwelling now owned by Robert E. Adams. He removed his family to Waterford, Wis., in the spring of 1844, where he died October 1, 1869. His widow resides with the family in Waterford, Wis.

Family:

1. *Henry K.*, b. in Fair Haven, Feb. 28, 1820; d. Jan. 28, 1841, aged 20 years.

2. *Delia*, b. in Fair Haven, Jan. 16, 1823; m. Dr. Geo. F. Newell, Dec. 22, 1843. They removed to Waterford, Wis., with the family, where they still reside. They have three children: Henry B., aged 24, who is practicing medicine with his father; Ellen B., aged 22, m. Charles Gipson, and resides at Elkhorn, Wis.; and George E., aged 19, who is studying medicine in Michigan University.

3. *George W.*, b. Jan. 17, 1824; m. Emily Hoover, Dec. 10, 1852. They reside in Racine city.

4. *William C.*, b. July 30, 1826; m. Ann Hoover, March 24, 1855. They reside in Waterford, Wis.

5. *Edward*, b. May 9, 1828; d. in Racine county, Oct. 17, 1846.

6. *Mary Ann*, b. April 19, 1830; m. Wm. B. Powell, in Wisconsin, Oct. 10, 1854, and removed to Marshalltown, Iowa.

7. *Sarah Jane*, b. Nov. 3, 1832; m. Augustus Sicard, May 20, 1857, and removed to Marshalltown, Iowa.

8. *Elizabeth*, b. June 9, 1837; m. Alonzo Pierce, in 1857. They reside in Waterford, Wis.

9. *Ellen*, b. Oct. 30, 1842; d. Feb., 1844.

GEORGE SHIRLAND, a shoemaker, who worked for Jabin Bosworth, bought of Chauncey Goodrich 12 acres of land, the place where he lived, from the south-west corner of Benjamin Cutler's first division, now owned and occupied by Hiram Briggs, in February, 1821. He deeded it back to Mr. Goodrich in November, 1826, and went away to the West for a number of years, after which he came to West Haven and died. He married a daughter of Elijah Tryon, and is said to have had a son, *Henry*.

JOHN SUTLIFF, a tailor, worked in Albany, N. Y., removed to Salem, Washington county, and there married Eurania Binninger, eldest daughter of Isaac Binninger, by whom he had eleven children, born in Salem. Leaving his farm in Salem, he came to Fair Haven in 1835, having bought in June of that year, of Stephen Ransom, of Salem, the " Bristol farm," so-called, which Enos Bristol had sold to Mr. Ransom in January, 1831, now owned and occupied by Wm. L. Town. He worked at his trade on his place, and owned land north of the village, where John Moore now lives.

His first wife died in Salem. He married Phebe Southard, for his second wife, after coming to Fair Haven. He married again, for a third wife, a Miss McNich, of Salem, N. Y., and, a fourth time, a Miss Crampton, of Poultney. She survived him, and died in 1869, in Tinmouth. He died in March, 1860, aged 83 years.

Family :

1. *Richard W.*, b. in Salem, N. Y., Feb. 6, 1810;

HISTORY OF FAIR HAVEN, VERMONT. 479

m. Laura Howard, in 1838, and has been the principal tailor of the town for over 20 years.

His family are: George, who died in Kansas, June, 1859, aged 18 years; Emmons, LeRoy, and Edith.

2. *Elizabeth*, m. Hiram Lyman. She d. in March, 1847.

3. *Edith.*

4. *Isaac*, m. Harriet McNeil, and has three children.

5. *Merritt*, resides in Vermontville, Mich.

6. *William E.*, removed to Benson in 1849, and there worked two years at tailoring, having learned the trade of his brother here. From Benson he went to Brandon, and carried on business there a few years, and thence removed to Lawrence, Kansas, where he is doing a thriving business. He married Jennie Sweet, in Bristol, Vt., and has three children.

7. *John B.*, learned the shoemaker's trade of Joseph Adams; went to Racine, Wis., and afterwards lived in Keeseville, N. Y., and in California. He is now in business with his brother, in Lawrence, Kansas. He married a Miss Hollister, from Ohio.

8. *Phebe Ann*, m. I. H. Allard; d. about 1861.

9. *Susan*, m. a Mr. Gates; is in Vermontville, Mich.

10. *Mary*, m. Christian Bowman, and resides in Topeka, Kansas.

11. *Charles Wesley*, m. Mary Delahanty, and resides in town.

LYMAN SHERWOOD was resident on the Dodge farm, south of Chauncey Wood's, in 1837, and sold the same to Obadiah Eddy.

CHARLES STRATTON. See p. 296.

DAVID STANDISH. See p. 296.

ROYAL R. STETSON purchased of Oren L. Williams, in Dec. 1847, the place now occupied by George W. Allen. He sold it to Cyrus Boardman, of Whitehall, N. Y., in January, 1853, having himself removed to Pomeroy, Franklin county, N. Y.

ISRAEL TROWBRIDGE—see pp. 32, 121—was a son of Isaac Trowbridge, of Stratford, Conn., and grandson of James Trowbridge, of Norwalk, and lately of Stratford, in April, 1716. He was baptised at Stratford, September 30, 1722, and married Mary, daughter of Peter and Mary Johnson, of Derby, Conn., previous to 1753.

In his family were:

1. *Mary*, the wife of Ralph Carver, of Castleton.

2. *Levi*. See below.

3. *Anne*, b. in Derby, May 18, 1763.

4. *Sarah*, m. Jeremiah Durand, in Derby, Nov. 12, 1772, and died there about 1777.

5. *Elizabeth*, m. Dr. Osee Dutton, in Derby, Jan. 19, 1773. They had a child John, born in Derby, Nov. 11, 1783, and resided there in April, 1796, when they deeded her share of her father's estate, 66 acres, to Samuel Tomlinson, of Woodbury, Conn.

6. *Abigail*, who never married, but made her home with Olney Hawkins, who had married her sister Sarah's only daughter, Hannah Durand.

LEVI TROWBRIDGE, b. in 1753, in Derby, Conn.; m. Hannah Smith, daughter of Capt. Benjamin Smith, of New Haven, Conn., December 29, 1782. He removed

HISTORY OF FAIR HAVEN, VERMONT. 481

to Fair Haven sometime between January, 1784, and June, 1786, where he resided until 1810, when he migrated to Washington county, Ohio, removing thence to Ames township, Athens county, in 1820. His wife died there in February, 1832, aged 73 years. In June, 1836, he removed to Swan Creek, Gallia county, where he died, December 14, 1843, aged 90 years; being smart and active, and able to walk several miles in a day, until taken down with his last sickness, "typhoid pneumonia."

His family were:

1. *Sarah*, b. in Woodbury, Conn., January 15, 1784; m. Caleb Wheeler. They came to Fair Haven, whence after Mr. Wheeler's death she removed to Athens county, Ohio, and there married Eliphalet Case. He died at Swan Creek, Gallia co., about 1845, and she went to live with her daughter in Bethel, Mich., where she died, about 1864. Her children were, John Wheeler, now residing in Millersport, Lawrence county, Ohio; David H. Wheeler, a Methodist minister, who was a Bible agent in Central America, and was killed there by the natives in 1856; Israel Wheeler is a practicing physician in Michigan; Jerusha Wheeler m. a Mr. Warner; is now a widow residing with a son at Walnut Fork, P. O., Jones county, Iowa; Irene Wheeler m. a Mr. Dean; is now a widow in Iowa; Sarah Case m. a Mr. Jones, and removed to Michigan, where she died.

2. *David*, b. in Fair Haven, June 13, 1786; removed to Ohio in December, 1810; m. Sophronia Howe, of Washington county, Ohio, daughter of Peter

Howe, of Poultney, Vt., March 7, 1813; removed to Swan Creek, Ohio, in June 1836, where he died, March 14, 1868, in his 82d year. His wife is still living, in her 80th year.

Their family, now living, consists of five sons and four daughters, who write their names " Trobridge," leaving out the *w*; A. V. Trobridge, is a druggist and postmaster at La Grange, Lucas county, Iowa; C. C. Trobridge is a farmer, in Tyrone, Monroe county, Iowa; F. N. Trobridge is a house carpenter at Red Oak Station, Iowa; was three years in the 2d Iowa cavalry; R. M. Trobridge studied law at Cincinnati, and has a farm near La Grange, Iowa, where he practices his profession; David S. Trobridge, resident at Swan Creek, Ohio, who was a soldier in the late war, and to whom the writer is indebted for the information here given. With him resides a widowed sister, Mrs. John C. Wilson, whose husband belonged to the 2d Iowa cavalry, and was killed at Farmington, Miss., in the advance on Cornith.

3. *Philo*, b. in Fair Haven, July 6, 1788; removed to Washington county, Ohio, in Dec., 1810; m. Martha Blake, about the year 1815, and moved to Swan Creek in 1838. From there he went to Moore's Prairie, Ill., where he died in March, 1856, his wife having died before him; only one son, Israel D. Trobridge, survives, at Chenoa, McLean county, Ill. He was three years in the war.

4. *Jacob*, b. in Fair Haven, Dec. 25, 1790. He was the first to migrate to Ohio, going there in 1806, with one Carver, a carpenter, and helped to build a large

HISTORY OF FAIR HAVEN, VERMONT. 483

flouring mill at Marietta. Thence he went to Cincinnati, about 1812, or '13, and enlisted in the army. He was taken prisoner at Gen. Hull's surrender of Detroit. He married Miss Sarah Shepard, at Cincinnati. She died in 1822, and he married Polly Boomer, and took up his residence at Swan Creek, Gallia county, where he died, April 19, 1867. He had two sons and two daughters by his first wife, the eldest son being three years in the Indian wars. By his last wife he had four sons and four daughters. Three of his sons, Isaac, John, and F. M. Trobridge, reside in Ohio, and one, Lemuel Trobridge, resides at Paris, Ill. They were all in the last war.

5. *Chauncey*, b. in Fair Haven, March 21, 1794. He is said to have removed to Ballston, N. Y., about 1809, where he married a Miss Catherine Fish, and worked in a paper-mill. He had two daughters; the eldest, Annie E., married a Mr. Ogden, and resides at Pontiac, Livingston county, Ill. Starting to go to his daughter's, with his wife and younger daughter, he got only as far as Michigan, where he sickened and died, July 27, 1869.

6. *Archibald*, b. in Fair Haven, Nov, 30, 1796; went to Montreal, Canada, where he married a French lady, afterwards removing to Mendota, Minn., in 1858, where he died, Nov. 24, 1858. Alfred P. Trobridge, of St. Paul, Minn., was one of his sons.

7. *Anna*, b. in Fair Haven, Dec. 7, 1798, removed with her father to Ohio, and married Lemuel G. Brown. She lived in McArthur's town, Vinton county, Ohio, and died in the spring of 1863. Her husband died

a few hours before her, and they were both buried in in the same grave. They had a son, Perley, who was Captain of Co. B., 18th Ohio Vols., and a son, Lemuel, who was wounded at the battle of Chickamauga, and died of his wounds at Chattanooga, in Dec., 1863.

8. *Hannah P.*, b. in Fair Haven, July 6, 1802; m. Dec. 10, 1826, to A. T. Blake, who has a large farm at Swan Creek, Ohio. They have two sons living, Wm. D. Blake, who belonged to the 77th Ill. Infantry, and C. B. Blake, who was Lieutenant in the 4th Virginia Vols., and is now a merchant at Crown City, Ohio.

Capt. Elijah Taylor. See p. 68.

John W. Throop. See p. 80.

Asa Tyler lived on Hampton Flat in 1787, and occupied the farm in Fair Haven, which he sold in August, of that year, to deacon Timothy Brainard. From 1807 he resided on the Cleveland farm, in Fair Haven, until about 1826. He was a shoemaker, and had two sons, *Harvey*, and *Nathan*.

Hiram Thomas resided on Mr. Esty's farm, on Scotch Hill, after the departure of the Vaughns, occupying a log house. He came from Benson, and had a family of boys. He removed to Illinois.

William Town, b. in Hebron, N. Y., Dec. 25, 1797; m. Christian White, in Ludlow, Mass., December 27, 1820; came to Fair Haven from East Whitehall, N. Y., in March, 1854.

Family:

1. *William Lyman*, b. in Pawlet, Oct. 8, 1821;

HISTORY OF FAIR HAVEN, VERMONT. 485

m. for his second wife, Mary Kirby, of New Haven, and has one child, Clara.

2. *Ellen* and *Martha*, twins; d. April 28, 1823.

3. *Alonson W.*, b. in Hubbardton, March 8, 1824; resides in Middle Granville, N. Y., and has eight children.

4. *Mary J.*, b. in Pittsford, Feb. 24, 1826; d. in East Whitehall, N. Y.

5. *Alphonso W.*, b. in Moriah, N. Y., Feb. 28, 1828; lives now in Union Mills, Erie county, Pa., and has three children.

6. *Francis A.*, b. in Moriah, N. Y., April 14, 1830; lives now with his second wife in Saratoga, N. Y., and has five children.

7. *Ruth A.*, b. May 3, 1832; m. Lewis D. Allen, and resides in town. Children: Melissa A., Lewis D., and Minnie M.

8. *Edwin R.*, b. June 3, 1834; m. Sarah J. Eggleston, of Saratoga, N. Y.

9. *Hannah M.*, b. Aug. 4, 1836; m. Samuel James, and has three children.

10. *Sarah S.*, b. June 10, 1839; d. Nov. 30, 1841.

11. *Franklin A.*, b. Nov. 17, 1841, in Poultney; m. Helen Clyne.

12. *Emerancy C.*, b. Aug. 26, 1844; m. Edwin R. Bristol.

ETHAN WHIPPLE, SEN., son of Capt. Benjamin Whipple, was born in North Providence, R. I., Feb. 13, 1758. He served in the Continental army in Rhode Island, the summer he was 20 years old. After leaving the army he appears to have worked at carpenter work in Providence, and there married Miss Elizabeth Green, in April, 1782. He bought one-half of Lemuel Payne's right of land in Fair Haven, of Beriah Mitchell, in August, 1784, Jesse Whipple buying the other half. His wife died in February, 1786, at 22 years of age, leaving one son, *Joseph*, and he removed to Fair Haven this same year. See p. 67. The land on which he located is the farm now owned and occupied by John Allard. In September, 1788, he purchased of Joshua Angell, of Smithfield, R. I., a half interest in the right of John Payne, Jr., which was located next south of his farm, to be paid in "silver or neat cattle, or in wheat at cash prices"—and subsequently he purchased of Col. Lyon the other half, and 64 acres lying north of his own, on Samuel Allen's right. He took the freeman's oath here in September, 1788, and in November he married Abigail Hawkins, a daughter of Charles Hawkins, for his second wife, and by her had eight children. She died February 12, 1813, in her 49th year.

He married the third time to widow Lydia Church, December 2, 1815, and had three children.

By his second wife his children were:

1. *Betsey*, b. June 30, 1788 or '89; m. Elias Hickok.

2. *Anna*, b. Dec. 14, 1790—called "Nancy ;" m. Isaiah Inman, Jr., of Hampton, Jan. 13, 1811.

3. *Sally Myra*, b. Oct. 1, 1792; m. Samuel Warren Guilford.

4. *Ethan Benjamin*, b. Oct. 16, 1794; d. Dec. 10, 1795.

5. *Ethan Benjamin*, 2d, b. Nov 10, 1796 ; m. Betsey Petty, niece of Samuel Petty, and resides in Illinois.

6. *Abigail*, b. June 12, 1800 ; m. Isaiah Inman, Jr., as his second wife, in March, 1827.

7. *Amy*, b. July 23, 1802 ; d. in 1815.

8. *Mary*, d. May 27, 1805.

By his third wife :

1. *Mary*, d. when 10 or 12 years of age.

2. *Newton*, d. at same time.

3. *Caroline*, b. April 27, 1821 ; m. Faxon Eddy, and now lives in Marquette, Mich.

Mr. Whipple continued to reside on his farm until the spring of 1831, when having sold the place to Adams Dutton, of Castleton, he purchased the house and lot where Charles Clyne now resides, on West street, of Joseph Adams, and removed into the same, where he died, December 18, 1836, aged 79 years.

Mr. Whipple was one of the selectmen of the town in 1792, and continued such till 1796. He was again chosen in 1802, '03 and '05. He was town treasurer from 1793 to 1813, and town clerk from 1809 to 1813, thus taking an active and leading part in the affairs of the town.

JOSEPH WHIPPLE, son of Ethan, born in North Providence, R. I., Nov. 13, 1783, came to town with his father when only three years of age. He married Anna Hawkins, a niece of Charles Hawkins, Sen., Oct. 23, 1806, and resided on the place where Peter Paradee now lives. He died August 28, 1853. She died September 5, 1854.

Their family were:

1. *Eliza Green,* b. March 1, 1809; m. James M. Chase, in Fair Haven, whose children are Nancy M., Ann Eliza, Theodore W., John B., Emma V., Mary L., Stella G., and Sarah V.

2. *Cyrus C.,* b. April 10, 1811; m. Rebecca M. Fish, in Fair Haven, April 12, 1836. They have one child, Ellen, who m. Norman Batchelder, now of Ypsilanti, Mich.

3. *Joseph,* b. Aug. 22, 1813; m. Eliza Culver, daughter of David Culver, in 1838, and now resides in Mansfield, Tioga county, Pa.

4. *Harris,* b. in 1815; m. Sylvia Hawkins, and is now postmaster in town. Their children are John, Sarah, and Mary.

5. *Benjamin,* who resides in Hamilton, N. Y.

6. *William,* m. widow Nancy Griswold, and resides in Crown Point, N. Y.

7. *John N.,* d. March 8, 1833.

JAMES WITHERELL, late of Detroit, Michigan, formerly of Fair Haven, Vt., was born in Mansfield, Mass., June 16, A. D., 1759. His ancestors emigrated from England soon after the arrival of the Mayflower. When the roar of artillery on Bunker Hill started the Colonies to arms, he volunteered, June, 1775, with his townsmen to go to the siege of Boston. After the British had been compelled to evacuate Boston he served with the "grand army," as it was called, during the whole war until it was disbanded at Newburgh, in 1783. He was at the battles of White Plains, (where he was severely wounded,) Rhode Island, Stillwater, Bemis' Heights, and at the surrender of

HISTORY OF FAIR HAVEN, VERMONT. 489

Burgoyne at Saratoga. He was in camp at Valley Forge through the terrible winter of starvation and suffering, and in the following summer at the battle of Monmouth, and bore a part in many other actions of lesser note. During the latter part of his service he held a commission in the 11th Massachusetts Regiment on the Continental establishment. On the disbanding of the army in 1783, he found himself in the possession of seventy dollars in Continental money, the avails of eight years hard service. With this he treated a brother officer to a bowl of punch, and set out penniless to fight the battle of life. The world was all before him—where and what to choose; and he chose Connecticut, and the profession of medicine. Having acquired his profession he started north to what was then called " the new State," and by some " the future State"—Vermont. This must have been about the year 1788. He stayed awhile with Samuel Beaman, Esq., in Hampton, and then went to Fair Haven, then a new and sparsely settled town.

He first located to practice his profession about a mile west of the " city," as it was then, and for many years afterwards, called. The late Major Tilly Gilbert studied medicine with him, and bore the title of Dr. Gilbert for years after. About 1789 the young Dr. married Miss Amy Hawkins, the youngest daughter of Charles Hawkins, Esq., and a lineal descendant of Roger Williams, who with his family, had then lately removed from Smithfield, Rhode Island, to Fair Haven.

Judge Witherell, in early life held many offices;

490   HISTORY OF FAIR HAVEN, VERMONT.

among others associate and chief justice of the county court of Rutland county, member of the Governor's Council, and of the Legislature. In 1807 he was elected to Congress and had the pleasure of voting for the act abolishing the slave trade, which was passed in 1808. While in Congress he was appointed by President Jefferson one of the judges of the supreme court of the Territory of Michigan, and soon after resigning his seat in Congress, started on his long journey to that almost *terrà incognita*—Michigan. The territory was then a vast wilderness, its jurisdiction extending from the great lakes to the Pacific ocean, and containing some three thousand white inhabitants, scattered along the margin of the lakes and mouths of the rivers. The duties of his office were arduous, the governor and judges constituted the legislature of the territory, and were required to act also as a land board in adjusting old land claims, and in laying out a new city—Detroit.

In 1812 the war with England was declared, and Judge Witherell, being, in the absence of Governor Hull, the only revolutionary officer in the territory, was appointed to command the "Legion" ordered out to defend the territory. He was soon after appointed to command a battalion of volunteers.

On the surrender of Detroit he refused to surrender his corps, but let them disperse wherever they chose. In 1810 Judge Witherell removed his family, consisting of his wife and six children, from Fair Haven to Detroit, but the hostilities of the savages, who were hovering about Detroit in vast numbers, induced Mrs.

HISTORY OF FAIR HAVEN, VERMONT. 491

Witherell and the younger children to return on a visit to Vermont, in the autumn of 1811.

The surrender of Detroit made Judge Witherell, his son James C. C. Witherell, (who was an officer in the volunteer service,) and his son-in-law, Col. Joseph Watson, prisoners of war, and as such they were sent with the other prisoners to Kingston, C. W., and then paroled and rejoined their family, who had assembled in West Poultney, Vt. After being exchanged he immediately returned to his duties as judge and continued in the same office for twenty years; at the end of which time, he, with the consent of President Adams, exchanged the office of judge for that of the Secretary of the Territory.

The above was prepared for this work about five years ago, by Judge Witherell's youngest son, Benjamin F. H. Witherell, who was himself a judge in the circuit court of Michigan, and a highly respected and influential citizen of Detroit; but who has since also passed away.

Judge Witherell, Sen., died at his residence in Detroit, January 9, 1838, and at a meeting of the bar of the supreme court of Michigan, held the following day, and presided over by Hon. Henry Chipman, resolutions of respect and mourning were adopted.

He studied medicine with Dr. Billings, of Mansfield, Mass.; came to Fair Haven in 1789—see p. 76—and married Amy Hawkins, Nov. 11, 1790, having the following family born in town:

1. *James Cullen C.*, b. July 14, 1791; entered Middlebury College in 1808 or '09, but left and

492   HISTORY OF FAIR HAVEN, VERMONT.

removed to Detroit with his father's family in 1810; was there taken prisoner by the English at the surrender of the city; was paroled and went to Poultney, where he remained an invalid for about a year, and died Aug. 26, 1813.

2. *Sarah Myra*, b. Sept. 16, 1792; m. Col. Joseph Watson. She died in Poultney, March 22, 1818, in the 25th year of her age.*

3. *Betsey Matilda*, b. in 1793; m. Dr. Ebenezer Hurd.

---

*MONODY.

TO THE MEMORY OF SALLY M. WATSON.

[This was supposed to have been written by a sister of George Warren, who was residing in Fair Haven at that time.]

Low in the grave, where solemn darkness reigns,
  The friend, the sister, and the wife is laid ;
Slow moulder to the dust her dear remains,
  And pensive yews the sacred relics shade.

The spring returns, but ah! to her no more
  The spring its wonted animation brings ;
While weeping friends her early fate deplore,
  The plaintive muse her rustic requiem sings.

'T was her's to cheer, to bless, and to console,
  To give connubial life its sweetest zest ;
To cause the white winged hours more blythe to roll,
  And check the sigh from sorrow's heaving breast.

Elate she left the city's* brilliant scene,
  The midnight ball and splendid revel gay,
Well pleased to seek her native village green,
  Amid the scenes of early youth to stray.

Here was the scene to pensive memory dear,
  Here her loved babe's unconscious ashes sleep ;
And all the mother yearned to drop a tear
  On that spot, where erst she loved to weep.

Ah! little dreamed the friend her worth, who knew
  And hailed her presence with a kindred joy,
That her warm heart, to love and friendship true,
  So soon would rest beside her sleeping boy.

Ah! little thought the friend, within whose heart
  Her worth, her tenderness and virtue dwell,

*Washington.

4. *Mary Amy*, b. Oct., 1795; m. Thomas Palmer. He died in Detroit, Aug. 3, 1868. Mrs. Palmer still lives, occasionally visiting her native town, and has contributed to the interest and value of this volume. She has two children living : Thomas W. Palmer, in Detroit, and Julia Elizabeth, who is married to Henry W. Hubbard, and resides in New York.

5. *Benjamin F.*, b. in 1797; d. June 22, 1867.

6. *James B.*, b. May 12, 1799; became a midshipman in the U. S. Navy, and died Oct. 20, 1822, of a malignant fever, on board the U. S. ship Peacock, during a passage from Havana to Hampton Roads.*

That while he wept in agony to part,
Her tender accents breathed a last farewell.

Pale sleep the moonbeams on her lowly grave,
And round that hallow'd spot young sylphs shall stray ;
And while night's tears the pensive snow drops lave.
The sorrowing muse thus pours her plaintive lay.

And hark ! responsive to the rustic notes,
Seraphs repeat to us the soothing strain,
And soft and low the melting music floats ;
Forbear to weep—for her to die was gain.

Fair Haven, April, 1818.   A STRANGER.

---

*TO THE MEMORY OF JAMES B. WITHERELL.

Tho' lost to friends, to country, and to fame,
Ere glory's annals had enrolled his name ;
And with his brave companions doomed to sleep
In the rough bosom of the stormy deep ;
Tho' Art no monumental tribute raise,
No trophied marble to record his praise ;
O ! say, shall the remembrance of the brave
Forever perish in oblivion's wave?
Will not the tributary muse bestow
Some mournful chaplet to adorn his brow?
In her sad strains hapless fate rehearse,
While sacred *friendship* consecrates the verse.
What opening virtues grac'd his youthful mind ;
The *hero* and the *scholar* were combin'd ;
A glorious emulation, and so rare
That all might envy, tho' so few can share ;
Averse to foolish overweening pride

494   HISTORY OF FAIR HAVEN, VERMONT.

7. *Benjamin F. H.*, m. Mary Ann Sprague, of Poultney, in 1823, and had five children : Martha E., d. in 1847; James B., was lost at sea, in 1861; Harriet C., m. Friend Palmer; Julia A., m. Henry A. Lacy ; and Charles I.'

SOLOMON WILDER was 'of Whitehall,' in March, 1795, at which time he bought of his brother-in-law, John Morrow Ballard, the Ballard farm. From this time he resided on the farm, mortgaging it to John White, of Whitehall, in February, 1798, and selling off 42 acres from the east side, in January, 1809, to Solomon Wilder, of Brattleboro, and deeding the balance to his son Keyes, in June, 1811, when he is reported as at Athens, N. Y. He married a daughter of Joseph Ballard, who is reported to have been in some degree of Indian origin, and his wife, Betsey, was propounded to become a member of the Congregational church in August, 1805. He is said to have died at Olean Point, Alleghany county, N. Y., and in the deed of Mr. White to Mr. Kidder, in September, 1815, Mr. Wilder is said to be deceased. His wife, we are

---

So oft to vice and ignorance allied,
Which swells the selfish and contracted mind
Beyond the sphere for which it was designed ;
A generous spirit marked his short career,
And rising greatness was implanted *there.*
Ardent for fame, impatient to sustain
Columbia's glory on the raging main,
The young aspirant left his native shore,
To which fate doom'd him to return no more !
Alas ! untimely lost in youthful bloom,
An early victim to a wat'ry tomb.
Accept, lamented youth, this friendly lay,
'Tis the last tribute that the muse can pay ;
One who but lately knew, yet knew thee well,
And bids thee now a long, a last farewell.

                                        N. B.

HISTORY OF FAIR HAVEN, VERMONT. 495

informed, removed to Camelius Lake, N.'Y., and died there.

Family:

1. *Diana*, m. a Fish, of Mass.

2. *Terza*, m. her cousin, Joshua Holt, of Hampton, March 24, 1811; was married by Rev. Mr. Cushman, in Fair Haven.

3. *Phebe*, m. a Jencks, (?) 1816 (?)

4. *Keyes*, was of Dryden, Cayuga county, N. Y., in Feb., 1816, and sold B. Ellis 28 acres of land.

5. *Mahala.*

6. *Beulah.*

7. *Elliot.*

THOMAS WHITEHOUSE, called "General," was a nailer, and is said to have come here with Col. Lyon at an early day. He married Patty Marshall, February 26, 1795; and appears to have resided the following year in Whitehall, his first child, *Elizabeth*, being born there February 25, 1796.

Col. Lyon deeds him a half acre of land, ten rods on the front by eight rods deep, on the north side of the highway, and eastward from L. J. Stow's present store, in May, 1897, and he appears to have resided here from that time, having children born in town as follows: *Thomas Chittenden*, July 20, 1798, and *Enos Marshall*, Dec. 23, 1800.

He sold the place to Salmon Norton, July 11, 1803, and soon went away himself to Eddyville, Ky.

Col. Lyon writes to Dr. Witherell concerning him, in January, 1805, as follows: "General Whitehouse is doing well. He has resumed his former steadiness and good nature; has renewed his age, and wishes he had Patty again. If she will go to him let her have money to bear her expenses; the children as they grow up may follow."

In the call for a town meeting in January, 1827, there is an article "to see if the town will take any measures to defend against an order of removal of Thomas Whitehouse from Poultney to Fair Haven," and the selectmen were authorized to use their discretion in the case.

ABIJAH WARREN. See p. 80.

GEORGE WARREN, associated with the business of the town, as a paper manufacturer, from 1813 to 1827 —see p. 146—came from Millbury, Mass., about 1812; was a musician; was captain of the militia; held the post office in the town, and was W. M. of Morning Star Lodge, F. & A. M., in 1824, '25, and '26. He had two brothers, Jarvis and Oliver, and a son, *George*, who is now in the music business in New York. He went from Fair Haven to Albany, and engaged there in the hardware trade, dying of paralysis about 1845 or '46.

BENJAMIN WARREN, a brother of Gideon Warren, of Hampton, N. Y., was in the wheelwright business in town in 1831 and '34. He married Sarah, daughter of Moses Sheldon; has a son who is a lawyer in Shreveport, La., and another, *Henry*, born in Fair Haven, now resident in Westport, N. Y. He himself resides in Elkhart, Ind.

BENJAMIN WATSON took the freeman's oath here in July, 1791, resided with Joshua Quinton at a later

period, Mr. Quinton having married his dau
He is said to have been drowned through the ic
the eastern shore of Castleton Pond—Lake Bon
—on a Christmas eve.

COL. JOSEPH WATSON m. the eldest daugh
Judge Witherell, and owned property and resid
a while in the town, as early as 1814. He d
Washington, D. C., and left two children.

JAMES Y. WATSON, keeper of the jail in Sale
Y., came to Fair Haven in the spring of 1814
ing Mr. Safford's farm of 130 acres, now occupi
Myron D. Barnes. He sold the farm in 1826 t
ner Ames, of Orwell, and went back to Salem, w
he removed to Racine county, Wisconsin. He
married Susan Stone, a sister of Lewis Stone.
died Oct. 12, 1820, leaving four children, a
married widow McFarland, a sister of his first
He is said to be living in Waukesha, Wisconsin.
children were: 1. *Susan*, m. Edmund King
2. *William*, m. a widow Cady. 3. *Asa*, dec
4. *Thankful*, resides in Wisconsin.

EBENEZER WALKER was here and took the free
oath in 1801 ; worked in the saw-mill for Tilly (
in 1804 ; removed to Castleton and died there.

HEZEKIAH WHITLOCK, b. May 30, 1770 ; rei
from Danbury, Conn., to Castleton, Vt., prior to
From Castleton he went back to Danbury and
married Naomi Taylor, January 8, 1797. Sh
born February 3, 1774.

While in Castleton, November 25, 1805, h
chased of Cornelius D. Board, of Castleton, th

acres of the second division of Israel Trowbridge's right, lying along Castleton town line, in Fair Haven, and took up his residence on the same, at the corner of the road where his grandson, Edward Whitlock, resides. He died on his farm, December 31, 1855, aged 85 years.

Family:

1. *Matthew*, b. Dec. 12, 1797; d. in Hubbardton, Dec. 17, 1850, where his widow still resides. His eldest daughter, Jane, married Francis Gault. His second daughter, Sarah, married Levi Spencer.

2. *Amy*, b. Dec. 8, 1801; d. Aug. 1, 1809.

3. *Joshua*, b. Dec. 14, 1803; m. Louisa Lewis; has one son, Edward

4. *Luman*, b. Oct. 12, 1806; d. June 8, 1807.

5. *Sally*, b. Oct. 22, 1808; resides with her brother, Joshua.

ENOS WELLS, of Poultney, married Anna Ballard, daughter of Joseph Ballard, of Fair Haven, and purchased of Danforth Ainsworth, in August, 1807, a part of the old Ballard farm, which had been given to Drusilla Holt. Mr. Wells died soon after, and his wife and family removed to the farm in Fair Haven, but sold it in November, 1813, to Barnabas Ellis, and bought a place in the village, where the drug store now stands.

Mrs. Wells' family were:

1. *Roxana*, m. first, Maj. Horace Olds, of Poultney, but left him and m. David Brainard.

2. *Docia*, m. James Satterlee, a merchant in Middlebury, in 1819. Their daughter m. Judge Phelps.

HISTORY OF FAIR HAVEN, VERMONT. 499

3. *Anna,* d. in Poultney.

4. *Marcia,* d. in Fair Haven.

5. *Lucia,* m. Erwin Safford.

6. *Electa,* m. Dr. Pearce, of Troy, N. Y.

7. *Polly,* d. in Fair Haven.

·8 and 9, *Pamelia* and *Daniel,* deceased.

THOMAS WILMOT came from Poultney and purchased the Lyon tavern of Isaac Cutler, in September, 1809. He is said to have been a silversmith, and to have introduced silver-plating machinery and work from New Haven, Conn.; having a shop just west of his house. See p. 129. He died January 16, 1813, aged 39 years, and his widow conducted the hotel for many years afterward. She resided after 1826 in the house built by Col. Lyon, where Mr. Knight's hotel now stands, and removed to Silver Creek, N. Y., about 1837.

Mr. Wilmot had a son, *Thomas,* who went to South Carolina and died there; a son, *Eben,* who died of delirium tremens in town, September 10, 1831, aged 25 years, and a daughter, *Ann,* who first married Randall Rice, and afterward Dr. Spencer Ward.

LANSON WATKINS came into town from Poultney; was a millwright; purchased the farm where Zenas C. Ellis now resides, of Beriah Rogers, in January 1809, and sold the same to Barnabas Ellis, in May, 1818. He married Nancy McFarland, of Hampton, and in 1812 had two children in the public school. He removed to parts unknown.

CHAUNCEY WARD, son of Barnard Ward, b. in Poultney January 12, 1790; came hither about 1812, and in May, 1815, bought of Tilly Gilbert two and three-fourth acres of land where Josiah P. Willard now resides, building thereon a one-story brick house. In 1818 a fire, set by him in a log heap back of his house, ran through the woods as far north as Ethan Whipple's. He sold his place to Chauncey and Ebenezer Langdon, and Nathaniel Hart, of Castleton, in 1818, and removed to Athens, O., in 1820. He was a Methodist minister and preached in Gallipolis, O. He married Perley L. Scott, a daughter of Paul Scott, September 12, 1811, and had three children born in Fair Haven : *Paul Scott*, b. July 21, 1813 ; *Samuel Newell*, b. April 15, 1816 ; *Delia Delight*, b. Feb. 6, 1820.

His wife died in Athens, O., Aug. 8, 1825, and he married Hannah T. Brown, who died July 29, 1828, when he married again to Patty Haywood, of Gallipolis, O. He now resides in Amesville, Athens county, Ohio.

DR. SPENCER WARD, b. January 7, 1806, in Poultney; studied medicine with Dr. Theodore Woodward, of Castleton, and came to Fair Haven in 1833, to practice his profession. While here he married widow Ann Rice, the daughter of Mrs. Lucy Wilmot. In July 1834, he took a lease from Mrs. Wilmot of the Lyon tavern, at a yearly rental of $150 for five years. He went away to Silver Creek, N. Y., in the fall of 1836. His first child, *Martha R.*, was born here in July, 1837, and the family removed to Silver Creek in Sept., 1837. Mrs. W. died in May, 1853.

ISRAEL WARD resided in the town about 1838, on

HISTORY OF FAIR HAVEN, VERMONT. 501

the place now owned by Mrs. Wiggins, and at one time owned and occupied by Daniel Rhine. Mr. Ward removed to West Castleton, and has a son, *Stephen*, now residing in Hubbardton.

ALLEN WEBSTER occupied the grist-mill house in 1814.

ELIHU WRIGHT must have been in town near the beginning of the century, and remained till about 1835. He married Minerva McArthur, daughter of Charles McArthur, and resided on a part of the old McArthur farm. He is said to have gone away to Coldwater, Mich.; to have become quite wealthy, and to have hung himself. He had three sons, *James*, *Harry* and *Willis.* James lived with Wm. C. Kittredge in 1835; married Fanny Hodgins, and removed to Napierville, Ill.

SAMUEL WOOD, SEN., son of Edward Wood, of Hartland, Vt., came to Hampton, N. Y., about 1815, where he worked at his trade as a carpenter, and purchased a part of the old Cleveland farm, in Fair Haven, of the heirs of Pliny Adams, of Hampton, in 1818. Renting his farm to Jonathan M. Huckins, and John Eddy, he continued working at his trade, and built the old brick meeting house in Rutland, in 1820. About 1821 he moved on to his farm and built the brick house so long occupied by him, and yet standing on the top of the hill. The farm had been called the "Tyler farm;" Asa Tyler having occupied it while it was owned by Mr. Adams. Mr. Wood added to it by purchase of 60 acres which had been set to Albert Cleveland in the division of the Cleveland estate, buying of Daniel Smith, March 17,

1826; and also 16 acres purchased of Keeler Hickok, in May, 1829. He deeded five acres of his farm to his son Samuel, September 1, 1838.

He died at his home, August 6, 1847, aged 67 years. The farm was sold—about 170 acres—in February, 1862, by Fayette and James H. Wood, to Reuben T. Ellis, and from him passed to its present owner, Ebenezer Gould, of Hampton, in March, 1865.

Mr. Wood married Sabrina Andrews, of Claremont, N. H., June 2, 1812.

Family:

1. *Samuel*, b. May 20, 1814, in Hartland; m. Clarissa M. Gray, and has three children: Marion S., Nelson S., and Emma J.

2. *Sophia*, b. Aug. 25, 1816; m. Benjamin F. Lyman.

3. *William W.*, b. Aug. 13, 1818; d. in Wisconsin in 1848.

4. *James H.*, b. Dec. 21, 1821; m. first, Esther A. Lyman, daughter of Eleazer Lyman, of Hampton, by whom he has one son Myron. She died June 19, 1851, and he married, second, Mary Richards, of Poultney, by whom he has two sons, Edward and Freddie.

5. *Fayette*, b. July 20, 1823.

6. *Lucy Loraine*, b. March 8, 1827; m. James M. Dewey; d. in town in 1870.

CHARLES WOOD, brother of Samuel, came to Fair Haven previous to 1817, and m. Eliza, eldest daughter of Oliver Kidder, November 30, of that year. He settled on the south part of the old Cleveland farm, where he died in February, 1832, in his 40th year, and where his widow and children, *Chauncey* and *Phebe* still reside.

JOHN D. WOOD, b. in New Hampshire, December 17, 1821 ; m. Lemira A. Hastings, of Woodstock, Vt.; came to Fair Haven from Bridgewater, in the spring of 1844; worked the farm owned by Barnabas Ellis— now J. W. Esty's—two years; worked in the marble mill and on the slate quarries until, in 1858, selling his place in the village, he removed to the Chauncey Goodrich farm where he now resides. His wife died October 14, 1850,. aged 33 years, and he afterwards m Mrs. Helen Ranney Smith. His children by his first wife, were : *Mary E.*, d. Jan. 21, 1867, aged 22 ; *Horace*, d. Feb., 1858 ; and *Martha*. By his second wife he has *Alice*, *Addie*, and *Nellie*.

THOMAS WOOD. See p. 108.

THE WILLARDS, of Fair Haven, came from West Windsor. There were six brothers, all masons by trade, and all, or all but one, came to Fair Haven, to wit: Oliver, Azel, Jacob, Simeon, Hosea, and Dennison.

JACOB WILLARD, a practical mason and active business man, came from West Windsor, in March, 1816. In September following, he bought of David Rood the farm on West street, previously owned by Dr. James Witherell, Mr. Rood's house on the north side of the road being the same which Dr. Witherell had occupied, and that and Olney Hawkins' being the only houses on the north side. A small dwelling house stood where Mr. Wescott's house now stands on the south side, which had been owned and occupied at an earlier date by Silas Shirtliff, and later by John Kingsland. It was occupied by John Ruggles in September, 1816.

In March, 1818, Mr. Willard, in company with his brother Azel, bought of Paul Scott the old Isaac Cutler farm and tavern, about 63 acres, it being occupied at the time by "old Mr. Abel Parker," he and Chauncey Ward having occupied it together as early as Feb., 1813.

In July, 1822, he sold about 60 acres of his Rood farm to Cephas and Lyman Carpenter; Cephas Carpenter having purchased the farm adjoining on the west, of Olney Hawkins, the previous summer.

Mr. Willard carried on a large business at his trade, employing a number of workmen, and having several apprentices, among whom were Bowman W. Dennis and Hosea and Dennison Willard. He and his brother Azel, built a large "stack" 20 feet or more square, on the flat below Carver's Falls, in 1825, for John P. Colburn, James Y. Watson, and Jacob Davey, they proposing to build an extensive furnace at that point, but abandoned the project, and the stack fell to the the ground.

In 1826 Mr. Willard went to Westport, N. Y., to build a large brick store, and was there taken sick and died, October 4th, in his 34th year. His remains were brought to Fair Haven and interred.

His wife was Thankful Stone, a sister of Mrs. James Y. Watson. She afterward married Abraham Sharp, and died February 23, 1835, in her 40th year.

HISTORY OF FAIR HAVEN, VERMONT. 505

Mr. Willard left two children:

1. *Simeon*, who is in California; and 2. *Jacob*, who resides in Chicago, Ill., having first married Helen Stone, of Vergennes, and after her decease, a Miss Baber, of Keeseville, N. Y.

AZEL WILLARD, an elder brother of Jacob, who had married Hannah Cady, at West Windsor, in 1812, came hither in 1817, moving into the Rood house, on West street. In March, 1818, he and his brother bought Paul Scott's place, and he moved into the house on the same. He bought out his brother's interest, in January, 1821, and sold the place to Cyrus Graves, April 4, 1825. In January, 1832, he purchased of Harvey Howard, administrator of Sylvanus Morton's estate, five acres of land where his son, Josiah P., now resides, which had been owned by his brother Jacob, at the time of his death, and on which there was a small brick house, built by Chauncey Ward. In March following, he bought fifteen acres of land adjoining the other, of Chester Howe. This extended to the old burying ground eastward and to the river on the south, and was the same on which Parkill and Crane had built a distillery and dwelling house in 1820.

Mr. Willard's son, Azel, rebuilt the brick dwelling house, in September, 1840, as it now stands, and here Mr. Willard resided until his death, which occurred March 10, 1865.

Family:

1. *Azel*, b. in West Windsor, in Sept., 1814; was employed in a mercantile house in New York in 1835, '36 and '37; commenced trading in Fair Haven in

1839, after Col. Allen's removal from the old store, where the new bank building now is, to John J. Davey's. He built the house where R. E. Lloyd has lately resided, in 1842, occupying the front part as a store. He was postmaster from 1841 to 1845, when he removed to Hartford, N. Y. He married Miss Mary Doane, of Hartford, in Sept., 1841, and has one son. Mrs. Willard died in Hartford, and he now resides, with his second wife, in East Poultney.

2. *Josiah P.*, is now resident on the home place. He married Lucy Spink, and has one son, Ira, who is a teacher of music.

3. *Hannah*, d. in 1839—a young and beautiful woman.

SIMEON WILLARD came from West Windsor, in 1818; m. Hannah Carpenter, and removed to Vergennes. He died in Malone, N. Y. His family were: *Sylvester*, who resides in Malone, and *Edson*, of Nashville, Tenn.

HOSEA WILLARD is now a resident of Vergennes, where he m. Betsey Benton. His children are: *Electa, Harvey, Hosea*, and *Mary D.*

DENNISON WILLARD was for some years resident in Fair Haven, owning the place where Col. Allen now resides, and afterward that occupied by Griffith O. Williams. He removed first to Vergennes, in 1839. He now resides in Malone, N. Y. He m. Miss Clementine Roberts, of Whiting, and his family are:

1. *Martha*, m. Dr. Manley, and resides in Columbia, Ky.

2. *Frank*, d. in California about 1859.

3. *Sarah*, and 4. *Charles*.

HISTORY OF FAIR HAVEN, VERMONT. 507

JOSEPH WARNER, originally from Massachusetts, came from Chelsea, Vt., to Fair Haven, in March, 1827, buying at that time of Olney Hawkins the place then occupied by John Parkill. He made a number of other purchases in town, but sold this place in April, 1831, to his· uncle, John Warner, his brother Luke occupying it at the time.

John, said to be of Rutland, in May, 1832, gave a power of attorney to Luke to sell the place, containing about 60 acres, and he sold it to Stephen Fish, in October, 1835.

He purchased the home farm of Cephas Carpenter in March, 1828, and appears to have resided on the place till 1833. It was sold to Chester Howe, from whom it passed into the hands of Abraham Graves. Mr. Warner is said to have been implicated with Howe in the forgery of a note against Worcester Morse, and to have gone away in haste. He is said also to have a son now in New Bedford, Mass., who is quite wealthy.

LUKE WARNER, brother of Joseph, is reported to have been a merchant in Pepperell, Mass He was here in April, 1831, and lived where John Parkill had lived. He left about 1835, and died somewhere in Pennsylvania, where he has a son, *Luke*, now residing.

MARTIN WIGGINS, a most respectable Irishman, of the earlier times, was in the town and worked for Mr. Gilbert about 1835. In Sept. 1841, he bought the place where his widow and children now reside, of Israel Ward. He died March 14, 1854. His children are: *James, Sarah, Mary, Eliza*, and *Daniel.*

JEREMIAH WESCOTT came from Clarendon about 1839. He bought the farm now occupied by his son, David P., of Preserved Fish, of Ira, in October, 1835, and his son-in-law, Samuel P. Curtis, occupied it for three or four years thereafter. Mr. Wescott, with his son, Jeremiah, carried it on till about 1855, when David P. succeeded to the care of the same.

He died in August, 1856, aged 72 years. His wife was Welthy Potter, and their children were: 1. *Amos*, now in Clarendon; 2. *Clarissa*, m. Samuel P. Curtis; 3. *George*, deceased; 4. *David Potter*; 5. *Jeremiah*, m. Helen Parker; d. Sept., 1868, aged 47; 6. *Phebe J.*, deceased.

DAVID P. WESCOTT, m. Lovisa Atwood, of Chittenden, and came to his father's place in Fair Haven, in February, 1855. Jeremiah deeded him one-half the farm in October, 1856. His children are: 1. *Eugene L.*; 2. *Emma Georgianna*; 3. *Charles David*.

HAMILTON WESCOTT, came from Milford, Otsego county, N. Y.; worked for Abram Graves in Fair Haven, in 1839 and '40. In March, 1852, he purchased Mr. Graves' farm and moved on to it. His wife was Abigail Bates. She died while on a visit at Milford, March 20, 1860, leaving five children: *Zilpha A., Reuben L., Hamilton M., Henrietta Jane*, and *Alice Rose*. Mr. W. afterward m. Mrs. T. J. Page, of Rutland, daughter of Dyer Townsend, of Wallingford.

DR. THOMAS E. WAKEFIELD, b. in Manchester, March 15, 1821; spent his youth in Granville, N. Y.; studied medicine with Dr. Charles Backus; attended lectures at Pittsfield, Mass., and Castleton, Vt., and came to

Fair Haven in October, 1842,

has been the leading physician

Miss Mary F. Fuller, from West

ELISHA VAUGHN, SEN., was in

He worked for Jacob Davey, bur

here. His wife's name was Ab

1. *Elisha*; 2. *Harvey*; 3. *Mar*

son, who lived in Major Gilbert's

road," where Charles Hawkins

was in the war of 1812; 4. *J*

Gibbs; 5. *Abiah*, m. a Kenyon,

ELISHA VAUGHN, JR., bought t

south of the Appleton lot—now

Esty—in August, 1815, of Noah

There were 42 1-2 acres of this

of it on the 4th division of Step

acres on the 3d division of Asa

had bought of Benjamin Carver,

ruary, 1815. Vaughn built an

place till 1838. He sold it to

1835, with 15 acres on the east,

of Adams Dutton, in April, 18

with his family to Coldwater,

Vaughn married Clinthia Mc,

Lieut. Charles McArthur, of Scot

and had a family as follows: 1.

3. *Charles*; 4. *Clinthia*; 5. *Al*

Of these Charles is said to be

ing.

JEDEDIAH VAUGHN is said to he

pleton lot, next north of Elisha's

He bought land of Tilly Gilbert in November, 1826, and in June, 1828, he deeded to his mother, *Abiah* Vaughn, " as a security for her support during her natural life," a lot of land south of Elisha's, where he had a log house, and resided. This land Abia quit-claimed back to him, September 24, 1836, and he deeded it the same day, as 24 acres, to Elijah Esty. The house was afterward occupied for some years by Hiram Thomas and family. Mr. Esty built a new frame house in the place of the old log one.

APPENDIX.

APPENDIX I.

Names of the original proprietors of Fair Haven, as found in the Charter of the town granted at Manchester, October 27, 1779, and signed by Gov. Thomas Chittenden, at Arlington, April 26, 1782, most of them being non-residents :

Ebenezer Allen, Isaac Clark, Samuel Herrick, George Foot, Jesse Belknap, John Grant, Oliver Cleveland, John Smith, Gilbert Mallery, Aaron Adams, James Brookins, Elisha Hamilton, Wm. Seymour, Daniel Owen, Stephen Pearl, John How, Benjamin Cutler, Derrick Carner, Isaac Knapp, Ira Allen, Elisha Baker, Nathaniel Smith, Joseph Averiss, Lemuel Roberts, Jonas Galusha, Zadoc Averist, Noah Allen, Matthew Lyon, Ebenezer Frisbee, Lemuel Payne, Joseph Haven, Wm. Williams, Ezra Allen, Ralph Watson, Stephen Mead, Stephen Fay, John Payne, Jr., Nathan Allen, Stephen Rice, Asa Joiner, Samuel Allen, Jacob Ruback, Philip Priest, John Fassett, Jr., Nathan Clark, Eleazer Dudley, Elisha Ashley, Stephen R. Bradley, Jesse Sawyer, Wm. Ashley, Oliver Sanford, Asa Dudley, Solomon Wilder, Israel Trowbridge, Elisha Clark, Elijah Galusha, Wm. Stewart, Cephas Smith, Samuel Josiah Grant, Andrew Carner, Robert Clark, Thomas Chittenden, Solomon Lathrop, Hope Lathrop, Thomas Ashley, Benjamin Richardson, Jonathan Brooks, Thomas Taylor, David Wheeler, Giles Pettibone, Noah Smith, John Hamilton, Samuel Kent, Israel Smith, Elizabeth Chittenden, Benjamin Everist. 1 share for a seminary or college in the state. 1 share for the first settled minister in the town. 1 share for the support of the ministry. 1 share for a county grammar school. 1 share for the benefit of the schools in the town.

APPENDIX II.

To the Hon. General Assembly of the State of Vermont, convened at Bennington, 13th June, 1781 :

The petition of the subscribers, being settlers and inhabitants of a tract of land called Greenfield, showeth that they did, in the year 1779, enter a petition in the Secretary of State's Office in said State, for the following tract of unappropriated land : Beginning at the south-east corner of Skeens' Patent, called Skeensborough ; thence east to the old Hampshire line, two and three-fourth (2 3-4) miles ; thence north on said line unto the south-east corner of Fair Haven ; thence on the southerly line of Fair Haven to the head of East Bay ; thence south until it reaches one-half mile west of the north east corner of Skeensborough ; thence east one-half mile to said corner ; thence south on the east line of Skeensborough to the first bounds ; containing about three-fourths of a township of six miles square ; which your petitioners then prayed might be granted to them, but it being west of the formerly west line of this state, your honors did not see fit to grant the same, and as said described tract is now included in the present bounds of this state, and the petitioners are now actually settled and improving the same, and are willing and desirous of being under, and having such privileges as incorporated towns in said state do enjoy, therefore for their own happiness and interest, and for the interest and benefit of said state, the petitioners do most earnestly pray that said described tract may be granted and incorporated to them at your said session, by the name of Greenfield, under such restrictions and reservations, and for such conditions as your honors in your wisdom shall direct, and do ever pray :

Abel Parker, Asahel Holmes, James Fuller, William Church, Samuel Church, Jonathan Meacham, Joseph Ballard, William Smith, Gideon Warren, Joseph Hyde, Isaac Craw, Nathaniel Galusha, Solomon Cleveland, Ebenezer Kellogg, Joseph Kellogg, Abner How, William Brooks, Benjamin Gideon, Isaac Harlow, Samuel Allen, Ebenezer Hyde, Joseph Hyde, 2d, Obadiah Winches, Peter Fuller, Abraham Sharp, Ogden Mallory, Enoch Cleveland, Josiah Squier, Benoni Hoskins. Nicholas Spoor, Lemuel Hyde, Wm. Paris Meacham, Stephen Pitkin, Abiel Hoskins, Ebenezer Mallery, John Meacham, John Charter, Oliver Cleveland, Ebenezer Welton, Bishop Warren, Joseph Adams. Jedediah Blackman, Jeremiah Adams, Elisha Allen, Caleb Warren, Silas Fletcher, Eli Freeman, Simeon Hotchkiss, Elisha Kellogg, Jonathan Hall, Derrick Carner, Isaac Race, James Adams, Peter Christie, James Brooks, Benjamin Parmenter, Stephen Holt, Nathaniel Smith, Asa Warren.

Greenfield, June I, 1781.

APPENDIX III.

To the Hon. General Assembly of the State of Vermont convened at Bennington :

Whereas, The petitioners are in actual possession of an ungranted tract of land lying within the limits of this state, beginning at Skeensborough Falls, in the deepest channel, and running on Skeensborough north line eastwardly to the north-east corner of Skeensborough ; thence east to Poultney river ;

thence in the channel of said river to the falls at East Bay ; thence in the channel of said Bay to Lake Champlain ; thence in the channel of the Lake to the bounds begun at. Your petitioners do pray your honors to grant to them the above mentioned tract by the name of New Cheshire.`

Skeensborough, June 2, 1781.

Lemuel Bartholomew, Joseph Mack, Barnabas Moss, Enos Stone, Benoni Hurlburt, Charles Smith, Robert Fuller, Henry Francisco, James Gilmore, Peter Christie, James Adams, James Christie, Robert Adams, Joseph Hoskin, Wm. Morse, Caleb Hurlburt, Robert Smith, Daniel Willard, Thomas Morrison, Abiel Haskin, Nathaniel Miller, Chas. Blinn. Joseph Carver, John Charter, Jeffery Donnavoe, Timothy Spaulding, Jonathan Lines, Benjamin Ufford, Mr. Carpenter, Daniel Hurlburt, Richard Bartholomew, James Wilson, John Wilson, John Moss, Benjamin R. Moss, Seth Bartholomew, William Hurlburt, John Vandozer, Lemuel Bartholomew, Squier Bartholomew, Eliezer Hurlburt.

APPENDIX IV.

To the Hon. General Assembly now sitting in Bennington, State of Vermont :

Whereas, We, the inhabitants of Fair Haven, who are now your honors' petitioners, have been greatly injured in our persons and property by a number of evil minded persons, who have a grant of said Fair Haven from the Hon. General Assembly, in October, 1779. Yet we suppose that the grant was obtained through some misrepresentation, or evil design in those persons, but through inadvertence in your honors ; as you were not made sensible of our former settlement in said town by any of those persons ; but through their low cunning, have endeavored to get a grant of said town, and turn our families into the open clemency of the weather, without giving us the least opportunity of securing ourselves in any shape, we being persons who had for a long time before improved the land, and were determined to petition your honors the first opportunity ; but were cut short by those persons, who never gave us the least opportunity to be represented in the petition, which we think is cruel and hard, and which will tend to abridge us of our rights and privileges, unless some method is taken by your honors to redress injured justice, and prevent these persons from disturbing us in our possessions, as we are persons who have left the southern parts of the New England states of America, and have fled to Vermont to resume its liberties and promote its interests by cultivating its lands, and by defending the liberties of our country, and we find ourselves under the necessity of lifting up our earnest prayers to your honors, that we may be redressed in this case and quieted in our possessions, and we flatter ourselves, as your honors are now informed of the true state of our situation, that we shall find favor in your sight, and your petitioners, as in duty bound, shall ever pray.

Joseph Carver, Joseph Haskins, Jonathan Hall, Benoni Hurlburt, John Vandozer.

Fair Haven, Feb. 23, 1782.

514   APPENDIX:

REMONSTRANCE OF BENONI HURLBURT.

Whereas, It appears that one certain Joseph Carver, a transient person, said to be an inhabitant of the State of Rhode Island, not having the fear of God before his eyes, without my consent, by a petition signed by himself and others, made use of my name, which I aver to be without the least knowledge or consent of mine, which is not only against my will but against my interests, I do hereby remonstrate against any act or thing being done in answer to said petition, and I further declare that I do not hold my interest in said town by virtue of possession only, but by virtue of the grant made to proprietors, who have not disturbed me in my improvements, but otherwise, have granted me the privilege of covering and retaining my possession.

Given under my hand at Cheshire, this 26th day of May, 1782.

BENONI HURLBURT.

APPENDIX V.

LICENSE FOR RETAILING LIQUORS, JUNE 14th, 15th, AND 16th, 1802.

At a meeting of the Civil Authority and Selectmen of the town of Fair Haven, for the purpose of giving license to persons to mix and sell strong liquors . . . on the 14th, 15th, and 16th of this instant, June, in order to accommodate the persons attending the Regimental Review in said Fair Haven, agreeably to an act of the General Assembly, passed at Vergennes, in Nov., 1798; accordingly there is hereby licensed for the purpose aforesaid, Josiah Norton, Tilly Gilbert, Wm. Hawkins, Olney Hawkins, Isaac Cutler, Philip Allen, David Erwin, Ira Durand, Curtis Kelsey, Jr., and Paul Scott.

Fair Haven, 8th June, 1802.

J. WITHERELL, Judge ; JOSIAH NORTON, Justice Peace ; ETHAN WHIPPLE, Justice Peace ; SAMUEL STANNARD, TILLY GILBERT, Selectmen, WM. HAWKINS, Grand Juror ; NATHANIEL DICKINSON, Constable.

REPRESENTATIVES OF THE TOWN IN THE GENERAL ASSEMBLY.

Matthew Lyon, 1783, '84, 1787. '88, 1790, '91, 1793, '94, '95, '96.
*Simeon Smith, 1789, '92, '97,
James Witherell, 1798, '99, 1800, '01, '02.
*Oliver Church, 1803, '06, '07, 1810, '11, 1819.
Isaac Cutler, 1804, '05.

* Belonged in West Haven.

Salmon Norton, 1808, '09.
Tilly Gilbert, 1812, '14, '32.
Ethan Whipple, 1813.
*James W. Rosman, 1815.
Thomas Christie, 1816.
Moses Colton, 1817.
*Erastus Coleman, 1818.
John P. Colburn, 1820, '21, '23, '24, '25, '27.
*Artemas Wyman, 1822.
George Warren, 1826.
Ira Leonard, 1828, '29, '34. '39.
John Jones, 1830.
Wm. C. Kittredge, 1831, '33, '37, '47, '48, '49, '56.
Barnabas Ellis, 1835, '36, '42.
Adams Dutton, 1838.
Joseph Sheldon, Jr.,.1840, '41.
Asahel H. Kidder, 1843, '44.
Jonathan Capen, 1845, '46.
Abram Graves, 1850, '51.
Artemas S. Cushman, 1852, '53.
Joseph Adams, 1854, '55.
Hiram Hamilton, 1857, '58.
Samuel Wood, 1859, '60.
Ira C. Allen, 1861, '62.
Corril Reed, 1863, '64.
Joel W. Hamilton, 1865, '66.
Horace G. Wood, 1867, '68, '69, '70.

* Belonged in West Haven.

TOWN CLERKS.

Eleazer Dudley, 1783, '84.
Michael Merritt, 1785, '86.
Silas Safford, 1787, '88.
Stephen Hall, 1789.
Frederick Hill, 1790, '91.
James Witherell, Dec. 26, 1791, '92.
John Brown, 1793 to Feb., 1801.
Josiah Norton, 1801, '02.
Tilly Gilbert, 1803 to '08 ; 1814 to '32.
Ethan Whipple, 1809 to '13.

Benjamin F. Gilbert, 1833 to '54 ; 1856 to '58.
Jonathan Capen, 1855.
Corril Reed, 1859 to '70.

DELEGATES TO THE CONSTITUTIONAL CONVENTIONS.

Simeon Smith, 1771.
Matthew Lyon, 1793.
Ethan Whipple, 1814.
John P. Colburn, 1821.

Moses Colton, 1828.
William C. Kittredge, 1836.
Abram Graves, 1843 & '50.
E. H. Phelps, 1870.

STATISTICS OF THE CENSUS.

Number of inhabitants in 1860,....................................1378.
   "   "   "   " 1870,....................................2208.
   "   " dwellings " " .... 391.
   "   " families "   " .... 452.
Total value of productions of the town for the year ending June
   1, 1870,.................................,....................$425,050,00.

CPSIA information can be obtained
at www.ICGtesting.com
Printed in the USA
LVOW10s0257060318
568771LV00009B/113/P